The Character of Human Institutions

The Character of Human Institutions

Robin Fox and the Rise of Biosocial Science

Michael Egan, editor

Routledge
Taylor & Francis Group
LONDON AND NEW YORK

First published 2014 by Transaction Publishers

Published 2017 by Routledge
2 Park Square, Milton Park, Abingdon, Oxon OX14 4RN
711 Third Avenue, New York, NY 10017, USA

Routledge is an imprint of the Taylor & Francis Group, an informa business

Copyright © 2014 by Taylor & Francis.

All rights reserved. No part of this book may be reprinted or reproduced or utilised in any form or by any electronic, mechanical, or other means, now known or hereafter invented, including photocopying and recording, or in any information storage or retrieval system, without permission in writing from the publishers.

Notice:
Product or corporate names may be trademarks or registered trademarks, and are used only for identification and explanation without intent to infringe.

Library of Congress Catalog Number: 2013039631

Library of Congress Cataloging-in-Publication Data

The character of human institutions : Robin Fox and the rise of biosocial science / Michael Egan, editor.
    pages cm
    ISBN 978-1-4128-5377-4
    1. Fox, Robin, 1934- 2. Anthropologists--England--Biography. 3. Anthropologists--United States--Biography. 4. Physical anthropology. 5. Sociobiology. I. Egan, Michael, 1941-, editor.
    GN21.F6Z64 2014
    301.092--dc23
                                                                2013039631

ISBN 13: 978-1-4128-5377-4 (hbk)

David Jenkins

On Reading 'Participant Observer'*

Antelope

Defies chronology as a master trope
Weaves tapestries of twisted rope
And bits of bone and air
And travels light.
Crooked warp, angled weft, Antelope
Breathes no noisome complaint
Nor ruined lament
Nor tale of otherworldly firmament.

Instead he puzzles through
The randomness of animals
Who, despite all odds surpass their kind
Invent language and divine
The meaning of their fate. Antelope braids
Mystery from human sociability.

With prolixity Antelope wends
No dance nor skate nor yeasty brew
Nor chart and skew of kinship terms
Beyond their ability to convey
Connections primordial and fey.
Still, without weave or trace
Or dreaded count of shuttled thread,
Without Trickster's antlered mask,
His girls provide the point at last.

Note

* Antelope (man) (*kütstiwa*) was the name the Indians of Cochiti Pueblo in New Mexico gave to Robin Fox, because of his springy walk, they said.

Contents

Dedication
On Reading *'Participant Observer'*
David Jenkins   v

Foreword
Robert Trivers   xi

I   Personal and Confidential

Introduction: Mainstream Maverick
   Michael Egan   3

1   This Guy, Fox
   Lionel Tiger   23

2   A Tribute and Personal Thanks
   Michael T. McGuire   41

II   Popularity and Drink

3   Writing Popular Anthropology
   Kate Fox   53

4   Drink and Duty: Extreme Drinking Rituals in the British Army
   Anne Fox   69

III   Laughter and Happiness

5   Understanding Laughter
   Sir Antony Jay   89

6   Joyous, Equal, and Free: Conditions of Felicity in
Human Organizations
Charles Macdonald   111

IV   Kinship and Incest

7   Kinship Constructed Us: Primate Kinship
and Cultural Anthropology
Linda Stone   135

8   Lighting the Red Lamp of Incest
Alexandra Maryanski and Jonathan Turner   161

9   Darwin and Cousin Marriage in England
Adam Kuper   183

V   Self and Epic

10   The Image of the Good Imperial Education
Alan Macfarlane   205

11   The Ethnography of the Self:
Anthropologists' Autobiographies
David Jenkins   221

12   The Universal Epic: A Research Challenge
Frederick Turner   249

VI   Nature and Society

13   From Human Nature to Human Society: Why
Anthropology Cannot Ignore Biological Constants
Bernard Chapais   273

14   The Changing Nature of Human Nature
H. Dieter Steklis   307

15   Science and Anti-Science in Anthropology:
A Look Back
Melvin J. Konner   329

VII   Finale

16   The Consumerist Cosmos
     Howard Bloom   345

17   Last Word: The Razor's Edge
     Robin Fox   349

Contributors   367

Index   373

Foreword

Robert Trivers

In the early 1970s Robin Fox and I became fast and firm friends. I loved his sense of humor, his countercultural mind, and his devotion to building what he called "biosocial science," that is, social life understood in terms of natural selection. Regarding his sense of humor, the very first time I met him he had us in stitches as he acted out the unexpected positive effect on his sexual attractiveness from continuing to wear the Nazi jackboots that were part of his costume in a college play. Much more recently, he gently implored my colleagues to adopt language on "expectations" regarding incoming student behavior that sounded a lot less "North Korean."

My affection was strengthened when he and Lionel Tiger became the research directors of the Harry Frank Guggenheim Foundation in the early 1970s. The National Science Foundation had just turned down my grant proposal for $7000/year on the grounds that theoreticians need only "pencil and paper." (I had also been hoping for a research assistant.) Robin and Lionel promptly supported three years of theoretical work, including my paper (with Hope Hare) on haplo-diploid kinship systems (e.g., ants and bees), and the unusual opportunity to test kinship theory in a precise way. Most agreeably, I remember the research proposal as being one-page long!

Certainly Robin and I were thoroughly naïve about how easy it would be to create biosocial science for humans. In the '70s we alternated between buttonholing people at conferences to explain why natural selection was the key to understanding life and (at the same time) predicting that in twenty years it would be impossible to walk down the hall of a social science building without hearing students say, "I wonder why natural selection would favor *that*?" Trust me, it is now forty years later and you can walk down almost any such hall in the United States absolutely certain you will hear no reference at all to "natural selection" and a lot to "the cultural construction of reality." But the influence of the "biosocial orientation," as Robin predicted, has been variously influential in such areas as biology, primatology, psychology, medicine, psychiatry, economics, ecology, history, literature, and law and among a dedicated minority of anthropologists, political scientists, and sociologists, to say nothing of the steady flow of popular books that seem to appeal to the general public. If the social sciences and humanities have remained stubbornly closed to the evolutionary idea, the intellectual world at large has seen its wisdom.

Robin's lifelong special expertise has been kinship. In 1962 he deftly reconciled the Freudian approach to incest with that of Westermarck (from the 1890s). In his most recent book, *The Tribal Imagination*, he delves into kinship systems among Australian Aborigines, in modern Iraq, in the Bible, and in Malory's *Morte D'Arthur*, among other societies and literatures. He memorably said that the clue to understanding the origins of human kinship was that while other primates have kin, only we have in-laws. In 1964 he traveled across London to meet William Hamilton just as Bill was publishing his famous kinship approach to natural selection based on genetic relatedness. It was impossible to understand Bill in person, so Robin asked him to send along his manuscripts, which, in turn, were equally impenetrable, leading Robin to later describe the exchange as "one of the great moments in the history of science that never happened." Robin, in turn, published *Kinship and Marriage* in 1967, which I avidly consumed and thought presented wonderful intellectual challenges to those interested in anthropology. In the '70s, when students came into my office and bemoaned that Hamilton and I had left them with nothing to do, I would tell them they suffered from a lack of imagination and shove Robin's book into their hands. "So you say you understand Hamilton. Here are all the anthropological facts, beautifully organized—just make sense of them in terms of inclusive fitness—why parallel cousins instead of cross cousins, and why is one system much more frequent than the other?" Alas, yet another great moment in intellectual history that is yet to happen. In 1972 Robin and I were side by side in a publication celebrating the centennial of Darwin's theory of sexual selection: I on parental investment and Robin on kinship. In 1975 Robin published *Biosocial Anthropology*, including a memorable chapter by Hamilton, but by then social anthropology was busy renaming itself *cultural anthropology*, the better to rule out the very biological arguments that Robin saw as important.

Robin has a contrarian streak that I like to imagine I share. If you tell Robin what the consensus of opinion in a discipline is, he will assume, as a rule of thumb, that it is mistaken. If I see a crowd of people running in one direction, my first impulse is to run in the opposite direction. Of course, we do not always share the same view—on the value of group selection for evolution or Hezbollah for Lebanon—but when I differ from him I note such differences with caution; he may easily be right on both.

Robin has been called "the last anthropologist," and this has an ominous ring to it. We know that it takes a very long time for "last" to arrive, but sadly Robin may be one of the last of the great social anthropologists in our lifetime. His vision of unifying physical and social anthropology is completely unfulfilled. Indeed, the absurdity of the current approach within cultural anthropology is captured nicely in *The Tribal Imagination*, where Robin mentions being called a "realist," which he took as a compliment only to find out it had been meant as an insult. He goes on to say, "I have also been accused of being heterosexual, bourgeois, Eurocentric, and male. I admit to all four." He says he forgot to add "white." When these are the terms of the discussion, nobody is advancing anywhere quickly. And it may be a very long time indeed before we have someone like Robin who masters all of anthropology, from kinship right on up. This excellent book gives us a taste of such an organism and why it so valuable to have at least one of them around.

I

Personal and Confidential

Music of the Spheres

Who choreographs the dance of life,
God, or Balanchine?
No. Mendel and his wrinkled peas:
Or something in between.

Who orchestrates the song of youth,
God, or Borodín?
No. Jacob, Monod, Watson, Crick:
A regulator gene.

Who promulgates the will to live,
God, that passerby?
No. Mindless little molecules
That don't know how to die.

1

Personal and Confidential

Introduction

Mainstream Maverick

Michael Egan

Jonathan Benthall, director of the Royal Anthropological Institute, 1974–2000, wrote to Robin Fox: "Yours is the kind of work that will be rediscovered and better appreciated once you are dead." Robin, who had a good relationship with Benthall, fully agreed. His wife Lin, to whom he read the letter, said that his reaction to the remark was delighted laughter. He always saw himself as an individualist and an antinomian—his favorite self-description. "Some people," he wrote in *Encounter with Anthropology*, "are born with different drummers banging away in their cradles." But inevitably the nonconformist, the contrarian, the maverick, and the fringe innovator will not receive the usual insider rewards and ritual honors, and in Robin's case does not expect or want them. They go, in his opinion, to those who repeatedly confirm what we already know, not to those who constantly challenge the received wisdom, even if this ultimately is the way that knowledge advances. But Robin's skepticism is grounded in an idea—the idea that in any analysis of human behavior the effect of evolution and adaptation cannot be ignored. So this book is a celebration of both the man and the idea.

The skeptic is not honored in his own country, or anyone else's for that matter. So this is why a few of his friends (initially myself and Ramón Jiménez) decided he needed a celebration, a recognition that was outside the insider network. We quickly aroused the support of Lionel Tiger and Michael T. McGuire and then all the other distinguished contributors who enthusiastically helped to form this volume. I am not an anthropologist (I know Robin as a friend through his work on the Shakespeare authorship question). But I am an editor, so I took on the task. To compile this introduction, I assembled some facts and comments from his work and from his friends and colleagues, and I asked questions of Robin as well.

The Character of Human Institutions

An introduction should start with the usual appreciation of the "life and works," but as Lionel Tiger says in his chapter, "This Guy, Fox," the only person who can really write an adequate account of Robin's life and work is Robin. His interests are so multifarious and his command of languages and disciplines so unusual that there is no other person who can truly give an account, much less an assessment, of the totality of his work. His contemporaries have praised him lavishly enough for one thing or another (in 2011, for example, the journal *Society* devoted a whole issue to his work titled "Taming the Savage Mind"), but not one of them would claim to know it all and be able to assess it all. One review editor complained that to deal properly with one of Robin's books he would need four different anthropologists, an evolutionary biologist, a philosopher, a historian, a political scientist, a poet, a classicist, and an expert in comparative literature fluent in at least six languages. Robin's description of himself is as an "essayist." And one reason his insights are often overlooked is that most of his books are collections of essays, across a whole range of often disparate topics, so they do not get read by specialists wearing professional blinkers. But they are driven by the idea of what he calls the "biosocial orientation," and when this book was proposed to him he agreed if it was to be "as much about the fulfillment of the idea as about the peculiarities of one mind."

When Rutgers promoted him to university professor—the highest rank it can give a faculty member—he chose the title "of social theory" rather than "of anthropology." This was because he has always seen the social and evolutionary sciences in general as being only part of the Enlightenment search for the "Universal History of Mankind": the total account of how man and civilization came to be and why they are the way they are.

Robin regards being a professional anthropologist as one of the many accidents in his life. After his graduation from the London School of Economics (1957), he really wanted to go to Cornell and do a philosophy thesis (on free will, the naturalistic fallacy, and rational ethics), but it didn't work out. Even within anthropology proper, where, as he insists, he earns his living, he has been called "the last anthropologist" because no one else has the breadth of knowledge and experience of the whole of anthropology that he shows in his work. To him, this is just "being an anthropologist" and is one reason he came from the United Kingdom to the United States: to be part of a science that embraced all "four fields" of evolutionary, linguistic, cultural, and archaeological anthropology. For twenty years at Rutgers he taught a four-fields introductory course; after he stopped, it was no longer taught, and the department he had struggled to keep unified split like so many others into cultural and evolutionary anthropology. He refuses to accept this distinction. He is just, he insists, carrying out the High Mandate (he always uses capitals for this) of Morgan, Tylor, and Malinowski, in the embrace of Darwin and the evolutionary perspective. Once you have this mandate and this perspective, he claims, you can move anywhere and tackle any problem in the intellectual universe, if you are willing to do the detail work that is needed.

This, for him, has involved (among many other things) the writing of an American Indian grammar; conducting original research on primate society and evolution; studying the evolution of brain and behavior and relating this to the incest taboo; becoming one of the world's leading experts on kinship systems and the leading educator on kinship; writing a definitive encyclopedia article on Native American religion; doing detailed historical research on land tenure in Ireland; covering the history of American constitutional and family case law in analyzing Mormon polygamy cases; knowing all the works of Swinburne and Browning and relating them to original theories about the brain and memory; inventing original statistical measures for demographic research on Tory Island; examining the role of incest in Western literature, from the Old Testament to Nabokov; working on the cognitive abilities of newborns; looking at the history of ideas from the sixteenth century and how the agenda of the social sciences was created; taking an entirely fresh look at Hume on the nature of causation; reanalyzing the Theban trilogy of Sophocles as it reflects the continuing struggle between kinship and the state; studying the archaeology of SW Florida and the origin of complex society; and the list goes on and on.

But the list does not include his original creative writing in prose and verse and his translations of classical, French, and Gaelic poetry, all done with humor and an ease of composition that professional authors envy. "You write like an angel," Kurt Vonnegut told him. "If I had known anthropology could be such fun, I would never have given it up." Robin treasured this compliment, along with Iris Murdoch's calling *The Violent Imagination*, "A free, wild book . . . a beautiful, strange work." Many of the people he admires and whose ideas have influenced him, and who have been his friends, have been, like Vonnegut, from outside the academy or on its fringes: Ashley Montagu, Robert Ardrey, Desmond Morris, David Attenborough, Antony Jay, William Golding, John Pfeiffer, Doris Lessing, Barbara Ehrenreich, Richard de

Mille, Helen Fisher, J. T. Fraser, Phillis Chesler, Owen Harries, Howard Bloom and many others.

The best thing we can perhaps do, then, is to listen to his own account of his life and work from various sources. This will not do justice to his verse, which the editor of *Light*, John Mella, compared to "W. H. Auden at his best," and the poet and critic Frederick Turner (one of our contributors) has described as being "As good as anything in the journals, and a hundred times smarter." The latter of course does not always endear a poet to his contemporaries, but to give the reader a flavor of it we have included some of Robin's sonnets and short verses on the title pages of each section of the book. That Robin moves between cynicism and outright romanticism will not surprise his closest fans. He never usually uses punctuation, but to make it easier on the reader I have added some—except for the Mandelbrot Sonnet, which appropriately defies punctuation.

A Short Biography

We can start our account of Robin's life with an adaptation of the biography from his website, partly his own, partly a publisher's summary, to get some of the facts and chronology on the record.

What follows is a publisher's summary, so please bear with the impersonality:

> Robin Fox was born in the Brontë village of Haworth in the Yorkshire Dales, at the height of the Great Depression in 1934. He had very little schooling during WWII, moving all over England with his soldier father, and his mother, then an army nursing aide. (See the dedication to *Kinship and Marriage*.) After a narrow escape from death by bombing he pursued his early education through the Army, the Church of England, public libraries, and the BBC, more than through formal schooling. Then through a series of scholarships—one of them to the Grammar School in the village where the Brontës were born—he made his way to the London School of Economics in 1953, and did his undergraduate degree in Sociology (First Class Honors). This included a heavy dose of Philosophy and Social Anthropology, with much influence from Karl Popper, Ernest Gellner and Raymond Firth—and occasional interaction with Bertrand Russell.
>
> He went to Harvard for graduate work in the Department of Social Relations where he found himself—under the tutelage of Clyde Kluckhohn, Evon Vogt, Paul Friedrich and Dell Hymes—in New Mexico, where he studied language and society among the Pueblo Indians. He concentrated on the Pueblo of Cochiti, on the Rio Grande, on which he wrote his Ph.D. thesis (submitted to the University of

Introduction

London and examined by Firth, Edmund Leach and Daryll Ford). A revised version of the thesis with his analysis of the evolution of Pueblo kinship systems and the "Crow-Omaha" question was published as *The Keresan Bridge: A Problem in Pueblo Ethnology*, 1967. This logico-conjectural attempt to reconstruct the history of kinship terms was completely against the grain of Functionalist orthodoxy in England at the time, and equally critical of the prevailing American theories of Acculturation.

He returned to England where he taught for four years at the University of Exeter, starting fieldwork on Tory Island, a remote Gaelic-speaking community off the coast of Donegal in Ireland (his mother's family, also called Fox, came from Ireland.) He wrote his first museum-series publication *Kinship and Land Tenure on Tory Island* (1966.) His work on the island eventually resulted in a book *The Tory Islanders: A People of the Celtic Fringe* (1978), for which the University of Ulster awarded him a doctor of science (D.Sc.) degree. He then returned to the LSE for four more years, lecturing mainly on kinship, and producing the widely used text translated into many languages, *Kinship and Marriage: An Anthropological Perspective* (1967): still in print after forty-five years, and with no rivals in the meantime.

He had published what became a classic paper, "Sibling Incest," in the *British Journal of Sociology* (1962), where he again defied the overwhelming consensus of opinion on the incest taboo and revived the neglected theories of Edward Westermarck. Under the influence of such figures as John Bowlby, David Attenborough (who was his student for a while), Robert Ardrey, Niko Tinbergen, Desmond Morris, Michael Chance and Lionel Tiger, he became interested in Ethology—the science of the evolution of behavior. He gave the first primate behavior and human evolution lectures in the department, co-teaching with the primatological anatomist John Napier from the Royal Free Hospital School of Medicine. He and Tiger wrote a paper on "The Zoological Perspective in Social Science" (1966). This was one of the first salvos in the great debate on the nature/nurture issue that was to flare up in the sixties and seventies. He added to it with his Malinowski Memorial Lecture of 1967 on "Aspects of Hominid Behavioral Evolution" delivered to an audience appreciative of the effort, but perhaps puzzled by the material and the neo-Darwinian approach. During this time he saw three daughters into the world, Kate, Ellie and Anne. (See the dedication to *Encounter with Anthropology*.)

Rutgers University offered him a chair of anthropology in 1967, and the chance to start a new department, including Tiger. This has grown to be a major research department and graduate program. In 2009 its two degree programs (evolutionary anthropology and cultural anthropology) were ranked in the top ten in the country. He and Tiger completed their joint work, *The Imperial Animal*, in 1970, a book that galvanized the nature/nurture debate and, hitting the rising tide of feminism, provoked a mix of enthusiasm and vituperation.

He spent an academic year at Stanford University School of Medicine (Department of Psychiatry) as an NIMH fellow, studying behavioral biology and the brain with David Hamburg and Karl Pribram.

In 1972, The Harry Frank Guggenheim Foundation, through its president Mason Gross, ex-president of Rutgers, made Tiger and Fox joint Research Directors, and started a program of support for work particularly on violence and dominance. The list of their grantees is a Who's Who in the early development of bio-social science and of what came to be known as "sociobiology." (See the chapter here by Tiger.) They worked for twelve years with the Foundation, and during that time he did original research with Dieter Steklis, another of our contributors, among Macaque monkeys on an island off Bermuda and vervet monkeys on St. Kitts. He produced several books, including *Encounter with Anthropology* (1973) *Biosocial Anthropology* (editor, 1975), *The Red Lamp of Incest* (1980) and *Neonate Cognition* (1984, edited with Jacques Mehler of CNRS.)

During this same period he was a visiting professor at Oxford, Paris (*Ecole des Hautes Etudes en Sciences Sociales*), California at San Diego, and the *Universitad de los Andes* in Bogatá, Colombia, where he did a "participant observer" stint as a bullfighter. In 1985 Rutgers made him a University Professor, the highest honor it can give a faculty member. He wrote *The Search for Society* (1989), his "equal time response" to the interpretive anthropology of Clifford Geertz, and *The Violent Imagination* (1989), a book of essays, verse, satire, drama and dialogue. He was then a Senior Overseas Scholar at St. John's College, Cambridge, and wrote a series of related collections of his essays. The first was *Reproduction and Succession* (1993), relating his part in both the appeal of a Mormon policeman to the Supreme Court, and the famous "Baby M" surrogate mother trials in New Jersey. Then followed *The Challenge of Anthropology* (1994), and *Conjectures and Confrontations* (1997). In 2000 he added significantly to the material in *The Violent Imagination*, plus a foreword by his neighbor and friend Ashley Montagu, which came out as *The Passionate Mind*. He has published a number of controversial papers on contemporary affairs in *The National Interest*—nationalism, the nature of war, the Northern Ireland problem, the "end of history"—and a series of brisk exchanges on human rights, mostly with Francis Fukuyama and Amnesty International.

And now Robin continues in his own voice:

The dry bones of biography do not convey the richness and excitement of a life lived between the two worlds of Europe and America, and amongst some of the most energizing ideas of the century. To try to capture some of this I have completed a memoir of the first forty years of my "accidental life," called *Participant Observer: Memoir of a Transatlantic Life* (2004). In the meantime I live on a small farm near Princeton, New Jersey, with my wife, Lin, an ex-teacher

Introduction

of health sciences at Kean University. (See the dedication to *The Passionate Mind*.) We have a winter retreat on Sanibel Island in SW Florida, where I pursue a research interest in the archaeology of the Calusa Indians with the help of local boatmen and sailors. When not working I try my hand at art (pastel and watercolor), music (choral singing—from madrigals to barbershop, classical guitar, songwriting) and follow college football, especially the Scarlet Knights: an acquired passion replacing ancestral rugby.

Lin, a longstanding member of the US Green Building Council, works on her project to educate us on The Healthy House. Two of my daughters, after education in England, France, the USA and Ireland, live and work in England. Kate is a director of the Social Issues Research Center in Oxford and has written a best seller: *Watching the English*. (Kate is married to Henry Marsh CBE, who was the subject of the award-winning film *The English Surgeon*.) Anne, having studied in the old USSR (Leningrad), founded and runs Galahad SMS Ltd., a social-science research firm. She has earned a Ph.D. from Imperial College London on the drinking culture of the British army, and produced my latest grandson. Ellie lived for nine years in the Bekaa Mountains of Lebanon with her husband and my other four grandsons (and now a great-grandson). She and they speak fluent Arabic. They were rescued off the beaches in the great escape of 2006 and now live in New Jersey. (See the dedication to *Reproduction and Succession*.)

I teach courses (including freshman seminars) on the origin and fall of civilizations, the history of anthropology, comparative mythology, incest in literature, and American Indians. My latest book is *The Tribal Imagination: Civilization and the Savage Mind* (Harvard 2011). I am also working on my other interest in the Shakespeare authorship question where I favor the 17th Earl of Oxford as an alternative candidate. I am especially interested in the role of the Grammar Schools in the making of the Tudor miracle and the modern world. In response to the events of 9/11, I became an American citizen in 2002: better late than never. I am deeply fond of, and grateful to, the USA (and especially Rutgers) for the chances and rewards it has given me, while never losing my affection for my native British Isles.

In *Participant Observer: Memoir of a Transatlantic Life*, Robin told the story of his first forty years (1934–1974). This very unusual autobiography, told in the third person, has been compared to both James Joyce's *Portrait of an Artist* and Laurence Sterne's *Tristram Shandy*. E. O. Wilson dubbed it "high-table picaresque." Robin describes it as "fact loosely based on fiction" and typically links it throughout to Robert Browning's *Sordello*, perhaps the most obscure long poem in English. The original title was *Dancing for the Woolworth Ladies*. There is really no substitute for reading it, but here is an introduction, again adapted from a website:

> I listened, jaw-sagging, as a brilliant young anthropologist, Robin Fox, lectured on the intricacies of kinship systems.

(David Attenborough: *Life on Air: Memoir of a Broadcaster*, 2002, as cited online.)

> *Participant Observer* is the story of how Robin Fox, now one of the most prominent anthropologists of our time, born in England in the Great Depression, managed against the odds to get to the point described by David Attenborough: at the London School of Economics in the mid-sixties. It goes on to tell how he went on from there to become a pioneer of what Robert Ardrey called "the revolution in the social sciences"—the revolution that, after a hundred years, took Darwin seriously in the study of human behavior.
> In the autobiographical tradition of Lévi-Strauss's *Tristes Tropiques*, but crossed with a good dose of *Angela's Ashes*, Fox, acting as the independent narrator of his own life, takes us on an exuberant romp through the thirties to the seventies of last century, over several continents but mainly Europe and America. It is a personal, historical and intellectual journey, which is at once intriguing, hilarious and moving. Without ever mentioning his own name, or any dates, he looks for all the impingements that caused the protean shifts in this sprawling mini-saga of the adventures of a child of the meritocracy.
> From the proverbial humble beginnings, in a family whose income was "a shilling a week less than Frank McCourt's" he became one of those at the center of the great debate of the century: the contention about the nature of human nature in a world that had learned, or failed to learn, from Darwin. But it was a long road, peppered with strange events, brain-bending ideas, odd adventures, dangers and sorrows, loves and losses, and a spectacular cast of lively—often very strange—characters. From Bertrand Russell and Noam Chomsky, to Margaret Mead and Konrad Lorenz, via William Fulbright, Kingsley Amis, and Lionel Tiger, among many, many others. Throughout all this he floats, like Christopher Isherwood's camera, at once observant and baffled, interested and amazed, sympathetic and cynical, but eternally curious.
> He feels he has been the observer of a series of endings: the last gasps of now extinct ways of life. He saw the last of the old steam-powered northern-English wool towns of the industrial revolution; of the pre-industrial Hardy countryside of southern England; of the ancient Grammar Schools before their destruction by what he calls doctrinaire socialism; of the old London School of Economics when it was still an international family, not just a big college; of the brave but

failed experiment that was Talcott Parsons' Social Relations Department at Harvard; of the innocent but troubled America of the fifties; of the last gasp of traditional Indian life in New Mexico; of "genteel Jane Austen England" in Devon; of peasant-crofter life in the Gaelic-speaking Irish islands; of the old American rah-rah men's college at Rutgers and Princeton; of the amateur bullfight in provincial South America; of the already commercialized Hippie life of San Francisco; of the intimate and eccentric world of anthropology before its rapid expansion in the seventies; and of the whole "deferential society" wounded in the sixties and seventies, and beginning to be erased by political correctness and egalitarian dumbing down in a world changed utterly by the baby boom, the pill and Vietnam.

Interests

Robin's latest book, *The Tribal Imagination: Civilization and the Savage Mind*, is dedicated to Claude Lévi-Strauss and Ernest Gellner. Gellner's influence, like Darwin's, "saturates" (his word) everything he does. Gellner, he says,

> inoculated me from relativism in all its forms. He saved me from the spell of Wittgenstein; no good fairy ever put a kinder gift into an infant's cradle.

The book deals with perceptions of time, human rights, Iraq and democracy, sectarianism and animal dispersion, the two sets of the Ten Commandments, incest and in-laws, incest in literature, male bonding in the epics, poetry and the brain, seafood and civilization, Morgan and the study of the tribes, Popper and the meaning of civilization, and the two traditions of thought he feels drive Western culture. Its basic premise is what has always been his premise: human nature is fundamentally tribal, and the future of civilization depends on dealing with that stubborn fact.

The following is from the book's "Prologue: The Miracle and the Drumbeats" and shows how he came to anthropology through the philosophy of history and how that is where he thinks it truly belongs. ("The Miracle" was Ernest Gellner's term for the "curious concatenation of circumstances" that produced modern Western science and capitalism.)

> A little background is in order to put these essays into context, both personal and professional. The question of the rise and fall of civilizations has intrigued me since my schoolboy interest in Arnold Toynbee in post-WWII England when we were desperate to know

what went wrong. A second-hand copy of the abridged edition of *A Study of History* was the most thumbed and annotated tome in the small collection that my very small allowance permitted. I augmented this with Edward Gibbon's *Decline and Fall of the Roman Empire* (school library) and H. G. Wells' *The Outline of History* (a gift from my mother) and the game was afoot. What was civilization? Was its appearance inevitable? How had it arisen from the primitive tribal condition and why did it seem so vulnerable and so inevitably to fail? Was civilization indeed an advanced stage that left the tribal behind, or was the tribal always with us in some form, beckoning us back? How far from the tribal state could we stray without going adrift and foundering? For Toynbee the threatening tribes on the fringes of civilization (the "external proletariat") were never as dangerous as the "failure of will" inside civilization itself.

Well-stocked public and college libraries sent me to Schopenhauer and Nietzsche, to Hegel and Marx (and more interestingly, Engels), to Schweitzer, Sartre and Spengler, and produced a lot of information and even more puzzlement. This was somewhat stressful for a young fellow whose main interests were in politics, rugby, girls and music, more or less in that order. Serious injury took me out of sports and opened a window for the exploration of ideas. But for the injury you might now be reading the memoirs of a sporting cabinet minister. Who knows? I was immensely fortunate to find a sympathetic degree course in sociology at the London School of Economics in the early 1950s. We were encouraged to read the philosophers of history even though the prevailing empiricism did not hold their methods in high regard. I had to deal directly with Karl Popper and his criticisms of Historicism. I was smitten with Popper and took his point, but still thought the questions could be asked in a way that was subject to falsification. Popper himself asked them in his own way, which became my way.

I did not find either British Empiricism or Continental Existentialism much help in this matter, but I did find the sociology of knowledge and comparative sociology more than enough to compensate. I was led to Max Weber and Herbert Spencer, to Emile Durkheim and the developmental anthropologists, particularly E. B. Tylor and James Frazer. I was in fact specializing in social anthropology, but found to my disappointment that in the form of Functionalism it had not only abandoned the questions that drew me to the study of the tribes, but it positively banned them. There was no point, I was told, in dealing with known error, however interesting it might be. So Freud and Jung were out too.

At Harvard in the 1950s I found the questions still alive among the Americans (Sorokin, Kroeber, Steward, White). Freud was front and center, but mostly the clinical Freud not the philosopher of history, while Jung, in whom I had really become interested, was not even mentioned. In any case I got skillfully sidetracked to the Pueblos of the Southwest and sociocultural anthropology and, to be fair, it has made me a decent living. But the questions still nagged. As I watched anthropology drift further and further away from them, I finally, in the London of the 1960s, discovered Darwin and the relevance of Darwinism to the questions. It was meeting John Bowlby and Lionel Tiger that gave me the nudge that turned into a push that became a vocation. Anthropologists, embarrassed by the *laissez-faire* capitalist propaganda of Social Darwinism (so-called) and by the ugly use of Darwinism in Germany and among advocates of racism generally, scooted in the other (ideologically safer) direction, energetically disavowing their own heritage and their purpose and status as a science.

But my curiosity was still there with Toynbee and Spengler and Spencer and Morgan, with Freud and Popper and all those for whom the question of the origin, nature and viability of civilization was an issue that could not be avoided. I found through the amazing upsurge of developments in social biology and evolutionary science, combined with comparative ethnography (anthropology's precious archive of human social behavior in pre-literate societies) a route back to the question of civilization and the savage mind. I have been exploring it ever since.

Prelude

This section was written for the same "Prologue"—it was intended to show how Robin's other works were a prelude to this latest book. In the end it was not included, so we can use it here to fill in the details and bring the story up to date.

Many of the things I have written earlier would sit happily with this volume in spirit if not in detail (new findings pour in daily). These perhaps start with my essay on "Sibling Incest" in 1962 where I proposed a "law" of incest avoidance (see the chapter by Maryanski and Turner here) and tried to reconcile Freud and Westermarck on the incest taboo. This was followed by *Kinship and Marriage* (1967), a book mistakenly assumed by many to be a "textbook" conveying received wisdom. While it is an introduction to the study of kinship it is also an original contribution which argues that human kinship rests logically on the playing out of four simple premises: (1) women bear the children, (2) men impregnate the women, (3) men exercise control, (4) primary kin do not mate with each other: gestation, impregnation, domination and hybridization. The basic human relationship, I argue, is the mother-child unit not the nuclear family. This position was arrived at on logical not biological grounds; it was nevertheless dear to John Bowlby, the Darwinian psychoanalyst who had introduced me to the idea of Ethology—the science of the evolution of social behavior. He liked a paper I had written on the success of healing rituals in the Pueblos (1960), but insisted I should understand the evolution of the emotions that these rituals tapped into. I never looked back.

All of *The Red Lamp of Incest*, for example, where I maintained, following Freud and triangulating him with Darwin and Lévi-Strauss, that "we constantly reproduce that which produced us" belongs in this company. I tried to marry Freud (on the emotions) and Lévi-Strauss (on the intellect,) to the process of evolution and what we then knew of primate behavior and behavioral neurology. I argued that the crucial factor in human evolution—and particularly the rapid evolution of the brain—was the growth of neo-cortical control over the emotional system. This was an outcome of the struggle between older and younger males for control of the females, and was the source of the arch-rule of the incest taboo. This process underlay the propensity to make and follow rules in general and kinship rules in particular. It was, as the subtitle says, "the origin of mind and society," and much of what is constant in human mental and social systems derives from it.

Most commentators, even the friendly ones, didn't seem to get it, treating the book solely as a contribution to the incest question rather than the question of the evolution of mind and the force of the moral imperative: the question posed by Hume to Kant, Kant to Durkheim, Durkheim to Bergson, Bergson to Lévi-Strauss. . . . The Harvard philosopher Willard van Orman Quine however thought the chapter on "The Matter of Mind" was completely compatible with his own materialist views on the subject. Mind as we know it had to come from somewhere. The edited volumes *Biosocial Anthropology* (on primate kin and human kinship) and *Neonate Cognition* (where I inverted Descartes: "Sumus Ergo Cogitamus") belong here, as does the early collection *Encounter with Anthropology* ("The Cultural Animal"). *The Keresan Bridge*, while concerned with a seemingly narrow problem in Pueblo ethnology (and the famous puzzle of "Crow-Omaha" kinship systems) still stresses the fact that human kinship systems evolve in predictable patterns and that we cannot escape the deep-time dimension by a simplistic appeal to social functions or acculturation.

The essays from *Reproduction and Succession* on "The War between Kinship and the State" (Mormon polygamy, surrogate mothers, Greek tragedy, especially *Antigone*, and the avunculate—the special relationship between a man and his mother's brother) have a place here. The book was in fact a commentary on Sir Henry Maine's theory of the historical shift from the law of status to the law of contract. *The Search for Society*, where it was the issue of "Consciousness out of Context"—my own phrasing of the "novel environment hypothesis"—also belongs. The further we move away from the Paleolithic norm, the more extreme become the conflicts that consciousness faces.

I introduced the idea of the "ethosystem" in which the organism and the environment that it modifies with its behavior, exist in a positive feedback loop: an idea that has been re-invented recently as "niche creation." I tried to trace the history of ideas on individualism and society to see where the empiricism, progressivism and relativism of the social sciences came from. I started with Bacon, Hobbes and Locke and the idea of the mind as a *tabula rasa*—a blank slate, and hence the hostility to "innate ideas" (or innate anything). In the process I tried to reconcile the division between the Durkheimian and Darwinian views of social life—a division which underlies the schism in the social sciences, by showing how "social facts" can also be biological facts. There also I defined instinct as "the organism's demand for an appropriate environment." An inappropriate environment can wreck the patient work of natural selection. Nature and nurture need each other; there is no "nature/nurture question" except for the question of how they interact.

In place here would be the subjects from *Conjectures and Confrontations*: bureaucracy, nationalism, innovation, self-interest, sexual conflict in literature, the moral sense, and left-wing archaeology. In "The Biosocial Orientation" I invoked Robert Merton's distinction between "theory" and "orientation" and it holds here. I am not pushing any kind of systematic theory, only suggesting an intellectual orientation, which may draw on many theories. Go where the questions lead; use what theories and data you need. Add also the essays on food, sex, orgasm, incest, menstruation (in Macaques), aggression, myth, rules and war in *The Challenge of Anthropology*, where I re-iterated my "law of the dispensable male." This book includes my personal favorite: "Prejudice and the Unfinished Mind," which held that prejudice is not so much an abnormal form of thinking as thinking is a normal form of prejudice.

That particular essay took off from the early work of Nobel laureate Daniel Kahneman and his colleague the late Amos Tversky, which was revealed to me in Jerusalem. There (in the essay, not in Jerusalem) I investigated, with the help of David Hume, Paul Robeson, Charles Lamb, Captain Kirk, and Mr. Spock, four insistent mental Drumbeats. These are: (1) that we must make causal connections; (2) that we must attribute responsibility for actions; (3) that we must think in terms of stereotypes; (4) that we must prefer intuition to logic in uncertain situations. Note the "must"—that is the link and the nub.

Even *The Tory Islanders*, a study of the social structure of a remarkable Irish island people, fits in here. At its core is the analysis of how family, clan, marriage and household articulate around the inheritance of land and the manning of boats. The fulcrum on which this pivots is the brother-sister bond and the mother-child bond, and the tension between the consanguine family and the necessity of marriage: many married couples did not move in together; each partner stayed in the natal home—"natolocal residence." It thus explores these universals in their Celtic particulars.

The verse, drama and essays in *The Passionate Mind* (incorporating *The Violent Imagination*) have their place on the list, perhaps especially the dialogue "Design Failure" on the tyranny of ideas, and the opener on "The Conference of Foules" where the battery hens gather to analyze their sad condition, or the story of the crucial stages in evolution told in "Evolutionary Poetics." My personal favorite is "The Jesus Tapes: We Are Not Alone"—a blank-verse monologue in the style of Browning where Jesus is revealed to be an alien spirit trapped in a human body in a vain attempt to elevate mankind. Jesus has little sympathy with anyone except Pilate and Judas. The readers might prefer "The Trial of George Washington"—which is what it says. The trial is for treason of course.

And there is always the impudent attempt to solve it all at one fell swoop that Lionel Tiger and I bounced off the world in *The Imperial Animal*, in those verdant years when it all looked so temptingly easy. Our notion of a "behavioral biogrammar"—inspired by Noam Chomsky's theory of generative grammar, (we even proposed a "culture acquisition device") was not so far off the mark. The basic grammar of behavior was given by evolution but it could produce an infinite number of behavioral languages. This might have been a better model than the "software" analogies that became popular with the advent of computers, although we couldn't resist the metaphor of behavioral instructions as being "in the wiring" of human nature.

Much of what follows in this book is about what Tiger and I called "behavioral gibberish." This results when you feed organisms information that does not accord with the biogrammar. Garbage in: gibberish out. We looked at the "primate baseline" and its transformation by the "hunting transition" to what was the human default system of tribal society and mentality. Then we tried to see how the industrial world was either in synch with or inimical to this default system. It is that simple and that complicated. Our epigraph from Jacques Monod's *Chance and Necessity*, that "every living being is also a fossil," is at the very heart of it. We put it in French because Monod's book hadn't been translated when we were writing. This gained us no brownie points with the yahoos of course, who saw it as up-front proof of our unregenerate élitism.

Colleagues and Students

The range and depth of issues and problems Robin has studied are superbly represented in the essays that follow. But the contributors are not students or disciples, although all have been influenced by his ideas. As Lionel Tiger notes, there is no school or sect of Foxism, no body of doctrine, no devoted followers, no concentrated accumulation of narrow and repetitive research. He does not think that way; that is not how he organizes his life and thought. His analysis of academic sects (in *The Tribal Imagination*) puts them at no level higher than the most primitive of doctrinal schisms with their prophets and acolytes. His attention is always on a problem and how to solve it, not on a doctrine and how to promote it. This is perhaps why he seems so often to be the mediator between fiercely battling colleagues—often their only mode of contact, and always the friend of each: Robert Ardrey and Ashley Montagu; Margaret Mead and Derek Freeman; Rodney Needham and David Schneider; Rodney Needham and Claude Lévi-Strauss; Konrad Lorenz and Daniel Leherman; and others he prefers to keep to himself.

Robin has however always been close to his students because he is, in his own estimation, an eternal student, and teaching is just "encouraging the curiosity of others." His students, he says, seemed often to be refugees from difficult relationships with other faculty, and their affection for him is as an academic rescuer, friend, and unwavering supporter. They have almost all done theses and pursued careers on subjects far removed from his core interests. He likes that because, he says, he learns such a lot from every new topic. From the symbolism of Basque violence, to de-Stalinization in Mongolia, to political songs of the Greek diaspora, to Lakota ceremonial costume, to Reform Judaism in Israel, to the Delaware Indian *Walam Olum* as a nineteenth-century hoax, to the meaning of gorilla vocalizations, to the role of women in rebuilding Germany, to the geomantic symbolism of Mayan architecture. These are just the most recent, to which I should add that for space reasons Robin's students are not represented in this book (though Alan Macfarlane did attend his lectures at the LSE).

Biosocial Science

Robin Fox has been hailed as one of the founders of biosocial science. One anthology (Caplan 1978) even included the young Tiger and Fox as "Forerunners of Sociobiology" along with Darwin, Spencer, Huxley, and Kropotkin! The psychiatric anthropologist Roland Littlewood recently called him "our most outstanding biosocial figure in social anthropology" because he "stays close to the central concerns of the discipline . . . before he interprets these through a Darwinian lens." (Littlewood 2011.) But Robin does not sit easily with the idea of creating new disciplines. To him they inevitably become new orthodoxies.

Although adversaries like to categorize in order to dismiss, Robin has never, for example, been a "sociobiologist" in any but the most general sense. He supported (and helped to fund) the sociobiological endeavor from its beginning and is very close to many of its principals, especially E. O. Wilson and Robert Trivers (and was to William Hamilton.) He is firm that he has learned a great deal from its exploration of ultimate causes in evolution, but he has also been one of its critics. He has favored the development of an approach that emphasizes the integration of ultimate *and* proximate causes in the evolution of human action: one represented in this volume by Melvin J. Konner, Bernard Chapais, and Dieter Steklis (and note the implicit debate between them on the nature of human nature). He had other differences from the sociobiological mainstream: always, for example, he championed the idea of group selection against the almost total (and even passionate) consensus that favored individual selection (Fox 1997, chap. 7.) He has lived to see the idea revived and renewed by some of the leaders of the movement, such as E. O. Wilson and David Sloan Wilson (2007/8.) His work on the avunculate (in *Reproduction and Succession*, where sociobiology was seen as one of six ways to view the problem) was equally critical of the explanatory power of "paternity certainty" and the "maximization of reproductive success." (See Fox 1996, for his comments on the idea, history, and various branches of sociobiology.)

Robin does not want to create new intellectual boundaries. His intention is always subversive: he seeks constantly to erode them by conjecture and refutation (after Popper), not to support them by constant reconfirmation. We can find numerous examples where he has happily accepted evidence or analysis that contradicted one of his key hypotheses and has changed his theory in consequence; for example, on the age of learning the incest taboo; on the mechanisms of the classical Murngin kinship system; on the most rudimentary form of human social organization; on the role of female choice in human evolution (Sullerot 1978); and on the conditions for the origin of civilization. One of the most recent was Bernard Chapais's reworking of his hypotheses about the origins of human exogamy (marriage out). But hear what Chapais, whose contribution is a centerpiece of this book, says about him under the heading of "The Deconstruction of Exogamy":

> Armed with a solid background in the anthropology of kinship, Robin Fox tackled the literature on kinship and behavior in nonhuman primates in a series of articles that appeared in the 1970s and in a book *The Red Lamp of Incest*. His insights, thirty years later, appear remarkable.... Fox's comparative studies constituted a major leap toward an understanding of the origin of human society.... In the 1970s Fox, as a social anthropologist, was almost alone and well ahead of his time in his efforts to understand and extract the significance of the primate data for human society. More than ten years were to elapse before Fox's ideas were taken up in a comprehensive manner and the decomposition of exogamy significantly furthered. (*Primeval Kinship*, pp. 120–121)

Introduction

In this as in other matters Robin was "well ahead of his time," thus leaving many of his contemporaries and elders baffled and defensive, and often just avoiding his bolder ideas. (This avoidance was the subject of Jonathan Benthall's consoling letter.) However, Bernard Chapais says in his introduction to *Primeval Kinship* (2008) that if he had not dedicated the book to his parents he would have honored Claude Lévi-Strauss and Robin Fox together. Robin says he would have been embarrassed but certainly delighted with the association. Peter Wood, writing in *Society*, said, "With the death of Claude Lévi-Strauss in 2009, Fox is perhaps the most important living exponent of the tradition in anthropology in which the study of kinship was indeed the central intellectual enterprise." Of all his contemporaries Robin respected Lévi-Strauss as *"le maître."* While he disagreed with him often, most notably on the incest taboo, he always saw his own thinking as a constant creative dialogue with that of the French genius. Does he consider himself in the same class as Lévi-Strauss? He says absolutely not. He told one of his wives to lower her early expectations of him: "I am not a prince," he said. "You'll have to settle for a superior frog."

Robin was hailed by a recent reviewer as a thinker who, in an age of overspecialization, "refuses to be an amateur at anything." His influence, his insistence on a "biosocial orientation," has been subtle, but it has been everywhere, not only in anthropology but also in literature, politics, the arts, and sciences. It's not so much that he bridges the two cultures of humanism and science, he simply refuses to recognize the dichotomy, in the same way that he refuses to recognize the distinction between cultural and evolutionary anthropology. In his original version of *The Violent Imagination* he included scientific articles among the verse, satire, dialogues, and drama. Needless to say, publishers were baffled, and the articles had to go. He has been called a maverick, and by any usual standard he is, but he likes to insist that he is ultimately totally mainstream; the rest of the world is out of step. He is, according to one of his own accounts, simply following Bronislaw Malinowski's dictate that culture should be studied as a response to human needs if we wish to understand the nature and fate of civilization.

The very diversity and the exceptionally high standard of what follows in this book from his colleagues and friends (and his daughters) testifies to his belief in the unity of the arts and sciences in the exploration of human nature; what E. O. Wilson was to call "Consilience." Gathered here are eight social anthropologists (two of them historians, one a poet), two neurobiologists (both primatologists), one neurobiologist who works with primates, two sociologists, a Shakespearean scholar, one poet and literary scholar, one biological anthropologist who is also a poet and an MD, one public servant and famous playwright, and one brilliant synthesizer and musical entrepreneur who is not easily classifiable. Eight are from the United States, five are from the United Kingdom, three from Canada, and one from France. They all differ in their specializations. What they share is Robin's broad mandate for a view of humanity that looks beyond narrow professional boundaries and to a resurrection of anthropology in its widest and most basic sense: the total study of mankind, past, present, and future.

If Robin's evolutionary view leads him to a general pessimism about the human future, he still seems to retain a small spark of hope. As he noted in *Search for Society*, given our capacity to create hideous cultures we have to hope that there is something in human nature that will, in the name of common humanity, always stand up to the tyranny of culture. If there is not, then we are in serious trouble.

One of Robin's most challenging books was aptly named *The Challenge of Anthropology*. The challenge is to look beyond the limits of "disciplines" to the greater vision of the wholeness of humanity and its universal history and to try to see the implications of this for our collective future. He resists the description of "the last anthropologist" and says he is just a foot soldier in the ongoing battle for what his friend Napoleon Chagnon calls "the conscience of anthropology"—something superbly illustrated by the essays in this book. As early as *Encounter with Anthropology*, and perhaps still remembering the thesis he never got to write at Cornell, he was arguing that the social sciences were subdisciplines of moral philosophy, that we have to know what we *are* to know what we should *do*. To quote his oft-used aphorism: "We have no choice but to be human."

Work on this book was complete when we learned that Robin Fox had been elected to the National Academy of Sciences (2013). It seems a fitting way to end this introduction.

References

Caplan, Arthur, ed. 1978. *The Sociobiology Debate: Readings on Ethical and Scientific Issues*. New York: Harper and Row.

Chapais, Bernard. 2008. *Primeval Kinship: How Pair-Bonding Gave Birth to Human Society*. Cambridge, MA: Harvard University Press.

Fox, Robin. 1960. "Therapeutic Rituals and Social Structure in Cochiti Pueblo." *Human Relations* 13:4, 291–303.

———. 1962. "Sibling Incest." *British Journal of Sociology* 13:128–50.
———. 1978. "La selection sexuelle et le role du choix feminin dans l'evolution du comportment humain." In *Le Fait Feminin*, edited by E. Sullerot. Paris: Fayard.
Fox, Robin 1996. "Sociobiology." Edited by Adam and Jessica Kuper. *The Social Science Encyclopedia*. 2nd ed. London: Routledge.
Fox, Robin, and Lionel Tiger, 1966. "The Zoological Perspective in Social Science." *Man: The Journal of the Royal Anthropological Institute*. NS. 1:1, 75–81.
Littlewood, Roland, 2011. *Society*, 48:6, 481–82
Wilson, David S., and Edward O. Wilson, 2007. "Re-thinking the Theoretical Foundation of Sociobiology." *The Quarterly Review of Biology*, 82:4, 327–48.
Wilson, David S., and Edward O. Wilson, 2008. "Evolution 'for the Good of the Group.'" *American Scientist*, 96:380–89.
Wood, Peter, 2011. "Drumbeats in Modern Life." *Society*, 48:6, 474–77.

Books by Robin Fox

Kinship and Land Tenure on Tory Island. Belfast: The Queen's University of Belfast, Ulster Folk Museum, 1966.
The Keresan Bridge: A Problem in Pueblo Ethnology. London: Athlone Press/ New York: Humanities Press, 1967. (2004, Oxford/New York: Berg.)
Kinship and Marriage: An Anthropological perspective. 1st ed. Baltimore & London: Penguin 1967. 2nd ed. Cambridge/New York: Cambridge University Press, 1983.
The Imperial Animal (with Lionel Tiger), 1971. New York: Holt Rinehart and Winston 1971. 2nd ed. New Brunswick, NJ: Transaction Publishers, 1998.
Encounter with Anthropology. New York: Harcourt, Brace, Jovanovich. 1973. 2nd ed. New Brunswick, NJ: Transaction Books, 1991.
Biosocial Anthropology (contributor and editor.) London: Malaby Press, 1975.
The Tory Islanders: A People of the Celtic Fringe. Cambridge: Cambridge University Press, 1978. (Notre Dame: University of Notre Dame Press, 1983.)
The Red Lamp of Incest: A Study in the Origins of Mind and Society. 2nd ed., Notre Dame, IN: University of Notre Dame Press, 1983 (Original, New York: E. P. Dutton, 1980.)
Neonate Cognition: Beyond the Blooming Buzzing Confusion. (Contributor and editor with Jacques Mehler.) Hillsdale, NJ: Erlbaum, 1985.
The Search for Society: Quest for a Biosocial Science and Morality. New Brunswick, NJ: Rutgers University Press, 1989.
Reproduction and Succession: Studies in Anthropology, Law and Society. New Brunswick, NJ: Transaction Publishers, 1993.
The Challenge of Anthropology: Old Encounters and New Excursions. New Brunswick, NJ: Transaction Publishers, 1994.
Conjectures and Confrontations: Science, Evolution, Social Concern. New Brunswick, NJ: Transaction Publishers, 1997.
The Passionate Mind: Sources of Destruction and Creativity. New Brunswick, NJ: Transaction Publishers. 2000.

Participant Observer: Memoir of a Transatlantic Life. New Brunswick, NJ: Transaction Publishers, 2006.
The Tribal Imagination: Civilization and the Savage Mind. Cambridge, MA: Harvard University Press, 2011.
Shakespeare's Education: Schools, Lawsuits, Theater and the Tudor Miracle. Buchholz, Germany: Verlag Uwe Laugwitz, 2012
Website: www.robin-fox.com.

1

This Guy, Fox

Lionel Tiger

For some unaccountable reason it's compelling to begin this document with the wholly irrelevant remark that one of the most perilous elements of working with Robin is his preposterous capacity to remember, and worse to sing, the endlessly coy and clever operettas of Gilbert and Sullivan—all of them, it was once threatened by the chap himself—and so, dull association with him never was. And by way of literary gossip, when we worked together at the Harry Frank Guggenheim Foundation (more later) we were fortunate to have a splendid colleague in our office of three. Karyl Roosevelt had come to New York from Chicago where she had been the secretary of Saul Bellow. He regretted her leaving and grandly recalled her for the final preparation of his last manuscripts. Among other things, she told Bellow that one of her new employers could recite most of Swinburne and sing Gilbert and Sullivan by heart. Nobelist Bellow wrote her a card advising testily: "Your new employer sounds like a jerk." Robin, who loved Bellow's novels, prized this above all other literary compliments.

Kinship and Marriage

The second much more germane datum was his description of his commute to central London to the London School of Economics and Political Science, where he taught, from the modest suburb in Surrey where he lived. He would install himself in one of the characteristic separate third-class carriages of English trains and therein work, for one thing, on his manuscript for his fundamental and classic text *Kinship and Marriage*. The same crowd of professional men also rode the train and shared the carriage regularly. Later he found out they all thought he was an electrical engineer because he was forever working on charts and graphs, the same charts and graphs that permitted him to describe human kinship in the most parsimonious and accurate manner. The book was published by Penguin Books (sainted and sacred to us all at the time). It has seen endless reprints and translations, established his reputation as an international kinship master in one precocious fell swoop, and brought him to the respectful attention of intellectual peers such as Rodney Needham and the secular pope of kinship analysis, Claude Lévi-Strauss. And for a usefully oxygenated and exhilarating description of Robin's comments on the function of systems of kinship in mediating between senior and young males, read in this volume the remarks of neuropsychiatrist Michael T. McGuire. For McGuire, Robin's books were not only deliverers of fact but also promoters of intellectual well-being.

But for those of us in Robin's milieu of baffled aspirants seeking full adult status, worse even than his hard-science reputation among commuters because of his kinship charts was the appalling and depressing fact that his epically concise and far-reaching *Kinship and Marriage* took him all of six weeks to write. How on earth? The four-minute mile, or three actually, is a rebuke to us all. He insists there was nothing remarkable about it: the stuff was all in his head; he only had to put it down. Handel, he points out, wrote the whole of *Messiah* in the same time—a typical Robin comment that could be either true modesty or subtle boasting. But it's clear from his body of work that he writes with dreamy clarity and with fully justified heft and has done so with unwavering quality throughout his long career. What was and is his secret? At various times he asserted vaguely that this efficiency was caused by nothing more noble than near penury and the lure of the moneybags that his Penguin editor had no doubt promised.

Let's consider this. Perhaps he was driven by penury and wrote quickly because of it. This even the most warm-hearted inspection of his arrangements could support. To a foreigner like me, his family's residence was typically cozy, well-managed, and characteristic of the lot in life, which was quite little, of English academics. What was however a (clear to me) dramatic local symptom of the cash-strapped state to which he referred, was the dented automobile he had purchased, very, very used (for forty-five pounds), from Her Majesty's Royal Mail. It was barely large enough for two adults and three ebullient little girls but had wheels and provided transport. However, it boasted one compelling penury indicator—a hand crank! The venerable vehicle on occasion (and in an English winter) required an aerobic joint-wrenching episode to achieve liftoff. Nevertheless, for a hazily ambitious potential book writer such as I concede I was, his equable confession about his absurdly speedy work could not have been more functionally and appropriately demoralizing no matter how his car sprang into life.

However, when we later did write a book together, it took not only six weeks nor even six months but closer to two years. Surely I slowed him down. And yet let it be said that the process of working with Robin was never marked by surliness, evasion, and laziness. Perhaps we were, working together, less swift than Fox on his own. We fell into a work pattern that invariably required a warm-up of several hours of jokes, gossip, fruitless strategies about taxes, and the inevitable soap operas intrinsic to establishing a new department (in 1967) in a new college in an old university in a lavishly turbulent country that was new to both of us. Also, duets may be more complicated than arias and take more than double the time because of this.

Beside any point as both these vignettes may be, they nonetheless each reflect an element of the unusually productive and entertaining pleasure it's been to endure association with Professor Fox. The first vignette reveals the ongoing skill and intricacy of his inner and outer life of mirth, fun, and irony. The second shows the intellectual athleticism that has enabled him to grab large subjects, master their weight, and then parse the complexity of human action. He has done this in a series of sentences and books that have ranged from the reveries of primates to what was on the minds of writers and talkers of Greek myths. He moves easily from the evolution of the brain to the mindlessness of the postmodern spasm about nothing much other than reveries of postsabbatical scholars about their Left Bank longings. Perhaps his intellectual breadth and his control of widespread allusion derives from his here-and-there education, mainly in church schools because of his father's military career, rather than from the firm and uniform curricula of most schools of the time. Robin's father was posted to Afghanistan in the 1920s, where he took a photo with a Brownie box camera of the king of Afghanistan being flown to safety in British India, fleeing from a Russian-inspired rebellion. This was the first time the British army had ever used a plane in a military operation. When in later years Robin told his then-retired father that the Russians were in Afghanistan, the old soldier asked, "When were they ever out?" The senior Fox also predicted that the world would end in Afghanistan!

Il Miglior Fabbro

The challenge in writing about Fox's professional life is that the only person who can with proper perspective and adequate breadth account for it is the man himself. Furthermore, despite my close association with him, which has been both a privilege and a hoot, I am technically unable to replicate (and often comprehend) the intellectual management that has governed so much of his work. I hope it is clearly humble and not boastful to recall what T. S. Eliot wrote in a dedication to Ezra Pound: "*Il miglior fabbro*" (the better worker).

However, there's no room for coyness here. Robin and I were aware from the very outset of our connection that it was not floated on weak beer. This was baldly stated in the absurdly and now-charmingly grand title of our initial paper, "The Zoological Perspective in Social Science." It extended for all of six closely printed pages in *Man: The Journal of the Royal Anthropological Institute*. Evidently some readers thought it was so bizarre and impolite that it had to have been written by the gringo, me, and that Robin had used his local connections to help me out. Others thought it was a gross mishap caused by Robin, which the addition of my name was supposed to mitigate.

No, it was neither. Robin and I had both been at a 1965 conference of the Zoological Society of London organized by Julian Huxley and held at the London Zoo. It turned out to be sharply consequential in the development of a biology of behavior. During the conference, Fox and I were introduced to each other by Anthony Forge who had been a fellow student of mine at the London School of Economics and was now a colleague of Robin's there. He decided we had some common interests, even if they were strange. In the movie version of this tale we were supposed to have met outside of, not in, the gibbon cage. As I recall, we had a brief chat, appearing to size each other up agreeably, and then Robin suggested we meet at his office the following week.

We did. My recollection about what specifically happened is somewhat unclear, except for its intensity. In essence, we were scouting out an intello-military terrain and evaluating our forces. After a while it seemed clear we were in the war, or were at least qualified as fresh reserve troops with a new approach perhaps. Then as we talked, it got even better in the *esprit de corps* department. Suddenly it seemed appropriate to begin to write down what we were talking up. And it was appropriate too that our adventure began at the London School of Economics, which was at the time a boisterous haven for intellectual aspiration of the highest and most acerbic order. A recent biography (by John Hall) of our teacher, friend, and colleague Ernest Gellner—a mainstay of the joint—is remarkably redolent of the rah-rah noncampus spirit of that special urban haven. In fact, when there was a student strike and sit-in, which utterly perplexed the administrators of a school boasting special (bourgeois) proletarian status, Gellner and anthropologist (Sir) Raymond Firth (a man of almost preposterous grace and intellectual skill) formed committees to represent the students' issues. Fox was on both of them. This was done at considerable cost to their reputations in the councils of faculty in the Senior Uncommon Room. They even wrote a letter to the *Times*, which was then regarded as a gargantuan act of social concern if not a hubristic reach for national status. (Hall's otherwise excellent book misses this episode.)

Ockham's Razor

The first words of that paper in *Man* clearly assert what we had in mind: "The relevance of new data to a discipline is not always immediately appreciated." It is appealing to cite much of the text because of its impact and quality—in our view. Instead, we will make it available on our respective websites. But our implacable intent was to change the rules of what social scientists should know about biology, but more aggressively, and what we all had to know. The law of parsimony had to be obeyed throughout social-science land. We worked at the LSE building on Aldwych, near Fleet Street, where Steven Sondheim's barber wielded his razor. We were immensely fond of Mr. Ockham's very own blade, and it was our favorite work tool too.

Of course, many primatologists were already using it. But we had a new concern: to establish that not only should social scientists know about evolution and the inner squishy bits such as the brain of the human animal that they study, but that biologists should also learn about sophisticated social science because this would reveal the important ways in which their subjects conform to some of the same regularities sociologists know so well.

To put it succinctly, we saw no reason for the (boringly persistent) division of the traditional university into faculties of natural and of social science. First of all, this coerced the extraordinary conclusion that social behavior was not natural. It reified the nature-culture boundary, a wheel-spinning adumbration that had been a thriving industry in academe for nearly ever. And it condemned social scientists to formal and usually belligerent avoidance of precisely the kind of transformative bioscience represented in the conquest of DNA and the literally thrilling discoveries about human evolution and primatology. Much of it derived from Africa as we discovered how ancient our species is, where it came from, and perhaps why it has succeeded so.

Zoon Politikon

Oh, for the good days of Aristotle, who announced, "Man is by nature a political animal." While troops of political scientists pondered "political," the important phrase "by nature" was almost completely ignored. All this seemed so obvious and vital to us that we felt a clear call to find a rooftop from which to advertise our better mousetrap.

How? By writing a book, of course. But Fox was in London, and I was at the University of British Columbia. I'd had a year's research leave when I first encountered Robin. How could I get another? Fox wrote a cleverly dramatic letter to my departmental chairman, revealing how we were about to do great things, had book projects and contracts, and could I please be released for yet more time. As luck would have it, the wonderful Canada Council and the new Killam Foundation awarded me the first ever fellowship for frankly interdisciplinary work, which provided more time in London.

Rutgers University was the State University of New Jersey, and it had no formal anthropology department, in part because Ashley Montagu, who became a friend to us both and to Robin's family, had a one-year appointment that he continued to claim for years after he was off the payroll. The university president, Mason Gross, was angrily reluctant to allow in any other of that academic tribe.

But in 1965–1966 a new college focusing on social science was to be established, and surely anthropology was to be part of it, and to their enormous credit the leaders of the college asked Robin (who was barely thirty) to chair and establish the department. He'd be delighted, he said, but only if I would join him as his wingman during our revolution. To make a not-long story really short, I moved to Rutgers at the end of 1968, fortified and well-launched with one of those hot John Simon Guggenheim Fellowships. We were in business, and in pleasure.

In our introduction to Transaction Publishers' new edition of *The Imperial Animal* we described our collaborative process in response to many questions about it, such as whether we fight, who wrote what, and why did we bother. Our rule was that every sentence had to be written in the physical presence of the other. We were playing jazz, and everyone had to be in tune. Almost immediately, our respective native intellectual arrogances surfaced, and we were both completely unfazed by the other who deemed a paragraph farcical and rewrote it to his face. We knew different things, and we each could bring to the project a different array of data, general principles, and experiences in the field: Robin among Celtic fishermen and Pueblo Indians and me among Canadian scientific bureaucrats and Ghanaian officials and politicians during Ghana's movement to independence.

Behavioral Biogrammar

But what we shared most and best was the obligation to subject everything to the lens of evolutionary biology, such as it was at the time. Robin, because of his training in linguistics at Harvard, was one of the few people I knew who fully understood the technical complexities of Noam Chomsky's new work on linguistic nature and its connection to evolutionary preparedness of infants to learn skills adults cannot master easily. (Fox had heard Chomsky's early lectures at MIT.) We adapted the notion of universal grammar to behavior and defined the "behavioral biogrammar." We sent the relevant chapter to Chomsky lest we be traducing him. He replied to say that there was "no other way of doing serious social science" than the way we were proposing. We kept in touch with him, and while we remained very friendly, my belief is that he could see that we were potential and fundamental critics of the political correctness then marinating in the United States and decided to include us out. Karl Popper, another of our teacher-heroes, wrote to tell us that he thought the claims of the book were capable of being tested and could generate many "vulnerable hypotheses"—in other words, we were doing science. This was the highest of high praises from the master of scientific method.

We shared Chomsky's view about the only way to write a serious book. We created one that divided forms and structures of society in a manner that permitted the use of the biological lens. Our chapter titles give the flavor: *Beginning Biogrammar* (on the basics); *Political Nature*; *Bond Issue One—Women and Children First*; *Bond Issue Two—Man to Man*; *Give and Take* (on exchange and economics); *The Benign Oppression* (on initiation and education); *Good Grooming* (on physical and emotional health); *The Noble Savage* (on aggression and war); *The City of Man* (on the human future).

The Imperial Animal

Meanwhile, in the discipline we were evidently disturbing the natives, especially the calorie-counting protein-drives-behavior theorists at Columbia Anthropology. They called us "the Rutgers Zoo"—which I learned just recently from Scott Atran, a student there at the time. Morton Fried of that department wrote a gravely false review of my *Men in Groups* in *Science*, in which he compared it to conjuring up phlogiston. (For her part, Margaret Mead, also of that department, wrote a very favorable review of the same book, however in *Redbook*.) A Columbia graduate, Judith Shapiro (later president of Barnard), wrote a review for *Natural History* that was not only gracelessly untutored but also accused us of writing our book mainly for the money—end of the intellectual story. We were going to sue the magazine for libel but were informed they had only one extra nickel and not to waste our time. In England, *The Imperial Animal* encouraged the uninterestingly boisterous Sir Edmund Leach to fill a page of *New Society* with a bafflingly critical and self-righteous review, which among other things accused us of not knowing the work on Australian kinship written by Warren Shapiro. Warren—surprise, surprise—was already a member of our department, chosen on the basis of that outstanding work. (See Fox's commentary on it in *The Challenge of Anthropology*.)

Our book did well. It had first been with Random House, the publisher of *Men in Groups*, but it turned out their editorial team couldn't deal with the book. So we took it to Holt, Rinehart and Winston to an editor and friend there, Steven Aronson, who performed an exquisitely detailed and brilliant edition of the manuscript. The book was on the short list as a Book of the Month selection but became a Featured Alternate instead. It was acquired for translation in about ten languages. For the German edition, we were unusually fortunate that the publisher asked Konrad Lorenz to write an introduction to the book. And then Lorenz won the Nobel Prize!

Here is one vignette. Before the book came out in German, we were invited to the Max Planck Institute in Sieweisen to give a talk about our work. Lorenz, who directed the institute, was there. We each talked for thirty minutes, and evidently, for the first time in the history of the institute, without an interruption from Lorenz.

Overall, publication of *The Imperial Animal* was a pleasure. It infuriated many anthropologists and other social scientists to say nothing of worthy concernocrats who accused us of being politically Paleolithic. Our commitment to human nature as an idea meant, to them, that we had implicitly or outright restricted options for social betterment and the fundamental improvement of mankind. We stood squarely in the way, for example, of creating New Soviet or New Chinese Man. Somehow, the connection between human nature and human rights completely eluded these confidently thoughtful ideologues, and they tried to make our collegial lives miserable. Let it be said that while they did in some minor ways, Fox and I luxuriated in a cool breeze of analytical confidence. Still, some collegial aggression hurt, such as when the American Anthropological Association (from which both of us had resigned because of its outrageous treatment of Napoleon Chagnon) created an award for anthropologists who communicated well with the public and made its first presentation to Steven Jay Gould. Gould was of course not an anthropologist but a contentious charter member of the PC claque that negatively reviewed books such as ours for the *New York Review of Books*. At the same time, Clifford Geertz told Robin he could only attend the social science seminar at the Princeton Institute for Advanced Study as long as he did not mention biology. Geertz had perhaps the best and certainly the most prestigious job in the social sciences and motivated a bilious billow of self-righteous postmodernism that sharply limited his and the discipline's impact on real knowledge. On his death after a painful illness I was asked to write an obituary, which I called "Fuzz, Everything Was Fuzz."

The HFG Foundation

Then our yacht came in. Mason Gross had retired as president of Rutgers and had been asked to preside over the Harry Frank Guggenheim Foundation, which had been delivered some $18 million to study what Guggenheim thought were the pan-human bases of human aggression and inequality. Gross was uncertain he could deal with this material, but when he went to a bookstore to buy B. F. Skinner's *Beyond Freedom and Dignity*, which had been recommended, he also noticed *The Imperial Animal*—both on the bottom of bookstore shelves. He knew and liked Robin (they shared a passion for college football) and bought both books. Skinner sharply offended his Oxford philosopher's soul, but he admired *The Imperial Animal*. That evening he called Robin to ask whether we would help out creating and directing a program for the foundation. Robin called me on a very cheap long-distance call, because it was so short, and soon we were co-research directors of the HFG Foundation and stayed for twelve years. The foundation bought half our time from the university so we could advance its work and our own, and we were able to fund some of the founding figures of what is now familiar and accepted science. We provided Daniel Kahnemann and Amos Tversky with their first grant and supported Jane Goodall, Richard Dawkins, E. O. Wilson, Michael T. McGuire, David Hamburg,

Robert Trivers, Gordon Orians, Donald Symons, William Irons, Paul Ekman, Martin Daly, Robert Sapolsky, Mildred Dickeman, Napoleon Chagnon, Robert J. Lifton, Jonathan Winson, Herb Terrace, Desmond Morris, the Canadian Peace Research Institute, and an extensive list of others.

Later Years

It was all beyond exciting. We decided to cap grants at $35,000 to provide scholars the precious free time that is difficult to get from agencies accustomed to large complex projects. We refused to pay "overheads," which we thought was a kind of racket designed for military researchers. Once I had a Stanford vice president fly in to see me to argue for overheads on a modest grant on incandescent principle. But we repeated our position and suggested that his office tell Professor X that a valued grant was unavailable to him because Stanford wanted its customary 45 percent. Of course X got the grant.

Working with Fox was always vivacious and efficient. We had two deadlines a year for applications, but more often than not we would be in informal discussion with potential grantees for long before they produced any paper. We had no magisterial forms and simply asked applicants to say what they wanted to do, why, how, and what it would cost a thrifty foundation. While we each might become informally responsible for one or other of the applications, we made all the decisions together about which grants to recommend to the foundation's board of directors. The board included, at various times, Bill Baker, the director of the spectacular Bell Labs; James Edwards, the governor of North Carolina; Ed Pendray, one of the founders of NASA; and Generals Jimmy Doolittle and James Gavin, two of Robin's WWII heroes. (His father was on the push to Arnhem with Gavin.) There were also several of Guggenheim's business associates and a few relatives. These included Roger Straus, the publisher who was never our fan and who routinely sought funds for his distinguished friend Susan Sontag, who endlessly and fruitlessly proposed film work on Palestinians.

Overall, the board and its chairman, Peter Lawson-Johnson, appeared to approve of what we did and saw it as appropriate to the donor's intent. Our later years with HFG were bolstered by work with Karen Colvard, who had tired of carrying priceless paintings around the European masters department of Sotheby's and had applied for the far less glamorous job we offered. Hers was the last interview of the day, and she was completely promising. When we announced it was time for a postwork drink and asked what she wanted, a double bourbon, Fox and I glanced at each other and told her she had the job, which she has still, having ennobled it in a major way.

But again, the main impulse was scientific, and there was nothing more exhilarating than receiving or working with applications that wielded Ockham's razor like a sushi master.

Innate Conservatism

I suspect Fox humored me in some of my well-meaning initiatives, such as with the Canadian Peace Institute and a few other similar adventures. Perhaps he thought I merely suffered from Canadian foibles. But again, the discussions about our ranking were always cordial, swift, and without reference to the status folderol so central to so much big science. Robin, I should note, was far less sympathetic to left-wingy causes than I was. Some of this stemmed from his self-described "innate conservatism" and admiration for Burke and Popper. But at the same time, I suspect it was partly because he had worked during summers for British Railways and observed the ticket fiddling, coal stealing, gambling, and other reflections of proletarian ethics. This did not compel him to support the political party of their choice or to believe with George Orwell (whom he greatly admired) that salvation lay with the proles.

Fox can mesh two seemingly contradictory positions with a synthesis that reveals unexpectedly common elements to both sides. Think of his very early work on the incest taboo, described here by Maryanski and Turner, where at one stroke he reconciled two positions that had been held for almost a century to be irreconcilable. He brought together Durkheim and Darwin in a virtuoso act of intellectual chutzpah, and did the same (I am told) with the British "descent theory" and the French "alliance theory" about the fundamentals of kinship theory. I'm sure this underlies an overview of the human condition that enables him, despite his often being a hard-hitting critic, to survive under the radar of conventional thinking without ever appearing aggressive. Come to think of it, I am hard-pressed to identify an incident that prompted his full anger, unless it was the easy target of metastasizing university administrations.

This is not to say that he is without angularity and a raucous sense of personal recklessness, despite spending much of his life in disabling pain as a result of a rare form of arthritis. Once, in California, he elected to parachute out of an airplane simply because he had never done it and was offered the opportunity. With little instruction, he made a perfect jump from 5,000 feet and sent me a telegram simply saying "Geronimo!" He went deep-sea fishing with the Tory Islanders in the North Atlantic in a small open boat. He could not swim, but then, he liked to point out, neither could they. It was considered useless. If you fell overboard in the freezing Atlantic, swimming only delayed the inevitable. Another time we were lecturing at the Universidad de Los Andes in Bogotá and were staying with its founding president. Mario Laserna had founded the university at the age of twenty-six and had on his board Johnny von Neumann, David Rockefeller, and Albert Einstein! Not only that, but he raised bulls for fighting and just happened to have a bull ring on his farm outside Calí in the south. Of course Robin had to fight one. Mario (a Kantian trained in philosophy at Heidelberg) provided him about twenty minutes of largely theoretical and attitudinal instruction about how to do this thing. With *élan vital* that was simply nuts, Robin (emboldened, he insists, by *coca* and *aguardiente*) went ahead with the show, despite having to substitute for a professional matador who had just been gored in the leg. After some terrifying (to me, anyway) moments, he managed to complete his task and come out alive. The crowd loved it, and because of the white jeans he was wearing dubbed him "El Gringo Blanco."

Fox and Bull

Robin is always knitting. There's always an article or book or comment or poem or song or painting on the hop. He was involved with a coauthor in developing a script for "To Hang George Washington Was Our Worst Mistake," which reviewed the major American founding event on the assumption the other side won. (Excerpts from this were eventually published in *The Passionate Mind*.) His story of his half-life, *Participant Observer*, ran to a trim 575 pages. It follows there's a whole equivalent other life to come should he decide to break away long enough from his intricate studies of myth, literature, and evolution. He, perversely or not, always says he would have preferred to be a composer, especially of songs, or an astronomer.

Final Grades

How did the same old story—the fight for love and glory—turn out for that guy Fox? Love is not my business except to comment that he is relentlessly thrilled with his three daughters and performs the requisite deep fret and bubbling joy about all their doings. He used to make up sentimental and funny songs for them when they were small, and which they still remember. Two of his daughters, Kate and Anne, are represented in this book, while a third, Ellie, copes briskly with four alarmingly tall and aspiring grandsons (a great-grandson arrived at the time of this writing). His warm and rock-solid marriage of thirty years to Lin Fox is its own message about his glad skill at domesticity and connection.

And glory? Not many young anthropologists are invited to drinks with Claude Lévi-Strauss to celebrate inclusion in the prestigious series "Les Essais." Few are invited to be a visiting professor at Oxford and Cambridge and Paris and California. He was the youngest English anthropologist to deliver the Malinowski Memorial Lecture and be promoted to professor and chair of a department at whatever age he was. Few have enjoyed such a steady rate of publication over decades by major houses. Few have such an unstoppable and fertile brain and—coming guardedly back to Messrs. Gilbert, Sullivan, and Swinburne—few can boast such useful and coherently integrated memory of the acres of pages he has read and reviewed. The Rutgers Zoo he established in 1967 has grown into a major contributor to the discipline. A panel of peers identified it in 2009 as one of the ten best American anthropology departments—and this in a state with the second-lowest per capita expenditure on higher education in the country.

But apart from his departmental work and our shared gig at the HFG Foundation, Fox has stimulated no movement, produced no "school" of automatic acolytes funded by giant grants and earnestly supporting a particular flavor of social science. This would be too boring for him, inadequately vulnerable to startling new research plans and no unexpected melding of hitherto disparate stuff. While having many good friends among ex-students, the very idea of devotees and followers is anathema to him. Go and do your own work, not mine. Fox never said "credo," and he has had to endure reading about the proud rediscovery of the biosocial and other wheels from their eager new adepts. These *wunderkinder*, anxious to push their own originality, fail to know the often prominently published existing work on which they base their surprising new findings, their delighted rediscovery of the obvious that had been articulated so much earlier.

Private Intellectual

Has this guy Fox no faults? He admits to many, including an overabundance of self-pity with an exaggerated sense of injustice, a running internal struggle between ambition and procrastination, chronic impulsiveness, and even more chronic impatience. Once he has worked on a problem to his own satisfaction, he wants to move on—sometimes even before he has finished. He has drawers full of things he never completed because they became too routine for him. Many of these were important enough (often about abstruse theoretical problems in kinship), and he knows that according to the customs of the profession he should have gathered research assistants, applied for grants, and carried them to fruition. Even so, he feels guilty rather than annoyed when his colleagues "discover" the same solutions years later: as though he "let the side down"—something his rugby-playing soul cannot easily live with.

He can alternatively become totally obsessed with one idea and worry it like a terrier and to the exclusion of matters he should be attending to. He disappeared from the world while combing through Swinburne to find out how many times and how the master rhymed "death" and "breath"—data that became central to an argument about social rules, the brain, and memory (Fox 2008/2011). When bored with a conversation or meeting or lecture, he sings Gilbert and Sullivan in his head, and he has a tendency to put what's happening under his skull above what is going on in his immediate world. His daughters used to summon him back to reality with "Earth calling, Daddy! Come in, Daddy!" He was, they said, on Tralfamadore again. Kurt Vonnegut aficionados will get the reference, and readers will be surprised (or not) to know that Kurt and Robin were great fans of each other's work and carried on a hilarious correspondence over the years. His shallow capacity for boredom leads him to finish off the sentences of slow speakers. He genuinely thinks he is just showing an interest in what they say. They inevitably find it irritating. But this is only with his peers; his numerous friends among Pueblo Indians, Irish crofters, sailors and fishermen, and farming neighbors, who seem to remember him largely for his singing ability, show him to be just at home, if not more, outside of the academy as in.

Is Fox a "public intellectual"—that semi-celebrated rarity? He has certainly supported his share of lost-and-won public (and mostly unpopular) causes: single mothers, nursing mothers, surrogate mothers (Baby "M"), Mormon polygamists, the rights of homosexuals and foxhunters, and the right to a dignified death of one's own choosing. He also supports the truly hopeless cause—given the power of orthodoxy—of the Earl of Oxford as the real author of Shakespeare's plays, which he knows almost as well as Gilbert and Sullivan and Sherlock Holmes. He was one of the first critics to spot the phoniness of Carlos Castaneda's "Yaqui" ("Yaquitiyaq" he called it) and in consequence survived a knife threat from a drug-crazed disciple, and he formed a lifelong friendship with the arch-exposer of Carlos, Richard de Mille. In what he describes as a pilgrimage, Robin personally carried the voluminous, witty, and altogether strange and unlikely correspondence between de Mille and Rodney Needham to a safe resting place in the archives of All Soul's College, Oxford. His most public of stands was his opposition to the so-called Seville Declaration on Violence, which was endorsed by several pious disciplinary associations: anthropology, psychology, sociology, and the gaseously pompous UNESCO of the 1970s and 1980s. He saw it as both wrong and as a sanctimonious piece of academic McCarthyism. He more or less single-handedly demolished it, beginning with his observation that this modern Sevilliana recalled nothing better than the earlier Inquisition so bloodily resident there.

But if anything, he is a private intellectual, able to convulse a small party with his anthropological evisceration of Star Trek as a tribe and Mr. Spock as, of course, a rendition of perfect rationality—no emotion, just the facts, the facts. He can become a firework at an academic meeting, riffing broadly and deliriously about arcane philosophical points. Once at a meeting sponsored by *Le Maison des Sciences de l'Homme* in Paris he delivered an unforgettable song (which I have forgotten) about kinship systems. I think it was called "The Cross-Cousin Rag."

I know it had a verse in French dedicated to Lévi-Strauss that was sung in the manner of Charles Asnavour. I haven't since dared to ask him to repeat it, with equal fear that he would or wouldn't. Private intellectual at an antic salon. Incisive tutored hilarity, but never mean.

When I retired formally from Rutgers, there was a gracious departmental dinner. Robin was ill and unable to attend but contributed to the embarrassingly warm event a high-protein, high-glucose account of our "great adventure," which it was, and still is. Even after all these years, I was still more than a little moved and surprised by his insistence that meeting me outside the gibbon cages had totally changed his life (even for the better). We have been self-condemned to revise the courtroom in which social science is evaluated while the trial is on, and having a larky brilliant buddy made all the difference. Am I proud and overjoyed because of my, so far, endless association with this mirthful skeptic? All I can think of to conclude is to cite what Isaac Bashevis Singer said during the inevitable *New York Times* interview when he won the Nobel Prize for Literature: "Mr. Singer, do you believe in free will?" "Do I believe in free will? Of course. I have no choice."

Editor's Note

Following are the words for "The Cross-Cousin Rag," including the Charles Asnavour version of verse one. Robin notes that the second verse refers to the George Homans and David Schneider argument (in *Marriage, Authority and Final Causes* 1955) that marriage with the mother's brother's daughter was prevalent because it was "sentimentally appropriate"—an argument famously disputed by Rodney Needham in *Structure and Sentiment* 1962.

The Cross-Cousin Rag

I'll give my sister, to my wife's brother,
'cos he gave his sister, to me.
It's a small affair that is quite easy to arrange,
among the Kariera it's called sister exchange.
Though something much grander, is done by the Aranda,
both of them are el-em-en-ta-ree.
So I'll give my sister, to my wife's brother,
'cos he gave his sister to me.

I'm going crazy for my mother's brother's daughter,
and she's going nuts over me.
I'd like to court the daughter of my paternal aunt,
but although I know I oughter, I find I just can't.

You see my mother's brother, was just like my mother—
I kept going round there for tea.
That's where I interacted with my mother's brother's daughter,
now she's going to marry me (not Rodney Needham)—
she's going to marry me (it's asymmetrical)—
she's going to marry me!

Je donnerai ma soeur, monsieur
au frère de ma femme monsieur,
parcequ' il ma donné sa soeur.
Une petite affaire, rien de mysterieux,
chez les Kariera c'est l'échange des soeurs.
Une forme plus grande, s'trouve chez les Aranda,
mais tous les deux sont él-é-men-tair-e.
Je donnerai ma soeur, monsieur,
au frère de ma femme, monsieur,
parcequ'il ma donné sa soeur.

References

Fox, Robin, and Lionel Tiger. 1966. "The Zoological Perspective in Social Science." *Man: The Journal of the Royal Anthropological Institute* NS. 1(2):75–81.

———. 1967. *Kinship and Marriage: An Anthropological Perspective.* London: Penguin. (2nd ed. Cambridge University Press, 1983).

———. 1994. "Will the Real Murngin System Please Stand Up?" In *The Challenge of Anthropology: Old Encounters and New Excursions.* New Brunswick, NJ: Transaction Publishers.

———.2000. *The Passionate Mind: Sources of Destruction and Creativity.* (Incorporating *The Violent Imagination.*) New Brunswick, NJ: Transaction Publishers.

———.2004. *Participant Observer: Memoir of a Transatlantic Life.* New Brunswick, NJ: Transaction Publishers.

———. 2008. "Playing by the Rules: Sound and Sense in Swinburne and the Rhyming Poets." *Philosophy and Literature* 32:217–40.

———.2011. *The Tribal Imagination: Civilization and the Savage Mind.* Cambridge, MA: Harvard University Press.

Hall, John M. 2010. *Ernest Gellner: An Intellectual Biography.* London/New York: Verso.

Skinner, B. F. 1971. *Beyond Freedom and Dignity.* Indianapolis: Hackett.

Tiger, Lionel. 1969. *Men in Groups.* London: Thomas Nelson.

Tiger, Lionel, and Robin Fox. 1971. *The Imperial Animal.* New York: Holt, Rinehart and Winston.

2

A Tribute and Personal Thanks

Michael T. McGuire

Robin Fox is graced with a gifted brain and the motivation and passion to use it. He has done so for decades to the benefit, education, and inspiration of thousands, many of whom would savor the chance to contribute to this volume. I am one of those fortunate enough to be invited to do so.

My field of work is brain-behavior research, not an area that might suggest that Robin's writings would be at the top of my reading list. They arrived there in a curious way.

Surviving in the world of medical research means that one is continually writing applications for research funds and research progress reports to funding agencies. For me, these activities began some six weeks in advance of the dates they were due. Soon they became all consuming. It didn't matter whether I was sleeping, taking a shower, driving to work, or eating lunch. Nothing else was on my mind. And when they were finalized and sent off to various agencies, there I was, "brain dead." Familiar tasks seemed unfamiliar, and often painful. Concentration for more than a few seconds was impossible. Normal conversations were a burden and usually irritating. Call it fatigue. Call it exhaustion. Call it poor planning. Call it all three. Whatever it's called, the brain was dead.

At those moments I did one of two things. I picked up the dictionary or a book by Robin Fox. Interesting as it is, the dictionary was never helpful. It did little more than remind me of the words and rules of grammar I seemed to have forgotten.

Robin's writings were another matter. He thinks, and does so with ease. He is generous with his ideas. He invites readers to share his findings and insights. Ideas don't frighten him—he is incapable of having a dull thought. Years before others, he tackled complex and contentious issues that begged for attention and insightful interpretations.

His prose is easy, flowing, and clear. Like T. S. Eliot, he is a master of the long sentence filled with nested ideas and inferences. And as I read through his writings, new thoughts popped into my brain. The blood began to circulate again. It usually took several weeks before I was back to normal. During those weeks Robin's books were my constant companions.

Four Selections

What follows are four selections from his writings with comments about their influence on my life. They are not offered as selections of his most important and influential writings—other contributors to the Festschrift are far better qualified to make such judgments. They are selections and comments best thought of as personal remembrances.

1. In commenting on the human condition, he wrote,

> The basics remained the same: zealotry, xenophobia, greed, lust, gullibility of the many, and power hunger of the few; the evil dominance of the idea by which we live and for which we will die and which is wrong; the search for meaning that is our original sin and that either elevates us to godhead or reduces us to foaming fanatics when our answer is threatened. All these were surely there from the start of our humanity. But what we find hard to imagine is that they could work together and harmonize and produce, for the species, a positive result.... This does not seem possible to our modern fragmented consciousness, where every frenetic addition to our already overburdened civilization seems to produce a serendipitous disaster. (*The Violent Imagination* 1989, p. 3)

Attending medical school in the 1960s and 1970s had its special appeal. We were members of a select group, or at least we imagined we were—during those years six students applied for admission for every one that was accepted. Medical research was in the early moments of its post–World War II exponential output of new knowledge. Journals with international circulations promised that the knowledge would be disseminated worldwide. The first groups of "international doctors" were fanning out across the globe to establish clinics, teach, and tackle long understudied diseases such as malaria and sleeping sickness. The United Nations had established a health division. The United States and other governments provided cash to support health over disease. Those were heady days. And those of us who at first were medical students

A Tribute and Personal Thanks

and then young doctors were part of the evolving picture. Excitement, optimism, and the urge to cooperate—all were in the air.

Sure, the Cold War was on. But Russia was far away and, anyway, none of us knew any red-blooded Russians. And, yes, John F. and Robert Kennedy were assassinated. And, yes, through many of these years antiwar protests took place and medical clinics were filled with healthy young men who claimed they were gay to avoid induction into the military and a trip to Vietnam. Still, a sense of optimism and cooperation prevailed. Better times were in the making.

Shortly after graduation from medical school I began a career in research. Aside from conducting experiments and engaging in the already mentioned writing of funding applications and research progress reports, it also meant attending scientific meetings, giving lectures, and participating as a member of large-scale, multidiscipline research projects. And during my early years in these activities I sensed that somehow—the "how" was never clearly articulated—they would organize themselves, meld into a coherent picture, and give my life a special meaning. If not this week, then surely the next.

Then disconcerting signs began to appear. At research meetings there were rumors about investigators falsifying research findings. There were violent critiques of competitors' research. There were moments of character assassination. Hypotheses that had been in the public domain for years were claimed as original, and threats of lawsuits for intellectual theft were aimed at others who believed the hypotheses were their invention. Who published first and most often in prestigious journals and who accumulated the largest funding support for research became steps on the ladder to high status and influence. At times, colleagues stopped speaking to each other. Political preferences began to divide faculties. The political conservative in those years, as is largely the case today in large state and private universities, might as well have been a leper. Demanding chairmen of medical school departments required adherence to their views among those faculty that wished to keep their jobs. Medical schools and research laboratories openly competed for prestige and funding dollars. Accompanying these signs was a change in the teaching priorities of universities, which diminished their traditional job of graduating well-educated young men and women to that of assuring that they obtained a job. The university had relinquished its position as the house of dispassionate knowledge and followed in the footsteps of Henry Ford and the assembly line—or was it a conveyer belt? And where was the cooperation?

The Violent Imagination

All of these happenings were mulling around in my brain when, following the submission of a funding application, I opened *The Violent Imagination*. Although inventively written and perfectly clear in its message, it was very unpleasant to read. Robin was on target. I had been one of the many gullible ones living in a world of fragmented consciousness full of zealotry, xenophobia, and greed. The question then became, could I escape from my consciousness?

2. In addressing the notions of autonomists and behaviorists who believed and perhaps still believe that they could change society for the better if only they could put their finger on how to do so, he wrote,

> I have another vision of what has happened in history. The successive stages of progress are simply different experiments in departing from the basic pattern. . . . They are not in fact "progressive states" at all; it is simply that changes in technology allow us to try different experiments. The knowledge and techniques used in trying are cumulative, of course. But this only means that we can attempt more bizarre designs for living than previously. But they never work in the way that the primitive total societies work because they can never be total societies: societies that tap the whole range of human needs and satisfactions for each and every member. These they fragment, and most so-called social pathologies are desperate attempts to heal the fragmentation or, if you like, the alienation and anomie. (*Search for Society*, 1989, pp. 212–13)

I'm a psychiatrist by training, a neuroscientist by occupation. In 1989, the prevailing belief among those working in these fields was that solutions to both minor and major mental disorders were only a few years away. Annual prevalence statistics revealed that disorders were gradually increasing not only in real numbers but also as a percentage of the population. Disappointing? Yes. But the trend was easily ignored. Funds for research were plentiful. Research papers appeared weekly, suggesting that it was becoming increasingly possible to pinpoint the causes and cures of disorders. Progress was in the making in clinics and laboratories.

As to fragmentation? Not us! Maybe somewhere else. Maybe in the wave of revolutions that were just beginning in Poland and would trigger the implosion of the USSR. Maybe in China at Tiananmen Square. Maybe in the Middle East with its then emerging assertive terrorism. Maybe at home among the cults of the time or among organized religions that were becoming increasingly hostile toward one another. Or maybe it was

Hollywood or politicians and their politics. Or maybe it was all of these. Whatever it was, fragmentation in the efforts to identify the causes and cures of mental disorders seemed remote from the events of that not uneventful year. With the combination of brains and energy devoted to decoding mental disorders and their causes, solutions were imminent.

It's not that the idea of fragmentation was new in 1989 or even a century earlier. It's either the dominant theme or an inescapable subtheme through much of recorded history and no doubt well before. Rather, it was the idea that the fragmented brain full of millions of facts, theories, plans, and deadlines rejects and denies its state and occupies itself otherwise. Recognizing this idea had no appeal. Denial did. And even at those brief moments when some feature of fragmentation was identified, it wasn't clear what to do. In fact, recognition made things worse because one had to acknowledge that one was both a contributor and a victim. Better to sweep such ideas under the rug for another time and get on with writing another funding application and curing mental illness.

And how easy it was to get caught in the fragmentation and for a few moments experience it as rewarding. For example, during the 1980s, the laboratory that I directed published a series of novel findings: (1) The level of the neurotransmitter serotonin is close to twice as high in the brains of dominant compared to subordinate male vervet monkeys. (2) When animals change their social status, their central nervous system serotonin levels change as well. (3) Submissive displays by subordinate animals toward dominant animals are the critical causal trigger for these changes; eliminate or reduce the number of subordinate displays received by a dominant male and his serotonin level declines. In effect, information from the environment was changing the brain's chemical profile of its recipient. It's not that this idea was truly novel or counterintuitive. At the time it was known that information from the environment such as news of the death of an important person, an unexpected promotion, or winning the lottery affected the mental states of recipients. Nonetheless, it seemed novel to others. Reporters suddenly swarmed the laboratory. The *New York Times* featured a special article. *Newsweek* followed. Offers for tenured professorships at Ivy League colleges arrived as did invitations to lecture around the world. And literally overnight, my life changed. Students lined up for an opportunity to work at the laboratory. Funding agencies and private institutions offered support. I was suddenly a celebrity. My position in the science hierarchy shot up hundreds of points on the academic Dow Jones, and no doubt my brain's serotonin level rose as well. But how long would all this last?

And again, how dead right Robin was. How right he was about how fragmented society had been through much of history, how it still was in 1989, and, by implication, how increasingly fragmented it would become in the following two decades. And how right he was about how easy it is to get caught up in ongoing events, especially those that provide momentary pleasure. And undeterred by facts and context, each year someone somewhere announced a new social formula to solve the world's ills, which of course were viewed as the work of a few individuals or nations or groups with perverse motives or who were exercising archaic economic or political strategies. Are such formulas themselves products of social fragmentation? Who else but Robin was asking this question?

As the 1990s unfolded, the autonomists and behaviorists were no longer the primary architects of the social blueprints being offered for the world's ills. Other scenarios had attained higher priority. The prevalence statistics of minor and major mental disorders would continue to rise for the next two decades. And for the most part, the engine of medical research would remain on full throttle. Only recently have investigators begun to consider the possibility that some mental illnesses might not be curable, even if their causes can be identified. And then of course there is smoking, cancer, obesity, addictions, aging, political and religious wars, and economic recessions.

3. Following another six weeks devoted to writing a funding application, I found myself still thinking about the question: can I escape from my fragmented consciousness? I recalled a comment by Miguel de Unamuno in *Tragic Sense of Life*, "try to fill your consciousness with the representation of no-consciousness, and you will see the impossibility of it," and the effort of Edmund Husserl that he describes in *Cartesian Meditations* about wiping his consciousness clean and starting to think again. It was at this moment that I picked up the *Red Lamp of Incest*:

> Durkheim and Mauss may be wrong to locate the processes of conceptual thought in society in the sense that the individual acquires them through socialization, but in an evolutionary perspective, they may be right. That is, in the evolution of conceptual thought via language, pressures toward social classification may have been supremely important, and these would have become true "selection pressures" demanding mental equipment that could cope with them. But these conceptual processes concerned with the ordering of social relations were being programmed into hominid individuals by natural selection over time, not induced by socialization in each succeeding generation. (*The Red Lamp of Incest* 1980, p. 187)

In a vague way I knew this, but not usefully until I read it. Was this then an answer? Or, at least, a partial answer? At first I was unconvinced. After all, Robin would likely agree that growing up as a Zulu or an Eskimo or the heir apparent to the British Crown would be associated with very different ideas, worldviews, brain information libraries, preferences, and conceptual thought.

Conceptual Processes

But then my life changed. At the time I had two teenage daughters that were very social and very serious about it. My attention turned to their age group. Since 1969, for part of each year, I worked in the Eastern Caribbean studying monkeys, but I had paid far more attention to the monkeys than the local humans. That year—1980—West Africa was added to the list of working sites.

As I traveled from one site to another, it gradually became clear: "conceptual processes concerned with ordering of social relations were being programmed into hominoid individuals by natural selection over time, not induced by socialization."

Wherever I went the social relations of children were more the same than not. Often I did not know their language. Nonetheless, they played, gestured, fought, strutted, and avoided authority the same way as at home. It didn't matter where I was. It could be a train station, an airport, or a remote village where children had never seen a "white man." Or it could be in homes, at schools, or on playing fields. The social programs were as one, even though the language, religion, political system, and local customs differed dramatically.

I hadn't fully answered the question about escaping from my consciousness, but in a way it seemed I might be halfway there. That is, it might be possible to jettison and replace many of those thought programs induced by socialization while those gifts of natural selection dealing with social relations would likely remain intact—it's hard to change millions of years of programming.

I took a sabbatical leave for six months to read and think and enjoy my children. Each week I made minor progress. The social programs for which my parents were responsible were the easiest to identify. Not all were questionable—they were decent and devoted parents. As I wandered through the later years of my development, the sources were more difficult to identify. Clearly, I had acquired and accepted all kinds of ideas about morals, responsibilities, and social rules whose origins were not clear. Time passed. I imagined I had made considerable progress in clearing my brain of many irrelevant, indefensible, or junk ideas and rules. As expected, the ordering of social relations remained as they were.

When I returned to the halls of academia, they seemed stranger and more distant than before.

4. In discussing critical questions and ideas in anthropology, he wrote,

> The revolutionary response to this, judging from the end product—that is, the social/breeding system of *Homo sapiens*—was the dual invention of initiation and alliance. There was no way, once the status of *Homo* was achieved, that the free-for-all competition of the males could continue. On the other hand, the rapidity of brain evolution could not have occurred without a highly assortative mating system in which only selected male genes were transferred to successive generations. The consequence was the evolution of a system geared to the control of the young males' access to the breeding system and the control of the allocation of mates by the older males. (*The Challenge of Anthropology* 1994, p. 17)

By the time *The Challenge of Anthropology* was published I was a senior member of a medical school department in a university. Among other things, this entailed sitting on committees that decided whether assistant professors should be advanced to the position of associate professor with tenure.

It was no secret to any of us that older males and females—parents, priests, nuns, rabbis, teachers, the police, and others—actively involve themselves in trying to control the access of young males to hometown breeding systems. Was movement up the academic ladder a proxy for such access? Were associate professors with tenure more likely to gain access? And were we, the judges of these young academic aspirants, inadvertently geared to control such access?

Academic Hierarchies

Yes . . . of course! Couched in the rules and traditions of academic advancement that are trademarks of universities in the United States, these committees controlled the access of males into the upper levels of the academic hierarchy.

It is easy to be skeptical of the proxy hypothesis. The average age of the assistant professors was about thirty and most had long before acquired membership in the local breeding system. But what if older males, irrespective of age, were programmed to control the access by younger males, irrespective of their age?

What were the indications? Where was the evidence? Not surprisingly it was right in front of us. It was there in our deliberations. There were the rules about how an evaluation was to unfold: essentially the quality, relevance, and quantity of the aspirant's work were to be judged by knowledgeable older colleagues. And these judgments we made. But by the time those meetings were finished, the personalities of the aspirants—the vast majority of whom were males in those days—were part of the discussion along with the never quite asked but always present question, "Is he one of us?" And often it was these factors that swayed decisions.

Was I perhaps wondering whether those young men might have been suitable mates for my daughters. The question had not occurred to me until I sat down to write this.

This contribution to the *Festschrift* ends as it began: as a tribute and personal thanks to Robin Fox. It might be viewed as the story of my many wake-up calls. In a sense that's true. And to the degree that it is, Robin has provided many critical wake-ups. Could there be a more fitting way to characterize his writing?

Robin, the people that have most influenced my thinking are Giambattista Vico, Robin George Collingwood, William James, William Osler, Stephen Pepper, and you. That's good company. And should some modernist, postmodernist, or post-postmodernist mention to you that those on this list are the "old guard" and "their time has passed," just inform him that their ideas have withstood the test of time and lived through the ups and downs of decades of fragmentation and that much of what they wrote and nearly the entire corpus of what you have written remains as relevant today as yesterday.

References

Fox, Robin. 1980. *The Red Lamp of Incest*. New York: Dutton.
———. 1989. *The Search for Society*. New Brunswick, NJ: Rutgers University Press.
———. 1989. *The Violent Imagination*. New Brunswick, NJ: Rutgers University Press.
———. 1994. *The Challenge of Anthropology*. New Brunswick, NJ: Transaction Publishers.
Husserl, Edmund. 1960. *Cartesian Meditations*. Dordrecht, the Netherlands: Kluwer.
Unamuno, Miguel de. 1954. *Tragic Sense of Life*. New York: Dover Press. (English translation originally published in 1921.)

II

Popularity and Drink

Snowflakes and Similes

An unrhymed sonnet

Each snowflake is a frozen memory
Of thirty thousand random drifting feet.
That crystalline descent, so intricate,
So infinite in its particulars,
Its influence from all the elements
Could never be the same for each, but though
No two can be alike, all must observe
The laws of hexagons and fractal trees.
This is an endless source of similes,
Which fall like snowflakes through a mental void,
No two the same, but when they incarnate
In words, each is compelled to make its mark
With a comparative conjunction and
To follow rules of syntax. Form Is All

3

Writing Popular Anthropology

Kate Fox

This contribution to the volume honoring my father is the transcript of a very informal little talk that I have given to anthropology students at a number of universities in the United Kingdom (including Oxford, London, Sussex, Kent, and Oxford Brookes) and elsewhere (including Brown, Tirana, and Pisa). At my father's insistence, I have not attempted to rewrite this talk as a more formal article or chapter, but have deliberately left it as a verbatim transcript, with all the casual language and chatty delivery that one would expect at a friendly gathering.

I was invited to give these talks when my book *Watching the English: The Hidden Rules of English Behaviour* became, much to my surprise, a popular best seller. A few brave heads of anthropology departments felt that their students (and some faculty members) might benefit from hearing about my approach to writing "pop anthropology." For some strange and probably subversive reason of his own, my father feels that my thoughts on this subject deserve a wider audience and wants them included in this book.

The Talk

By inviting me here to talk about my work, our host is committing a minor heresy, or at the very least sticking his neck out a bit! My books have until very recently been pointedly ignored by the academic world—they are pop anthropology, written for a mass audience, and therefore not worthy of being taken seriously or reviewed in proper academic journals, or in fact even acknowledged at all. My stuff is normally not even considered worthy of being sneered at, which is remarkable, as most academics dearly love to sneer at things. You would think they would have jumped at the opportunity.

Okay, joking aside, I was asked to talk here about the sort of anthropology that I do and specifically why my latest effort—rather to my surprise, I have to say—has become a popular best seller. This is *not* going to be about popularizing anthropology in general or what other much more important popularizers have done. I'm not an expert on the history of the discipline, and there are others far better qualified to talk about this, such as Jeremy MacClancy, a professor of anthropology at Oxford Brookes University, who has written excellent books on the subject.

All I can really talk about with any authority is my personal experience in writing this stuff, how I came to do it, and how it has been received. So I'm afraid this may all sound horribly self-centered and self-important, and even less academic than the work itself. It is also impossible to talk about why one's work has been successful without sounding dreadfully arrogant (even though in my case it is almost entirely down to good luck). But that is what I have been asked to do here, so I hope you'll forgive me.

When I was approached a few years ago by David Mills, a lecturer in pedagogy and the social sciences at Oxford University, who wanted to interview me for *Anthropology Today*, he presented this as a way of getting academic anthropologists to pay attention to my work and take it seriously. My initial response was something along the lines of, "Yeah, right—and pigs might fly!" I also had to tell him that I am not particularly hankering after attention from the academic world, and as my books are clearly not written to impress academics, I can hardly grumble when they are not impressed.

And to be brutally honest, I said, I don't really *care*. My book *Watching the English* has now sold about half a million copies, and at the time it was selling about three thousand copies a week, which is more than most academic monographs sell in their entire lifetime. It has had loads of rave reviews, it has being translated into lots of foreign languages; I have given talks at all the big literary festivals; and I even gave the frightfully prestigious Christmas lecture at the Royal Geographical Society. Plus, there are all the usual endless media interviews and so on. Sorry, this sounds insufferably braggy, but there is a point to it, which is that I'm getting more attention than I either need or want, and certainly more than I deserve. So why should I care that a few fusty old anthropology journals turned up their noses and refused to acknowledge my existence or that university departments were not exactly falling over themselves to invite me to speak or give me honorary doctorates or whatever?

Preserving Anthropology

David told me that I *should* bloody well care, not for my own sake, but because apparently anthropology as a discipline is seriously losing ground. Did you know this? Students are defecting in droves to subjects such as cultural studies, media studies, and so on, things that sound cooler, more relevant, and quite frankly more fun than anthropology. He said that my book was exactly the sort of thing that could give anthropology the publicity and image boost that it desperately needs.

Now, I suppose I could be horribly cynical and ask whether it really matters that anthropology is in decline. I mean, does the world really *need* more social anthropologists? But actually I'm *not* that cynical, and I *do* think that the world needs more anthropologists—or at least a hell of a lot more than it needs yet another batch of media studies graduates!

At any rate, I think that the insights and understanding of the world that trained anthropologists like you can provide are useful and worth preserving. And I have to say that of all the letters and e-mails I get about *Watching the English*, those that always make me happiest are the ones from people saying that the book has inspired them to study anthropology. At another university where I gave a talk recently, the head of the anthropology department told me that when he asks prospective students in interviews what got them interested in anthropology, over 50 percent say that it was reading *Watching the English*. And a lot of the fan mail I get is from people who tell me they didn't even know what anthropology *was* until they read my book, which makes it sound fascinating and lots of fun.

Which it is, right? I'm afraid I'm very out of touch with how the subject is being taught nowadays. Do you find it fascinating? Is it fun? Is it exciting? I hope it is. If not, I have been giving people a completely misleading impression, and they are going to be severely disappointed. I do try to point out, though, both in the book and when I give talks and interviews, that what I do is not generally regarded as "proper" anthropology.

As well as my work not sounding academic enough, the more traditional, macho school of ethnography also regards me as a pathetic wimp because I do not do my research in remote, uncomfortable places with monsoons, mud huts, and malaria. This is, or at least used to be, a kind of initiation ordeal that one was expected to undergo before being allowed to write one's monograph and call oneself an anthropologist.

Trouble is, I have this wimpish aversion to all that dirt, dysentery, killer insects, disgusting food, and primitive sanitation. I prefer to do my research in cultures with indoor plumbing, where you can get a decent cup of tea and maybe indulge in a bit of retail therapy after a long hard day of participant observation.

Now, I know that things have changed from the days when it was all about exotic and uncomfortable locations. Anthropology has "come home," and more and more graduates are studying aspects of modern, industrialized Western cultures. There are even "corporate anthropologists" working in big companies and "retail anthropologists" working in market-research organizations, consultancies, and so on. So the problem some academic anthropologists have with my books is no longer quite so much the subject matter; it is more the informal, chatty way I choose to write about it. Purists are suspicious of the random cross-disciplinary mix of research methods I use, plus maybe the fact that I have the temerity to come up with a big unifying theory or two sometimes, rather than confining myself to "thick description" and observing the currently fashionable taboo on ever making a definitive statement about anything.

Shining Example

I did study "proper" anthropology at Cambridge but got bored and fed up with it after two years, so I changed subjects and took a degree in philosophy instead. This was despite my immense good fortune in being more or less born to be an anthropologist. Seriously. My father—who is Robin Fox, a much, much more eminent anthropologist—began training me as a participant observer when I was still in my cradle—literally. Although in my case this was a Cochiti Indian cradleboard, a legacy of his own fieldwork in New Mexico.

I could not be allowed to lie in a pram or cot, staring at the ceiling like any other baby. Oh no, I had to be strapped to a board and propped upright at strategic observation points around the house. Presumably I was supposed to be studying the typical behavior patterns of an English academic family. I suppose I should be grateful that he didn't demand a forty-page dissertation on the subject. That sort of thing came later, when I was about five.

Well, I'm only half-joking! I'll give you an example. I remember very clearly the first wedding I ever went to, when I was just five years old.

Some cousin or friend of my mother's was getting married, and my father decided the day before that this would be a good opportunity to give me a lecture on rites of passage, theories of pair bonding, the wedding customs of various cultures, and the intricacies of matrilateral cross-cousin marriage—with diagrams. My mother, who also slightly overestimated my mental age, took it upon herself to explain the facts of life—sex, where babies come from, and so on.

I found it all fascinating, and at the church the next day, I found the ceremony equally riveting. Like any good student, I had a lot of questions, and during a moment's silent pause (I think it was just after the "speak now or forever hold your peace" line), I turned to my mother and in a very loud, piercing whisper asked, "Is he going to put the seed in now?"

My father was disappointed that although I had clearly grasped the essential points, I had got the chronological order of things muddled. I think he gave me a C minus. He never had much of a concept of childhood—to him I was just a rather short student. By the time I was seven, I had figured out that the only way to get and hold his attention was to ask intelligent questions. If my question was smart enough, the answer might be a twenty-minute lecture—that is, twenty minutes of his undivided attention! Wonderful!

When I was about nine or ten, he even let me come to a few of his real lectures at Rutgers. I sat in the front row, paid close attention, and tried to think of an intelligent question to ask at the end. It was pretty much like dinnertime at home. I actually understood a fair amount of these lectures, *not* because I was a particularly bright child, but because my father firmly believes that if an anthropological concept or insight is of genuine worth and importance, it can, *and should*, be explained in terms that a nonacademic can understand, even a very small nonacademic. If my work now has popular appeal, it is largely thanks to his shining example.

This training from my father carried on right up until I went to university, by which time I had absorbed not only some of his knowledge but also much of his rather maverick attitude and writing style, something we proved when he came to Cambridge as a visiting fellow at St. John's during my first year. We decided as an experiment and private practical joke to have him write one of my essays for me. I copied it out in my own handwriting, and it came back from my supervisor with a comment scrawled on it that said, "This is exactly the sort of flippant, journalistic stuff I've come to expect from you, Kate—very clever and entertaining, as usual, but *when* are you going to learn to take this subject seriously?"

My father roared with laughter when he read this, and as you may have gathered, I never did learn to take anthropology very seriously. Although I do have to say that the reason I switched to philosophy was mainly because I became frustrated with what I saw as the wooliness and lack of intellectual rigor in most current anthropological writing. It all seemed very sloppy and undisciplined, and I wanted to learn to argue clearly and logically. As it turned out, the degree in philosophy was probably much better training for writing popular anthropology than continuing to study anthropology. It taught me a lot about clarity and precision, about defining one's terms and avoiding woolly thinking or careless use of language. (Whether I've managed to apply all this is for others to judge, but at least I know how it *should* be done.)

Blurbs and Bars

The other lucky accidents that helped to train me as a writer of popular anthropology were working first as a freelance copy editor for various academic publishers; then writing ads, advertorial, and theater reviews for a local newspaper; and then—especially—working as a full-time copywriter at Oxford University Press. My job there was to write book blurbs for catalogs and leaflets, at a rate of about forty blurbs a day.

These had to give the gist, in just a few lines, of what were usually very dense and abstruse scholarly books and monographs, and to do so in a way that would make more than the usual tiny handful of people actually want to buy them. So it was all about being very clear, very concise, and at the same time very persuasive—making something dry and complex sound interesting and exciting. In other words, pretty good training for a popularizer!

Of course, I did not know then that that was what I wanted to be, but I did know that I wanted to do research. So I left publishing and joined a small social science research company as codirector with my friend, the social psychologist Dr. Peter Marsh. At the time, he was mainly doing consultancy work for some of the big breweries and pub companies, doing research on aggression and violence in pubs and designing training programs for pub managers on how to prevent and manage these things—how not to get beaten up, essentially.

So that's what I did for several years, conducting research and writing research reports on violence in various contexts (such as pubs, nightclubs, betting shops, gas stations, and department stores) and writing training programs and producing training videos for the staff and managers of these places. Again, this was all about clarity, making the often quite complex psychology of aggression and violence accessible to non-psychologists, night club bouncers, bar staff, retail sales staff, and so on. We did research on violence and public disorder for the government as well, and these reports had to be accessible for politicians, who, believe me, require even more "dumbing down" than night club bouncers!

Social Issues Research Centre

It was more good training. But after some years Peter and I were both getting fed up with only doing research on the downsides of social behavior: disorder, drunkenness, deviance, dysfunction, delinquency, and other bad things beginning with "D." So we founded the Social Issues Research Centre and branched out. I started doing research on such things as flirting and courtship, body image, gossip, risk taking, crying, cyber dating, individualism, horseracing, motherhood, patriotism, friendship, young people's attitudes and lifestyles, the social impact of mobile phones (cell phones), social and cultural aspects of drinking, the effects of health scares, the psychology of smell, and the cultural meaning of chips (French fries).

As you can imagine, this was much more fun than all the violent stuff. I'm still doing a lot of this, alongside writing books. Much of SIRC's research is commissioned by government departments or the European Commission, but some of our studies are funded by private-sector companies: the mobile-phone study was for British Telecom, for example; the one on smell was for The Body Shop; I persuaded the British Horseracing Board and the Tote to fund my research on horse racing; and the study on crying was for Kleenex.

The companies mainly commission these studies for information and insight, but also in some cases for the public-relations benefits—to have their names associated with interesting and important research. So although the research is conducted in *exactly* the same way as an ESRC project or any other academic study, using *exactly* the same research methods, the reports have to be written in a style that is accessible and entertaining for nonacademics. Often I end up writing the press releases as well. Again, all of this may be useful training for writing popular anthropology.

My books are written in very much the same style as these more lighthearted research reports, trying to get the right balance between information, analysis, and entertainment, or rather, trying as best I can to make the information and analysis not only accurate and enlightening but also amusing and entertaining.

The only difference is that in the books—well, in the two most recent ones—I write in the first person singular: I actually use the word "I" as opposed to saying "we found that" or "our findings indicate that" in the conventional academic manner, which I still use in research reports. In the books, I make it all much more personal. There is no hiding behind the traditional "we" or littering the thing with citations to back up every other point that I make.

And I don't just give the readers my findings; I try to give them a bit of a flavor of how those findings were found. It's like in math when the teacher says you have to show all the workings out: you can't just put down the final answer but also have to show how you *got* to that answer. So in my books, people get the workings out, the stories of my fieldwork—what I saw, the hunches I had about possible explanations, and the sometimes rather unorthodox experiments I conducted to test those hunches—and of course a lot of the hiccups, stupid mistakes, embarrassments, and red herrings: the deceptive tactics I used to elicit information from informants; and so on: all the stuff that academic writers tend to keep rather quiet about. This way, people have told me they feel that there is a real person coming off the page and talking to them, not some exalted omniscient boffin but someone they can identify with, someone who makes doofus mistakes and gets scared, fed up, tired, and has bad days and embarrassing moments and so on.

Pride and Prejudice

But writing popular anthropology isn't just about taking your completed PhD thesis and sexing it up with a few anecdotes and confessions from your fieldwork and a bit of self-deprecating humor. It's more like taking the raw data, findings, analysis, and insights from your PhD fieldwork and writing them up in a completely different way.

The research I do, apart from maybe the slightly unusual field experiments that I mentioned, is no different from yours. I do use some methods that are more associated with social psychology than anthropology, such as national surveys and formal focus groups and experiments, but also a lot of traditional participant observation and long individual unstructured interviews and so on.

My book *The Racing Tribe* is basically a standard ethnography, based entirely on three years of participant observation at racecourses, among horse-racing people and race goers. *Watching the English* draws on over a decade of my research at SIRC on different aspects of English life and culture, using pretty much every research method known to social science, *plus* three years of intensive participant observation and interviews specially conducted for the book. The only difference between this and the research you would do for a PhD or academic book is that I get paid more and I'm not obliged to drink a lot of inferior sherry.

One can take all that research and write it all up as a PhD or an academic monograph, or one can take the same findings and analysis but write it up as a popular best seller. If you want to do the latter, probably the most important thing you have to be prepared for is swallowing your pride, a lot, and steeling yourself against the prejudices of the academic world. As I said earlier, if you are not writing to please or impress your academic colleagues, you can't very well complain when they are neither pleased nor impressed—not even when they sneer at and patronize you, which they will. Unless of course they simply ignore you, which you may find even more irritating.

And it's not just after the book comes out that you have to swallow your pride—it's in the writing of it. Here is an example. I don't know if any of you saw the mini-debate about my work in *Anthropology Today*. It started with an editorial by David Mills, who interviewed me and then wrote an editorial arguing that the academic world should pointedly stop ignoring my work because, whether they like it or not, it has become sort of the public face of anthropology.

His piece was a bit condescending, but essentially fair enough, and I thought it was very brave of him to say anything positive about me at all in a major academic journal. But then an even more unlikely thing happened, which was that another academic anthropologist, Keith Hart, professor emeritus of anthropology at Goldsmith's College, University of London, whom I've never met, wrote a comment piece in *Anthropology Today*, accusing Mills of being patronizing and undervaluing my work. Hart insisted that *Watching the English* and my arguments about national character deserve to be taken seriously in their own right, that this is a genuinely important and original book, not just a piece of frothy harmless popularizing.

To be honest, I thought that might be going a bit too far. And when I was invited to write a response to both these articles, I included a line to the effect that "I'm not really sure *Watching the English* either deserves or would stand up to the kind of earnest academic attention that Dr. Hart is demanding for it."

But I did take exception to one somewhat dismissive line in David Mills's original editorial about my book, where he rather sniffily asks, "Since when have the linguistic conventions and social rituals around alcohol consumption offered insight into national character, whatever that may be?" I pointed out that actually the linguistic conventions and social rituals of alcohol consumption provide a great deal of insight into cultures and cross-cultural differences—and that I am by no means the first person to say so.

The best-known advocate of the study of drinking in this context is of course Dwight Heath, who said that "just as drinking and its effects are embedded in other aspects of culture, so are many other aspects of culture embedded in the act of drinking," (Heath, 1991). (A wonderful line, which I did actually quote in my book.) I sort of figured that any academic anthropologist reading my book would be familiar with the work of Heath, Mary Douglas, and many others on this subject, so I didn't need to spell it all out for them with names and dates in brackets.

Obviously, I did need to spell it out: some academics clearly need the security of seeing citations such as (Heath 1991, 1995) and (Douglas, 1987) before they will accept that an author—particularly a "pop" author like me—might be making a valid point. It is that safety-in-numbers thing that academics do and that I do myself when I'm writing more academic research reports. It is as though we expect that every statement we make or idea we put forward is going to be challenged by someone saying, "Oh yeah? Who says? You and whose army?" So we can't say anything without quickly reassuring people that Professors Tom, Dick, and Harry said much the same thing in 1987, 1993, and 2004, and therefore it must be true, or it must at least be a concept worth taking seriously.

A statement, concept, or idea without a string of names and dates attached to it looks rather lonely and vulnerable—a sort of Billy-no-mates statement, a friendless social misfit of a concept, with spots and bad breath, that no one wants to be associated with.

But you can't litter a popular book with a lot of names and dates, so in *Watching the English* I couldn't constantly invoke deities such as Heath and Douglas to support my claims about alcohol and culture. And there are many other instances like this in the book, where I could have made my arguments more palatable to academic readers—and shown off my extensive reading, countless surveys, painstaking fieldwork, command of tricky jargon, and so on—but chose not to for the sake of keeping the tone light and accessible to the general reader.

Having said that, I did point out in *Anthropology Today* that there are also undoubtedly many areas where I had no reading or specialist knowledge to show off, even had I wished to do so. Sometimes I'm dumbing down; sometimes I'm just dumb.

Jokes and Jargon

Anyway, this is what I mean by having to swallow your pride when writing for a popular audience. You absolutely cannot show off. In fact, you must deliberately hide any cleverness or expert knowledge you may have. I allowed myself only a very occasional little in-joke for more academic readers, and then only when I could be sure that it wouldn't spoil things or be confusing for nonacademic readers.

To give just one very trivial example, there is a section in the introduction to *Watching the English* titled "Participant Observation and Its Discontents"—an obvious jokey reference to Freud, for those who know, but still a perfectly understandable heading for those who don't, particularly as I immediately explain what is meant by participant observation. This is incidentally one of the very few technical or jargon terms that I use in my books. Mostly, I very carefully avoid them.

Okay, I do occasionally, when absolutely necessary, use a few somewhat technical terms such as *liminality, cultural remission, endogamy, empiricism, rites of passage, totem, acculturation, commensality,* and so on, but I always explain them and try to find a way of explaining them that is self-mocking rather than superior or condescending—a way that gently pokes fun at academics and our silly private languages.

For example, this is my very brief explanation of participant observation in *Watching the English*: I say that the term "essentially means participating in the life and culture of the people one is studying, to gain a true insider's perspective on their customs and behavior, while simultaneously observing them as a detached, objective scientist. Well, that's the theory—in practice it often feels more like that children's game where you try to pat your head and rub your tummy at the same time."

In *The Racing Tribe*, I actually took this one step further, and instead of having the usual compulsory chapter agonizing over the ethical and methodological difficulties of the participant-observation method and the role of the participant observer, I borrowed the language of self-help psychobabble—you know, the whole you-must-nurture-your-inner-child business—and expressed the problem as an ongoing battle between my inner participant and my inner observer.

Throughout the book, I described the bitchy squabbles that these two inner voices engaged in every time a conflict arose between my roles as honorary member of the racing tribe and as detached scientist. Given the deadly serious tones in which this subject is normally debated, I did not expect academics to take very kindly to my poking fun at it all in such an irreverent way, so I was very surprised when I got a letter from a lecturer at the School of Oriental and African Studies, saying that he was actually using my *Racing Tribe* book to *teach* the participant-observation method! This chap must have a good sense of humor.

And there must be others like him, as *Watching the English* is now also on the syllabus at a number of universities, some of which are now flying me around the world to give lectures to their students about it. So there is a warning for you: you do your best to be a maverick, nonacademic iconoclast, and they turn you into a bloody textbook!

Anyway, that was just by way of illustration—just some of the ways in which it is possible to write a kind of anthropology that appeals to a much wider audience, providing you don't mind making a bit of a fool of yourself. I am probably not explaining it very well. There is an Italian student who has just written her whole master's thesis on my use of language in *Watching the English*, so perhaps it is more difficult than I think it is!

But when I decided on the title for this talk—*Writing Popular Anthropology*—although I chose the title myself, I was not entirely sure about it, but I couldn't put my finger on why I was a bit unsure. Eventually I realized that it was because I never actually set out to "popularize" anthropology or to be a "popularizer." I just set out, with each book, to research and write a book on a subject that I found anthropologically fascinating, and to try to do so in such a way that a lot of other people would find it fascinating as well. It certainly was not just a case of taking other people's complex ideas or research and dumbing them down for a popular audience, as my books are entirely based on my own ideas and original research.

Do Methods Matter?

Because I am lucky enough to work outside the academic establishment, I am also free to use whatever research methods I choose, without worrying about boundary disputes between academic disciplines or whether a particular technique that I want to use counts as anthropology or should more properly be called social psychology, sociology, or whatever. At the moment, for the book I'm researching now,

I'm wiring people up to heart monitors and GSR and EEG machines. Is that anthropology? Dunno. Who cares? Does it really *matter*?

As I don't have to conform to a particular set of academic expectations, I can even invent my own research methods when it suits me. For example, when I was working on the Englishness project, people kept mentioning this habit the English have of saying sorry when someone bumps into us, even when the collision is clearly the other person's fault. Although I was pretty sure I had experienced this myself, it is one of those things we do not really notice because we take it for granted, so I thought I had better do the proper scientific thing and actually test the theory in a field experiment or two. So I spent many days in crowded places such as train stations and shopping centers and accidentally on purpose bumped into people to see how many of them would say sorry.

(If you want to try this one yourself, you have to make the bump seem convincingly accidental. I found that the best method was to pretend to be searching for something in my shoulder bag. With my head down and my hair over my eyes, I could still see my target and then calculate my trajectory to achieve a relatively gentle bump while giving the impression that I was genuinely distracted by my bag fumblings.)

This experiment actually got off to a rather poor start, as I kept messing it up by blurting out "sorry" before the other person had a chance to speak. In the end, I managed to control my knee-jerk apologies by biting my lip really hard.

I tried to make the experiment as scientific as possible by bumping into a representative cross section of the English population, in a varied sample of locations around the country. And in fact the English lived up to their reputation. About 80 percent of them said sorry when I crashed into them, even though all the collisions were clearly my fault.

These findings would of course tell us little or nothing about Englishness if the same results were obtained in other countries, so by way of "controls" I diligently bumped into as many people as I could in France, Belgium, Italy, Russia, Poland, and Lebanon. Because even this was not a representative international sample, I also bumped into tourists of different nationalities—including American, German, Japanese, Spanish, Australian, and Scandinavian—at various tourist-trap locations in London and Oxford.

Only the Japanese seemed to have anything like the English "sorry" reflex, and they were frustratingly difficult to experiment on as they seemed to have this knack of sidestepping my attempted bumps. I am not saying that the other nationalities were rude or anything—most of them just said "Careful!" or "Watch out!" or the equivalent in their own languages, and a lot them were positively friendly—they would put out an arm to steady me or check to make sure I was okay before moving on. But the automatic "sorry" did seem to be a peculiarly English response.

There simply isn't time here to go into all the conclusions and explanations I drew from this experiment—you'll just have to read the book if you're interested. But when I put my findings from the bumping experiment together with some of the excellent work of the sociolinguists Brown and Levinson on their concepts of "positive" and "negative" politeness, it all started to make sense. And, yes, I gave them due credit in my book, although it was difficult to quote them directly, as I had trouble finding a single sentence in their book that a nonacademic would understand.

Is my bumping experiment "anthropology"? This testing of unconscious social reflexes certainly helped me (and my readers) to understand the unspoken rules, norms, and values of the culture I was studying. Isn't that what anthropology is supposed to be about?

Image Problems

But whether you like my pick-and-mix approach to methodology or not—and indeed whether academics like my writing style or not—both of those recent pieces in *AT* pointed out that they have to acknowledge that anthropology has a bit of an image problem at the moment, and that books like mine are helping to change that image.

Some of the reviews for my books give an indication of the nature of this image problem. There was one (ludicrously and embarrassingly overly flattering) review that said, "Kate Fox is a social anthropologist, but that does not prevent her from writing like an angel." Another one said, "Fortunately she does not write like an anthropologist, but like an Englishwoman—with amusement, not solemnity, able to laugh at herself as well as us."

Now, as well as being far too kind to me, I actually think these reviewers are being a bit unfair. What they really mean is that I do not write like an *academic*. Anthropology is no more turgid or jargon ridden or inaccessible than other academic disciplines. But it is certainly no less so. I read some great books while I was researching *Watching the English*—really fascinating ethnographic studies of British subcultures such as Goths, bikers, and clubbers—and it seemed such a shame that they couldn't have been written in a less academic style so that people outside our own cliquey little academic subculture could enjoy and learn from them as well. But most cultural anthropology is written in a dialect that only other members of this elite academic tribe understand. And this discipline has even less popular appeal because it has become so "micro"; all ethnographers are allowed to do nowadays is take one tiny aspect of one tiny social group and describe it to death!

That's fine, I suppose, but just as I can't complain about academics not being impressed by my work, or ignoring it, because it is clearly not written for them, academic anthropologists cannot complain about declining student numbers and being ignored by the general public if they are clearly not writing for this wider audience.

Surely it is not *that* difficult to write about the complexities of human life and culture in clear, unpretentious English? And maybe even try to entertain people a bit instead of trying to impress them? I can only assume that academic anthropologists are deliberately *choosing* impressive obfuscation. In fact, I know at least one who feels obliged to do this. He has written some beautifully lucid, unaffected, and illuminating books, so when I came across one by him that read like the usual opaque, cryptic stuff, I expressed disappointed surprise. "It's ridiculous," he sighed, "but I have to churn out one or two pretentious ones like that occasionally or my colleagues stop taking me seriously." How sad, and what a waste of his time and talent.

More recently, I had lunch with two very talented anthropologists, one of whom had written a book that won the Margaret Mead Award, which is at least partly awarded for "accessibility." Her colleague asked her, "So, when you were writing that one, did you *intend* to make it readable?" I burst out laughing, and to give them credit, they only took a few seconds to see why. But they candidly admitted that had I not been there, this would not have seemed a bizarre question at all. We ended up discussing the unspoken rules of the academic anthropology tribe to which they belong—specifically, I asked, at what stage in one's academic career would it be "safe" to write a *truly* popular book? Having tenure would be an absolute minimum requirement, they concluded, and even then . . . hmm, no, safer to wait for a full professorship.

On a happier note, a friend told me the other day that he had seen my book *Watching the English* in the humor section of a bookshop and asked whether he should have complained that it wasn't in Anthropology. I said no, not just because I thought it would sell better in the humor section, but because the sort of anthropology I do is actually not that far removed from stand-up comedy—at least the kind of "observational comedy" stand-up routines that involve a lot of jokes beginning with,

"Have you ever noticed how people. . . ." The best stand-up comics invariably finish this sentence with some pithy, acute observation on the minutiae of human behavior and social relations.

Anthropologists and other social scientists try very hard to do the same, but there is a crucial difference. The stand-up comics have to get it right. If their observation does not ring true or strike a chord, they do not get a laugh. And if this happens too often, they do not make a living. Social scientists, however, can talk utter rubbish for years and still pay their mortgages. But at its best, I think that social science can sometimes be almost as insightful as good stand-up comedy. And that's the best I can do by way of a punch line, so I'll stop. Thank you.

References

Fox, Kate. 1999. *The Racing Tribe: Watching the Horsewatchers.* London: Metro Books. (New Brunswick, NJ: Transaction Publishers, 2005).

———.2004. *Watching the English: The Hidden Rules of English Behavior.* London: Hodder and Stoughton. (2008).

4

Drink and Duty: Extreme Drinking Rituals in the British Army

Anne Fox

Some years ago, on a warm night in September, somewhere in the hills of Wales, while engaged on a participant-observation study of the drinking habits of the British Army's infantry soldier, as a young private's boot firmly married my face to the mud and dust on the floor of a four-ton lorry, it occurred to me that perhaps I should have chosen a gentler tribe for my PhD fieldwork. On the night in question, a group of drunken and amorous officers had vehemently insisted that I join them in the town to drink and dance until the wee hours. I escaped only with the cunning assistance of a group of privates who unceremoniously stuffed me under the bench of a transporter lorry and feigned drunken stupor on top of me. It was at times like these that I wondered why I had not chosen "the song cycles of Welsh ladies' quilting circles" as a subject for my PhD rather than the drinking culture of the British Army.

In support of my thesis, the Ministry of Defence (MoD) had astonishingly granted me unprecedented access to both recruits in training and serving soldiers. In 2001, I was the first (and probably the last) female civilian ever allowed to "join" the British Army as a researcher and to shadow groups of young infantrymen through the rigors of basic training. Six months of intensive fieldwork, followed by several more years of research piggybacked on my role as a consultant to the MoD, built the foundation for my thesis. In this chapter I will spare the reader the bulk of my conclusions and just skip straight to the gory bits.

For soldiers, beer is associated with nearly every aspect of life. The money that is left from their pay, after all deductions have been accounted for, is commonly referred to as "beer tokens."

A sergeant tried to explain to me how important beer is, even out in Iraq:

> An evening was put aside in Iraq to drink. You could only have two cans. But, I can't explain it: it made all the difference. Alcohol has a way of changing people. That word "alcohol" just changes people: it changes the atmosphere. As a human race, we've built the thing up to something more than it is. You could have a "stand down" with cokes but it wouldn't have been the same. It is a big part of Army life, but I can't explain how or why. It doesn't make you soldier any better and it can't help you perform any better. It's just the norm.

Most informants did not think too deeply about the association of soldiers and drinking. Some shared the views of Wellington, who famously commented that soldiers are

> the scum of the earth . . . fellows who have enlisted for drink—that is plain fact.

This view is echoed, for example, in the words of a modern infantry sergeant:

> All the young lads want to do is drink. For them it's, you know, "Join the Army; see the world; get shit-faced."

Do British Army soldiers drink more than their civilian counterparts? A survey of 8,686 armed forces personnel by Fear et al. (2007) found that 67 percent of the men in the armed forces drink at levels deemed "hazardous," compared to 38 percent of men with similar drinking patterns in the UK civilian population. Soldiers' group drinking resembles the drinking patterns of young men in civilian society: but when subsumed into the military ethos, it is subtly transformed into a purposeful, semiorchestrated activity. While a similar process of drink ritualization may occur among other groups of civilian males, it is the facilitation and exploitation of this "natural" process by the military organization that distinguishes the practice as a key feature of the organization's culture and strategy.

The ritualistic, orgiastic group-drinking behavior of British infantry soldiers shares features with other warrior practices throughout history and among many other extant military groups worldwide.

Far from being a mere adjunct to military life, or relief from it, the unique British Army drinking culture is an integral and vital feature of the business of soldiering. The main aim, or "product" of this business is "combat readiness." In literature on military strategy, combat readiness and effectiveness are often measured not just by material might or technological advantage, but also by the level of group identification and cohesion among the fighting men. It has long been assumed that men do not necessarily fight for high ideals, but for their mates, and thus the encouragement of friendship and loyalty is a key component of military strategy (Cox 1995). Research has demonstrated, time after time, that there is a "strong relationship between cohesion, soldiers' level of morale, and combat efficiency" (Stewart 1994). The "Code of Conduct in the Armed Forces" introduced in January 2000 calls team cohesion an "overriding imperative" (Ministry of Defence 2000). Group drinking is used to create cohesion among men. As one lance corporal put it, "Alcohol glues us together."

The British Army exerts a strong organizational influence on the drinking culture. New recruits are actively initiated into this drinking culture and encouraged to view drinking as their reward. Although the drinking practices of the British infantry often result in costly consequences, they are ultimately an adaptive, beneficial element tuned to the military purpose. It is for this reason, my research concluded, that the drinking culture exists and persists, despite periodic opposition from the public.

Drinking alcohol has become institutionalized in the British Army. Alcohol is also used by the chain of command, not only as a means of developing a unit's cohesiveness but also to create and maintain formal and informal power structures and to test a soldier's endurance and "hardness" toward the horrors of battle. British Army servicemen use alcohol to define individual status and group identity and to construct the characteristic hegemonic military masculinity that is seen as the ideal soldier type. Army drinking rituals serve to consolidate social bonds, to service debts, to provide rewards and gifts, to self-medicate against depression, and to reinforce the values thought necessary for a good soldier to embody: aggression, strength, manliness, courage, good humor, sociability, and trustworthiness.

At the start of my fieldwork, my hypothesis was that members of an organization so bound by a multitude of rules would be more in need of and more likely to engage in "cultural remission" (or the undoing of the rules on as many occasions as they could) than other groups. Blinded by the common explanations given by soldiers of all ranks for this behavior, I accepted that drinking occasions were opportunities for the men to "let their hair down" and "relax the rules a bit."

I assumed that the very heaviest drinking binges by soldiers and officers alike were an act of temporary collective rebellion against the order—an expression of individual freedom. By going through the training process with soldiers, however, what I found was that the apparently rebellious, excessive, out-of-control drinking behavior that characterizes the infantry soldier's off-duty time is, in fact, an order-preserving ritual, the near-sacred significance of which is taught through drinking occasions that are carefully stage managed by the "elders" of the tribe. Young recruits are manipulated into the belief that heavy drinking *is* rebellion, a transformative expression of freedom. This allows the army to preserve order by scripting and orchestrating a form of rebellion that is, ultimately, congruent with the overall organizational goal in the infantry of maintaining unit cohesiveness and thereby enhancing combat readiness.

By simultaneously teaching soldiers to prove their loyalty and manhood through drink, and conditioning them to accept drink as a reward, the organization achieves its operational aims of "unit cohesion" with minimal expense. While mass drinking sessions create the illusion of rebellion against hierarchy and discipline, these sessions, and their accompanying games, also serve the operational aims of hardening and bonding men. The ability to drink is, to the British soldier, the insignia of a warrior—associated with manliness and strength. Not only is this a chemical fallacy (drinking reduces testosterone levels dramatically), but it is a social one as well. What drunkenness does achieve, I found, is to give men in a homophobic and "macho" culture a "cover" for physical affection, which, among soldiers, seems also to be important for bonding and survival. Extreme drunkenness often allows soldiers to express their "feminine" aspects: emotion, affection, sensitivity, and so on.

Historically, love between men did not carry with it the negative taint that it does today, and according to classical literature and art, some armies relied on such love to bond the soldiers. In traditional warrior societies, this was understood as a necessity for survival and celebrated in verse epics. The great poetry of such epics as *Gilgamesh*, the *Iliad*, *Beowulf*, the Irish *Tain Bo Cuilinge*, the *Chanson de Roland*, the *Morte d'Arthur*, and others is the poetry of lament over the loss of the "companion"—the "comrade"—the oath-bonded fellow warrior. Anthropologist Robin Fox, in a study of the highly emotional male bonding in Western epics, remarks that

> something even more basic than physical homosexuality is involved. This is perhaps only doubtful to those who have not served actively in wars and been through repeated battle experiences. The depth of emotional attachment between men of the same platoon or company who have shared terrifying experiences and risked their lives for each other is real and always moving. It may not these days be expressed in powerful epic verse—it probably never was, this was the contribution of the poets. But no one who has witnessed the reunion of those baptized together in fierce battle, or seen the tears shed over fallen comrades, can doubt that this is one of the most powerful emotional bonds known to us. (Fox 2005)

Fox (2005) argues that the male-male bond is at least as strong in terms of its evolutionary importance as the male-female bond. Simple impregnation ensures the process of reproduction, but males who must absolutely trust each other in warfare—for whom it is literally a matter of life and death—must form a deeply ritualized emotional bond. Those in army management understand the importance of this bond. When asked how one trains a man to enter a combat situation in which he might be killed, all officers and NCOs repeat the mantra, "Men die for their mates." The challenge for instructors at infantry army training regiments is not necessarily to develop strong bonds between recruits in the training platoon—as they will all eventually be split up among other battalions—but to teach them the bonding process itself. It is my argument that alcohol plays a key role as the ritual object in this bonding process. Those recruits who refuse to accept the ritual object or to use it according to the ritual script are jeopardizing their acceptance into this society of men. The scripted process of inebriation and affection is a bonding ritual between men akin to sexual bonding between men and women.

Drinking Rituals

The British soldiers' night out might seem, on the face of it, a wild, unregulated affair. Closer inspection, however, reveals a degree of ritualization in these drinking events and outings. The carefully planned pub and club circuit, the timing of drinks, the ordered escalation of "disinhibition," and the "storying" of events the day after, mapped the route of a transformative, communal journey. What is different, then, about soldiers' drinking?

In the course of my research over a decade, I observed numerous drinking rituals among British Army soldiers. Most of the heaviest drinking was celebratory, but the "excuses" for celebration ranged from the end of an operational tour, to welcoming a new soldier, to its being "Wednesday." A common initiation practice is to make the new member of the group drink the top shelf—that is, a shot from each one of the bottles. Variants include the "top-shelf teapot" in which a shot from each bottle is poured into a teapot and the new member must drink the lot through the spout. Although such initiation rituals are, I was told, officially banned by the army under Queen's Regulations, I had evidence, right up until 2010, that they were still occurring on a regular basis.

A feature of the British Army's drinking culture (and that of other military groups) is the practice by some, most infamously by the "elite" or specialized fighting units, of drinking games that involve nudity, humiliation, extreme drunkenness, and the ingestion or scattering of bodily fluids such as vomit, urine, and fecal matter (see Ehrenreich 1997; Beaumont 1976; Bryant 1974; Winslow 1999; and McCoy 1995). In the course of this research into the British Army's drinking culture over the past decade, a comprehensive collection of anecdotes regarding such practices has been recorded, and a few witnessed firsthand. Although some could be "urban myths," many stories were corroborated by credible witnesses or other data such as disciplinary records.

The meticulous and fastidious care that recruits are expected to demonstrate in their dress, posture, and speech at nearly every waking moment is sharply contrasted with the careless, unhygienic, and vile behavior that they are often expected to engage in when drunk. Group drinking sessions seem to offer a "time out" from this fastidiousness.

Very few of the experienced infantry soldiers I spoke with were shocked by such activities. Although ostensibly homophobic and decrying anything remotely "gay," several of my older informants in the infantry (particularly those from the "elite" regiments) confessed to having taken part in such things as drunken "daisy chains": a ring of soldiers connected through anal penetration. One sergeant was clear that such acts were about bonding and trust, and his explanation echoed the themes of male bonding in the aforementioned great epics:

> For a soldier, deployment for six months is the most intense period he's ever had with anyone, even his wife. On tour, they are pissing, sleeping, shitting, eating together. It takes a special person to fix a bayonet and kill someone at close quarters. You need to know the person next to you. The comradeship in war is something that is immeasurable, and they can get closer to that through the escapism

that alcohol gives them. How much closer can you get to your friends than having intercourse and doing things like daisy chaining? It's like a marriage, isn't it?

Many people would argue that you never know someone's capabilities until they have been tested to the full extremes, both mentally and physically. As a soldier, they will have to do some pretty unnatural things—taking a bloke's life—and who else understands them? Their wife never sees this—the true him.

The collection of games favored by some of the "elite" regiments includes the "digestive biscuit" game, or "speckles," which involves a deposit of feces (known by many soldiers in Cockney rhyming slang as Eartha Kitt) sandwiched between two digestive biscuits. Competitive drinking tasks bring the group in a closer and closer circle around the biscuit until one player commits an error. This results in a fist or beer glass being brought down like a gavel on the biscuit, showering all in the vicinity with "shit crumble." The person with the fewest "speckles" on his face has to eat what is left of the biscuit.

Another favorite is a variant of the classic "boat race" drinking game that requires participants to vomit into a glass and then pass it along for the next person to drink and then vomit into before handing it to the next man. In another variant, players alternately piss or vomit into the glass. Another version of this is known as the "soggy biscuit." Soldiers in a circle masturbate (known as "hand-to-gland combat") and ejaculate onto a digestive biscuit. The last one to deposit has to eat the biscuit.

Although I initially attributed this kind of behavior to "hazing" or initiation rites, I was interested to find that, although new members of a battalion are frequently forced to drink copious amounts of alcohol in their welcoming rituals, the particularly vile drinking games occur even more frequently among tightly bonded older and established groups of infantrymen. Some officers suggested that this always has been a particular feature of the male combat soldier.

What is the significance of these rituals, and what part does alcohol play?[1] Are we right in calling them rituals at all? In d'Aquili's (1993) analysis, to be classed as a ritual, an event has to be "structured or patterned," and it has to be "repetitive"—that is, "to occur in the same form or nearly the same form with some regularity." Moore and Myerhof (1977) also saw a ritual as "repetitive," "stylized," or "orderly," even "acted." In his study of "The Myth-Ritual Complex," Eugene d'Aquili

(1993) asks what is meant by ritual behavior and comes up with four criteria:

1. It is structured or patterned.
2. It is rhythmic and repetitive (to some degree at least), that is, it tends to recur in the same or nearly the same form with some regularity.
3. It acts to synchronize affective, perceptual-cognitive, and motor processes within the central nervous system of individual participants.
4. Most particularly, it synchronizes these processes among the various participants.

Although d'Aquili is speaking of religious ritual, it is obvious that this applies to many secular rituals, including the soldiers' drinking sessions. Additionally, ethanol can facilitate criteria two, three, and four in the brain. The effectiveness of ritual in this synchronization depends on a particular process of brain stimulation.

To summarize, there are two basic processes related to the two hemispheres, left and right, of the brain. The left hemisphere (dedicated to analytic, verbal, and causal thinking) is related to the *ergotrophic* or energy-expanding functions of the sympathetic and central nervous systems. The right hemisphere (which governs emotional, visual-spatial, and creative or gestalt activity) is related to the *trophotrophic* or energy-reducing (calming) functions of the peripheral and central nervous systems: those that maintain the baseline stability of the organism.

Normally the hemispheres function by rapid alternation, but over-stimulation of either hemisphere by collective ritual activity can result in the two firing together. This causes a chemical "spillover" from one hemisphere to the other (via the *corpus callosum*), with consequent feelings of the falling away of individual consciousness, the loss of boundaries and distinctions, the oneness with others, the embrace of opposites and contradictions, and the feeling that death is not to be feared. The only other physical experience that comes close, d'Aquili (1979) says, and that in fact involves the very same neurological processes, is orgasm.

Intense collective ritual activity, particularly activity involving rhythmic movement, drumming and dancing, dramatic repetitive chanting and display, can produce, at its extreme, trance conditions. But before the trance state is reached, this collective ritual activity produces feelings of a euphoric synchronicity with the other performers, leading to the sense of total group belonging and collapse of the sense of self. (Intense meditation can get the same results, but it is individual, not collective.) Psychoactive substances can also be used to reach or enhance these states, and, of course, as anyone who has ever participated in group drunkenness will attest, alcohol is often a favored support substance.

Grooming and other group actions have an undeniable physiological component: a trigger to the reward system. So the feeling of euphoria and oneness with the group (which Victor Turner (1969) calls *communitas*) is not purely spiritual; it is physical. As alcohol so perfectly mimics this physiological response, it is my contention that drinking can recreate the internal physiological sensation of group synchronicity, of *communitas*, of flow. In the context of group drinking rituals, this propensity can trigger a powerful bonding response. In the absence of physical contact between members of a group, it is my hypothesis that alcohol's actions on the brain serve to give language (verbal communication) a more physical component and thus bring us closer to our primate feelings of group safety.[2]

A chimpanzee will usually come to the rescue of another who is making a distress call. But Dunbar (1996) reports that they will do so far more quickly and consistently if the two chimps have been recent grooming partners. Soldiers talk of drinking partners in a similar way. Drinking together implies a bond that extends to protection in times of danger. So alcohol allows secular ritual to feel transformational, thus taking it into the realm of the sacred.

According to Mary Douglas (1987) and other authors (Tiger 1969), to be effective, bonding requires ritual, and, in turn, for its operational units to be effective, the army requires bonding. If alcohol plays the role in army bonding that we have described, then we should expect to see the elaboration, even extreme elaboration, of bonding rituals involving alcohol in situations where extreme bonding is seen to be necessary.

But how to explain the more extreme rituals involving ingestion of body fluids, excreta, and the like? Erving Goffman (1961) describes enforced acts of defilement as part of the total institution's strategy of mortification of the self by "contaminative exposure." Outside of the total institution, he explains,

> the individual can hold objects of self-feeling—such as his body, his immediate actions, his thoughts, and some of his possessions—clear of contact with alien and contaminating things. But in total institutions these territories of the self are violated; the boundary that the individual places between his being and the environment is invaded and the embodiments of self profaned.

Goffman claims that this mortification of the self by contaminative exposure can be "amplified" when "the agency of contamination is another human being." The consequence of forced interpersonal contact, public nakedness, or, in the case of the games described above, forced contact with the excreta of others, is a "forced social relationship."

In the case of prisoners, the purpose of this would be the complete subjugation of the individual to the authority: forcing the person to accept that the boundaries of his self are under the control of, and in essence merged with, the institution. But in a military organization, the contaminative exposure may serve a different purpose: to physically merge the boundaries of self between soldiers in a tight-knit unit, a merger that Victor Turner sees as a central function of ritual. The group ingestion of each other's ejaculate, urine, vomit, and feces could perhaps be viewed as akin to group sex—a complete dissolution of personal boundaries. It could also be viewed as a kind of group confessional: as in ancient British funerary rites, an individual takes on the role of "sin eater" for others by ingesting something that had been placed on the corpse or, in this case, something that had passed through another's body. That which is excreted from one person, that which is dirty, polluted, and unholy, is willingly ingested by another in an act of extreme bonding. It is perhaps symbolic of the final mutual sacrifice that these soldiers may be faced with.

These excremental and sexual rites are not an invention of the British Army: they are found in many cultures. Klein (1993) talks of the rites of the Aztec goddess Tlazolteotl, known as the "goddess of divine excrement" and the "Eater of Ordure," who transforms human and animal excrement into fertile earth. A penitent's confession to Tlazolteotl of one's sexual transgressions could rid him of all corruption: the rites of such a confession involved eating one's own filth to restore moral and physical equilibrium (Klein 1993).

Army officers see a practical function in the rites: the sensitization of soldiers to the realities of battle. One senior officer of the parachute regiment admitted that the vile and violent drinking games do occur, but insisted they have a training purpose. Although a serviceman or woman of any regiment or corps might encounter horrific sights and smells on the battlefield, he explained that the men of specialized infantry regiments are more likely to do so, being the first to be dropped into a situation. A civilian who encountered something horrific, he explained, such as a decaying or mutilated corpse, might immediately freeze and go into shock or be overcome with nausea or dizziness. Although the soldier might vomit as well, he is expected to carry out his duty without losing his head. If he has experienced these feelings before, he is more likely to "soldier on" in the face of horror. Kirke (1994) claims that this capability is what makes the military group unique:

> Military groups can be considered special in many ways because of the unique requirement that they should operate effectively under extreme stress, and indeed continue to do so even after suffering sudden and traumatic reduction through casualties.

In her book, *Ecstasy, Ritual and Alternate Reality* (1988), Felicitas Goodman concludes that

> we have a biological propensity for experiencing both the ordinary and the alternate reality. In the long run ... humans cannot tolerate ecstasy deprivation. The religious trance is an indestructible part of our genetic heritage. No amount of urban living can change that.

We have seen in the work of d'Aquili and Turner how ritual behavior can induce trance states through neurological processes. Goodman suggests not only that this is possible, but that it may be functional or necessary to relieve the harshness of real life by giving us, however briefly, access to another perceived reality. If this is true, then perhaps the strictness of the soldier's everyday life necessitates periodic forays into some form of alternative reality. This then takes group drinking beyond simple explanations of cultural remission and into the sphere of symbolism. The drinking group of soldiers is transformed into something else.

Alcohol itself has been described as a "transformative" or "transitional" substance, helping us make the transition from one state to another, or from work to nonwork. According to Hajar (2000), the etymology of the word "alcohol" probably derives from the Arabic word *al-kol* or *al-ghol* (from which we derive our English word *ghoul*), which translates simultaneously as either a shape-changing genie (or spirit) or a substance that can take away or cover up the mind (Hajar 2000). Douglas (1987) identifies one of the key functions of ritual, and of drinking, as "the construction of an ideal world." Rudgley (1993) invoked "the universal need for liberation from the restrictions of mundane existence" that can only be satisfied by experiencing "altered states of consciousness." The drinking place itself can become a kind of alternate reality where one can reconstruct oneself as one wishes (Rooney 1991; Mandelbaum 1965; Gusfield 1987).

Part of this process of transformation can involve purging the body, ridding it of the contamination of ordinary existence. Emetics are an essential part of many rituals. Many soldiers felt that "a good binge" once in a while cleansed the system and restored health.

> You vomit so much that it just purges your system. The next day you, after you get over it, you feel much better for it.

> The alcohol purges your system, like, of toxins and poisons. It's good for you.

For others, this "purging" had more to do with rebalancing mental, rather than physical, health, and they described the postbinge feeling in an almost spiritual vein:

> You feel like a new man.

> Sometimes you just have too much on your mind. When you get absolutely rat-arsed, you clear it all out, and after, you can think clearly again.

> It's like starting over. Wiping everything out and starting over.

In other cultures, beliefs about the spiritual cleansing properties of alcohol are more explicit. In Mexico, for example, many still believe that alcohol banishes evils from the soul (Palofox 2001).

In some African cultures, alcohol is not only a passage to the realm of the dead, but a link to the spiritual realm through the offering of drink. Igor de Garine (2001) describes a legend of the Tupuri people of Northern Cameroon in which death itself began with drunkenness, when drunken villagers were mistaken for the dead and were buried. Ancestor worship is also prominent in Dupa religion (Northern Cameroon) where the spirits of the dead are given offering of *bumma* (fermented sorghum or millet beer) throughout the year. Not even death, however, releases a person from cravings: the cause of illness among villagers is most often diagnosed as an ancestor's craving for *bumma* (de Garine and de Garine 2001).

Can we therefore see ritual drinking of any kind as symbolic of life and death itself? Anthropologists have thought so. Arnold van Gennep (1960) saw in the rites of passage frequent examples of the liminal phase involving "death to the world." The initiate is symbolically killed and then restored to life as a full member of the tribe.

In her article "Wine and Men in Alsace, France," Isabelle Bianquis-Gasser (1992) argues that the ancient association of the vine with the cycles of life and death persists in the modern man's drinking patterns. Drinking to the point of unconsciousness, she says, causes men to lose their "mundane awareness" and, by their subsequent regeneration, symbolize immortality (Bianquis-Gasser 1992). She also suggests that women find their immortality primarily through bearing children and therefore do not need to experience it symbolically through drink.

Clifford Geertz (1966) says,

> In a ritual, the world as lived and the world as imagined, fused under the agency of a single set of symbolic forms, turns out to be the same world.

Again, he is talking about sacred rituals, but I am led by my observations to the conclusion that army drinking rituals, while not ostensibly religious, often have the character of a semisacred, scripted rite and seen in this vein can be analyzed as performing a symbolic function. What the army drinking sessions symbolize depends on the company and the context, but there is always the power of the idea of drinking to loss of consciousness in the company of comrades. To some degree, communal drinking by young soldiers can be analyzed alongside "rave-style" drug-taking sessions as a form of secular worship, extreme examples of what has been called "civil religion" (Bellah 1967). But with the soldiers, the real possibility of death and killing raises this ritual activity to a level of significance well above the celebration and commiseration of civilian drinking in sports clubs or all-male parties.

Much of the vocabulary that soldiers use to describe the state of extreme drunkenness revolves around euphemisms and metaphors for death. They say, for example, "I was mortalled/comatose/dead to the world/five feet under/one foot in the grave/coffined/ slaughtered/ cadaverous/worm food," and so on. On one occasion, when I was truly frightened by the amounts that recruits were drinking, I felt compelled to explain to them the possibility of alcohol poisoning and brain-stem death. They were morbidly fascinated by this information, but not out of concern for their own safety. What they wanted to know was how close they could get to the boundary between life and death. There then ensued a bragging match about which of them had ever come the closest to death.

Battle and the Hunt

Because the business of soldiers is battle, to what extent does the drinking session become symbolic of battle? And is this in turn built on the emotions and cognitive scheme of the hunt?

Certainly, many soldiers go out for a night's drinking as if preparing for a hunt. As many soldiers explained to me, there are several goals to be achieved by a good night out. The first, as any soldier would agree, is bonding, just to be with your mates. The second is to "pull" or achieve a sexual conquest. The third is to engage in a good fight. Whatever the outcome, the language used to describe the night evokes the primeval hunt. There is preparation, coordination, strategy, costumes, the plan, the route, the thrill, the chase, the capture, the prey, the kill, the conquest, the victims, the "scene of destruction," the feasting, the celebration, and the journey home on the shoulders of one's comrades.

If the emotion of battle and the willingness of men to engage in it is predicated on our evolutionary hard-wiring for the hunt, then the enemy become akin to prey. But the aim in the hunt is not to chase the prey away, but to capture it, to possess it, to eventually transform it into one's own flesh by eating it and wearing its skin.

The aggressive power necessary for the hunt may have its evolutionary origins in mating fights, yet the organization necessary for the hunt is driven by group male cooperation while their focus on females and children is suppressed. Following Lorenz's contention that all bonding evolved concomitant with aggression, Tiger (1969) argues that all male bonding requires a consummatory stimulus to end the aggressive or competitive impulse. Sexuality and aggression are cohabiters in the male psyche. Littlewood (2002), for example, argues that there is a Dionysian sexual ecstasy in human hunting not unlike that of competitive sport. The drive to capture, possess, and consume that which is hunted translates into a sexual consummation. In our hunting past, both the hunt and the primitive battle would have had a similar consummation: killing, feasting, celebrating, sexual conquest. In modern warfare, however, battle (certainly by British Army soldiers) is no longer consummated in a period of rape and pillage, nor do the preparations for battle now promote these as the soldiers' reward. Military engagement no longer always ends in killing, and if it does, the dead enemy is often miles away. The soldier in theater can spend days and days without firing a single round, or even seeing what he is firing at.

I believe that the frustration of modern warfare fuels the male drinking culture that precedes and ends the tour of duty. In a drinking session, the soldier recreates the hunt with all the elements of this evolutionary "master pattern" (Tiger 1969): the bond with other males, the chase, the excitement, the conquest, and, through drunkenness, its completion or consummation.

However repetitive this may sound, we can never lose sight of the fact that organized drinking among recruits and serving soldiers always takes place within the context of the preparation of men for battle, for killing at firsthand, for facing the often horrific death of comrades, and ultimately for facing the strong possibility of their own deaths at the hands of an equally determined enemy. Human beings have always confronted the possibility of death with ritual of some kind. Death is, in Lévi-Strauss's sense, the ultimate "contradiction" that we must overcome, and ritual is our way of overcoming it.

Over and above its other functions, the organized drinking practiced by recruits and soldiers, organized by NCOs and officers, and tacitly encouraged by the army chain of command, has heavy elements of ritual, as understood and analyzed by anthropologists and psychologists. At both the functional and symbolic levels, the unofficial extreme ritual drinking sessions do for these men what the official ceremonies of military life cannot do, or can only do in less intense and less extreme ways: they prepare them for battle, and for the death that is always a very possible outcome of their particular vocation.

For the British Army, there is a functional crossover between the natural desires of young males to bond with other men and to engage in high-risk, "hunt-like" activities, and the Army's mission to create bonded groups of fighting men. Certain group-drinking practices serve both as a substitute for the hunt and also as a ritualized means of transcending death and returning to vitality through the literal or symbolic use of violence.

The notion of alcohol as the ritual object used in the warrior-hunter male process of bonding is not a novel one. What I hope is novel is the idea that an organization of the size and complexity as the British infantry uses this ancient process as part of military strategy. I do not wish to be an apologist for vile, aggressive behavior occasionally perpetrated by groups of drunken soldiers, I merely hope that by illuminating such behavior from within, with the glow of anthropological insight, rather than from without with the glare of media spotlights, that a real understanding of the behavior might be achieved. Perhaps this in turn might lead to methods of training infantry soldiers that harness the natural power of the aggressive and affectionate male bond without resorting to the alcohol-induced simulation of the real thing.

Notes

1. While these practices are facilitated by extremely heavy drinking, it must be noted that alcohol does not *cause* this kind of behavior. In fact, I observed on several occasions that a placebo usually works just as well as a trigger for drunken behavior.
2. For more on the origins of drunkenness see A. Fox and M. McAvoy (2010).

References

Beaumont, R. A. 1976. *Military Elites*. New York: Bobbs-Merrill Co.
Bellah, R. N. 1967. "Civil Religion in America." *Daedalus* 96:1–21.
Bianquis-Gasser, I. 1992. "Wine and Men in Alsace, France." In *Alcohol, Gender and Culture*, edited by D. Gefou-Madianou. London: Routledge.
Bryant, C. D. 1974. "Olive-Drab Drunks and GI Junkies: Alcohol and Narcotic Addiction in the US Military." In *Deviant Behavior: Occupational and Organizational Bases*, edited by C. D. Bryant. Chicago: Rand McNally.
Cox, A. 1995. *Unit Cohesion and Morale in Combat: Survival in a Culturally and Racially Heterogeneous Environment*. Fort Leavenworth, KS: Army Command and General Staff College, School of Advance Military Studies.
d'Aquili, E., C. D. Laughlin, J. McManus. 1979. *The Spectrum of Ritual: A Biogenetic Structural Analysis*. New York: Columbia University Press.
d'Aquili, E. 1993. "The Myth-Ritual Complex: A Biogenetic Structural Analysis." In *Brain Culture and the Human Spirit*, edited by J. B. Ashbrook. Lanham, MD: University Press of America.
de Garine, I., and V. de Garine, eds. 2001. *Drinking: Anthropological Approaches*. New York: Berghahn Books.
Dunbar, R. 1996. *Grooming, Gossip, and the Evolution of Language*. London: Faber and Faber.
Douglas, M., ed. 1987. *Constructive Drinking: Perspectives on Drink from Anthropology*. Cambridge: Cambridge University Press.
Ehrenreich, B. 1997. *Blood Rites: Origins and History of the Passions of War*. New York: Henry Holt.
Fear, N .T., A. Iversen, H. Meltzer, L. Workman, L. Hull, N. Greenberg, et al. 2007. "Patterns of Drinking in the UK Armed Forces." *Addiction* 102:1749–59.
Fox, A., and M. MacAvoy, eds. 2010. *Expressions of Drunkenness (Four Hundred Rabbits)*. New York: Routledge.
Fox, R. 2005. "Male Bonding in the Epics and Romances." In *The Literary Animal: Evolution and the Nature of Narrative*, edited by J. Gottschall and D. S. Wilson, 126–44. Evanston, IL: Northwestern University Press.

Geertz, C. 1966. "Religion as a Cultural System." In *Anthropological Approaches to the Study of Religion*, edited by M. Banton A.S.A. Monograph No. 3. London: Tavistock Publications, 1–46.

Goffman, E. 1991. *Asylums: Essays on the Social Situation of Mental Patients and Other Imates* London: Penguin Books.

Gusfield, J. R. 1987. "Passage to Play: Rituals of Drinking Time in American Society. In *Constructive Drinking: Perspectives on Drink from Anthropology*, edited by M. Douglas. Cambridge: Cambridge University Press.

Hajar, R. 2000. "Alcohol: Friend or Foe? A Historical Perspective." *Heart Views* 1(9).

Klein, C. F. 1993. "Teocuitlatl, 'Divine excrement': The Significance of 'Holy Shit.'" In *Ancient Mexico Art Journal* 52:3.

Littlewood, R. 2002. *Pathologies of the West: The Anthropology of Mental Illness in Euro-America*. New York: Continuum International Publishing Group.

Mandelbaum, D. G. 1965. "Alcohol and Culture." *Current Anthropology* 6(3):281–293.

McCoy, A. F. 1995. "'Same Banana': Hazing and Honor at the Philippine Military Academy." *The Journal of Asian Studies* 54(3):689–726.

Ministry of Defence. January 2000. *The Armed Forces Code of Social Conduct Policy Statement*, D/SP Poll 2/50/1.

Moore, S. F., and B. G. Meyerhof, eds. 1977. *Secular Ritual*. Netherlands: Van Gorcum, Assen.

Palafox, R. A. 2001. "Cantinas and Drinkers in Mexico. In *Drinking: Anthropological Approaches*, edited by I. de Garine and V. de Garine. New York and Oxford: Berghahn Books.

Rooney, J. F. 1991. "Patterns of Alcohol Use in Spanish Society." In *Society, Culture and Drinking Patterns Reexamined*, edited by D. J. Pittman and H. R. White. New Brunswick, NJ: Rutgers Center for Alcohol Studies.

Rudgley, R. 1993. *The Alchemy of Culture: Intoxicants in Society*. London: British Museum Press.

Stewart, N. K. 1994. "Military Cohesion." In *War*, edited by Lawrence Freedman. Oxford: Oxford University Press.

Tiger, L. 1969. *Men in Groups*. London: Granada Publishing Limited.

Turner, V. 1969. *The Ritual Process: Structure and Anti-Structure*. Chicago: Aldine Publishing Company.

Van Gennep, A. 1960. *The Rites of Passage*. Chicago: Chicago University Press.

Winslow, D. 1999. "Rites of Passage and Group Bonding in the Canadian Airborne." *Armed Forces and Society* 25(3):429–57.

III

Laughter and Happiness

No-Win Situations

The democratic roundabout
Makes sure the people never win,
For if they throw the rascals out
They vote the other rascals in.

The virtues of the questing mind
Are not as they are billed,
For in the country of the blind
The one-eyed man is killed.

Vishnu in his lotus dreaming stirred
and moved one shoulder slightly. Mountains fell.
Continents shifted. Empires collapsed.
Received ideas appeared ridiculous.

5

Understanding Laughter

Sir Antony Jay

It started with Machiavelli. I had grown up in institutions—school, college, regiment, the BBC—and even as a freelancer I had worked with several others. They were all very different, and yet it seemed that beneath the differences there was an underlying identity. But I had no idea what it was until I read *The Prince* and realized that Machiavelli's analysis of Italian Renaissance states and the rules for running them were pretty much identical with those for a twentieth-century corporation. The states had barons and courtiers, alliances and takeovers, rulers and subjects, which corresponded exactly with the structure and behavior of the modern business. The book I wrote about it, *Management and Machiavelli*, must have struck a chord because it is still in print after forty-three years, but I was still unsatisfied. Why were they the same? Was there some underlying unity to all human organizations? Obviously I didn't know, and didn't think I ever would.

Everything changed when I read Robert Ardrey's *African Genesis* and *The Territorial Imperative*. Of course there was an underlying unity, and it was formed by our evolution as social hunting primates. That was why we formed small work groups that were why we had status hierarchies that were why we applied territorial emotions to defend our customer base and market share. That was why five hundred or six hundred was about the limit for a business that one team could run; that was why ten (the hunting band) was about the limit for a work group, a section in the army, or a football team.

It all seemed so obvious that I was astonished by the passionate opposition, almost enmity or even hatred, that it stirred up in the world of social science. The social scientists were prepared to accept that our physiology was the result of our evolution, but fought to the death against the idea that the same might be true of our psychology and the behavior that arose from it.

There seem to have been two reasons for this. The first was that if it were true, then they were seriously unqualified to study human society. Disciplines such as evolutionary biology, animal behavior, and neuroscience were now central to our study of human behavior, and they were not part of the social scientists' intellectual tool kit. The second reason was political rather than academic: Marxists needed to believe that the mind of the citizen was *tabula rasa*, a blank slate on which anything could be written. The old ideas could be wiped off and replaced with new ones. You could see this in the argument that it was only social conditioning that made girls want to play with dolls and boys with guns. If this wasn't true, their whole theory of society was built on sand.

One of the barriers to the acceptance of the theory of behavioral evolution was that Bob Ardrey was not a qualified academic. In fact, he was a trained statistician, but he did not belong in the world of social studies. He wrote plays and film scripts and published in popular magazines, and so could be dismissed as "just a journalist." What was needed was academic respectability. That is why it was such a great moment when two serious and distinguished young academics published a book that supported and developed the theory of evolutionary behavior and planted ethology right in the heart of social studies. The book was *The Imperial Animal*, and the scholars were Lionel Tiger and Robin Fox.

Robin has been one of my heroes for many years and the most important of the scholarly influences on my understanding of the ancient survival imperatives that make human beings behave in the way they do. It has taken over forty years for the idea he grasped so early to be given even a grudging half-acceptance in the wider community, and the battle is not won yet. I suspect his reputation will grow higher and higher in the years ahead as the wider public comes to understand the primitive origins and evolutionary substructure of human behavior and as the academic community comes to acknowledge Robin's role in analyzing, developing, and spreading that understanding over a lifetime of scholarship.

I personally owe Robin a professional debt on two different accounts for his work and for his correspondence over the years. The first is as a management writer and consultant for the understanding he gave me of business management that can only be understood by recognizing the tribal roots and evolutionary origins of corporate organization and behavior. They were particularly important when I started my own business. The second is as a comedy writer, for the insights he gave me into the primitive collective tribal emotion that takes over a group of four hundred people when they become an audience. To a comedy writer, one of the most interesting and important expressions of tribal group emotion is laughter, and what follows is a lecture I gave on this subject to an audience of about four hundred people at the Royal Institution in London.

I don't know if you've ever thought about comedy and laughter, about what makes us laugh, and why. But if you do stop and reflect on it for a moment, you can see that there's something very odd about it.

Physiologically, laughter is a form of threatening behavior. A baring of teeth, a shortening of the breath, a rapid spasm of the diaphragm accompanied by a sort of baying noise. It is the sort of behavior we associate with aggression, alarm, warning, and hostility.

Socially, it is as far as we know universal to the species, not only all round the world, but also as far back in our history as we can trace it. It is also essentially a group activity: we do sometimes laugh when we are on our own, but it is unusual. Certainly, if I find myself sitting opposite someone on a tube or bus who is laughing all alone, I tend to get out at the next stop.

So we have this aspect of human behavior that is a primitive, universal manifestation of group hostility, and yet which we associate not with pain or fear but with some of the warmest, happiest, and most relaxed and relaxing of life's experiences. There is even some evidence in the work of Norman Cousins that it can be positively therapeutic not only for mental illness but for some physical illnesses too: patients who watch comedies undergo beneficial biochemical change. Why? How did it come about?

I cannot produce for you this evening a watertight theory of comedy and laughter. But as a writer and producer I have been trying over the past twenty-five years to create comedy and provoke laughter, and I have come to a view about it that I would like to share with you this evening. I hope you will forgive me if my approach is somewhat autobiographical and anecdotal, but I believe I shall be able to explain my ideas better if I can recreate some of the experiences by which they were formed.

I first started to think about it when I saw a performance called "The Hollow Crown" at the Royal Shakespeare Theatre. It was an anthology of writings by British monarchs, and it included the passage from Queen Victoria's diary where she describes her coronation. As it happens, I had read that passage to myself a little while earlier and remembered being mildly amused by it. But in the packed theatre, with Peggy Ashcroft

The Character of Human Institutions

taking the part of the young queen, I fell about with laughter, like the rest of the audience. There is a passage where she recounts how poor old Lord Rolle, who was eighty-three, knelt down to kiss the robe and keeled over and rolled all the way down the altar steps. I had read these diaries to myself and been privately amused, but only in the theatre did I discover they were funny.

I also remember an example of the opposite. One of the funniest cinema experiences ever, for me, was watching the sequence of the hall of the nodding heads in "Road to Morocco" with Bob Hope and Bing Crosby. When the film came on television I made a point of staying in to watch it. I didn't laugh once. It was quite amusing, but the magic simply wasn't there.

But perhaps the most vivid and thought-provoking of all was at the National Film Theatre in 1958. I was talking to an audience of some three or four hundred people about television and current affairs, which is where I was working at the time. The organizers had brought in a gigantic, twenty-foot television screen so that we could all watch part of Panorama live during the evening. It was from the outset a risky idea, because the audience of mostly young teachers and students were clearly not devoted fans of Panorama. It was not helped when it emerged that the item was an interview with the chairman of the British Electrical Equipment Federation about electrical safety in the home. It was not the most riveting subject, but worse was to follow. The chairman had a luxuriant, wavy RAF moustache, and as the interview began, the massive set developed a sort of line wobble so that a huge ripple ran across the screen right along the line of his moustache. The first time a few small groups got the giggles. The next time, it spread dangerously. By the third time they were cackling like the audience for Charlie's Aunt.

And then the worst happened. Once the audience had started laughing, they were looking for something else to laugh at. And at this point the chairman was talking about plugs and sockets. Inevitably the audience saw the sexual imagery, and after that you could hardly hear a word of the interview. They might have been watching Max Miller at his best, or indeed worst. Obviously the rest of the evening, which was me, was a terrible anticlimax. It was not an act I ever wish to follow again. But the point is that all over Britain millions of our fellow citizens were watching the same program without a smile, just occasionally nodding with agreement, or more likely nodding off to sleep. And yet four hundred people in the National Film Theatre were roaring with laughter at it.

I said earlier that I had been working with audiences for twenty-five years. In television parlance I have been doing so for thirty-five years, but the first ten years were programs for the home audience, with no studio audience and no laughter, except perhaps for the occasional titter from the camera crew. From those programs I learned nothing about comedy, audiences or laughter. We had nightly audiences of some eight million people who in fact did not add up to an audience at all. But in 1963 I produced a program—an anthology of entertaining excerpts from English literature performed by actors—that we felt needed an audience. It was my first experience in producing for live audiences, and the program was a flop, more or less, and the audience a disaster. There was hardly a murmur from them throughout the series—which needless to say was not continued. But the next year I left the BBC and helped to develop a comedy series with David Frost called "The Frost Report." This came under Light Entertainment Department, and it too had a studio audience. They laughed like anything, and the program was a great success.

What was the difference? Obviously the material was different, but that wasn't the heart of it. It was something to do with the audience. The first audience was about eighty people, and the requirements of camera movement and fire regulations meant that they were split up into four quite small groups. The second audience was in a proper television theater, two hundred and fifty or so people in a more or less solid block, separated from the cameras. That seemed to be close to the heart of it. The first audience was not an audience. The second audience was.

So when is an audience not an audience? Over the years I have discussed this with professional colleagues, and there seems to be six principal factors that help to make a group of people into an audience.

First, absolute numbers help. We came to the conclusion that for practical purposes we needed a minimum of two hundred. Four hundred was even better. We never got near a thousand, but we felt that with that many you would be in danger of losing contact with some of the people at the back and on the fringes.

Second, concentration and dispersal are essential. Two hundred might be an audience in a small auditorium, but scattered around the Albert Hall or Wembley Stadium they certainly would not be. Conversely, a hundred in a room that could really only hold seventy might well become an audience.

Third, darkness sets the mood. The more brightly lit the audience, the harder it is for the performers. But if the performers are brightly lit and the audience is in almost total darkness, it is much easier.

Fourth, it helps if they are not too far from the performers.

Fifth, it is better if they know each other, as with coach parties or clubs, than if they are complete strangers.

Sixth, it helps if they already know the principal performer, provided they like him or her, of course.

If you look at all those requirements together, it is clear that they all point in the same direction: the need for the individual members of the audience to lose their individual identity, to be confident that they won't be picked out separately, to merge into a single group identity, and to become part of a singly indivisible unit called "the audience." I remember when I first started teaching, a wise old master told me, "If you go into a classroom and encounter chaos and pandemonium, it's no good shouting "Shut up!" You have to say, "Shut up, Robinson!" Then the people realize they can be singled out and punished as individuals, so they stop. They're also curious to see what on earth Robinson was doing. It helps if there is a boy called Robinson in the room, but it's not essential."

It is also essential—as that advice also illustrates—for the audience to be focused on, and to accept, the performer or performers. I once asked the 1950's French existentialist singer Juliette Greco how she approached the audience. She said, "I just try to turn the whole audience into one man and make him love me. And if I can't, I go home." This sense of unity is at the heart of it. Henry Bergson in his essay on laughter tells the story of a church where the priest was preaching such a moving sermon that everyone was weeping. All, that is, except one man. One of the sobbing congregation turned on him and asked him why he remained unmoved while everyone else was in tears. "Oh," he said, "that's all right. I don't come from this parish."

All of us, I am sure, are aware of this mysterious, powerful force that we get caught up in when we merge our identity with the rest of the audience. We encounter it powerfully with community singing, and songs have often been a powerful instrument in cementing and expressing group unity: "Onward Christian Soldiers," "Abide with Me," "The Marseillaise," "John Brown's Body," "Pack Up Your Troubles," "Bless 'em All," "'Ere we go, 'ere we go, 'ere we go again."

Many of us will also have experienced the difficulty, almost the wrongness, of singing one of those "membership" songs when too many nonmembers are present. In the words of the psalmist, "They that led us out captive required a song from us: sing us one out of the songs of Sion. How shall we sing the Lord's song in a strange land?"

But whereas an army or a football crowd arrives with an identity and an ethos, a group of people who turn up for an evening in the theater—or the Royal Institution—are by no means instantly or automatically an audience, nor do they know what sort of audience they are going to be. That is something they have to discover after they have arrived. They start as a group of strangers in a hall. What is it that makes them become an audience, and what is it that determines the sort of audience they become? We have already talked about the conditions necessary to turn a group into an audience—numbers, darkness, proximity, and so on—but although they are necessary conditions, they are not sufficient conditions. You need something more.

The folklore will tell you that when making a speech you much always start with a joke. Like most folklore beliefs it is not completely true, but there is a truth hidden somewhere inside it. The first person to help me toward the answer to this question was Robert Ardrey, probably best known as the author of *African Genesis* and *The Territorial Imperative*, but also previously a successful playwright and Hollywood scriptwriter. He told me that if you are writing a comedy you had better make sure there are not any laughs in the first ten minutes; that, he said, is the time when you have, in his phrase, to "organize your audience." That is when they all have to find out together about the situation and come to a collective, shared understanding of the characters, their hopes and fears, and their relationships—all the foundations on which you are going to build your two hours of comedy. Too many laughs too early on and the foundations will not support the edifice—it will start to show cracks by the middle of act 1.

This creates a special problem for television audience shows because the home viewer needs programs to start with a bang, but live audiences very rarely start with a bang. The answer, all round the world, is the warm-up. This is a session with the audience before the start of the recording or transmission, to turn them into an audience before the television show begins. There are comedians the home audience never sees who are regularly hired as warm-up artists to perform this essential function. We used one for the very first "Yes, Minister," but it only half worked. He certainly got all the audience laughing together, but his type of humor was, well, shall we say not the same type as the program's. So when recording began, we had an audience all ready and organized for the sort of show they weren't going to get. It took some time to turn them round. After that we made sure that our three principal actors all talked to the studio audience and got them laughing before the recording began, and that worked very well.

We had stumbled on the fact that it is not enough for a group of people to become an audience. They must become *your* audience. In the last few weeks I have been to two one-man shows in London: one was by Peter Ustinov, the other by Frankie Howerd. Their styles of comedy could hardly be more different: Ustinov's was educated, sophisticated, and elegant; Howerd's was broad, basic, and vulgar. Both were terribly funny. The two audiences showed tremendously different characteristics. In fact they could well have been composed of exactly the same individuals, but the two artists turned us into two very different units. It was as if they had become our temporary leaders, like the ancient "Lord of Misrule," the jester who is made king for a day. For a couple of hours they made us see the world through their very different eyes, as Brutus and Mark Antony once make the Roman mob see Julius Caesar through very different eyes.

By about 1970, I had been involved in the production of quite a number of programs with audiences, and I was beginning to understand audiences and laughter a bit better. But I had actually written virtually no comedy to be performed in front of audiences myself. Then I went to a showing of some industrial training films. They were very boring, and yet people were paying large sums of money for them. These two facts in conjunction were as close to an inspiration as struggling freelance filmmakers ever get. I started to think about writing training films. My mind went back to my national service days. Some of the most powerful, memorable, and effective films I was shown were comedies. I still remembered some of them clearly after twenty years. And for soldiers, training was literally a matter of life and death. There were also, incidentally, some good dramas, but comedies seemed especially powerful in stopping us from making dangerously silly mistakes.

Surely, I felt, this principle could be applied to management training? But if so, I needed a partner who knew about comedy writing, and preferably someone who could play comedy too. Fortunately I had worked on two series with John Cleese, and for the next seventeen years, on and off, we wrote and he acted in some forty of fifty comedy training films. Indeed we haven't stopped yet. I learned a great deal from those films, and from John, but three lessons in particular are relevant to our present inquiry.

Understanding Laughter

First, comedy always meant looking for someone doing something wrong. The great strength of comedy film was in exposing and correcting errors. If you needed to show the right way to, say, interview a candidate, then the comedy had to come from the candidate. The interviewer was the comic figure only when he was doing it wrong.

Second, you had to make your audience see how they looked to others. To train salespeople you had to make them see themselves through customers' eyes. The film had to make them feel like customers and to experience the process of selling with customers' emotions. Because all salespeople are also customers, the experience of being badly sold to was there inside them. It was there to be drawn on to help them understand and learn. But to do so, the film had, in Bob Ardrey's phrase, to organize them into a group of customers, not a group of salespeople.

Third, we discovered that the real power of the films was not just the identifying and lampooning of certain mistakes. They worked at their best when there was an audience big enough to laugh at the mistakes. We discovered that the laughter was in itself a powerful training instrument. It proved that all the others agreed that the particular sales approach was ridiculous. They told you by their laughter and simultaneously you, by laughing, told them. And you all took away the lesson that you didn't ever want to risk exposing yourself to that sort of ridicule. And the lessons lasted. A week or so after we released a film John and I had written on how not to chair meetings, I was chairing a meeting of the company and made one of the classic mistakes we had shown in the film. The rest of the board fell about with laughter. I went very pink and discovered that laughter is indeed not always warm and relaxing, and is fundamentally hostile, if you are on the wrong end of it. But I did not make that same mistake again.

I learned those three lessons, but I did not at the time realize quite how fundamental they were to the understanding of laughter. It was clear however that the comedy John and I discovered in customer relations and management had applications that went beyond the world of training. John used the discovery as the foundation for Basil Fawlty, one of the greatest customer relations disasters of all time. Some episodes of *Fawlty Towers* are still used for training in the catering industry. And I teamed up with another writer of our training films, Jonathan Lynn, to write a series that we treated almost exactly as if we were writing a training film for cabinet ministers. The only real difference was that we showed all of the mistakes but none of the positive lessons.

The Character of Human Institutions

Yes, Minister was the first time I had actually written, as opposed to producing, for a live performance in front of an audience. Live shows are performed in sequence, and audiences genuinely do not know what is coming next. Some audience shows are filmed first and then shown to an audience, with the laughter being recorded. Some are taped cold and canned laughter is then added from discs in the dubbing theater. But ours was performed for real in front of an invited audience.

The question did arise as to whether that particular program wanted or needed a studio audience. Johnny and I were always adamant that we did. We had a very neat and convincing argument; we pointed out that the show might be attacked in high places as a tasteless and not particularly funny assault on our cherished institutions, but if there was an audience there laughing away, at least they couldn't say it wasn't funny. You can't refute a laugh with an argument. Also, the complainer would look humorless, and there are few things more damaging in British public life than to appear to not have a sense of humor. The audience was therefore a valuable protection.

That was our best argument, but it was not our real reason. The real reason was that we just felt the performance of the program had to be as if it were a public event, not a work of art to be constructed and perfected in a studio and then displayed in its final form. The audience was an ingredient in the program, like the crowd at Wimbledon or the Cup final. The laughs were integral to the event. I have always felt there is something deeply wrong about comedies performed in television studies without an audience and—unlike films—without ever being destined or designed for laughter. I have seen skillful television productions of plays like *School for Scandal* and *L'Avare* performed in an empty studio to be seen at home by one or two people on a sofa, and I have been appalled. They simply were not the plays Sheridan and Molière wrote. For me at least, the point of writing comedy is to make people laugh. Audiences and laughter are intrinsic to the performance, not an optional extra.

In fact, we still get regular letters complaining about what the writer usually calls "intrusive, canned laughter" and telling us how much better the programs would be without it. Of course, you could produce them without the audience, but they would not be the same shows. For a start, Johnny and I would write them differently, and certainly the actors would play them differently. And the absence of laughter would change the nature of the event.

So, how do you set about making an audience laugh? Of course I can only speak from personal experience, but I suspect that my experience is not all that different from other writers of comedy. I do not know of any formula, but in the course of a couple hundred mornings sitting down with a blank sheet of paper, knowing you have to put down on it something that will make three hundred people laugh in some six months' time, you do end up building yourself a sort of scaffolding, a framework to hold on to while you work, and hopefully to stop you from falling flat on your face.

The minister and his permanent secretary were a good starting point because the relationship is kept going and kept stable not by being inherently peaceful but by a balance of powerful, conflicting forces. The two frequently have very different, even opposite, objectives, but they both need each other. The permanent secretary needs the minister to secure the department's budget, to pilot its legislation through the House, and to make its actions appear vaguely plausible to Parliament and the public. The minister needs the department for facts, speeches, advice, guidance, answers to awkward questions, and indeed the whole administrative framework that turns his policies into actions or, more likely, explains to him why it is not possible to do so, but offers him instead a much more practicable policy, beautifully worked out, which happens to have been left over from the previous government.

That conflict at the heart of the relationship, a relationship which, like a marriage, cannot be easily broken off or walked away from, was the foundation on which we built every episode. Next, we had to find a theme—an issue that divides politicians from civil servants: secrecy, publicity, civil service pay, civil service honors, the use of government authority and resources for party political advantage, and so on. Then we had to invent a story, and it was a requirement of the story that it should land one or other of the two principals, or preferably both, in a ghastly predicament, or preferably several ghastly predicaments.

We took great trouble to make the actual story as interesting and realistic a story as we could. This was originally an insurance policy. We were frightened that people would not laugh. But we felt that if we failed to make it very funny, at least people would be held and interested so that it wouldn't be a completely wasted half hour. They would have been held by the plot, involved in the fate of the characters, and interested by an insight into the way the government actually works. But although our underlying motive was cowardice, it paid off in three interesting ways. In the first place, all sorts of people in high places told us about and allowed us to use incidents and practices that we would not have been able to print as fact. The fact that we changed key elements and disguised it all as fiction made it safe for our informants.

The second payoff was that the world of fact in government, and I suspect in most institutions, turned out to be much funnier than any fiction we could think up out of our own heads. A scene of an important government meeting taking place in a sleeping compartment on the train to Blackpool was based on a true incident. So was the scene of a teetotal Islamic reception in the desert where the minister set up an emergency communications room into which the minister's party drifted from time to time to open their red boxes and surreptitiously top up their chaste orange juice with Johnny Walker Black label. In fact, if you think about it, we could never have dreamed up or indeed gotten away with, a plot that hinged on a schizophrenic climbing into the queen's bedroom in Buckingham Palace and cadging a cigarette off her, as actually happened in 1982. And the third payoff was that the more authentic the story and issues, and the more that people accept the reality of the world you create for them, the greater the comedy. Indeed, we came to realize that if an episode didn't seem to be coming out funny enough it was because we hadn't done enough research. So we went back to our sources, and sure enough, as we learned more and more, it all got funnier and funnier. So given a theme and a plot, how do you set about constructing scenes that will make people laugh? In one sense, I suppose there are hundreds of ways, but for practical purposes I finally winnowed it down, at least for my own satisfaction, to two essential conditions.

The first condition is that someone should be in a highly tense or emotional state about something he is trying to achieve or avert. There is no comedy if everyone is relaxed and reasonable. And this emotional state is always to some extent self-centered and self-absorbed. It can be simple absentmindedness, being wrapped up in your own ideas. More often it is vanity, greed, lust, terror, or social pretentiousness— probably any of the seven deadly sins will do—but at the heart of it is an objective pursued, if not necessarily at the expense of everyone else, then certainly without much concern for them. You only have to think of Malvolio, Falstaff, M. Jourdain, Harpagon, Sir Joseph Surface, Basil Fawlty, Alf Garnett, Captain Mainwaring—all of them self-obsessed, selfish egotists. And their self-obsession often blinds them to what is obvious to the rest of us, even to the extent that a comic character can convince himself that windmills are giants.

Understanding Laughter

And the other condition is that someone on the stage must be unaware of something the audience knows. You may remember the scene in *Much Ado about Nothing* where Don Pedro, Claudio, and the others plot to make Beatrice and Benedick fall in love with each other. It is vital that the audience knows it is a trick, but that Beatrice and Benedick do not. It is the foundation for those two wonderful comedic scenes when first Benedick and then Beatrice think they are accidentally overhearing a conversation about how much the other loves them. And that sets up the third comic scene when they meet alone for the first time after the trap has been sprung. And in the same way, in *Twelfth Night* the audience has to know that the letter Malvolio finds in the garden suggesting that his employer Olivia is in love with him is in fact a forgery cooked up by Sir Toby, Maria, and their gang. *Twelfth Night* is reckoned to be one of the most surefire of Shakespeare's comedies, and it is of course a treasure chest of facts known to the audience but not to someone on stage. Apart from the gulling of Malvolio, there is the fact that Viola is dressed as a boy, so Olivia does not know she is in fact in love with a woman, just as Orsino does not know that his new page boy is in fact a girl who is in love with him. And into all this comes Viola's twin brother, looking now exactly like her, and each thinking the other has been drowned. You can see why *Twelfth Night* is known in the profession as being actor-proof.

There is however an interesting point here. These two preconditions—someone in a high emotional state selfishly pursuing his or her own ends and someone on the stage not knowing something the audience knows—are also the preconditions of powerful, suspenseful drama. What is the difference? One of the best illustrations I know of is *Jamaica Inn*—the Hitchcock film was repeated on television recently. It's about a gang of wreckers on the Cornish coast, and our hero customs officer knows about them but is waiting to catch the "Mr. Big," the powerful but unknown figure he realizes is behind it all. He discloses all this to the lord of the manor. However, the audience knows, though the customs man does not, that the lord of the manor is himself the man behind it all. The scene where he explains it all and the lord of the manor nods sagely, congratulates him, and asks him how he plans to catch this mastermind is highly tense and dramatic. But it could also be highly comic. You hardly have to change a word if you simply cast someone like John Cleese as the customs man. The scene could play exactly as it is written and be extremely funny.

101

The only difference is that in the drama we want the customs officer to win. We care about him. We are on his side. In a comedy we are not on his side. We think that anyone that stupid deserves everything that's coming to him. We feel an awful glee in watching him dig himself deeper and deeper into the pit. In Bergson's delightful phrase, we suffer "momentary anesthesia of the heart."

There was a story in the *Times* a few years ago about a couple who went into a Chinese restaurant with their miniature poodle. They wanted the dog to be given some lunch in the kitchen, but because their waiter didn't understand enough English, they pointed at the dog, and then at the kitchen, and made eating gestures. They then waited a very long time, surprised that no one had brought them a menu, until the waiter came back with a very large dish covered with a big silver hood. I have to say that I found it a very funny story, but a number of people (including my wife) didn't think it was funny at all. And of course, they were actually right. And yet, is it a funny story or isn't it? It all comes back to what you think of the behavior of the poodle's owners. Did they act reasonably and suffer an unkind fate or did they act foolishly enough to trigger that momentary anesthesia of the heart?

Perhaps at this point I could attempt to summarize what we have established so far about comedy and laughter. There seem to be nine points:

- It is, physiologically, a reflex action of the sort we connect with fear, aggression, or threat.
- It is associated with pleasure, relaxation, and good fellowship.
- It is universal to our species and has been from as far back in our history as we can trace it.
- It is, at heart though not invariably, a group activity.
- It requires a group of people who one way or another have submerged their separate individualities into a single collective identity.
- It requires that the group accept the temporary reality, the point of view, in a sense of authority, of the performers and the performance.
- It is triggered by someone emotionally obsessed and absorbed in himself and his objectives at the expense of or to the exclusion of other people.
- The audience does not share those objectives or want him to achieve them. They are in fact hoping for his discomfiture, and their laughter expresses their pleasure when it happens.
- It requires someone on the stage to be unaware of something the audience knows.

Can we therefore hold that for a moment and move on to something else? Up until now I have been talking about the "what" and the "how" of laughter and comedy. Now I would like to move on and talk about the "why."

If laughter is so universal and ancient, it must surely have some survival value for the species or, to be more precise, must at least have had a survival value at some time in our evolutionary past. But what? I would like to put forward a suggestion as to what this survival value might have been. I was going to call it a hypothesis, but I learned recently that *hypothesis* is a term ascribed to a wild guess by a distinguished scientist. I am afraid that what I have to say meets only the first of those two conditions, so perhaps I had better call it a *conjecture*, though even that may turn out to have been too dignified a term.

I was in the BBC for nine years, as a trainee, a producer, an editor, and finally as a head of department, a manager. In the last year or two, as a manager, I became more and more interested in how the BBC worked or, to be more accurate, how it didn't work. Often it seemed that the corporation itself, its own organization, was the obstacle to the achievement of its aims. After I left, I worked with other organizations and found the same problem. What I didn't find was any "right" way of organizing. People had personal experience, isolated pockets of wisdom, little stores of maxims, but there was no general overall consensus, no unifying thesis.

And then I started reading Machiavelli's *The Prince* and discovered that he, back in the early 1500s, was grappling with exactly the same problem. He was talking about kings and princes rather than the chairman and directors, but if you made certain simple changes, the issues were identical. Corporations have their ranks and honors systems, their barons and courtiers, their campaigns and treaties, their territories and conquests, and all the apparatus of the city state. It was particularly interesting that the advice he gives on dealing with the rulers of a conquered state is identical to the advice modern management consultants would give on how to deal with the directors of a taken-over company. I found it absorbing, not just for the light that knowledge of history can throw onto questions of management, but also for the light that experience of management can throw onto questions of history. There were so many instructive parallels that I wrote a book about it all. But I still felt a fundamental dissatisfaction. Was this correspondence just an accident, an intriguing coincidence, or did it go deeper? Were ancient states and modern corporations in fact manifestations of some underlying and abiding reality about the way our species orders and organizes itself?

The Character of Human Institutions

At the time this seemed to be idle speculation about an unanswerable question. And then I started reading a book called *The Territorial Imperative*, which suggested that perhaps the question was not unanswerable after all. Parts of it seemed to be about exactly the same subject. Certainly no one with nine years' experience of BBC departmental infighting could doubt that the instinct for territorial aggression and defense was alive and well and living in Shepherd's Bush. Indeed, I have heard rumors that it can be encountered even in the pure atmosphere of academic institutions. It led me on to a small binge of reading around comparative ethology and evolutionary behavior. But in terms of what we are talking about this evening, the most important idea that occurred to me was that there might be natural, evolutionary types, indeed sizes, of human groups, and that the need to organize ourselves into such groups might be within us still.

The first and most immediately persuasive grouping was the ancient hunting band of not much more than ten adults. There is a lot of evidence, and a lot more personal experience and insight, to suggest that a genuinely cooperative working group becomes too unwieldy if its numbers get much over ten, and to be effective with a larger number you need to split into two or more smaller groups. It is unlikely that the change from hunting to farming in the past ten thousand years would have changed a behavior pattern we had evolved over millions of years as social hunting primates, though certainly we could learn to channel it differently.

But the more I read, the more it sounded as if there ought, somewhere, to be a larger grouping: what geneticists call a *population*. Technically, populations are groups of members of a species within which breeding is common and across which breeding is rare. And it seems that the higher up the scale you go, so to speak, the smaller these populations tend to be. A population of elephants is likely to be smaller than a population of fruit flies. Zebra, for example, tend to have populations of about a thousand. Simple arithmetic would say ten groups of ten make a hundred, but that seemed too small. Anyway, the ten groups were only the hunters; there would be children, mothers and perhaps old people back in the camp. So could it be a thousand? That seemed too large. In fact, everything I could find seemed to point to a number somewhere between four and seven hundred: schools, colleges, villages, parliaments, the Roman cohort, the modern battalion, the successful one-man business—all these seemed to suggest that there is an upper limit of six or seven hundred in an integrated

Understanding Laughter

human community, a community you could genuinely belong to, where everyone could know everyone else, where people would notice if you weren't there. It's about the largest number you can reach in the open air with the unaided human voice. Above that number, an organization could only work if you split into more groups.

What I have come to believe is that we still, today, carry within us, perhaps in some way in our brain patterns, a need or instinct to form or join or belong to units, to groups, that cannot easily grow to more than six or seven hundred in size and still hold together. "Tribes" is probably the best name. And it is within these tribes that we find reality and identity. Before industrialization, most of us would have found our tribe in our village. In urban civilization, most of us find it in our work, though many fail to and are stuck in lonely anonymous suburbs discovering the acutely demoralizing effect of detribalization.

As I said, this idea that we still have a natural human tribal size of about six hundred is at best a conjecture. If you find it unacceptable, you can look on it as just a metaphor. But for me it is the only remotely convincing starting point for our understanding of the "why" of laughter.

I see laughter, laughter at comedy, as being at heart a tribal phenomenon. It is tribal behavior, a collective tribal response to something the whole tribe recognizes and understands. When people tell you to start your after-dinner speech with a joke, when television comedy shows book warm-up artists, when Bob Ardrey talked about spending the first ten minutes of a stage comedy "organizing the audience," they are all saying that you have to turn three hundred or so strangers into an instant tribe: to stop them feeling like separate individuals and make them think, feel, act, and react like a single tribe and to make that tribe accept you as its temporary leader. And all the devices we noted earlier—darkness, close seats and rows, several hundred people together all looking at the stage—work to create, release, and focus this primitive tribal emotion.

When Rumford designed this theater, he designed what is almost the perfect place for a tribal gathering. There is no ambient light. It holds four hundred people, all close together, all focused on one point, and yet the most distant are still only a few feet away from the speaker. These Friday discourses are tribal events. Intellectually speaking, there was no need for you all to come here this evening. All the words you have heard could have been typed out and posted to you. But the fact that you chose to come, even though you may now be regretting the decision, shows that you know it would not have been the same. And the principal difference is that you have all heard exactly the same thing, you know all the others have heard it, and you know they know that you have. It becomes part of our shared knowledge and experience. If some of us meet up again next week, next month, or next year, we have this shared tribal experience to draw on.

Recently I met someone who turned out to have been in the same audience at Stratford some twenty or thirty years ago for the most disastrous first night of *Othello* in that theater's history. The bond was still there. We became immediate fellow tribesmen. We shared again that seven minute blackout when they couldn't get the bed through the gap in the wings, the moment Gielgud leaned against a pillar and we all thought it was going to crash down into rows A and B of the stalls, how his beard came half adrift and swung from one side of his chin like a pendulum, and how Iago rushed on and said, "Cassio dead and Roderigo slain!" and then saw the horrified Cassio in the wings waiting for his entrance and had to say rather sheepishly, "I mean, Cassio almost dead." We may also have read some of the same books and newspaper articles around the same time, but they were not memorable in the same way and could not form the same kind of bond.

But even if we accept that an audience is a primitive tribal gathering, why does a tribe have to laugh? Where is the survival value of laughter? Freud has suggested it is triggered by the violation of a taboo. Certainly the violation of a taboo can be very funny. But incest is taboo, and while the *Oedipus Rex* is one of the greatest plays ever written, there aren't a lot of laughs in the final scene.

Of all the people who have tried to explain laughter, I believe that Bergson has gotten closest to the heart of the matter. He points out that inflexibility is at the root of most comedy scenes. He also calls it "automatism" and "lack of elasticity." At another he talks about "fundamental absentmindedness." He says we laugh at this sort of behavior because someone is, for one reason for another, so locked into a pattern of thought or behavior that he is unaware that circumstances make that behavior inappropriate, like carrying on walking when there is a banana skin in front of you. "A comic character," he says, "is comic in proportion to his ignorance of himself." And, we might add, his unawareness of how he looks to others.

This seems to me to be very close to what I have found to work in comedy writing—someone bound up with themselves to the exclusion of others, and someone unaware of something the rest of us know. But what is its purpose? He sees it as a form of social gesture whose purpose is normative, to restrain eccentricity and promote a coherent, cohesive pattern of tribal behavior where people observe the world and the others around them and adapt accordingly, to bring the deviant into line. It is a wonderful essay, "La Rire" ("Laughter"), beautifully written and full of illuminating insights, and it is hard to quarrel with any of it. But I believe that the work of ethologists and others in the eighty years since he wrote it, and particularly the last forty, gives it an even more profound and precise evolutionary significance, and that it is the hunting tribe that supplies us with the key.

Clearly every member of a hunting tribe in a hostile world needs an acute sense of danger and an ability to communicate that sense of danger to all the others as quickly as possible. There was an interesting experiment on this subject with a shoal of fish, because they have this uncanny ability to move almost like a single organism, totally and instantly aware of what all the others are doing. How do they manage it? It was isolated to the part of their nervous system that senses danger, so they took one fish and removed from its brain the part that sensed and communicated danger. Then they returned it to the shoal. What happened? Well, there may be some deep parable here, but what happened was that this half-brained fish immediately became the leader. It swam blithely on, and all the others followed it. The experiment unfortunately did not go on to establish how long the shoal survived.

But obviously the behavior of every individual in a tribe surrounded by predators and perhaps hostile tribes, and hunting a swift and elusive prey, is crucial to the survival of the whole tribe. It is literally a matter of life and death. One person who is absentminded or ignorant of something he ought to know, or obsessed with himself and his selfish aims, can kill us all. He is a menace. You may have read about "fragging" in the Vietnam War—incidents where troops of American soldiers shot their officer when they believed he was leading them to certain and unnecessary death. In a hunting culture, as in war, inflexible, nonadaptive behavior, obliviousness of dangers, failure to be on the alert for warning signals—these are threats to life, and they must be stopped. Sometimes it is possible for the whole pack to bark a threatening warning to the members whose actions menace all the others, but not always.

However, there is a surer way, and that is to reenact the dangerous situations and the tribe-threatening behavior within the relative safety of the tribal gathering and in front of the whole tribe. We can all watch the approach of danger, feel the tension rise, and when someone does the foolish thing that precipitates that disaster and suffers the consequences (and serves him right) we can all snarl and yap and bay together to our hears content. And that tribal reaction—especially if it comes from everyone spontaneously and simultaneously—is a lesson of immense power for the whole tribe. It is not an intellectual lesson, but an emotional one: not brain learning but gut learning.

Drama and comedy are at their best real and true emotional experiences for the audience, vicarious emotional experiences but true ones. Our spontaneous, immediate laughter tells the others this is a true danger and a proper retribution, and theirs tells us, all at the same time. And we all learn not to do it ourselves, as a child learns not to put its hand in the fire again. Just as heroic drama, epic, gives the tribe positive models to follow, so comedy gives it negative models to avoid. Of course we all learn by firsthand experience, but firsthand experience may mean dying, which is of course one of the principal instruments of species survival by purely genetic evolution. But cultural evolution means that populations can transmit survival behavior by teaching and learning, not just living and dying.

The origins of comedy and laughter, I believe, lie in what I, if I were a sociologist, would no doubt call "the collective tribal transmission and reception of negative socio-behavioral models," but what I prefer to think of as primitive tribal training sessions: group behavioral training programs. The threatening, stupid, funny behavior teaches a lesson, the lesson stimulates laughter, the laughter reinforces the group's unity, and the group's unity reinforces the lesson. It affirms its truth and universality, and it signals its acceptance by the group, the tribe. The comedy identifies the dangerous, antisocial, self-centered behavior; it shows us how it looks from outside, as it were. And the laughter of the tribe inhibits it. It cauterizes it. It prevents any member from behaving that way ever again.

Clearly comedy has come a long way from the primitive tribal gathering. But I believe that we are still tribesmen and tribeswomen at heart and that the sense of community and fellowship and satisfaction we get from shared laughter is drawn from a profound ancient tribal emotion and survival need that is still very much alive within us all.

References

Ardrey, Robert. 1961. *African Genesis*. London: Collins
———.1966. *The Territorial Imperative: A Personal Enquiry into the Animal Origins of Property and Nations*. New York: Atheneum.
Bergson, Henri. 1959 (1900). *La rire: essai sur la signification du comique*. Paris: Presses Universitaires de France. (Translated by Cloudesley Brereton

and Fred Rothwell. *Laughter: An Essay on the Meaning of the Comic.* New York: Macmillan, 1914.)

Jay, Antony. 1967. *Management and Machiavelli.* London: Hodder and Stoughton

———.1971. *Corporation Man: Who He Is, What He Does, and Why His Ancient Tribal Impulses Dominate the Life of the Modern Corporation.* New York: Random House.

Tiger, Lionel, and Robin Fox. 1971. *The Imperial Animal.* New York: Holt, Rhinehart and Winston.

6

Joyous, Equal, and Free: Conditions of Felicity in Human Organizations

Charles Macdonald

> *Bay-bee'-mi-say-si replied in a laughing voice: "My life may be foolish, Waynaboozhoo, but I have a purpose in life as noble as yours. My purpose is to tease those who take themselves too seriously. I tease the human beings, I tease the buffalo and all the four-leggeds, and I tease the spirits, too. There is a place for foolishness in the Creation."*
> (Benton-Banai 1979, 54)

When asked to contribute to this volume honoring Robin Fox, I felt I was offered a rare occasion to show a token of my unconditional admiration for one of the great minds in my field. My reading of The Red Lamp of Incest (Fox 1983) was indeed one defining moment in my understanding of human social organization, how the interlocking of society and mind functioned and how pervasive were certain general but unnoticed principles in human behavior. For the first time I was apprised of the fact that, contrary to Lévi-Strauss's contention, the incest prohibition was not a cultural edict. His analysis of the naming system of the Tory Islanders is another of my favorite pieces of ethnology, the kind of deep, detailed and anthropologically illuminating studies that are the real gems in our laboriously plowed field. Looking at Robin Fox's numerous books and articles, I find there is hardly any corner of the ethnological field he did not explore with incredible sharpness, depth, and, I should say, unmatchable poetic flair. I could have written something on two of his favorite topics, kinship or personal names, but in the following contribution I shall address the twin concepts of communitas and structure that he discusses in the final chapter of his latest book, *The Tribal Imagination* (Fox 2011). He rightly points out that communitas (taken from Turner 1969) in dialectical opposition to societas is a state of being rather than a stage of social evolution. As such, it is a dimension of all societies. There is a release of tensions, dissolution of boundaries, a state of felicity in the communitas moment, an almost ecstatic liberation from the constraints of ordered social life. In this sense, communitas cannot exist without societas. This is certainly true for ritual events and privileged times when a crowd becomes one and a sense of transcendent unity pervades the collectivity. Is there, however, a possibility for communitas, or something like it, to exist outside and without societas? This is a question I will pose in the following pages.

What causes communities characterized by a high degree of personal autonomy and a lack of constraints because of an absence of rank and power to be cohesive and stable is a hard question to answer in an anthropologically cogent way. Having considered such a community in my field studies (Macdonald 1977, 2007), and after subsequent interpretive attempts, I have sought an answer in terms of values and attitudes and in a pervasive ethos predicated on something I call "conditions of felicity" of collective living (Macdonald 2008). The phrase is borrowed from linguistics, where it means "conditions for a speech act to be successful" (Austin 1962), and by it I simply mean conditions that enable interpersonal relations to happen and meet basic psychological and emotional requirements of the actors concerned in order for these relations to get established and recur. It is then an adaptation to sociality of Austin's definition, and somehow departing from it. If someone I try to engage in conversation turns around and does not acknowledge my verbal entreaties, I will say that the conditions of felicity for a social or interpersonal engagement are not met. The interaction stops there. If this person responds by looking at me and acknowledging by his entire demeanor my presence while uttering words that are consonant with the tenor of what I said, I will say that the conditions of felicity for our interaction are met. If, moreover, the response I get from the other person is so engaging and replete with warm feelings, I will not only continue the interaction but even wish for its renewal at some ulterior time. The supporting elements of these conditions here are attention given to the speaker, relevance of response relative to the words of speaker; facial and bodily movements expressing interest, pleasure, friendship, concern; and speech acts stating positive or warm feelings, respectful attitude, agreement, and so on.

Conviviality

Social scientists have used a number of terms to describe a state recognized as felicitous and conducive to a stable and repetitive interaction: togetherness, conviviality, empathy, intimacy, grace, immediacy, harmony, and so on. (see Bird-David 1994, 591, 594; Ingold 1999, 405, on intimacy; Macdonald 2008, 14–15, on harmony). Such a state has connections with such dimensions of sociality as solidarity, bonding, shared activity, consensus, and cooperation.

My approach is perhaps better defined as psychological anthropology rather than cultural psychology. It has, however, much in common with the concerns of anthropologists dealing with the "social and moral context of emotional experience" (Schweder, et al. i.p.) and particularly a context defined as "ethics of autonomy," "ethics of community," and the attendant "culturally valued aspects of the self" (Shweder 2003, 1120). Attitudes or dispositions I am looking for must have enough normative power to become institutionalized. They must be culturally encrypted and expressed in an idiom of moral goods, and they are likely to be found in various settings and in different cultural and historical contexts. I am seeking then a certain degree of generality and cross-cultural similarity at a subphenomenal level. Also, I shall focus on the psychological and moral factors conducive to stable bonding and positive relatedness, rather than those that are disruptive and conflict producing. Both sets of factors have a dialectical relationship with one another (Fajans 2006, 107). But it is not conflict resolution that is my main concern; it is rather the avoidance of conflict, even if these processes cannot be entirely separated. My starting point will be the notion of anonymity, which will lead to the twin notions of equality and reciprocal humility.[1]

I will further consider humor and laughter with an attention to healthy obscenity. In this excursion, I shall investigate two different kinds of collective entities: enclaved and nonenclaved. Nonenclaved aggregates are communities that are autonomous and live a life of their own in a geographically distinct portion of the universe, just what we call *ethnic groups* or *tribal societies* (Inuit, Palawan, Semai, etc.).[2] Although dependent to a certain degree on their human environment (made of hegemonic or nonhegemonic polities), they possess a self-contained reality and manage their own self-reproduction process.

The enclaved aggregates I have in mind are of two kinds also: cenobites that are embedded in a state organization but tend to live in complete self-sufficiency (hippie communes, libertarian movements, Amish communities, etc.) (Dentan 1992, 219; 1994, 73–74) and "intentional communities," fellowships or associations that meet occasionally and for a specific purpose only (Alcoholics Anonymous, adepts of the Japanese tea ceremony, deaf-mutes, etc.). All these different aggregates display some common or similar features in their ethos, moral values, and interactive habits. As I will try to show, a common thread is running through what appears as completely dissimilar situations and cultural settings. This thread is an attention to a strict equality of status, an insistence on the humble and nonaggressive, and at times spiritual, dimension of the interaction, resulting in an intriguing conflation between equality and spirituality.

Anonymity in AA

The fellowship of Alcoholics Anonymous (AA) has been an object of anthropological study, and a number of studies, books, and articles have been devoted to its investigation (among those see Cain 1991, Dentan 1944, Gellman 1964, Jensen 2000, Lechner 2003, Maxwell 1961, Millar n.d., Rudy 1984, Steinbring 1981, and Trevino 1992). My interest in this particular association, AA, stems from its obvious anarchic nature as an organization and from its resilience in an uncongenial environment. Born in 1935, AA has gone through all sorts of growing pains and travails but has remained a viable, productive, and successful association, without becoming a religious sect, a government-dependent agency, or a political movement, proof enough that an anarchic type of aggregate can survive true to itself in a nonanarchic "Babylonian" environment. So far it has resisted institutionalization very successfully. Fellow members of AA are peaceful anarchists—within the confines of their associative activities, that is—and inasmuch as they recognize no manner of chiefs or leaders within their association and at the same time fulfill a social function: they help addicted people get their act together and thus save society a lot of expenses and trouble.

I will now concern myself with the concept of anonymity, mainly because it is, according to AA's self-definition—as spelled out in the AA "Twelve Traditions"—the "spiritual foundation" of its traditions (Alcoholics Anonymous 1952, 188). Anonymity is further defined as "putting principles before personalities" (ibid.) and is linked with "sacrifice" (ibid.) and with "humility" (ibid., 192). Other explanations are given as to why anonymity is an important principle, especially regarding the image of the fellowship in the general public (ibid., 191).

In his penetrating study of the AA fellowship, Lechner spells out some of the main points of anonymity, especially the fact that it "protects members from the stigmatizing glare of outsiders" (Lechner 2003, 35). When speaking among themselves during a group meeting, AA members use their first names only or any names of their choosing. Conversely, "When members who know each other meet in public they do not disclose their AA identity to nonmembers" (ibid., 38). There is however a lingering confusion about the very concept of anonymity, one that I think needs untangling. What is "anonymity" exactly, and why should it be considered a "spiritual" foundation, even seen as a form of "sacrifice"? Why does anonymity translate into "humility"?

In most cases, personal names reflect the hierarchical aspect of society. Only in certain cases are naming systems structured so as to reflect, not hierarchy, or dominance, but friendship and dyadic egalitarian relations, or some other spiritual properties devoid of any ranking connotation (Macdonald 1999, 2006, i.p.) In European societies dominated by a binomial or trinomial naming system (first name + middle name + surname), the entire syntagm is attached to the person as a status-loaded member of a ranked society. In spite of egalitarian and democratic aspects, Western societies remain fundamentally hierarchical in most spheres of activity, and names point at least virtually to a social status within these hierarchical systems. Not using one's full name (the complete binomial or trinomial syntagm) amounts to hiding one's social status. In other words, it means presenting oneself as neither higher nor lower than anyone else. Anonymity in this sense means equality.

When addressing each other by their first names, or a nickname, AA members publicly establish the informal and fraternal (therefore humble) style of their interaction. In the English and French naming systems, being on "first-name basis" is obviously a sign of intimacy and equality (in French, pronouns underline this even more strongly: *tu* instead of *vous*). It is also a good gloss for the word "humility." The spiritual foundation of the fellowship is then rooted in the absolute equality of its members, not as members of any social, religious, or political group or organization, and therefore having no part in any kind of hierarchy. There is no social status in AA, whose members have no other self than the suffering alcoholic self.[3] They are socially "self-less." I wish then to close this section by the general conclusion that the most "sacred" (loaded with quasi-mystical value) principle in such a fellowship as AA is simply that: equality and reciprocal humility.

Let us note also that this kind of interaction between "pure selves" opens the way to what the AA people call "sharing." This transaction, a sharing of words, when a person tells his or her story, is seen as having healing power, promoting a therapeutic identification with the other.

The Japanese Tea Ceremony

This fundamental dimension of AA sociability—defined as "spiritual"—is present in a number of tribal societies where reciprocal humility is encouraged. It is also present in another and very different setting, that of the Japanese tea ceremony, an institution originating in Zen Buddhism. Like AA, aficionados of the tea ceremony form clubs or circles and meet to share tea in a formal and ritual way. There are schools teaching the art of preparing and serving tea and how to observe the numerous prescriptions attendant to its consumption. Adepts declare this activity to be imbued with the highest degree of spiritual and aesthetic reverence. What they actually do is as mysterious as the notion of anonymity in AA. There are many variants and ways to perform this highly sophisticated activity. Basically, however, the host prepares a mixture of green tea and offers it in a bowl (preferably ancient and meeting certain aesthetic criteria) to his guests. They sit in preordained arrangement and in turn sip the mixture and pass it around while offering appreciative comments. After drinking, they examine the utensils, the bowl, the tea caddy, and the like. Then they leave and go back to whatever they are normally doing (*Wikipedia* 2008). I always had difficulty seeing this as spiritually elevating until I happened to read the following description:

> The taste of a retired life of elegance has always been and still is the characteristic of the Japanese temperament, as is evident from the popularity of the philosophy of the *Cha-no-yu* or "Teaism," which enables even busy people to become temporary hermits in the Tea-room, to be in the world though for a while not of it.... The fixing of the size of the Tea-room as four and a half mats... indicate its descent from the cell of the Buddhist recluse Vimalakirrti who miraculously entertained in it the Buddha and 3,500 of his saints and disciples, and has as it were crystallized and handed down the mood of *Chomei* as a historical-philosophical "retreat" for all who wish to refresh their souls by temporary retirement. (Sadler 1972, iii, my emphasis).

In this passage the author reveals the ritual as belonging to a class of events long ago identified by anthropologists and folklorists. It is a *rite de passage*, and the ceremony itself is set in a mood of typical liminality, that is, in a situation of temporary separation from the everyday social world. Participants in the tea ceremony are temporarily extracted from their "busy" timetable and are placed in a "retreat" (away from the mundane) to "share" a beverage from the same bowl, thus indicating equality. For those familiar with Japanese society, one of the most obsessively ranked in the world, probably just behind the Indian caste society, a gathering of people of this kind is a "refreshment" for the soul. Very much like an AA meeting seen as an island of sobriety and serenity in a sea of Babylonian turbulence (Lechner 2003, 91), the tea ceremony is an island of calm equality in a sea of unremitting hierarchy and constantly pressing demands of rank. It is true, however, that the Japanese tea ceremony is also imbued with a sense of decorum and strict etiquette (guests and host bow to each other), and as such it keeps something of the external hierarchical space. And of course it also does not address a problem like AA does for alcoholic addiction. It remains that the liminal, out-of-the-world dimension of the whole process inures it from the usual pecking order to which individuals are submitted in the office and other public situations. Chanoyuists get together "in the world though for a while not of it," share something in strict equality within the confinement of a separated and spiritually protected space, and then go away with no binding commitment to each other. They just experience an order with no one giving orders. It is maybe what I called "harmony," a kind of emotional co-resonance between actors stemming from liminality and calm equality.

The above analysis must be seen in the wider context of Japanese cultural and social history. While originating in Zen temples in the thirteenth and fourteenth centuries, the ritual of tea ceremony evolved as an independent art form in the sixteenth century. "In the ritualized space of teahouses, merchants, lords, and monks could meet together as equals" (Ikegami 2005, 120). In her illuminating description of the *za* arts, Ikegami goes on to define the meaning of the tea ceremony as one marked by the "spirit of oneness," by equality and humility, by the "formation of congenial egalitarian relationships among the members," by "a sense of communal solidarity" (Ikegami 2005, 120–23), and by "a sense of ephemeral lightness" (94). There was "no formal organizational structure." Tea ceremonies, like other *za* arts such as the *renga* poetry, "constituted enclaves of free socialization in which people could temporarily suspend the application of feudal norms" (76, my emphasis). The room where the tea ceremony takes place can also be seen as a "free space of *mu'en* (no relation)" (122). Tea ceremonies became an instrument of political power. Shoguns such as Nobunaga and Hideyoshi used them to political ends, but the spirit of the tea ceremony was kept "in the open spirit of *za art*, in which participants socialize with one another without regard to formal status distinctions" (123).

Very clearly then, the tea ceremony had all the trappings of an "antistructure," negating social distinctions to the point of mixing the sacred and the profane, the marginal outcasts with the insiders, in an absolute contradistinction to any social hierarchy and by crossing major symbolic boundaries. In several important ways, but in quite a different style, this reminds one of European medieval carnivals.

Humor

In the preceding section, I established that equality and its moral and psychological expression of reciprocal humility were relational modes of interaction sought by actors. As such, they can be considered dimensions of what I called the conditions of felicity of a collective form of existence. Humility and a sense of strict equality within a shared space of interaction are felicitous. Members of such associations like them and deem them important. It allows them, nay, moves them powerfully, to repeat their interaction. But there are obviously a number of other dimensions that are at work to ensure interconnectivity among humans. Among those that seem specific to the kind of communality I am discussing are humor and laughter. I will consider situations other than those just described and more characteristic of nonenclaved communities.

The question of humor and laughter begs for some preliminary remarks. Anthropologists have paid some attention to this phenomenon, but probably not enough. Specialized studies exist however, and some ethnographic attention has focused on joking, humor, laughter, and so on (see, for instance, studies on South and North American Indian humor in Wallace 1953, Bernard 1975, Griffith 1975, Reifler Bricker 1980, Clastres 1989, and Beaudet 1996), but as L. Mintz remarked in a book review, "students are not trained to consider humor as a vital aspect of culture" (Mintz, 1986, 339). Merriment, especially when linked to sexual matters or scatology, may be seen as unsuitable or second-rate material for a sociological and anthropological study. There is clearly a "lack of scholarly attention to foolery" (Overing 2000, 64). This echoes another remark, bemoaning the dearth of obscene materials in Native American folklore: "Plain prudishness... is thus the first and most obvious reason for the scarcity of obscene materials" (Bernard 1975, 385). But prudishness is not the only reason.

The main reason, I submit, is that it is precisely "not serious." Seriousness in our intellectual tradition carries the meaning of "important," "that which really matters." Laughter does not matter. Joking, teasing, bantering, jesting, mirth, gaiety, glee, hilarity, and amusement in general are not "serious" activities and therefore are only peripheral to what is really functional in society. They are anecdotal and epiphenomenal, if not completely irrelevant phenomena in a "serious" theory of social life, lacking as they do the necessary gravitas with which to address essential and stately matters. The "serious" factor, leaning toward the "unhappy," the "sad," the "gloomy," and the "miserable" side of human affairs, tells us more that we tend to believe about what is really important in the working of human relations. This is a long and ancient tradition in the social sciences, and, as Sahlins has pointed out, it is consonant with the Christian mythology of the Fall, the "greater providential value of human suffering," the Augustinian and Hobbesian view of human nature as selfish and uncaring, and the Durkheimian view of society as coercive and humans as bottomless pits of unsatisfied desires (Sahlins 1996). The dim view Pascal had of any "distraction" comes to mind with a host of other examples, including the Sartrean primal experience of existence through nausea. We should, according to them, trust utter revulsion rather than pure joy when seeking the true core of humanity.

Anthropologists have dealt with the funny and the risible inasmuch however as laughter was part of an institution, enshrined in a tradition, and amenable to structural interpretation. Joking was fine as long as it clothed a serious rule. The "joking relationships" famously interpreted by Radcliffe-Brown is a good example of how an anthropological explanation of the funny factor skirts its essentially humorous content.[4] Radcliffe-Brown, it must be remembered, saw in joking relationships a sign of a structural incongruity: kinship relations that were both close and distant, "a compound of friendship . . . and hostility" (Radcliffe-Brown 1951, 20). Of course, there is nothing inherently funny about such a situation contemplated under the microscope of formal logic. The idea is that it allows an opening, a license to make jokes, to poke fun or hurl insults at each other across the kinship divide.

A recent article provides a good example of it (Siran 2006). In the African society described by the author, the Voute of Cameroon, matrilateral cross-cousins may not marry, but this form of marriage is nonetheless desirable. As a result, two matrilateral cross-cousins will tease each other in a most sexually provocative fashion. However, the "fun factor" remains peripheral, a skin-deep reaction as it were, and its essential funniness, the meaningful core of laughter, is not considered as a causal factor, nor is it explained in itself.

Humor or laughter is considered by anthropologists and folklorists as legitimate objects of study whenever it arises as part of an institution, such as the ritual clownery of the Hopi Indians (Courlander 1982; Clemmer 1995). But even in these cases, prudishness prevents a detailed description of what people really joke about when it comes to obscenities that "cannot be mentioned" (Clemmer 1995, 64). One cannot imagine a worse sin against the spirit of scholarly and scientific pursuit, and it just tends to prove how biased and limited in their vision of human nature our social sciences can be at times.

What does fun really do for people? Society, as we saw above, cannot be funny. It is a battlefield or a vale of tears, not a place for clowning around. The work of Bakhtin alone should have killed this prejudice long ago, but apparently it has not. The comic dimension in social life remains of anecdotal significance for most authors, with some exceptions. One is Overing's essay on Piaora humor, for whom laughter and the ludic is "an important clue to the very distinctiveness of [Amazonian peoples'] sociality" (Overing 2000, 64). She also proposes to place laughter in a conceptual framework shared by notions of equality, conviviality, and the aesthetics and ethics of everyday life (67–68, 76–77). Laughter is thus—at least among certain peoples—part of what I call the conditions of felicity of collective living and therefore possesses a positive and creative value in community building. So, I will from now on examine laughter and its derivatives as a "serious" factor. The seriousness of fun shall be revealed.

Inuit Humor

A sense of humor has been recognized by almost all authors among the Inuit. They tease each other and frequently practice various forms of buffoonery and self- or mutual-deprecatory joking in good humor and friendly merriment (Ager 1976). Their good humor and jollity was remarked upon by early travelers (Kumlien 1880). Playing games, singing songs, or while dancing, they display extreme jollity; they "prance around, chuckle, slap their knees, hoot," and "contort themselves and jump up and down with the fun of it" (Lantis 1946). An observer says that during certain dances "in which men and women ridicule each other in a friendly way ... sometimes everyone laughs so much that the dance gets temporarily out of step" (Ager 1976). More importantly, the same observer notes that any expression of emotions, especially those that are negative, such as anger or depression, must be suppressed, except for amusement and laughter (Ager 1976, 11). Among the Inupiaq, humorous mimetic dances are performed with a "humor-filled" style (Johnston 1980), and the same author notes the "ancient belief that a smiling visitor cannot be seeking blood-feud-vengeance" (ibid.). Similarly humorous and playful behavior is seen as a way to avoid conflict among teenagers (Condon 1987, 207). Laughter as an antidote against anger and violence is at work in two different kinds of circumstances: festive occasions and when two people meet occasionally or for the first time. In the second case, a humorous and mirthful countenance may have masked potentially hostile intentions.

Inuit are known as well for their method of conflict resolution by means of songs and laughter. Eskimo song duels have been shown to rely on mirth and good humor (Eckert and Newmark 1980, 192). Insults and mutual accusations between opponents were so aired. "The appropriate conclusion to the duel was for the audience's mirth to drown the bad feelings of the opponents, who were then expected to laugh off their animosities" (192). Although an ideology of "good will, cooperation and equality" characterizes Eskimo society, human relations were unstable, fragile, and violence never far. Murders were frequent (194): "beneath the surface of good will and harmony there existed intense pressures, suspicions, and hostility" (197). Among the North Alaska Eskimos, "violence was endemic," and "intrusions would result in quivering rage which could and often did lead to mortal violence" (Hippler 1974). Humor and warm companionship were then paired with a strong undercurrent of potential violence. In a note on child socialization, another anthropologist notes the complexity of affects involved in teaching the child the right attitude of *nallik* (peaceful and compassionate), the presence of what she calls "benevolent aggression" and ambiguous games played with children (Briggs 1987).

Going back to song duels and conflict resolution, Eckert and Newmark contend that the necessary ambiguity contained in irony is necessary to insure stability in interpersonal relationships because actors have to strike a balance between suspicion and distrust. Irony and humor maintain this equilibrium (207). The authors conclude that underlying the use of irony in song duels is "the feeling of a constantly flipping coin, by means of which anger becomes humor, enmity friendship" (208). Bad feelings are not removed but "converted into intense good feeling and jollity" (209). A "stable ambiguity" is restored (ibid.).

In sum, then, Inuit people maintain an essentially peaceful and friendly kind of sociality by means of a lot of laughter and merriment, thus promoting good feelings and at the same time disguising or diverting hostility and an undercurrent of great potential violence. In this complex arrangement of behavioral norms, reciprocal humility counts as one of the most important, laughing at and making fun of oneself being also attached to this attitude of self-disparagement, resulting in a complete rejection of rank. Humor promotes equality and creates conviviality.

Palawan Humor

If, in the above description, I replaced the name "Inuit" with the name "Palawan," I would not have to change much else. My own fieldwork among these most charming people, inhabitants of a Southern Philippines island, provides recollections of moments marked by intense gaiety, joking and bantering, horseplaying, making fun, and teasing and jesting in the most hilarious and outrageous manner. An inclination for bawdy humor was always present. My companions were doing exactly what Inuits were described as doing: "prancing around, chuckling, slapping their knees, hooting, contorting themselves and jumping up and down with the fun of it." Sexual references of the crudest nature were not uncommon.[5] A respected elder, for instance, would loudly announce in the market place his desire to commit incest with his granddaughter whose fragrance had ignited his lust. A distinguished old lady would be teased for past affairs, and she would, in front of an amused audience, reprove an ex-lover for his foul-smelling semen. While performing the collective plantation of rice in the swidden, a man would mockingly accuse his brother of consorting with his mother-in-law and ejaculating so much as to make the whole place slippery with semen. Listeners would be in stitches and could not catch their breath because of the extreme merriment caused by such wonderfully amusing inventions and other outrageous ejaculations. Many other occasions call for fun and hilarity; when watching a cockfight, men shout their encouragements in a shrill voice, gesticulate emphatically, contort themselves, jump up and down, and so on. But violence, as with the Inuit, is never far. Likewise, a Palawan informant told me not long ago, "If you are not joking, then you are angry" (*Baq diki ke megluluy, kaluq meiseg*).

The Palawan people I have studied over the years (Macdonald 1977, 2007) are indeed peaceful, nonviolent, and egalitarian in the extreme. They value self-control and permit no outward expression of negative emotions, especially anger. Similar to the Inuit concept of *nallik*, their most central moral value is compassion, *ingasiq*, and they tend to orient their behavior, especially when it comes to sharing, according to such a norm.[6] The profound similarity between the two cultures, Palawan and Inuit, goes beyond a simple resemblance or superficial universality of values. I hypothesize that it indexes their membership in a specific class of human cultures.

Going back to humor and laughter as a structural dimension in this mode of relationship, I could bring in another piece of evidence to support my thesis. The way Palawan people conduct a marriage ceremony (Macdonald 1972, 1974) is both puzzling and revealing. First of all, there is an element of buffoonery and grotesquerie in the ritual itself, at least in the highlands' non-Islamized version of it. At one point, a procession of individuals disguised in grotesque accoutrement will circumambulate the room around the bride and groom, who are seated together (Macdonald 1972). This is supposed to entice laughter. But this is not even the main point. The bulk of what we may call the wedding ceremony consists in a lengthy discussion between representatives of the groom and representatives of the bride. A central issue focuses on the marriage payment, or bride-price. As it turns out, this is always settled in a preordained manner, bride-prices amounting traditionally to a limited number of items (plates and other items of heirloom property) dependent upon the birth order of the bride or on previous marriage arrangements.[7] There is no real haggling, and in any case this aspect of the discussion occupies a small amount of time. The first and major part of the discussion is nothing but a protracted joke, or verbal play. Representatives of the bride, in whose house the wedding takes place, wonder why so many people have gathered in their place. Who are these strangers and why have they come? Is it with the intention of waging a war? To exterminate everyone and burn their houses? No, exclaim the representatives of the groom, it is with the most peaceful intentions. Then the former would retort, why have they come? They probably lost their way? Alas, they (the bride's people) are unable to indicate the right way; they cannot point to the right direction. No, exclaim the groom's representatives, no, no! They are not lost; they came with a purpose, and, to say the truth, they are actually looking for something. What they are seeking is a "chicken." Ah, but there are no chicken here; the poultry has been depleted. So sorry! Well, by "chicken" they mean a certain kind of "chicken," actually the "little chick of Kikilangan brook." Ah, so by chicken they mean "a girl."

Ah, but there are no girls here, only one girl they can think of, and, alas, she is unsuitable for marriage. She is "stupid," "lazy," cannot cook, and so on. It would be unfair to let anyone marry such an incompetent wife. To which the groom's people retort that they don't care. The groom loves her and is willing to give his life for her, and so on. And so goes the verbal play, mixing humor, mockery, and self-disparagement in a display of rhetorical skills whereby one party is forever dodging the real question, and the other one making his point patiently and with great indirectness. I have summarized some of it in the briefest manner but the exchange last for hours. The Palawan language calls it a *peribasa*, or "courtesy." It is a way to show respect and an exercise in humor. Now if we consider the fact that marriage is about the only event in the life cycle that is ritualized to some extent, the only occasion for a feast outside the periodic ceremonies linked with the rice cycle and the seasonal or solar cycle, and in sum the only ceremony ratifying a social contract—at least in the highlands—one can wonder at its unserious character, its playful conduct, and its humorous content.[8]

Finally, there is another important remark I have to make concerning the particular sense of humor displayed by almost all Palawan people I know, and that concerns something usually not mentioned for the reasons I suggested above, prudishness and a disdain for amusing aspects of social life. Palawan people, men and women, are thrown into undiluted mirth by the release of intestinal gases, or farting, known to them in the most apposite manner as "the anus's laughter," *kesit et ambut*. Passing wind is performed publicly, and the author of the fart makes a point to have everyone notice his resounding flatulence. Its release produces joyful comments. It entertains without fail. Now the possibility of public farting, and the various meanings attached to it, form one of the most revealing complexes of traits in any given culture. Its deep connection with laughter and humor, its sympathetic link with an ethos of freedom and equality, and its joyous mood of anarchic communality has been understood and explained by the Russian thinker and literary critic M. Bakhtin in his penetrating study of the medieval carnival and its attendant grotesqueries (Bakhtin 1970).

Laughter and the Grotesque

Bakhtin's analysis of medieval and early Renaissance folk culture is a study of the imagery generated by carnivals and the expression it found in the work of Rabelais (Bakhtin 1970). First of all, carnivals and feasts that belonged to this class of popular collective events were of considerable importance during medieval times, and huge amounts of time and energy were devoted to their preparation and accomplishment. The carnival world was a boundless world of humorous forms opposed to the serious tone of medieval and ecclesiastical culture" (Bakhtin quoted in Clark and Holquist 1984, 299–300). Halloween is a pale copy, enfeebled and watered down, of the collective, delirious, and cosmic frenzy of medieval feasts. These feasts were characterized by a certain conception of life and sociality. The grotesque was the proper style and essence of the spirit of carnival, and it primarily concerned the body, its presentation, and the values and ideas attached to its functions.

The grotesque body, the body of the folk culture of carnival, is endowed with properties at complete odds with the official ideology of the medieval church. It also contains defining elements intimately associated with a notion of social life in complete opposition to the hierarchical ordered social structure of the time. "The carnival spirit is fundamentally opposed to all hierarchies in epistemology, all canons and dogmas, for in carnival everything is constantly moving and changing" (Clark and Holquist 1984, 310). Carnivals were thus an expression of an anti-official ideology, and cultural anthropologists have long recognized their status as rituals of reversal (Turner 1977). We would say today that the grotesque image of the body projected in carnival was a political statement, and we would speak of the "politics of the body." Carnival was "a minimally ritualized antiritual, a festive celebration of the other, and . . . a gap in the fabric of society" (Clark and Holquist 1984, 310.) It was "an island in the sea of history" (301). Carnival included a number of important elements that we can find in the ethos of anarchic and gregarious communities, the sharing of food being one. It also and most prominently saw humor and laughter as crucial dimensions of a philosophy of nature and society, of the organic, human, spiritual, and cosmic universe. A primary element in carnival was indeed the "unabashed display of bodily functions, including defecation, copulation, and even labor and birth" (311).

The grotesque body is defined along several main lines. First of all, it is an open body, a body full of openings, such as the mouth, anus, and vagina. It is also a body with protruding parts: nose, breasts, phallus, and big belly. It is seen in its digestive and excretive operations: its vital and creative functions of copulation and birthing (Bakhtin 1970, 35). It is the opposite of a smooth, sealed, closed body. In the bodily imagery of carnival and of Rabelais's poetry, the lower part of its topography is given prominence (genital organs, behind, anus) as well as the inside of the body (intestines, stomach, uterus, bladder). Bodily fluids (urine, semen, sweat, excrements, saliva) are in conspicuous display. As such the bodily image is in complete denial of a vertical hierarchy. The so-called superior parts or functions (head, face, disembodied mind) do not take the lead. Instead of a vertical and static hierarchy of parts and functions, a horizontal and creative dynamic process takes place. Instead of an "upper" and a "lower," we have a "before" and an "after," an "inside" and an "outside." One aspect of this new situation is the replacement of the upper parts of the body by the lower parts, the face becoming ass and the mouth anus. This brings us back to the Palawan notion of farting as "the asshole's laughter." Farting is indeed included in the list of life-affirming bodily functions. In an episode of Rabelais's *Gargantua and Pantagruel, Book II*, a character is brought back to life by Panurge. The first sign of his return to life and proof of recovery is not breathing or eating, but farting. Farting thus appears as the "real symbol of life" (Bakhtin 1970, 380).

The body thus conceived in its grotesque ontology is also and primarily a joyous and fearless body, an entity whose primary energy is the force of laughter, which supersedes human hierarchies but also countermands a basic cosmic fear of universal destruction. Bakhtin sees laughter as endowed with a universal value of truth against the stupid simplification of a supposed "serious" life, an affirmation of vital and creative energy that is deeply ambiguous, ambivalent, complex, and regenerative (Bakhtin 1970: 127). Laughter and merriment stand in complete opposition to the serious attitude of Christian penitents, of the pious Christian spirit of constant atonement, and Christianity has of course attempted to ban laughter and humor from the life of the faithful. The popular novel *The Name of the Rose* by Umberto Eco, and the film based on it, have exposed the public to the idea of the subversive power of laughter and its attempted eradication by the clergy. Fundamentalist religious movements detest any form of mirth and gaiety. The grotesque spirit and hilarious madness of carnival are thus intimately associated with a spirit of festive joy and rest on the display of bodily functions and bodily substances positively valued as life-giving. The subversive quality of laughter in the context of folk carnival and grotesque artistry is another aspect of the same phenomenon because it elevates the lowly and debases the exalted. The seriousness of fun is thus vindicated, and the essential connection of laughter with the lower parts of the body and their excretive and assimilatory properties is amply demonstrated.

There is however another important dimension already mentioned, the ambivalent and complex nature of laughter, and a caveat must be posted at this juncture. Instead of fostering convivial energy and a friendly communion of souls, derogatory and sarcastic laughter can promote enmity and hatred. The Palawan ideas concerning this phenomenon are also a good example of its ambiguous nature. Laughter, as we have seen, and particularly the obscene and scatological aspect of laughter, is associated with joyful communality and a sense of egalitarian brotherhood. But in Palawan cosmology, as well as in the cosmology of neighboring people in Southeast Asia, laughing can be highly dangerous because it irritates Thunder himself. The anthropomorphic figure of this celestial phenomenon punishes people who laugh excessively or for the wrong reasons (Macdonald 1988). There are thus at least two kinds of laughter, one between humans that is almost mandatory and a sign of sociability and another that meddles with cosmic forces that are dangerous and forbidden.

Conclusion

The whole point that I tried to make in this paper is that throughout the world and in completely different cultures, under varied and very dissimilar appearances, some things are very similar, and among these things is a tendency for peaceful, serene, and joyous connections between individuals, with an assumption of strict equality between them. There are such "islands" in the sea of society (AA, tea ceremony), history (carnivals), and violence (peaceful societies among predatory states). If certain requirements are met, such as an assertion of equality through humor or sharing of food or beverage, or by other means such as anonymity and humble demeanor, then we can say that conditions of felicity are obtained for a certain form of aggregation. I suppose these conditions are at least necessary, if maybe not sufficient, to ensure a measure of stability and permanence for aggregations thus formed.

The different factors I have examined (anonymity, humility, humor) produce a certain atmosphere or mood to which I have applied the term "harmony," a concept that includes a certain number of semantic dimensions (Macdonald 2008a). One is the sense of order, although not a formal static order such as in a hierarchy, nor the mechanical order of an automobile engine, but an ever-changing, organic, and lifelike sort of order. Second, it may have the sense it has in music: the vertical dimension of communality. The vertical, like Bakhtin's "horizontal" dimension, are just crude topological approximations of something that should probably be defined in another language, mathematical maybe or, more appropriately, musical. It is a polyphony of voices singing together, and for this reason among others, harmony implies complexity.

When faced with harmony in humans, a member of a social system brainwashed since early childhood in the religion of rank and corporation, at all times wedged between two rungs of the social ladder, intent on showing a smooth and sealed exterior, convinced that sex is offending, and with a deeply rooted belief in the virtues of self-affirmation, a person like this one may have a difficult time understanding what is going on in the harmonious world of humble people and is unable to immediately comprehend the value and dignity they display. Let me illustrate this point thus. The Palawan people were extremely shy and still retreat in the face of any threat or aggression: they run away and think that flying is better than fighting. An early observer (Whitehead 1893) described them as "running away like fools." They also have a great sense of humor, but one that might not look quite palatable to some of us: they like to fart in public and mention sexual matters unabashedly. Also, they tend to a degree to avoid being in debt. As a result, "thank you" has been a recently learned formula of politeness. Like the Inuit companions of Freuchen (Macdonald 2008, n.14) they are apt to agree that "gifts make slaves." But precisely because they fart, never say thank you, and run away like fools, they are such fine specimens of the human race: joyous, equal, and free.

Acknowledgments

I am indebted to the Florence Gould Foundation for my stay at the Institute for Advanced Study, Princeton, during which I was able to prepare this paper. A preliminary version of it was presented at the Anthropology Club, New York State University at Buffalo, on November 24, 2008. I thank Robert Dentan and Richard Shweder for their insightful comments on a preliminary version.

Notes

1. See also Goffman's assumptions (Goffman 1983) and Grice's maxims of conversation (Grice 1975). I thank Barry O'Neill for pointing this out to me.
2. Nonenclaved indigenous communities can nonetheless be encapsulated, that is, geographically contained by surrounding dominant groups and societies.
3. By their first-name-only mode of address and reference, members of AA resemble Inuits and deaf-mutes (Macdonald 2006; Delaporte 1998).
4. See Graeber 2007, 16–19, for a similar line of thought.

5. Several other cultural communities in the same area, including the Hanunoo of Mindoro (H. C. Conklin, personal communication), also indulge in obscenity and bawdy humor.
6. Ingasiq has a large semantic field, from sympathy, to pity, love, understanding, generosity, and a general disposition to help and succor (Macdonald 2007, 136).
7. I am using the ethnographic present for something that is undergoing important transformations. The monetary value of the bride-price has become a very crucial issue, and its amount has significantly increased. The particular marriage ceremony I am referring to took place in the highlands in the early seventies.
8. Joking relationships as a way to alleviate the tension surrounding marriage and affinal relations among the Semai has also be noted by Dentan (2004, 180).

References

Ager, Lynn Price. 1976. "Eskimo Dance and Cultural Values in an Alaskan Village." *Dance Research Journal* 8(1):7–12.
Alcoholics Anonymous. 1952. *Twelve Steps and Twelve Traditions*. New York: General Service Office.
Austin, J. L. 1962. *How to Do Things with Words*. Oxford: Clarendon Press.
Bakhtin, Mikhail. 1970. *L'oeuvre de François Rabelais et la culture populaire au Moyen Age et sous la Renaissance*. Translated by A. Robel. Paris: Gallimard.
Benton-Banai, Edward. 1979. *The Mishomis Book: The Voice of the Ojibway*. St. Paul: Indian Country Press.
Bernard, H. Russel. 1975. "Otomi Obscene Humor: Preliminary Observations." *The Journal of American Folklore* 88(350):383–92.
Bird-David, Nurit. 1994. "Solidarity and Immediacy: Or, Past and Present Conversations on Bands." *Man* 29(3):583–603.
Briggs, Jean L. 1987. "In Search of Emotional Meaning." *Ethos* 15(1):8–15.
Clark, Katerina, and Michael Holquist. 1984. *Mikhail Bakhtin*. Cambridge and London: The Belknap Press of Harvard University Press.
Clastres, Pierre. 1989. *Society against the State: Essays in Political Anthropology*. Translated by R. Hurley. New York: Zone Book.
Clemmer, Richard O. 1995. *Roads in the Sky: The Hopi Indians in a Century of Change*. Boulder, CO: Westview Press.
Condon, Richard. 1987. *Inuit Youth: Growth and Change in the Canadian Arctic*. New Brunswick, NJ: Rutgers University Press.
Delaporte, Yves. 1998. "Des Noms silencieux. Le systeme anthroponymique des sourds francais." *L'Homme* 38 (146).
Dentan, Robert K. 1992. "The Rise, Maintenance, and Destruction of Peaceable Polity: A Preliminary Essay in Political Ecology." In *Aggression and Peacefulness in Humans and Other Primates*, edited by J. Silverberg and J. P. Gray, 214–70. New York and Oxford: Oxford University Press.
———. 1994. "Surrendered Men: Peaceable Enclaves in the Post-Enlightenment West." In *The Anthropology of Peace and Nonviolence*, edited by L. Sponsel and T. Gregor, 69–108. Boulder and London: Lynne Riener.

Eckert, Peneloppe, and Russel Newmark. 1980. "Central Eskimo Song Duels: A Contextual Analysis of Ritual Ambiguity." *Ethnology* 19(2):191–211.

Fajans, Jane. 2006. "Autonomy and Relatedness: Emotions and the Tension between Individuality and Sociality." *Critique of Anthropology* 26(1):103–19.

Goffman, Erving. 1983. "Felicity's Condition." *The American Journal of Sociology* 89(1):1–53.

Graeber, David. 2007. *Possibilities: Essays on Hierarchy, Rebellion, and Desire.* Oakland and Edinburgh: AK Press.

Grice, Paul H. 1975. "Logic and Conversation." In *Syntax and Semantics*, edited by P. Cole and J. L. Morgan, 41–58, vol. 3, *Speech Acts*. New York: Academic Press.

Griffith, James. 1975. Review of *Ritual Humor in Highland Chiapas*, by Victoria Reifler Bricker. *The Journal of American Folklore* 88(348):191–2.

Hippler, Arthur E. 1974. "The North Alaska Eskimos: A Culture and Personality Perspective." *American Anthropologist* 1(3):449–69.

Ikegami, Eiko. 2005. *Bonds of Civility: Aesthetic Networks and the Political Origins of Japanese Culture*. Cambridge: Cambridge University Press.

Ingold, Tim. 1999. "On the Social Relations of the Hunter-Gatherer Band. In *The Cambridge Encyclopedia of Hunters and Gatherers*, edited by R. B. Lee and R. Daly, 399–410. Cambridge: Cambridge University Press.

Jensen, George H. 2000. *Storytelling in Alcoholics Anonymous: A Rhetorical Analysis*. Carbondale: Southern Illinois University Press.

Johnston, Thomas F. 1980. "Alaskan Eskimo Music and Dance." *Current Anthropology* 21(3):370–71.

Kumlien, Ludwig. 1880. "Fragmentary Notes on the Eskimo of Cumberland Sound." *Science* 1(9):100–1.

Lantis, Margaret. 1946. "The Social Culture of the Nunivak Eskimo." *Transactions of the American Philosophical Society* ns 35(3):153–323.

Lechner, Thomas M. 2003. *Surrender without Subordination: Peace and Equality in Alcoholics Anonymous*. Buffalo: State University of New York at Buffalo.

Macdonald, Charles J-H. 1972. "Le Mariage Palawan." *L'Homme* 12:5–28.

———.1974. "Une discussion de mariage Palawan. Texte traduit et commenté." *ASEMI* 5:81–139.

———.1977. *Une Société Simple. Parenté et Résidence chez les Palawan*. Paris: Institut d'Ethnologie.

———. 1988. "Bons et Mauvais Coups de Tonnerre." *L'Homme* 28(2–3):58–74.

———. 1999. "De l'Anonymat au Renom." In *D'un Nom a l'Autre en Asie du Sud-Est*, edited by J. Massard-Vincent and S. Pauwels, 105–28. Paris: Karthala.

———. 2006. "Inuit Names: A Unique System?" Paper presented at the International Conference of Inuit Studies, Paris, 2006.

———. 2007. *Uncultural Behavior: An Anthropological Investigation of Suicide in the Southern Philippines*. Honolulu: University of Hawai'i Press.

———. 2008. "Order against Harmony: Are Humans Always Social?" *Suomen Anthropologi. Journal of the Finnish Anthropological Society* 33(2):5–21.

———. In press. "Towards a Typology of Naming Systems in Southeast Asia." In *Asian Names*, edited by Y. Zheng and C. J.-H. Macdonald. Singapore: NUS Press.

Maxwell, Milton A. 1961. "Alcoholics Anonymous: An Interpretation." In *Society, Culture, and Drinking Patterns*, edited by D. Pittman and C. Snyder. New York: John Wiley & Sons.

Overing, Joanna. 2000. "The Efficacy of Laughter." In *The Anthropology of Love and Anger*, edited by J. Overing and A. Passes, 64–81. London and New York: Routledge.

Radcliffe-Brown, A. R. 1951. "The Comparative Method in Social Anthropology." *The Journal of the Royal Anthropological Institute of Great Britain and Ireland* 81(1/2):15–22.

Reifler-Bricker, Victoria. 1980. "The Function of Humor in Zinacatan." *Journal of Anthropological Research* 36(4):411–18.

Rudy, David R. 1984. "Alcohol and Ethnography: A Case of Problem Deflation?" *Current Anthropology* 25:169–91.

Sadler, A. L. 1972. *The Ten Foot Square Hut and Tales of the Heike*. Vermont and Tokyo: Charles E. Tuttle.

Sahlins, Marshall. 1996. "The Sadness of Sweetness: The Native Anthropology of Western Cosmology." *Cultural Anthropology* 37(3):395–428.

Shweder, R. A., et al. In press. "The Cultural Psychology of Emotions: Ancient and Renewed." In *The Handbook of Emotions*, edited by M. Lewis and L. Feldman Barrett. New York, Guilford Publications.

Siran, Jean-Louis. 2006. "Idéal du mariage et plaisanterie." *L'Homme* (180):73–96.

Steinbring, Jack. 1981. "Alcoholics Anonymous: Cultural Reform among the Saulteaux." In *Alcohol and Native Peoples of the North*, edited by J. Hamer and J. Steinbring, 89–106. Washington DC: University Press of America.

Turner, Victor W. 1969. *The Ritual Process: Structure and Anti-Structure*. Chicago: Aldine.

Wallace, William J. 1953. "The Role of Humor in the Hupa Indian Tribe." *The Journal of American Folklore* 66(260):135–141.

Whitehead, J. 1893. *Explorations of Mount Kinabalu, North Borneo*. London: Gurney and Jackson.

Wikipedia. 2008. http://en.wikipedia.org/wiki/Tea_ceremony

IV

Kinship and Incest

Structural Sonnet

I cannot by summation of each part
Imply the living magic of the whole.
That would require a logic of the heart,
A limpid mathematics of the soul,
To grasp at once the juncture of green eyes
(That flash like timid emeralds in the night)
With an outrageous nose; to emphasize
The mouth when laughter sets the face alight;
To witness that sharp movement of the head
So quick that it eludes the startled hair,
And find for these a formula instead
To generate the surface magic there.
Then through its transformations I would see
The structure of my love's mythology.

IV

Kinship and Incest

7

Kinship Constructed Us: Primate Kinship and Cultural Anthropology

Linda Stone

> *"The potential for culture lies in the biology of the species."*
> —Robin Fox, The Search for Society

Robin Fox has made a number of significant contributions to kinship studies within anthropology. Here I focus on one thread of his work, namely, his analysis of human kinship in relation to that of nonhuman primates, in an effort to elucidate the origins and evolution of human forms. This work, while largely ignored within anthropology at the time (1975), has been more recently resurrected in primatology, where research on primate kinship has grown considerably over the years. This development is, in my view, a powerful one that carries implications for approaches to human kinship within cultural anthropology. I will suggest that it is now time to take a new look at Fox's initial insights into the evolutionary and biological bases of human kinship and his early call for a "biosocial" approach to the topic. While this reconsideration is unlikely to shift kinship away from its current grounding in cultural relativism, it will at the least support the reopening of interesting lines of inquiry for a scientific study of kinship and its evolution.

Kinship and Marriage

Before moving to primates, I will briefly mention some of Fox's other major contributions to kinship as these will emerge later in my discussion. In 1967, Fox published a text, *Kinship and Marriage*, a remarkable book that made a complex subject simple and an often boring topic lively and interesting. It sustained many cohorts of anthropology graduate students, who, without it, would never have understood the basics of anthropological kinship and many of whom would never have gone on to consider kinship as their own professional specialization. In this book and elsewhere (Fox 1994: 215–243) Fox explored the evolution of particular kinship terminology systems. Fox also developed new perspectives on the human incest taboo (1980, 1994: 29–38) and the avunculate (1993: 191–232). Finally, Fox has used kinship to analyze everyday events and issues in contemporary times, from Mormon polygyny (1993: 11–51) to political turmoil in Iraq (2011: xx), to name a few. Indeed, there seems no end to the arenas to which Fox is capable of taking kinship: in what should be considered a landmark in "applied anthropology," Fox used patrilineal descent ideology to interpret otherwise problematical lines of the Greek tragedy *Antigone*. (1993: 165–171). Throughout his work, Fox has argued for a scientific, multidisciplinary approach to kinship and culture; he has never shied away from questioning the origins of human society, even at times when the raising of these questions was dismissed as sheer speculation in anthropology.

Biosocial Kinship and the Crisis of Kinship Studies

Fox published his major article on primates, "Primate Kin and Human Kinship," in 1975. This work reflects one thing Fox has written about himself (1997: 2), that is, his willingness to master new disciplines. In "Primate Kin" Fox showed his new mastery of primatology; for his analysis he had amassed every shred of relevant primate data available to him at the time. He was among very few anthropologists to have even looked at primate social organization, and the only one to have studied primate kinship this extensively before.[1] Fox considered that there are two basic building blocks of human kinship. One, which he called "alliance," refers to relatively stable mating relationships. The second building block was "descent," which defines who belongs to what kin groupings. Fox's conclusion from his primate studies was that some nonhuman primates exhibit one of the two building blocks of human kinship but never both together.

For "alliance," Fox looked at primates who live in groups with one male, using hamadryas baboons as an example. These baboons consist of several females with their young and one male who mates with the females. These polygynous units are relatively stable and long-term, lasting year-round, even though the baboons have a breeding season. Young males are driven off at maturity and later use various strategies to secure their own polygynous units. This pattern with its distinct breeding units and long-term mating arrangements can be seen as a rudimentary form of what becomes marriage in humans.

Fox found "descent" among multi-male, multi-female species of Old World monkeys such as rhesus monkeys, vervet monkeys, and Japanese macaques. These species' groups consist of several males, organized in a dominance hierarchy among themselves, and groups of females who are organized into "matrilines" that may extend over a few generations. One unit, for example, might consist of an old female, her daughters, and her daughters' infants. Males usually disperse out of these units at maturity to join and mate within other groups. Within these groups, the different matrilines are ranked, and this rank is transmitted from a mother to her daughters over the generations. Clearly we have here a rudimentary kind of "descent," but because mating in these groups is relatively promiscuous and long-term mating units do not form, we do not have "alliance." Fox had found, then, the building blocks of human kinship among primates and had suggested that the uniquely human development was merely to put these two blocks together in one system in such a way that the pattern of descent would determine the direction of the alliances (i.e., descent group exogamy). Fox had rooted human kinship in our primate heritage, our evolutionary biology.

Fox had also given with this study a stunning example of the shape that a "biosocial" approach, in this case to kinship, might take. Throughout his career he has consistently fought for this approach in the discipline, generally "to preserve the uniqueness of anthropology as the evolutionary study of [humankind]" (1994: xii). Fox insists that the biosocial approach is an *approach*, not a theory: "I am not pushing any kind of systematic theory, only suggesting an intellectual orientation which may draw on many theories. Go where the questions lead, use what theories and data you need" (2011: 9). A clear statement of what a biosocial orientation does and does not mean is provided in the following:

> [T]he unity of anthropology, its uniqueness among the social sciences, lies in its devotion to the study of human societies as the product of evolution. This does not mean, as it seems to mean to some contemporary sociobiologists, that all and every piece of human behavior must be explained on the principles of Darwinian natural selection.... Most of the time, as I have always said, anthropologists operate several removes from this theory. We do not need to be always looking over our shoulders for Darwinian explanations.... We can go on collecting

our data and finding our connections and explaining these at a more proximate level. All I am saying is that in the end, the master paradigm that holds all this effort together must be the theory of natural selection and must connect us to our evolutionary past via the theory of the evolution of social behavior. (1994: xii)

Within cultural anthropology, a biosocial approach to kinship (or other topics) was not widely adopted. In addition, very few anthropologists picked up Fox's lead to incorporate primate data in the study of kinship.

One reason was that around the time of his work, kinship as a field of study was facing a crisis; it soon fell into a state of demise and later reemerged as a "new kinship" grounded in cultural relativism and constructionism. This shift was ushered in by writers such as David Schneider (1972, 1984) in the United States and Rodney Needham (1971) in England who felt that anthropological kinship categories were seriously out of touch with ethnographic reality. In Schneider's view, anthropologists had mistakenly assumed that all peoples understand and relate to their "kinship" in terms of biological connections through acts of procreation, as kinship is understood in the West. Many other peoples, he argued, construct "kinship" (or what, to outside investigators, looks like "kinship") on other bases, such as common residence, food sharing, rituals, and so on. Thus anthropologists had been misunderstanding other peoples' cultures and had been ethnocentrically imposing their own cultural categories on these others. Schneider also dismissed biology, not only from the study of kinship in particular but also from the whole of culture, on the basis that the cultural realm (to him, symbols and meanings) should be investigated as a distinct and separate domain. With respect to kinship, Schneider (1972) held that the concept as understood in anthropology was so flawed that it could not even be applied to Western societies; hence his declaration that kinship does not exist in any culture.

There followed a twenty-year period of near silence on the topic of kinship within anthropology. Paulo Souza (2003) held that this decline of kinship was also due to a broader "hermeneutic turn" within the discipline that questioned the basis of anthropological knowledge in general and that shifted the discipline away from affiliation with the natural sciences and toward the humanities. To this Adam Kuper (2003) added the impact of social and political developments in the outside world, noting, for example, that classical anthropological kinship collapsed as scholars, especially feminists, objected to the conservative implications concerning men, women, and the family in the work of sociobiology and evolutionary psychology. (Further critiques of Schneider and his impact on kinship are provided by Kuper [1999] and by Richard Feinberg and Martin Ottenheimer [2001]).

In the late 1980s, some of Schneider's followers critiqued categories such as "male" and "female" in a way similar to Schneider's treatment of kinship, holding that they, too, were cultural constructions, showing significant variation among different cultures. "Kinship," "male," "female," "procreation"—all of these were to be understood in terms of their local meanings within each culture separately (or emically). In an article that led this movement, Sylvia Yanagisako and Jane Collier claim that their analytical strategy

> rests on the premise that there are no "facts," biological or material, that have social consequences and cultural meanings in and of themselves. Sexual intercourse, pregnancy, and parturition are cultural facts, whose form, consequences, and meanings are socially constructed in any society, as are mothering, fathering, judging, ruling, and talking with the gods. (1987: 39)

Feminism and Kinship

Inspired by this position, a new group of largely feminist scholars resurrected kinship beginning in the 1990s. But this was a new kinship; indeed, the term "kinship" somewhat fell into disuse, and a broader concept of "relatedness" (introduced by Janet Carsten, 1995) came into vogue. The new kinship, purged of unwarranted assumptions about biology, focused on local meanings of relationships and moved into topics such as the New Reproductive Technologies, adoption, and gay and lesbian kinship topics that themselves challenged (Western) conventional ideas of biological reproduction. Discussions of kinship in relation to cultural constructions of personhood and bodies became popular, while locally understood human relatedness also came to be seen as often processual and performative (for reviews, see Stone 2004; Levine 2008).

In sum, as far as mainstream cultural anthropology was concerned, the period from the 1970s to the present was not a good climate in which to advocate a biosocial approach in anthropology. This did not of course discourage Robin Fox from doing so. Fox has been a firm critic of cultural relativism in general (1989, 11–34; 1994, xii–xiv and 363–80; 1997, 161–85) and particularly critical of the relativists' depiction of culture as detached from the process of evolution.

As for kinship, there were other critics of the new, relativistic kinship-as-pure-cultural-construction. Some objected to the sharp dismissal of biological reproduction (for example, the fact that women give birth to children) as universally significant to human relationships, however culturally constructed (Stone 2010). Others objected that the relativist/culturalist kinship was so closely focused on local cultural constructions that it undermined cross-cultural comparison (Carsten 2000, 22). (For some other criticisms of the new kinship, see Scheffler [1991] and Shapiro [2008]).[2]

In one respect, Schneider was right: humans do use bases other than biology or indigenous ideas about procreation to construct their kinship. In contrast to nonhuman primates, we *make* kin as well as grow our own. The only remotely comparable phenomenon among some primates is "adoption"—a deceased female's sister will often raise her orphaned infant. But among humans this creative aspect of kinship is pronounced. All of this was known by anthropologists well before Schneider. In the old days, this kind of creative making of kin was referred to as "social kinship" or "fictive kinship." Of course, Schneider objected that ethnographers mistakenly assumed that what to them was "fictive kinship," and thus modeled on or derived from real (biological) kinship, was also perceived in this way by native peoples. This, to Schneider, was an incorrect assumption and yet another illustration of how anthropologists were ethnocentrically imposing their own cultural ideas of biologically based kinship onto other peoples.

Given their framework of relativism, what Schneider and his followers overlooked was that nonbiological bases of kinship construction exist in all societies and for good reason: human groups can apply kinship flexibly to link up with or incorporate outsiders as well as to organize actual or presumed biological kin. In other words, in the course of their evolution, humans did not need to rely on exogamous marriage alone to forge non-kin interpersonal and inter-group alliances; they could do so through extension of kinship terms to outsiders or through rituals, acts of feeding, and so on, to establish kinship with non-kin or even strangers (Stone and Lurquin 2007: 225). The extension of human kinship beyond biological relationships serves to create networks of cooperative, political alliances across time and space and through levels of social organization beyond what is possible in the world of nonhuman primates. As Lars Rodesth and Richard Wragham write,

> [T]he myriad ways in which people conceptualize and act toward "kin" involve not only their knowledge of who is descended from the same ancestor or who shares the same bodily substance, but also their sense of who has been and should remain an ally in political competition (2004, 390). Humans, in contrast to, say, chimpanzees, are organized above the level of local groups and face political competition and violent inter-group encounters at higher levels. Given this political context, . . . [human] kinship is not so much used for political purposes as it is constructed for such purposes. . . . From an evolutionary point of view, the human capacity to create kin is adaptive and so "the cultural manipulation of kinship itself tends to serve biologically explicable goals." (Rodseth and Wragham 2004, 409, 412)

Thus, however much we find that biology or procreation is not locally conceived as a basis *for* human kinship construction, it does not follow that our evolution (and hence biology) was not a factor *behind* the human construction of kinship in the first place. Robin Fox (1979) has made similar points in his discussion of kinship categories as natural categories. As he notes, all societies classify kin; kinship terminology systems are a human universal, and there is a rather small and finite number of such systems.

> [O]ur uniqueness lies not in having, recognizing, and behaving differentially to different kin. . . . [I]t lies in giving this process names and rules of naming; in the classification not the kinship. (Fox 1979, 133)

What kinship terminology systems do, among other things, is draw distinctions between marriageable and unmarriageable categories of persons. As humans, with developing capacities for language and other mental abilities, rapidly migrated into different environments, kin classifications arose as means of flexibly regulating outbreeding. The circumstances of our evolution

> selected for speaking, classifying, and rule-making creatures *who could apply these talents directly to the breeding system.* (Fox 1979, 135)

Thus, like language ability itself, kin classification was selected for in our species and is *in* us. In a number of his writings, Fox (e.g., 1989, 21–22) has carried out thought experiments whereby a group of human infants is placed in a natural environment and somehow kept alive without exposure to any culture. The practical, let alone ethical, obstacles to a real experiment of this kind are obvious; but Fox imagines that over time, this group of humans would develop a human language, fully recognizable to linguists, and a kin classification system fully recognizable to anthropologists.

The New Primate Kinship

David Schneider once said to Robin Fox, "If primates have kinship, then I'll be a monkey's uncle." Fox's comment on this was, "He spoke too soon—but thereby hangs a tale" (Fox 1993, 193). Indeed, just as anthropological kinship was about to begin its demise, research on primate kinship was rapidly accumulating new data and improving methods of observation. Primates were found to have more kinship in terms of kinship recognition, recognition of others' kin, and the importance of kinship to social organization than was previously supposed. By the opening of the twenty-first century, Joan Silk (2001, 84) could conclude from a mound of evidence that human kinship bonds "have very deep roots in the primate order."

Even earlier, after Schneider had effectively erased conventional kinship and as the new kinship was emerging, developments were taking place within primatology that brought Fox's original work back to the fore. In 1991, a team of researchers (Lars Rodseth, Richard W. Wrangham, Alisa M. Harrigan, and Barbara B. Smuts 1991) claimed that hamadryas baboons actually exhibit Fox's "alliance" and "descent" in one system. These baboons consist of one-male polygynous units that are loosely organized into "clans" and above these "bands," based on common kinship through males. Fox (1991) agreed that this would be a case of "alliance" and "descent" in one system. But, as he had pointed out in his early (1975) article, finding a case like this among extant primates would suggest even more strongly that human kinship is rooted in our primate evolution, not just a creation of human culture.

This study by Rodseth et al. also concluded that among primates, humans are distinctive in that both sexes retain lifelong relationships with their consanguineal kin, regardless of which sex disperses out of the natal group. Among other primates, only one sex (the one that does not disperse) maintains lifelong recognition and ties with natal kin. It was this development among humans (which, for these authors, required language and symbolic ability) that allowed humans to ally with other non-kin groups to which a dispersing son or daughter had moved.

Most recently, primatologist Bernard Chapais published *Primeval Kinship* (2008), which holds that Fox had been on the right track in his attempt to understand the evolutionary roots of human kinship through comparing it with primate kinship. Like Fox, Chapais breaks down human kinship into components, but whereas Fox had proposed two such building blocks, Chapais proposes a longer list (twelve in all). Among these are pair-bonding (stable mating relationships), recognition of a mate's relatives ("in-laws"), and recognition of kinship through both mothers and fathers. These and other traits compose an "exogamy complex" that Chapais proposes is the core of human kinship. Like Fox, Chapais claims that it is the combination of the building blocks in one system that is uniquely human. Taken separately, the traits themselves are present, even if only in rudimentary form, among some primate species. Chapais goes on to suggest a likely sequence in which the kinship building blocks emerged in hominid evolution, and he proposes that the components of human kinship may have emerged, at least in some rudimentary form, before the advent of human language.

Important to Chapais's scheme is the idea that while a true tribal level of organization (a social entity consisting of several distinct local groups) is uniquely human, hominids may have developed a primitive (and prelinguistic) tribal-like organization in which the relationships among local groups were characterized by tolerance rather than hostility. In hominid evolution, according to Chapais, dispersing females may have served as peacemakers between such groups: "After pair bonds evolved, they could do so through two distinct routes: directly, via preexisting bonds with their natal kin, and indirectly, as intermediaries between their natal kin and their 'husband'—in other words, as connectors between affines" (2008, 219). Thus Chapais differs from Rodseth et al., who claim that language was needed for the development of tribes or alliances between non-kin groups. Chapais is suggesting that recognition between natal kin (parents and daughters, brothers and sisters) could have been maintained after separation (through dispersal of the daughter/sister) without language as long as contact between local groups was at least sporadic, as it may have been, for example, through group fissions into two or more groups. Chapais goes on to assert that a prelinguistic proto-tribal organization, itself a consequence of pair-bonding, was a prerequisite for other features of human kinship such as residential diversity, that is, residence patterns other than male philopatry/parilocality. Peaceful intergroup relationships were needed before males could move safely between groups, as they would in matrilocal or bilocal residences.

Along with the work of many other primatologists, Chapais's model reopens the issue of the evolution of human kinship and challenges the claim by cultural relativists that human kinship is pure cultural construction. It invites the development of a framework that can incorporate the biological, evolutionary, and cultural aspects of human kinship.

One possibility may be to view human kinship as human niche construction, borrowing the concept from Richard Lewontin (2000) and from F. John Odling-Smee, Kevin N. Laland, and Marcus W. Feldman (2003). This notion is similar to Fox's concept of "ethosystem" (1989, 106–26). The idea here is that organisms not only adapt to their environments, they make modifications to it. Organisms construct their own niches, and in this process, the alterations they make to their environments can potentially set up new selective pressures that affect the evolution of subsequent generations of organisms over time. To take but one easy example from Odling-Smee, Laland, and Feldman (2003), a beaver builds a dam that is literally inherited by its descendants. This environmental modification sets up selection pressures on particular beaver genes, favoring, say, sharper teeth, flatter tails, and so on, through which beavers adapt to the dam, dam maintenance, and further dam construction. In this way, over evolutionary time, the dam constructs the beavers as much as the beavers construct the dam.

Needless to say, humans with their culture are dramatic niche constructors who have made major alterations in their environments.

> [I]t is readily apparent that contemporary humans are born into a massively constructed world, with an ecological inheritance that includes a legacy of houses, cities, cars, farms, nations, e-commerce, and global warming. Niche construction and ecological inheritance are thus likely to have been particularly consequential in human evolution. (Odling-Smee, Laland, and Feldman 2003, 241)

Although prominent and often highly visible, what humans do culturally in terms of niche construction is in principle no different from what other organisms do.

In a niche construction framework, an organism's genes and the constructed niche are perpetually interlocked. Applied to humans this means that our cultural impacts on our environment are likewise interlocked with our biological evolution. In this way, niche construction is compatible with co-evolution theory (Cavalli-Sforza and Feldman 1981; Boyd and Richardson 1985; Durham 1991) whereby human biological and cultural evolution impact one another. Niche construction theory adds the concept of the niche, or arena in which this interaction takes place and through which selective pressures change. Within the concept of the human niche, there is no possibility of seeing any human adaptations as cases of biological determinism or cultural determinism. Nature and culture are in this view inseparable.

Niche construction writers contrast their approach with that of Dawkins's (1989) "selfish gene," whereby organisms are seen as passive vehicles through which genes struggle to replicate themselves. In contrast to these and some other evolutionary approaches, "We are proposing an additional role for phenotypes in evolution. Humans are not just passive vehicles for genes; they also actively modify sources of natural selection in environments" (Odling-Smee, Laland, and Feldman 2003, 281).

Using a niche construction framework, there are a number of ways in which we can see how the evolution of human kinship played a role in constructing us as a species. For openers, the development of exogamy (especially reciprocal exogamy) may have prevented our extinction as indicated long ago in Edward Tylor's famous remark, "Again and again in the world's history, savage tribes must have had before them the simple practical alternative between marrying out or being killed out" (1889, 267). In a somewhat less dramatic way, the evolving childcare assistance of grandmothers may have increased the longevity of postmenopausal females (the grandmother hypothesis). In this process, birth intervals in evolving humans may have shortened (Hawkes et al. 1998). Human pair-bonding may have resulted in the reduction of human sexual dimorphism as it was connected with reduced male competition for females (Chapais 2008, 255). Kinship may have even played a role in the development of human language. As Cavalli-Sforza (personal communication) pointed out, whatever selective advantage a new gene or genes behind language development conferred on our species, it had to have operated through a minimum of two organisms. An individual possessing the new trait would not be advantaged unless he or she had another with whom to communicate. Most likely such a new trait, or gene, would first appear among close kin and so be shared by, say, a mother (or father) and child or two or more siblings such that the first advantage of language development would be enhanced communication among close kin.

Fox suggested early on that the increasing size and complexity of the human brain, which ultimately led to language, were fostered by, among other things, developments in the hominid breeding system. He situated our early hominid ancestors within a "primate baseline," consisting of three units: adult males, juvenile males, and females with infants, each with its own reproductive interests. Most significant is that in this baseline, juvenile males are initially marginalized, excluded from the breeding system. In order to breed, they must work their way back into the larger society, and to do so, according to Fox, requires not aggressive displays or impulsive behavior but the development of mental constraint, control over impulses (equilibration). With this,

> the stage is set for the growing importance of equilibration and, hence, for the evolution of the brain to the point where we know it now, capable of language, rules, deferred gratification. (Fox 1980, 115)

Large-Game Hunting

For Fox, the hominid transition to large-game hunting accelerated this process, as it ushered in a number of changes in male-female relationships and mating strategies for the three units of the primate baseline.

These examples aside, the most significant ways in which kinship shaped our species have to do with the impact of the evolution of kinship on human society. According to Chapais (2008), the single most important development among our hominid ancestors that profoundly shaped our species was pair-bonding. By this he meant what Fox had termed "alliance," or stable mating bonds, inclusive of monogamous, polygynous, or polyandrous forms. For Chapais, the effect of pair-bonding on human society was equivalent to "the effect of bipedal locomotion on the use of the hand" (2008, 27). In his view, pair-bonding may have emerged as a male mate-guarding strategy under ecological constraints that favored females foraging in small groups. However it happened, once in place, pair-bonding ushered in a number of changes in human kinship and social life. To name but a few, pair-bonding fostered father-offspring recognition (a father is one's mother's relatively stable mate) and eventually recognition of other kin through the father (agnatic kinship). Pair-bonding and fatherhood further strengthened sibling ties. Pair-bonding was also crucial for the recognition of affines, "in-laws," and the development of a social structure beyond the local group (a primitive tribe), all of which were needed to set the stage for a truly human development: marital exchange.

In short, the evolution of hominid kinship from a pre-hominid baseline to a fully human form involved the construction of a societal niche that in turn shaped our species. We are still a group-living, kin-classifying, pair-bonded, largely exogamous species that recognizes consanguineal and affinal kinship bilaterally and over the generations.

Upon this, our culture, or symbolic capacities, developed, elaborating and considerably varying our kinship from one group to another. Many aspects of Chapais's work will be controversial (see Mulder 2008, Stone 2008, Wilson 2009), and his particular evolutionary scheme may be debated and amended in the years ahead. But for now this work demonstrates that a baseline, or what Chapais called the "deep structure" of human society, can be formulated on the basis of comparisons of human and nonhuman kinship. It has been to this possibility that Fox's pioneering work has led.

Implications for Cultural Anthropology

Recent decades of research on primate kinship have led to one conclusion: kinship is part of our biological and social evolution as a species. In the process of this evolution, kinship constructed us as much as we constructed, and continue to construct, it. If this contribution from primatology is accepted, a number of implications follow for the study of kinship within cultural anthropology. First and foremost is that the denial of any role for biology in human kinship becomes difficult to sustain. Given that extant primates exhibit as much kinship as they do, and given that the comparative study of primate (including human) kinship can now lead to reasonable reconstructions of the evolution of kinship in our hominid line, it follows that human kinship will be best understood within the framework of our biosocial evolution. Humans culturally create kinship, but they do so within the boundaries of their evolution as a species of primate. Kinship, then, is not purely cultural, and its cultural variations are not infinite. From an evolutionary perspective, the idea that many (non-Western) cultures construct their notions of "relatedness" on bases other than indigenous ideas of procreation becomes irrelevant, and the demonstration of yet other cases where relatedness rests on feeding, rituals, residence, and so on, becomes less interesting.

It is, of course, quite possible (some would say likely) that cultural relativists will ignore, or contest the relevance of, the findings of primatology. In this case, one consequence will, I think, be that the field of kinship as we have known it will migrate away from its homeland in anthropology, where it was nurtured, if also at times mistreated, and into other fields such as primatology and human evolutionary ecology. To some extent, this migration is already taking place. We will have, then, cultural relativists who study "relatedness," focusing on cultural variation and historical specificity. They may continue to emphasize cultural constructions of personhood and human bodies and to focus on kinship as process and performance. Others will study kinship (reformed, perhaps, from its pre-Schneiderian days) in terms of its evolution, transformations, and cross-cultural regularities.

On a positive note, rooting human kinship in our primate heritage may encourage some cultural anthropologists to focus on the similarities of human kinship systems rather that the differences and to seek cross-culturally valid connections between kinship and other aspects of human culture. For example, one recent analysis of patriliny, itself critical of cultural relativism in the realm of kinship, looks at cultures throughout Asia and the Middle East that combine patrilineal descent, patrilocality, socially strong patrilineages, and a cultural idea of patrogenesis (only males are considered able to generate other persons through procreative acts). The authors distill from these cultures a common concept of "lineal masculinity," that is, the notion of a male essence that flows to and through men over the generations (King and Stone 2010). Lineal masculinity shapes male identity and places emphasis on male achievement and male fertility. In form, lineal masculinity is strikingly similar from one culture to another, although its cultural expression is varied (for example, it is expressed through an idiom of honor in the Middle East in contrast to an idiom of purity or pollution in Hindu South Asia).

Another consequence of rooting kinship in our primate evolution is that it supports the reopening of questions of the origins, or initial formations, of components of human kinship, such as residence norms, modes of descent, and the incest taboo. These kinds of questions, vigorously debated in the nineteenth century and largely dropped in the early twentieth, are now being addressed again. For example, Knight (2008) revives Lewis Morgan's (1871) position (held before him by Johann Bachofen and J. F. McLennan) that matrilineal descent and matrilocality preceded patrilineal-patrilocal formations. Knight bases his argument on the widespread development of classificatory kinship terminology, itself based on the "equivalence of siblings." To Knight, the unity of siblings in turn implies a relative weakness in the marital bond: "There are good biological reasons why in any culture, a young infant might wish to stay close to its mother. Fathers, on the other hand, can come and go" (2008: 66). Where the marital bond is weak, "paternity certainty will be that much less likely and the scales will be tipped correspondingly toward matrilineal descent" (2008: 66).

Supporting early human matrilocality are discussions of the "grandmother hypothesis"—that selection favored the lengthening of women's postmenopausal lifespan, enabling them to increase their fitness (and that of their children) through caring for and provisioning their grandchildren (Hawkes 2004). With respect to matrilocality, the idea here is that because of paternity uncertainty, grandmother benefits more from provisioning her daughters' children than her sons' children. Hence, to benefit from grandmother allocare, mothers and daughters should remain together through matrilocal or bilocal residence (Alvarez 2004). Kit Opie and Camilla Power (2008) argue that by the stage of *Homo erectus*, infants' energy needs had increased to the point that provisioning by both grandmothers' and mothers' mates was needed. At this stage, mate provisioning of infants with animal protein was sporadic and likely a mating strategy, not a regular paternal investment, whereas grandmother provisioning from foraging provided steady though less nutritious food. In the view of these authors, "Only a female philopatry or matrilocal model permits allocare support from both female kin and male mates" (2008: 182). (Philopatry means staying in one's territory of origin.)

Looking at the issue further back in time, Chapais argues that "The fact that male philopatry characterizes our three closest relatives makes it likely that our common ancestor with *Pan* was male philopatric and hence that patrilocality evolved from male philopatry" (2008, 151). For Chapais, the development of residential diversity beyond patrilocality (i.e., matrilocality or bilocality) could only have come about after the emergence of the tribe because these new residence patterns required peaceful relationships between nonlocal groups. "Stated bluntly, males could remain as competitive and xenophobic as before at the between-tribe level and none the less move between distinct local groups that belonged to the same tribe" (2008, 240). As for the grandmother hypothesis, Chapais rejects the argument that it requires matrilocality or bilocality; it is, rather, compatible with male philopatry: "Under male philopatry, grandmothers would be better off taking care of their sons' offspring, even if this meant taking care of a nonbiological grandoffspring from time to time, than ignoring them" (2008, 245).

Genetic evidence for an early human pattern of residence is not yet definitive. One study (Seilstad, Minch, and Cavalli-Sforza 1998) comparing Y chromosome and mitochondrial DNA from populations in Europe and Africa found that, over the generations, females had been geographically more mobile than males, suggesting an early predominance of patrilocal residence. Another genetic study (Destro-Bisol et al. 2004) pointed out that all of these populations were from "food-producing" societies. This study compared Y chromosome and mitochondrial DNA among hunter-gatherers in sub-Saharan Africa and showed that, in this case, ancestral males had been more mobile than females, supporting matrilocal residence. However, this study also showed that social factors such as polygyny and intermating between food-producing and hunter-gatherer populations could also account for some of the genetic data obtained.

The Incest Taboo

Two other "origins" issues that had once preoccupied anthropology—the incest taboo and the avunculate—have been also recently readdressed. On the incest taboo, Fox (1980) had effectively corrected Levi-Strauss's (1969) assertion that it was a human cultural invention, necessitated by exogamy, that marked humanity's transition from nature to culture. Fathers/brothers had to renounce their daughters/sisters as sexual partners in order to exchange them for the daughters/sisters of other men. As Fox pointed out, primates and mammals generally avoid incest, often through dispersal of one or the other sex, or both, at maturity. Fox then formulated his own theory of the taboo, which combined ideas from Sigmund Freud and Edward Westermarck as well as drew upon primatology, neurology, and other sources. His work was recently picked up by two sociologists, Jonathan Turner and Alexandra Maryanski (2005), who updated and revised Fox's points, largely retaining his approach but dropping most of Freud. In addition, they posited that the emergence of the nuclear family in hominid evolution necessitated the development of cultural mechanisms to promote the avoidance of incest.[3] As for the avunculate, or special relationship between a man and his sister's son, it is built into matrilineal situations; the anthropological interest has been to explain its widespread appearance in patrilineal and bilateral kinship systems. Some nineteenth-century scholars had seen it in these contexts as a "survival" of an earlier human-wide matrilineal or matriarchal state. Lévi-Strauss (1969) saw the mother's brother as already present at the dawn of humanity, in his "atom of kinship," which included a man, his sister, his sister's husband (his brother-in-law), and their son(s). In this scenario, the mother's brother created, in a sense, the sister's son because he had renounced his sister as a mate and released her to the husband/brother-in-law. Lévi-Strauss had seen the incest taboo as the prime mover, the essential principle of humanity, and the avunculate as secondary, or derived from the incest taboo and female exchange.

Fox, by contrast, having dismissed the incest taboo as humanity's prime mover from nature to culture, saw the avunculate as "the defining principle of humanity and culture" (1997, 227). For this, Fox developed the very interesting idea that among humans the avunculate is an ever-present potential that can be activated as a parental strategy. Behind the avunculate is the brother-sister bond that itself rests on the common bond to the mother of this pair. But this brother-sister "pair" can be used for parental purposes, as a whole or partial alternative to the "pair-bond" of a mother and her mate:

> It seems to me a peculiarly human thing to allow the asexual brother-sister tie to take over certain aspects of the parental role from the husband-wife tie. This gives rise to avuncular responsibilities that may flower into full-blown matrilineal succession or inheritance, or to the classical indulgences of the patrilineal avunculate. (Fox 1997, 227)

Fox was not suggesting that this use of the mother's brother, which can over time result in a matrilineal situation, was primary in human evolution or a stage through which all humanity passed. Rather, he held that when in our evolution it became necessary to add males to mother-child units, adding mother's brother was an option, "a neat alternative whereby males do their mating jobs with one set of women and their parental jobs with another" (1997, 211). Like Lévi-Strauss then, Fox saw the mother's brother as "already there" in the "atom of kinship" but further back in nature than Lévi-Strauss would have him, that is, back further than the incest taboo or marital exchange.[4]

Avunculates and Matrilinleality

Strong brother-sister ties, relatively weak husband-wife bonds, and a built-in avunculate characterize matrilineal societies. There are also ethnographic cases where the sister-brother pair fully takes on parental roles to the exclusion of the sisters' husbands, as among the Nayar of southwest India in former times. The Nayar practiced a rare form of postmarital residence termed natolocal (after marriage a man and woman each remain with their own natal kin; brothers and sisters then reside together with the sisters' children). An intriguing case of sibling solidarity and natolocal residence comes from Fox's own long-term fieldwork (1960–1965) among the people of Tory Island, off the northwest coast of Ireland (Fox 1978). This case is particularly interesting in that the Tory islanders were not matrilineal (or patrilineal, where an avunculate, at least, is common) but cognatic (descent groups are formed by tracing descent through any combination of male and female links). On Tory, in the 1960s, natolocal residence (Fox coined the term) was not the most common form of postmarital residence (Fox found ten out of fifty-one married couples living natolocally during his fieldwork), although it was far more common in the past. As among the Nayar, natolocal husbands on Tory visited their wives in their homes and reproduced children with them; but unlike the Nayar case, Tory husbands maintained relationships with their children and participated to some extent in child care.

Fox analyzed natolocality as a potential solution to a Tory cultural paradox, or ambivalence, with regard to marriage. The Tory ideal was a conjugal family consisting of a married couple with their children living together in one household, "enshrined in the ideal of the Holy Family" (Fox 1978, 156). This unit was founded on marriage, of course, but then subsequent marriages in the junior generation (the married couple's sons and daughters) were seen as threatening to this initial family. Either a son's wife or a daughter's husband moving in would disrupt the peace and solidarity of this unit; on Tory this was considered an act of domestic treason. Neolocal residence (the couple sets up an independent household), although acceptable, was also a problem because it meant the loss of an original family member and was particularly considered wrong and disrespectful if aging or widowed parents were in need of close care by their children. Natolocal residence, then, within certain phases of the domestic cycle, was a way to combine both intact conjugal families and new marriages over the generations.

Yet another stab at the avunculate in patrilineal societies, also from an evolutionary perspective, has been taken by Maurice Bloch and Dan Sperber (2002). These authors take the point that all human societies trace kinship bilaterally and that humans have an evolved "psychological disposition" (following kin selection theory) to favor kin bilaterally. Because patrilineal systems gear the transmission of resources in one line only, the avunculate can act as a compensatory device, such that over the generations resources will flow bilaterally.[5] In their view, evolved psychological dispositions do not deterministically bring about cultural forms but lie behind the process whereby some cultural forms, such as the avunculate, are attractive and thus likely to spread and stabilize as cultural expressions. Block and Sperber offer their approach as an alternative to the strong relativism of much of current anthropology. While agreeing with David Schneider that human kinship is culturally constructed and that humans behave in terms of these constructions, it does not follow that biological and evolutionary factors should be abandoned in the study of culture "as though these [cultural] representations and the people who hold them had somehow floated free from the earth into the material clouds of history" (2002, 441).

Along with these renewed issues of the origins of particular components of human kinship and the depth of their appearance in our hominid ancestry are questions of what happened next. What kinship system(s) did early modern humans have—those anatomically modern humans who lived in Africa some 200,000 years ago? How did early human kinship evolve and diversify? What difference did fully human language make (or not make)?

The Crow-Omaha

Following Lévi-Strauss (1969), Fox (1967a) saw that terminology systems known as Crow-Omaha reflected societies in transition from "elementary" alliance systems (where rules specify into what groups a person may not marry and into what groups a person should or must marry) and "complex" systems (where there are only negative rules specifying into what groups a person may not marry). Fox developed his ideas further in a later essay called "The Evolution of Kinship Systems and the Crow-Omaha Question" (1994, 215–43) where he also wrote of the possibility that all Crow-Omaha systems derive from a Dravidian-type Ur structure, with their variations representing different degrees of transition away from that base (see also Fox 1967b).[6]

On the evolution of kinship terminology, Nicholas Allen (1986, 2008) contributed an intriguing "tetradic theory." According to this, the logically simplest form of a kinship classification system (assuming a small human group where every member is regarded as a relative) would use four terms and resemble an Aboriginal Australian four-section classification system. Allen posits the tetradic model as the earliest kinship classification system. He suggests that this model must have predated the settlement of Australia some 60,000 years ago, adding that "since systems throughout the world are also derivable from tetradic ones, presumably the invention preceded the dispersal from Africa" (2008, 112). For Allen, this tetradic model could have existed before the development of fully human language because the classification of people within this system could have been indicated through nonlinguistic symbols (haircut, body ornamentation, etc.). Fox applauds Allen's theory, noting that it is "close to my own thinking," although "his reduction is more logical" (2011, 72). Fox concludes that "He [Allen] completely, for me, demonstrates that all other kinship systems are derived from the rupture of the logically most primitive tetradic system" (2011, 74).

From a different angle and methodology (analyzing known or supposed transformations of kinship terminologies), Maurice Godelier (1998) and others (Godelier et al. 1998) have asked whether kinship terminologies and systems themselves evolved. In particular, "Is there any indication of irreversibility in these [terminological] transformations in the order in which one terminology replaces another (Godelier 1998, 386)?" Godelier's answer is yes. He proposes that the majority of cases analyzed by himself and others "seem to present themselves as a succession of different transformations, all starting from a terminology that is almost Dravidianate" (1998, 404).[7] Because a tetradic system is a simplified form of Dravidian, or Dravidian easily derivable from it, he seems to be in agreement with Allen.[8] Like Allen, Godelier also suggests that the first human kinship systems may have emerged before articulate speech.

Conclusion

Roy D'Andrade records a story told to him by Robin Fox in 1958. When Fox was an undergraduate at the London School of Economics, a professor, aiming to liven up a class, asked the students what they would do if they ended up working as anthropologists in as society without lineages: "The class went silent, and then, from the back of the room, a rough voice answered 'We'd cheer' (D'Andrade 2003, 310). D'Andrade reports that at the time he lacked the wit to ask Fox about the basis of this student boredom with kinship but that since then he came to understand one reason: classical kinship theory lacked causal models; it failed to explain why anything was the way it was. This lack of causal models, according to D'Andrade, likewise plagues interpretive/cultural relativist kinship, which will see the same fate as the earlier kinship studies.

> I believe the field is beginning to become weary of gender, personhood, the body and memory, just as it did with kinship studies in the fifties. What will another study of the symbolic systems contained in

narratives and rituals and other performances tell us? They may carefully describe certain symbolic systems and interpret their meanings, but why should anyone care? Theories which lack causal models can only describe. They can't discover why things are the way they are. (D'Andrade 2003, 314)

Perhaps an even newer anthropological kinship can begin to do so. This will be the challenge of the future of at least one line of kinship studies, a line stemming from the early work of Robin Fox, taking seriously the contributions of primatology, adopting scientific paradigms, and including perspectives of many disciplines. In this pursuit, the contribution of cultural anthropology, with its sensitivity to cultural context, commitment to intensive field research, and emic (insider) perspectives, can be to highlight cross-cultural similarities to reach generalizations and explanations of cultural phenomena. A world of questions about the origins of human kinship, its evolution, prehistory, history, present, and future awaits the next generation of kinship specialists in anthropology.

Notes

1. Fox himself has had firsthand experience with primate field research "[t]o keep myself honest" (1994: 315). See, for example, Steklis and Fox (1989), reprinted in Fox 1994, 319–32).
2. Fox has an interesting take on David Schneider and the demise of kinship. In *Participant Observer* (2004, 342) Fox describes himself as a "piggy-in-the-middle" of a great debate between David Schnieder and Rodney Needham over cross-cousin marriage. Schneider lost the debate; then

   > Schneider could not accept that he was wrong on the issue of cross-cousin marriage, but since he clearly was, the only tactic open to him was to question the category of "kinship" itself. His tactic was to take the criticism leveled against Morgan regarding the lack of fit between kinship terminology and biological relatedness, and make this into a case for abandoning the concept of "kinship" altogether. This was greeted with relief and enthusiasm by the hordes of baby-boomers flooding into anthropology. . . . Today most of so-called kinship studies, and a lot of current "cultural anthropology," are products of David Schneider's rearguard action and his intellectual scorched-earth policy. (Fox 2011, 97)

3. Although he does not cite Fox, Maurice Godlier uses some of the same elements in Fox's work, such as human brain development and the sexual division of labor, to construct his own theory of the incest taboo (see Godelier 1998, 406–12).
4. But for this to work, brothers and sisters would have to reside reasonably close together in adulthood. In Chapais's scheme (2008, 240–42 and 260–62)

the avunculate would have to await the emergence of the prelinguistic tribe because only then could the residential diversity required (that is, natolocal residence [brothers and sisters remaining together] or avuncolocal residence) have taken place.

5. I am not sure this is what Bloch and Sperber meant by a bilateral transmission of resources; they may have merely meant that transmission to a man's sisters' sons and his own sons is more bilateral that transmission to his own sons only. However, over the generations, a rule favoring the flow of resources to a man's own sons and to his sisters' sons would end up as fully "bilateral" in that resources would flow to a man's own sons, who in turn would have to transmit resources to their own sisters' sons, the original man's grandsons through his daughters.

6. For an interesting and full account of this issue, see chapter 11 and the appendix in Fox's book *The Tribal Imagination* (2011). This discussion covers the history of thought on kinship terminology and its possible evolution from Morgan through Lévi-Strauss, Fox's own work, and that of many others.

7. Thomas Trautman (2001), however, questions whether kinship terminologies evolve from an original Dravidian-like structure.

8. But see Godelier (1998, 405) and Allen (2008, 108–9) for where they disagree.

References

Allen, Nicholas J. 1986. "Tetradic Theory: An Approach to Kinship." *Journal of the Anthropological Society of Oxford* 17:87–109.

———. 2008. "Tetradic Theory and the Origin of Human Kinship Systems." In *Early Human Kinship: From Sex to Social Reproduction*, by Nicholas J. Allen, Hilary Callan, Robin Dunbar, and Wendy James, 96–112. Malden, MA: Blackwell Publishing.

Alvarez, Helen Perich. 2004. "Residence Groups among Hunter-Gatherers: A View of the Claims and Evidence for Patrilocal Bands." In *Kinship and Behavior in Primates*, edited by Bernard Chapais and Carol M. Berman, 420–42. New York: Oxford University Press.

Bloch, Maurice, and Dan Sperber. 2002. "Kinship and Evolved Psychological Dispositions: The Mother's Brother Controversy Reconsidered." *Current Anthropology* 43(5):723–34.

Boyd, R., and P. J. Richarson. 1985. *Culture and the Evolutionary Process*. Chicago: Chicago University Press.

Carsten, Janet. 1995. "The Substance of Kinship and the Heat of the Hearth: Personhood and Relatedness among the Malays in Pulau Langkawi." *American Ethnologist* 22:223–41.

———. 2000. "Introduction: Cultures of Relatedness." In *Cultures of Relatedness: New Approaches to the Study of Kinship*, edited by Janet Carsten, 1–36, Cambridge: Cambridge University Press.

Chapais, Bernard. 2008. *Primeval Kinship: How Pair-Bonding Gave Birth to Human Society*. Cambridge, MA: Harvard University Press.

Cavalli-Sforza, L. Luca, and Marcus W. Feldman. 1981. *Cultural Transmission and Evolution: A Quantitative Approach*. Princeton, NJ: Princeton University Press.

D'Andrade, Roy. 2003. "Why Cheer?" *Journal of Cognition and Culture* 3(4):310–14.

Dawkins, Richard. 1989. *The Selfish Gene*. 2nd edition. Oxford: Oxford University Press.

Destro-Bisol, G., F. Donati, V. Coia, I. Boschi, F. Verginelli, A. Caglia, S. Tofanelli, G. Spedini, and C. Capelli. 2004. "Variation of Female and Male Lineages in Sub-Saharan Populations: The Importance of Sociocultural Factors." *Molecular Biology and Human Evolution* 21:1673–82.

Durham, W. H. 1991. *Co-Evolution: Genes, Culture and Human Diversity*. Stanford, CA: Stanford University Press.

Feinberg, Richard, and Martin Ottenheimer, eds. 2001. *The Cultural Analysis of Kinship: The Legacy of David M. Schneider*. Urbana: University of Illinois Press.

Fox, Robin. 1967a. *Kinship and Marriage: An Anthropological Perspective*. Cambridge: Cambridge University Press.

———. 1967b. *The Keresan Bridge: A Problem in Pueblo Ethnography*. London School of Economics Monographs in Social Anthropology, No. 35. London: Athlone Press.

———. 1975. "Primate Kin and Human Kinship." In *Biosocial Anthropology*, edited by Robin Fox, ed., 9–35. New York: John Wiley and Sons.

———. 1978. *The Tory Islanders*. Cambridge: Cambridge University Press.

———. 1979. "Kinship Categories as Natural Categories." In *Evolutionary Biology and Human Social Behavior*, edited by William Irons, 132–44. North Scituate, MA: Duxbury Press.

———. 1980. *The Red Lamp of Incest: An Enquiry into the Origins of Mind and Society*. Notre Dame, IN: University of Notre Dame Press.

———. 1989. *The Search for Society: Quest for a Biosocial Science and Morality*. New Brunswick, NJ: Rutgers University Press.

———. 1991. "Reply to Rodselth et al.: The Human Community as a Primate Society." *Current Anthropology* 32(3): 242–43.

———. 1993. *Reproduction and Succession: Studies in Anthropology, Law and Society*. New Brunswick, NJ: Transaction Publishers.

———. 1994. *The Challenge of Anthropology: Old Encounters and New Excursions*. New Brunswick, NJ: Transaction Publishers.

———. 1997. *Conjectures and Confrontations: Science, Evolution, Social Concern*. New Brunswick, NJ: Transaction Publishers.

———. 2004. *Participant Observer: Memoir of a Transatlantic Life*. New Brunswick, NJ: Transaction Publishers.

———. 2011. *The Tribal Imagination: Civilization and the Savage Mind*. Cambridge, MA: Harvard University Press.

Godelier, Maurice. 1998. "Afterword: Transformations and Lines of Evolution." In *Transformations of Kinship*, edited by Maurice Godelier, Thomas R. Trautmann, and Franklin E. Tjon Sie Fat, 386–413, Washington DC: Smithsonian Institution Press.

Godelier, Maurice, Thomas R. Trautmann, and Franklin E. Tjon Sie Fat, eds. 1998. *Transformations of Kinship*. Washington DC: Smithsonian Institution Press.

Hawkes, Kristen. 2004. "The Grandmother Effect." *Nature* 248:128–29.
Hawkes, K., J. F. O'Connell, N. G. Blurton Jones, H. P. Alvarez, and E. L. Charnov. 1998. "Grandmothering, Menopause and the Evolution of Human Life Histories." *Proceedings of the National Academy of Sciences of the United States of America* 95:1336–9.
King, Diane E., and Linda Stone. 2010. "Lineal Masculinity: Gendered Memory within Patriliny." *American Ethnologist* 37(2):323–36.
Knight, Chris. 2008. "Early Human Kinship Was Matrilineal." In *Early Human Kinship: From Sex to Social Reproduction*, by Nicholas J. Allen, Hilary Callan, Robin Dunbar, and Wendy James, 61–82. Malden, MA: Blackwell Publishing.
Kuper, Adam. 1999. *Culture: The Anthropologists' Account*. Cambridge, MA: Harvard University Press.
———. 2003. "What Really Happened to Kinship and Kinship Studies." *Journal of Cognition and Culture* 3(4):329–35.
Levine, Nancy E. 2008. "Alternative Kinship, Marriage and Reproduction." *Annual Review of Anthropology* 37:375–89.
Lewotin, Richard C. 2000. *The Triple Helix: Gene, Organism and Environment*. Cambridge, MA: Harvard University Press.
Lévi-Strauss, Claude. 1969 (1949). *The Elementary Structures of Kinship*. Translated by James Harle Bell, John Richard von Strurmer, and Rodney Needham. Boston: Beacon Press.
Morgan, Lewis Henry. 1871. *Systems of Consanguinity and Affinity in the Human Family*. Washington DC: Smithsonian Institution Press.
Mulder, M. 2008. "Bonding as Key to Hominid Origins: Primatology Meets Socio-Cultural Analysis in a Controversial Account of Human Evolution." *Nature* 454:29–30. A review of *Primeval Kinship: How Pair Bonding Gave Birth to Human Society*, by Bernard Chapais. Cambridge, MA: Harvard University Press, 2008.
Needham, Rodney, ed. 1971. Introduction to *Rethinking Kinship and Marriage*, iii–cxvii. London: Tavistock.
Odling-Smee, F. John, Kevin N. Laland, and Marcus W. Feldman. 2003. *Niche Construction: The Neglected Process in Evolution*. Princeton, NJ: Princeton University Press.
Opie, Kit, and Camilla Power. 2008. "Grandmothering and Female Coalitions: A Basis for Matrilineal Priority?" In *Early Human Kinship: From Sex to Social Reproduction*, by Nicholas J. Allen, Hilary Callan, Robin Dunbar, and Wendy James, 168–86. Malden, MA: Blackwell Publishing.
Rodseth, Lars, Richard W. Wrangham, Alisa M. Harrigan, and Barbara B. Smuts. 1991. "The Human Community as a Primate Society." *Current Anthropology* 32(3):221–41.
Rodseth, Lars, and Richard Wrangham. 2004. "Human Kinship: A Continuation of Politics by Other Means?" In *Kinship and Behavior in Primates*, edited by Bernard Chapais and Carol M. Berman, 389–419. New York: Oxford University Press.
Scheffler, Harold W. 1991. "Sexism and Naturalism in the Study of Kinship." In *Gender at the Crossroads of Knowledge: Feminist Anthropology in*

the Postmodern Era, edited by Micaela di Leonardo, 361–82. Berkeley: University of California Press.

Schneider, David M. 1972. "What Is Kinship All About?" In *Kinship Studies in the Morgan Centennial Year*, edited by Priscilla Reining, 32–63. Washington DC: The Anthropological Society of Washington.

———. 1984. *A Critique of the Study of Kinship*. Ann Arbor: University of Michigan Press.

Shapiro, Warren. 2008. "What Human Kinship Is Primarily About: Toward a Critique of the New Kinship Studies." *Social Anthropology* 16(2):137–53.

Silk, Joan B. 2001. "Ties That Bond: The Role of Kinship in Primate Societies." In *New Directions in Anthropological Kinship*, edited by Linda Stone, 71–92. Lanham, MD: Rowman and Littlefield Publishers.

Sousa, Paulo. 2003. "The Fall of Kinship: Towards an Epistemological Explanation." *Journal of Cognition and Culture* 3(4):265–303.

Steilstad, M. T. E., E. Minch, and L. L. Cavalli-Sforza. 1998. "Genetic Evidence for a Higher Female Migration Rate in Humans." *Nature Genetics* 20:278–80.

Steklis, Horst D., and Robin Fox. 1989. "Menstrual-Cycle Phase and Sexual Behavior in Semi-Free Ranging Stumptail Macaques (*Macara arctoides*)." *International Journal of Primatology* 9(5):443–56.

Stone, Linda. 2004. "Introduction to Contemporary Directions in Kinship." In *Kinship and Family: An Anthropological Reader*, edited by Robert Parkin and Linda Stone, 331–41. Malden, MA: Blackwell Publishing.

———. 2008. "Kinship Back on Track: Primatology Unravels the Origin and Evolution of Human Kinship." *Evolutionary Psychology* 6(4):555–61. A review of *Primeval Kinship: How Pair-Bonding Gave Birth to Human Society*, by Bernard Chapais. Cambridge, MA: Harvard University Press, 2008.

———. 2010. *Kinship and Gender: An Introduction*. 4th edition. Boulder, CO: Westview Press.

Stone, Linda, and Paul F. Lurquin. 2007. *Genes, Culture and Human Evolution: A Synthesis*. Malden, MA: Blackwell Publishing.

Trautman, Thomas R. 2001. "The Whole History of Kinship Terminology in Three Chapters." *Anthropological Theory* 1(2):268–87.

Turner, Jonathan, and Alexandra Maryanski. 2005. *Incest: Origins of the Taboo*. Boulder, CO: Paradigm Publishers.

Tylor, Edward B. 1889. "On a Method of Investigating the Development of Institutions: Applied to Laws of Marriage and Descent." *Journal of the Royal Anthropological Institute* 18:245–69.

Wilson, Robert A. 2009. "The Primal Path to Kinship: A Critical Review of Bernard Chapais *Primeval Kinship: How Pair-Bonding Gave Birth to Human Society*." *Biology and Philosophy* 25(1):111–23.

Yanagisako, Sylvia Junko, and Jane Fishburne Collier. 1987. "Toward a Unified Analysis of Gender and Kinship." In *Gender and Kinship: Essays toward a Unified Analysis*, edited by Jane Fishburne Collier and Sylvia Junko Yanagisako, 14–50. Berkeley: University of California Press.

8

Lighting the Red Lamp of Incest

Alexandra Maryanski and Jonathan Turner

> "The subject is incest and the fascination of incest. Why the fascination? Because it is forbidden? But why is it forbidden— or is it always forbidden? The quick answer is—not always. But at the very least, the idea of it seems to make us easily uneasy, and at worst, downright hysterical."
> —Robin Fox (1980)

The Red Lamp of Incest! Has there ever been a more racy title for an academic book?[1] Its pages are equally colored with Fox's lively prose and salty sense of humor. Yet, the title and witty remarks belie what is an intellectual powerhouse of a book that tackles a longstanding problem: what is the origin of the incest taboo? While Fox has many claims to fame, both in anthropology and related disciplines (e.g., his *Kinship and Marriage* (1967) is still the most lucid and best book on kinship ever written and a must read in Maryanski's sociology course on social institutions), *The Red Lamp of Incest* (1980) is special for us because it paved the way for our own recent work, *Incest: Origins of the Taboo* (2005). But Fox's classic work harbors much more: the intellectual rebirth of Edward Westermarck. Thus, before turning to our intellectual debt to Robin Fox, we need to first take up his amazing (and little known) resurrection of Westermarck's thesis on the origins of the incest taboo and exogamy—a theory that is not only important in our work but has gained acceptance in both the social and biological sciences.

The Westermarck Effect

Edward Westermarck was a sociology professor at the University of London. In 1891, he published *The History of Human Marriage*, a magnum opus that reviewed the literature on kinship and marriage patterns in traditional and contemporary societies. In contrast to the prevailing sociocultural theories that the incest taboo originated to guard against sexual intercourse between near relatives and to assure that individuals marry out of their kinship groups, Westermarck argued that even the severest penalties cannot easily constrain the "sexual instinct." Instead, drawing upon evidence that animal inbreeding often resulted in reduced or malformed offspring (and generalizing it to humans), Westermarck proposed that to ensure fitness, natural selection had installed a cognitive function in humans that dampened sexual love between grown-up children reared together. Siblings typically exhibit this trait, but all individuals, related or not, when raised in the same household will typically evidence this same "conspicuous absence of erotic feelings" (Westermarck, [1991] 1922, 192). So Westermarck advanced the thesis that the genesis of the incest taboo and the need to marry out stemmed *not* from a horror of an arising sexual desire but, rather, from the activation of a sexual dampening trait that limited the "forbidden act" from happening in the first place. Knowing that his thesis would provoke controversy, Westermarck wrote,

> The objection will perhaps be made that the aversion to sexual intercourse between persons living very closely together from early youth is too complicated a mental phenomenon to be a true instinct, acquired though spontaneous variations intensified by natural selection. But ... this feeling ... only implies that disgust is associated with the idea of sexual intercourse between persons who have lived in a long-continued, intimate relationship from a period of life at which the action of desire is naturally out of the question.

Westermarck's thesis was greeted with enthusiasm by some scholars (Alfred Wallace wrote a short preface to the book), but overall it was summarily dismissed by such intellectual giants as Edward Tylor, Emile Durkheim, Sigmund Freud, A. R. Radcliffe-Brown, Sir James Frazer, and Bronislaw Malinowski, who all maintained that it was self-evident that the taboo exists to prevent incestuous acts from happening. By the 1920s, Westermarck's reputation was in steady decline: and by the time he died in 1939, his avoidance thesis was largely forgotten. Among supporters of Westermarck, the problem lay in testing his avoidance hypothesis because it required special environmental conditions without the conflating influence of the incest taboo (e.g., case studies of unrelated children brought up together). Among opponents, the problem lay in its incompatibility with the crop of newly minted sociocultural theories proposed by such luminaries as Talcott Parsons, who viewed the incest taboo as a means to reduce familial conflict and Claude Lévi-Strauss who proposed that because all animals engage in incestuous acts, rules against incest served to divide nature from nurture and to assure the corresponding rule of exogamy. In 1944, in an essay titled "Who Reads Westermarck Today," Knut Pipping, a sociologist and relative of Westermarck, expressed his heartfelt regret that his great-uncle's *"magna opera, The History of Human Marriage"* is now sadly *passé* and of little interest to anyone but historians.

Fox to the Rescue

While Knut Pipper was lamenting the decline in Westermarck's reputation, Robin Fox was busy working on getting it restored. Strolling down memory lane, Fox wrote in the preface to our recent book that his fascination with the incest taboo began in the early 1950s, when he was a sociology undergraduate at the London School of Economics. His first significant encounter, he said, was in a social anthropology course when the week's topic was the incest taboo. Anxious to impress his professor with his familiarity with trendy sociological explanations, he was well into his monologue when he was suddenly thrown off balance:

> I was trotting out all the standard sociological explanations for exogamy and the expansion of social ties and so on when Maurice Freedman, the great expert on Chinese kinship and later professor of anthropology at Oxford, obviously bored with this recitation, interrupted me: "Why can't we have a sexual free-for-all in the family and *then* marry out of it?" I was startled out of my sociological rut and launched on a lifelong intellectual adventure. (Fox 2005, ix)

His second meaningful encounter was at Harvard in the late 1950s in a conversation with John Whiting, who was discussing how opposite-sex youngsters during roughhouse games often get sexually aroused and then choked up emotionally, seemingly in frustration. "It immediately hit me," Fox said, "that this might be the foundation for Edward Westermarck's contention that siblings easily develop a 'natural aversion' to sex with each other at the onset of puberty" (ibid.). This insight led Fox to write "Sibling Incest" in 1962, where he proposed that Westermarck was pointing to a fundamental truth "that we were so against incest precisely because we *didn't* want to do it and so were horrified by those who did." While the paper itself got buried, Fox rendered up a great service in this early essay by coining the term "The Westermarck Effect," a telling phrase that is now common parlance in evolutionary-minded circles when discussing Westermarck's thesis on sexual avoidance.

The Red Lamp of Incest

By 1980, two decades had passed with Fox still searching for an answer to the same question: why is it that incest is not rampant among humans? Building on his earlier insights and the accumulated evidence from relevant disciplines—from anthropology to neurobiology to zoology—*The Red Lamp of Incest* weaved together these elements into a synthetic theory of the incest taboo. Sailing close to the edge at times but intent on getting answers, Fox pondered these questions: What is nature up to? Why have a taboo at all? Is there a horror of incest everywhere? If humans are not interested in incest, why do they detest those who engage in it?

Fox began his narrative with the *Westermarck effect* and what it can and cannot do. Opposite-sex siblings seem ripe for incest given that they grow up together and are usually fond of each other. But relatively speaking, he mused, there is little incest. Why? Is the human organism *primed* to receive anti-incest instructions? But what does it need to work? Selection works on probabilities rather than certainties, and, yet, nature would not leave it to chance; it must suppose a stable learning environment early in life (Fox 1980, 19). But what is this environment or mechanism? What does it need to work? Why does it not get activated sometimes? Here the *Westermarck effect* literally comes into play with a built-in natural sexual avoidance between siblings (or any youngsters growing up together). But if it doesn't get activated, the door is opened for incest.

To test his hypothesis, Fox compiled descriptive case studies of societies that ran along the following continuum: those where children are in close propinquity with lots of intimate fondling growing up, and those where children are in close propinquity but with little opportunity for touching or general physical contact. In the first, he found, there are few sanctions with lots of contact and sexual indifference at puberty; in the second, fierce sanctions and a repressive sexual environment. It was a self-fulfilling paradox: "Cultures which essay to prevent incest between siblings often manage to promote precisely the feelings they aim to inhibit, thus making the prevention more difficult and yet more necessary, in a never-ending vicious circle—a kind of parody of human good intentions" (Fox 1980, 19). So if the sexual environment is too rigid, the Westermarck effect will not get activated, and thus, strong anti-incest sanctions are likely to be imposed. If the environment is lax, with lots of cohesive play between the sexes, nature takes its course and the result is few strong sanctions. The Westermarck effect truly makes evolutionary sense, operating as it does in tune with a human neurobiology primed for fostering sexual indifference among youngsters raised together or variations depending on social environmental conditions. As Fox propositioned,

> The intensity of heterosexual attraction between co-socialized children after puberty is inversely proportional to the intensity of heterosexual activity between them before puberty. (ibid., 50)

After dispensing with the brother-sister issue, Fox's narrative shifted to the intergenerational parent-child problem. Again, like the brother-sister dyad, there is little adult-child incest. But when it occurs, why does it occur? The Westermarck effect applies primarily to youngsters growing up together, and so something else must be working here to prevent intergenerational incestuous intercourse. To explain parent-child incest, Fox turned to Freud, who had dealt mostly with parent-child incestuous cases. While Fox followed Freud's blueprints, he interlaced Freud's ideas with data from primates, neurobiology, and hominin evolution into a complex and integrative analysis of the origin of the incest taboo and exogamy.

As will become evident, we followed much of Fox's lead and strategy. Let us now summarize the elements that we drew from his great work and adapted to our approach along with an outline of our explanation for the origin of the incest taboo.

Fox's Synthetic Incest Taboo Theory

We asked Robin Fox to write a foreword to our book, with the much less interesting title of *Incest: Origin of the Taboo* (Maryanski and Turner 2005) because among all the various theoretical approaches to the topic of incest his came closest to our approach. Much like Fox's theory, our strategy draws from a broad mosaic of approaches and adds recent data from psychology, sociology, primatology, neurobiology, evolutionary biology, and research on incest rates in trying to explain the origins of the incest taboo. Moreover, Fox's statement of the problem of why a taboo would be necessary corresponds to our own, although we offer a slightly different slant on the issue of why a taboo is essential to human societies. Fox recognized that the human mating system—anchored as it is in a stable nuclear family—goes against ape behavioral propensities and, hence, the last common hominoid ancestor that we share with all present-day great apes. Sexual activity among great apes is mostly promiscuous, with the result that paternity is never known.[2] Moreover, most ape adolescent males and females leave their natal grouping at puberty and never return. Only male chimpanzees deviate from this dispersal pattern. Although a chimpanzee male behaves much like other apes by taking leave of his mother and younger siblings after puberty, he still visits them frequently because he never leaves the boundaries of his natal community. Because females (and all males, except for chimpanzees) depart their natal range after puberty, incest is avoided because these transfers greatly lessen the chances that brothers or fathers (by chance) might mate with their sisters or daughters. Yet, as Fox emphasized, sibling incest among humans would still be unlikely because the Westermarck effect produces sexual apathy when siblings are raised together and have close physical contact in play activities. Thus, the core problem of creating the nuclear family lay not with sibling incest but with incest between parents and offspring. For it is unlikely that a Westermarck effect is activated for parents, and it is certain that incest between parent and offspring would cause great strain on an early hominin nuclear family, just as it does for humans today. Yet, as Fox emphasized, this familial unit was essential to hominin survival in open-country savanna conditions.

Given the inherent dangers of living in open-country environments where predators abound, selection forces operated to make rather loosely organized, evolved apes more organized, especially around productive and reproductive functions. The family was the key to reproductive success while coordinated hunting and food gathering in bands anchored by a sexual division of labor in nuclear families was essential to productive success. For Fox, big game hunting was crucial in many ways: selecting on bigger-brained hominins who could better coordinate the hunt, while establishing a bond-generating system of exchange of meat from males for plant life from females. With larger brains, infant dependency would naturally increase, thus generating selection pressures for more permanent reproductive units, but these pressures would produce a unit in which incest of parents and offspring would also increase. For Fox, bigger brains involved the integration of prefrontal cortex with subcortical emotion centers like the amygdala, which would give hominins more capacity to inhibit emotions and to plan, think, and deliberate as well as to remember past events and to bring these memories to bear on the present situation. But while these cortical-subcortical connections may have helped adults inhibit sexual urges directed at their offspring, there was no biological mechanism or programmer, like the Westermarck effect for siblings, to actually reduce these incestuous impulses.

Fox's argument deviates from our own because he ad-opts a more Freudian approach, emphasizing the power struggle between older and younger males over access to females, which led to restrictions on sexual relations among closely related kin and, perhaps, to the evolution of guilt as an emotional response when these restrictions were violated (or even considered in the first place). As the brain of hominines grew, guilt and other moral emotions would increase, giving emotional teeth to an incest rule (Turner 2000; Turner and Maryanski 2005). But Fox continues the Freudian line of argument when he emphasizes that the sublimated sexual desires of the young are redirected toward increased commitments to the incest taboo, with this energy continuing into adulthood and leading to socialization of the next generation of young into the taboo. While this explanation is plausible, we took a somewhat different tack. Still, we share Fox's basic argument about the selection pressures that produced the nuclear family that, as it evolved, generated new selection pressure to inhibit sexual relations among family members (Turner and Maryanski 2005). For Fox, only the Westermarck effect (on the behalf of siblings) was available by nature to reduce sexual tensions in the evolving nuclear family. Fox's Freudian dynamics may operate, but we propose another explanation for the origins of the incest taboo.

Recasting Fox's Basic Argument

We began in the same place as Fox: the general promiscuity of great apes (who with humans form a monophyletic grouping or clade) and how to overcome this behavioral propensity in forming the nuclear family. We add a further problem: the relatively weak social ties among extant adult apes. Maryanski's (1987, 1992, 1995) network analysis of ape social structures, including a cladistic analysis of the strength of ties among extant apes, produced a reconstructed social structure of the last common ancestor (LCA) to apes and humans. Maryanski and Turner (1992, 2005, 2008) argued for a predominately weak-tie social network with few stable or close affect relationships among adult hominoids (Maryanski and Turner 1992, 2005, 2008) This method of systematics thus generated a primordial social structure that closely resembles the relational network of present-day orangutan populations.[3]

Space is not available here to discuss why the LCA population likely had a weakly tied social network. But, in short, this relational structure (along with female dispersal at puberty) seemingly enhanced fitness for middle to late Miocene hominoids after most ape species went extinct and monkey species began to proliferate, pushing the few remaining ape species with morphological features conducive to under-branch feeding to the terminal niches of the rain forest habitat where larger networks with intergenerational continuity could not be sustained (see Turner and Maryanski 2005, 2008, for a discussion).[4] But as the earth grew cooler during the late Miocene, the forests receded, opening up vast grassland ecosystems that became the new habitat for many Old World higher primates. An open-country environment is not a good place for a loosely tied primate. Savanna-dwelling ancestral monkeys would have had much less difficulty, as they do today, because they are already highly organized by male dominance hierarchies and tightly knit blood-tied matrilineages. In contrast, weakly tied hominoids would be easy fodder for predators.

Higher primates have other distinct disadvantages in adapting to grassy ecosystems: they are relatively slow moving (especially large-bodied hominoids); they have a reduced olfactory organ (so unlike most ground-dwelling mammals they cannot detect predators by olfactory cues alone); they are visually dominant (a sensory organ that is not automatically alerting and is useless after dark for detecting predators); and they can become highly emotional and draw attention to themselves. But the critical problem for hominoids trying to adapt to open-country living is their *lack of cohesive social structures* that can protect dependent offspring and their adult parents and that can coordinate foraging-hunting activities as well as mount a defense against large open-country predators. Thus, given the problems above, it is not surprising that most hominoids who left the forest environment died out, with humans the only hominoid that can now live on grassy plains or wide open woodlands. How, then, did our hominid ancestors beat the odds and survive?

The answer to this question is at the heart of any explanation of the incest taboo. Somehow our ancestors became better organized, keeping adults tied to a band and parents in a nuclear family. Thus, the first explanatory task is to determine how hominins became better organized; then we can begin to answer the question of how they resolved the potential inbreeding problems inherent in the nuclear family. For ape-style promiscuity did not vanish as *Homo* became more organized; rather, social organization put potential sexual partners in propinquity and then had to regulate sexual drives among hominins in the evolving nuclear family. As Robin Fox (1980) succinctly phrased it, strengthened ties and nuclear families lit the "red lamp of incest."

The Strength of Stronger Ties

Present-day common chimpanzees have stronger ties than the last common ancestor to humans and the great apes. Chimpanzee males do not transfer from their natal community at birth; rather, they stay in their community, wandering about, and, if necessary, defending their home range from incursion by males from other communities (Watts and Mitani 2001; Goodall 1986). They also sustain relatively strong relations with their mothers and brothers and notably preferred male "friends." (Lucas 2005; Mitani, Watts and Muller 2002). Thus, for reasons that are unknown, selection worked to enhance relationships within the home ranges of chimpanzees, and perhaps this modest enhancement of network ties can give us a distant mirror to see our last common ancestor to chimpanzees and hominins. If humans' hominin ancestors were anything like extant chimpanzees, then the potential problem of mother-son incest could exist because adult chimpanzee sons have quite strong ties to their mothers. Yet, incestuous relations between mother and son are very rare, and hence it is instructive to see how this potential inbreeding problem is avoided in chimpanzee communities. When a female is sexually receptive, local males will often line up and wait patiently for their turn, but there is a conspicuous male absent from this "hoi polloi" sexual activity: her son (Pusey 1980, 2005). Thus, there appears to exist a bioprogrammer in the neurology of the chimpanzee brain for avoiding sexual contact between mother and son, and if this programmer existed among hominins, it helps explain the strikingly divergent rates of incest between dyads in the nuclear family as well as the emotional reactions of the younger party to incest.[5] But let us not get ahead of our story of how stronger bonds were created among the ancestral *Homo* adapting to open-country conditions.

The Primal Horde

We can begin by reintroducing an old idea of the pre-family "horde." Let's assume that common chimpanzee social structure today was like that of our common ancestor—a big assumption, to be sure, although niche theory would predict relaxed selection pressures on chimpanzees that remained in the forest.[6] That being so, their existing tie patterns could be selected on to create a stronger structure built from the already moderate to strong ties among mothers and preadolescent offspring, mothers and sons, brothers, and preferred male friends. This would be the primal horde on which selection would have gone to work to forge the nuclear family and band. The primal, core ties would thus be the following (Turner and Maryanski 2005, 134):

1. Strong mother ties with prepuberty male offspring.
2. Strong mother ties with prepuberty female offspring.
3. Strong ties between mother and adult son.
4. Strong to moderate ties between male siblings and "best" male friends.

All other ties among common chimpanzees, including those between unrelated adult females who joined the community after puberty (and which Jane Goodall (1986) describes as having "neutral relationships"), adult males and females, mothers and their adult daughters, and fathers and their offspring would be unknown, weak, or nonexistent.[7] To create the nuclear family, some key weak or even nonexistent ties would have to be strengthened: the adult female to adult male sexual partner, the adult male to his offspring, and perhaps even adult female and male ties to their adult offspring. Strong directional selection probably worked rapidly on the tails of (bell-curve) trait distributions to strengthen those ties that might have constituted the horde. Mother and adult son bonds did not need strengthening because they already exist along with a strong sexual avoidance programmer. The already strong mother and dependent offspring bonds could be selected upon so that offspring perhaps stayed with mother in a stronger quasi-nucleated unit, at least for a time, into adulthood. Male friendship and brother ties could also be utilized to forge a larger quasi-kinship unit composed of mothers, adult brothers and their friends, and postadolescent females, and together these might mark the first evidence of the band structure typical of early hunter-gatherer humans.

The biggest obstacle would be strengthening adult female-male ties so that the latter would stay with his sexual partner and help protect their offspring. One clue to natural selection's handiwork is that the septum in humans—the source of the sex drive and the pleasure that it brings—is twice as large in humans than in the great apes, even when body size is controlled (Turner 2000, 91). This enlarging of an area already making apes promiscuous may indicate that deeper emotions, such as love and attachment, were being added to the pleasure of the sex act; this would, it seems, be the easiest route for selection to take because there was an extant subcortical area of the brain on which to select, thus making it unnecessary for natural selection to wait for point mutations to produce adult-to-adult "love" and commitment. Thus, even though the promiscuous sexual relations among adult hominoids would seem to be an insurmountable obstacle, enlarging the septum may have been the first step to forging something like the nuclear family. Moreover, as studies on voles document (Lim et. al. 2004), mutations on the single gene responsible for vasopressin in males and oxytocin in females could dramatically reduce promiscuity and increase male-female pair-bonding, although whether this occurred among *Homo* is unclear. Later, as humans general emotional capacities were enhanced (see later discussion) and as cognitive abilities grew to the point of being able articulate moral codes to which emotions could be attached, a full-blown nuclear family could have emerged, although just when is also unclear.

Building Solidarity among Low Sociality Animals

If we conduct a thought experiment on how humans generate social bonding and solidarity, we can see what selection had to do to relatively self-contained hominins to make their fluid group structures more cohesive. Humans bond by a series of emotion-arousing actions: opening rituals establishing a mood, common focus of attention, rhythmic synchronization of talk and body language, mutual emotional entrainment, symbolic representation of group, righteous anger over violation of group norms, and shame and apology rituals for those violating group norms (Collins 2004; Turner 2002, 2010). As Turner (2000) has argued in a number of places, natural selection first worked on the subcortical areas of the hominin brain where emotions are generated, first increasing the range of primary emotions that could be used to forge bonds, then mixing primary emotions to expand even further the range of emotions that could be used to forge bonds and sanction violations of expectations, and finally mixing the three negative primary emotions (i.e., anger, fear, sadness) together to produce the moral emotions of shame and guilt. This last step probably occurred only with *Homo sapiens*, but it was a critical evolutionary development because three of the four primary emotions—satisfaction-happiness, assertion-anger, disappointment-sadness, and aversion-fear—are negative. By combining them together, new emotions are produced that mute the power of each negative primary emotion alone and that drive individuals to monitor and sanction themselves, while increasing their desire to ritually make amends for transgressions to group norms.

Turner (2000) also argues that areas of the neocortex that give apes the fundamental ability to use symbolically based "language" (if taught)—that is, the association cortices around the inferior parietal lobe that evolved to facilitate the shift of primates from olfactory dominance to visual dominance (Geschwind 1965a, 1965b; Geschwind and Damasio 1984)—was usurped to build a language of emotions, revealing emotional phonemes strung together by a syntax to communicate meanings. This early language system was visual, relying on the already-in-place visual dominance of primates and their ability to use facial gestures to understand each other's likely courses of action (termed *role taking* in sociology or *perspective taking* in theories of mind). This language of emotions could be used to forge bonds, but it could also create emotion-based moral expectations for certain kinds of behaviors. By consistent arousal of the emotions attached to positive and negative sanctions for behaviors that meet or fail to meet expectations for group actions, an implicit, nonverbal *emotion culture* of norms can emerge and supplement the use of emotions to forge interpersonal attunement and interpersonal bonds. Groups could become more cohesive and thus able to coordinate defense, hunting, and gathering in ever more open-country savanna conditions.

Because the emotion centers of the brain already existed, natural selection would not have to wait for mutations as much as select on tail ends of distributions of emotion centers in the brain and, over time, increasingly connect these centers to the prefrontal cortex, once the neocortex of hominins began to grow with *Homo habilis*. Evidence for these changes in the human subcortex can be found in the comparative measurements of the emotion centers in the subcortical portions of the brain among extant apes and humans, with the areas most likely to generate and store emotional memories being about twice the size of those in great apes, again controlling for body size (Stephan 1983; Stephan and Andy 1969, 1977; Eccles 1989). Thus, natural selection had hit upon a fitness-enhancing solution to the low sociality problem of all apes: grow the emotion centers so that they can produce more variants and combinations of primary emotions that can be used to forge social bonds and to develop a proto-culture.

Once emotions, languages of emotions, and emotion-based expectations that could be positively and negatively sanctioned were in place, enlarging the neocortex to produce auditory or verbal language would only increase fitness that much more. Expectations could be articulated, valenced with emotions, and sanctioned with emotional responses to transgressions; and as this combination of emotions, culture, and interpersonal sanctioning increased group solidarity, the direction of selection was set for language and culture in the human measure. It may be that only with *Homo sapiens* that true articulated speech evolved (Enard et. al. 2002a, 2002b), but the neurological ground had been laid by millions of years of selection on emotion centers to produce a dramatically enhanced range of emotional phonemes, a grammar for emitting these phonemes to produce fine-grained meanings, and a proto-culture of emotionally based expectations. Once selection had gone this far, it was not a dramatic step to articulated speech and symbol-based culture in the human measure.

There is, however, a significant problem with using emotions as the basis for forming stable bonds: enhanced emotional attachments of adults to their offspring could potentially generate sexual attractions of adults to their offspring, thereby increasing the potential for incest. If hominins had something like chimpanzee sexual avoidance between mothers and sons, the likelihood of sexual attraction between members of this dyad would be reduced, and coupled with the Westermarck effect for siblings, the only remaining problem would revolve around the father-daughter dyad. For this dyad there would be no bioprogrammers for sexual avoidance. Why should there be? Father-daughter ties are nonexistent in chimpanzee societies (and just about all primate societies), and once an adolescent female departs her natal community, she and "father" are not even in propinquity for sexual activity. And this situation was probably the same for the early *Homo* lineage that first took up savanna ecology. But if increased emotional attachments among members of the emerging nuclear family kept adolescent females near her parents for a time, then the potential for incest would increase.

Current Incest Data and Evolution of the Incest Taboo

The data on incest among contemporary families is highly flawed for many reasons: selective reporting of incidence, secrecy, varying definitions of what constitutes incest, conflation of incest with highly politicized notions of child abuse, and other sources of bias (see Miletski 1995, for a long list of definitions of "incest" used by practitioners; and Turner and Maryanski 2005, 54–65, for a discussion of the methodological problems with data on incest). Yet, in looking at all of the data, some patterns are clear (Turner and Maryanski 2005, 65–79; Fromuth and Burkart 1989; Fritz, Stoll, and Wagner 1981; Finkehor and Russell 1984; Finkelhor and Hotaling 1984; Finkelhor, Hotaling, Lewis, and Smith 1990). First, mother-son incest appears to be the least frequent form of incest and, second, the only form of incest that leads to psychotic behaviors for the younger participant (the son). This suggests that incest in this dyad is crossing a hard-wired avoidance, much like that among chimpanzee sons and mothers, plus the most powerful tenet of the incest (i.e., mother-son incest is the most tabooed in virtually all societies). Perhaps the Freudian dynamics outlined by Fox are at work in making this taboo so strong, but we think that the combination of violating hard-wired avoidance between mothers and sons, coupled with violation of a powerful cultural taboo, is sufficient to cause severe psychotic responses among some sons. Third, stepfather and stepdaughter incest is the most common, followed by father-daughter incest, with daughters revealing anxiety disorders rather than debilitating psychosis. Fourth, sibling incest is the third most common, but incest among step-siblings may be as common as stepdaughter-stepfather incest. Moreover, father abuse of sons (physically or sexually) increases the likelihood that sons will sexually abuse their sisters. It also appears that incest is more common between siblings who are separated physically and culturally. If they cannot play and roughhouse as young children, the Westermarck effect is undermined—as Fox had emphasized in his analysis of sibling incest. The Westermarck effect is powerful, but only as long as children grew up in a cohesive environment with long-term physical contact. For example, in the early Israeli collective settlements where children lived together away from their parents' residential space and where parents actively encouraged romantic liaisons between kibbutz children, neither love affairs nor marriages occurred among individuals raised together in the same peer group (Spiro 1958; Talmon 1964) Indeed, a tally of the marriage records in 211 kibbutzim—2,769 of them—revealed only 14 cases where peer group members married each other, and these all occurred when one of the parties moved into the Kibbutz after puberty, when the Westermarck effect could not have taken hold (Shepher 1971). Later, when kibbutz settlements underwent major ideological changes (see Aviezer et al. 1994) and began to increase parent-offspring interaction and, thereby, to reconstruct the nuclear family (even so far as having children sleep in their parents' housing), sexual attraction between peers increased as socialization practices shifted to a daytime boarding school arrangement (see Maryanski, Sanderson, and Russell forthcoming for a discussion).

These patterns of incest might be what would be expected if the hominin ancestors of humans, who had to get better organized or die, were like chimpanzees with their hard-wired sexual avoidance between mothers and sons, sexual avoidance among siblings because of the Westermarck effect, female transfer at puberty from the natal community, and unknown paternity.[8] The hard-wired sexual avoidance in the mother-son dyad and the Westermarck effect on siblings could continue to work as selection pushed for a nucleated family structure. But for the father-daughter dyad, there would be no bioprogrammers for sexual avoidance, with the result that sex would be most likely in this dyad and require formation of an incest taboo to reduce sexual contact between fathers and daughters.

Inbreeding and the Incest Taboo

The need for the taboo would be all too evident when sexual partners sharing 50 percent of their genes have offspring. A very high proportion of offspring of these matings evidence obvious deformities at birth, such as cleft palate, encephalitis, retardation, and other physical deformities (Turner and Maryanski 2005, 53–81). Indeed, sexual relations among more distally connected kin, such as first cousins (who share only 12.5 percent of their genes, produce deformities in a significant percentage of offspring, although these deformities are not as severe or prevalent as in the case with offspring sharing 50 percent of their genes with a parent). Thus, late hominins and certainly humans would understand the dangers of sexual intercourse between closely related kin, and as both the cortical and subcortical portions of the brain grew, more culturally based taboos evolved and regulated intra-family conduct.

At first, the language of emotions—the fear and sadness of deformed offspring—coupled with emotionally charged sanctions against inbreeding may have been able to reduce rates of incest among hominins without the capacity to use verbal language. The language of emotions may have been sufficient, as sex was becoming so emotionally charged with the growing size of the septum. This emotional protolanguage may have begun as early as *Homo habilis*. Of course, with greater intelligence, auditory language, and culture, the taboo could become much more explicit and powerful with late hominins, perhaps beginning with *Homo erectus* but maybe only with *Homo sapiens*.

Selection pressures to reduce father-daughter sexual relations, coupled with powerful emotions such as love, attaching males to females and their offspring, to form the first nuclear families of hominins must have been intense because a nuclear family provides a stable organizational base for reproduction and production (through the division of labor between males and females in hunting-gathering bands). These selection pressures focused on the father-daughter potential for incest (given the lack of bioprogrammers generating sexual avoidance), but as the taboo began to emerge it would have extended to all close inbreeding, thus giving mother-son avoidance a cultural basis to reinforce the neurological wiring for avoidance and, at the same time, reinforcing in a cultural taboo the sexual avoidance between siblings generated by the Westermarck effect.

For the ancestors of humans to survive on the African savanna, they had to become better organized. Maryanski's cladistic analysis reveals that the last common ancestor to humans and extant apes was a self-contained hominoid, much like the orangutan, and mobile within a home range; and except for mother attachments to her prepuberty offspring, this ancestor had few strong ties and, hence, no intergenerational continuity in social structure. Given this ancestral legacy, early *Homo* living on a predator-ridden savanna had to get organized or die, as did most species of apes over the last ten million years. The last ancestor to hominins and our closest living relative, the common chimpanzee, had some footing for more organization as revealed in extant chimpanzee societies. This initial base of ties, revolving around strong ties between mother and her son, brothers, and selected male friends, is probably what allowed early *Homo* in open woodlands to survive. To build on this social structure required, however, that the two structures of all nomadic hunter-gatherers had to evolve—the band and nuclear family.

Our portrayal of the horde was perhaps the beginning of the band, but what of the nuclear family? Two hard-wired biological programmers for sexual avoidance exist among chimpanzees—the Westermarck effect for siblings and the avoidance of sexual contact between mothers and sons—and so these would typically keep the red light of incest from being lit for these dyads in nuclear families. The problem was sexual avoidance between promiscuous fathers and their female offspring, once selection increased the intensity and range of emotions. Now, males felt new emotions—perhaps the beginning of love and the attachment that it brings—for mates, but what was to keep these emotions from being transferred to female offspring? Thus, making hominins more emotional so as to form the nuclear family may also have made them more lustful, thereby setting into motion selection for a new mechanism of sexual avoidance between fathers and daughters. This mechanism may have initially been emotional, programmed into the language of emotions that was emerging in the hominin line. Seeing deformed offspring would generate strong emotional reactions that in turn would lead to proto-normative systems built upon emotions—revulsion of deformity and sanctioning of those relations generating this deformity. But this kind of quasi-taboo would take on even more power when articulated verbally and acknowledged, especially if emotions were attached to the moral codes against intra-family sexual relations and to the sanctions that would ensue when these relations occurred.

The evolution of the emotional capacities for guilt and shame—probably unique to human primates—would only give these moral codes against incest more power. And even though there were bio-programmers in place for sexual avoidance between mothers and their sons as well as siblings, a layer of moral codes against inbreeding would add power to these bioprogrammers. But for the father-daughter dyad of the family, where such bioprogrammers did not exist because they were not needed when paternity was unknown and females left their natal communities at puberty, the entire burden of sexual avoidance falls on the moral codes. Thus, without the one-two punch of biological and cultural programmers for sexual avoidance, it should not be surprising that incest between fathers and daughters may have been common among hominins, just as it is today in human families. And given the dramatically increased pathologies in some dysfunctional contemporary families (e.g., drug and alcohol abuse, physical neglect and abuse, spousal abuse, spousal conflict, and the like), even bioprogrammers can be disrupted, to say nothing of cultural codes. Still, all that was necessary for hominins was a significant reduction of inbreeding, especially among fathers and daughters, to enable bands of nuclear families to survive in open-country savanna.

Today, we must live with the simple fact that, for all its veneration, the nuclear family is not a natural form of organizing reproduction. Humans are still evolved apes who still share 99 percent of their genes with chimpanzees. We should expect, therefore, for incest to occur and for its consequences—inbreeding depression and deformity, coupled with severe psychological problems for the victims of incest—because the incest taboo will often prove ineffective in controlling sexual avoidance.

Robin Fox brought together a rich mosaic of concepts and data from diverse fields to offer what, at the time, was the most sophisticated theory on the origins of the incest taboo. Its basic tenets are essentially still correct over three decades since *The Red Lamp of Incest* first appeared. We not only learned from this brilliant book; we took most of its argument and recast it in minor, but perhaps critical or at least useful, ways. Works in the social sciences have very short "half-lives," but Fox's work on the origin of the incest taboo has stood the test of time. For he brought together new insights along with some of the key ideas from earlier thinkers on incest and, as we have tried to do in our *Incest: Origins of the Taboo* (2005), recast them in light of new data that was unavailable to Fox and to those earlier thinkers who inspired his great synthesis.

This is how science should work, especially explanatory science; each generation takes existing explanations and adds to them. The result is a more powerful explanation with the steady accumulation of knowledge. As John McLennan, who coined the term "exogamy" and who was among the first scholars to propose the horde arrangement and to trace the origin of human society wrote, "Whether we have hit the truth or not, we trust we have at least been preparing the way for those who in the fullness of time will reach it" (McLennan 1869: 408).

Notes

1. The name, Fox says, came from a poem by Jaques Prévert: "le lampion rouge de l'inceste." A "lampion" is small fairy light.
2. Chimpanzees (*Pan*) and orangutans (*Pongo*) are characterized as having promiscuous mating systems, while the gorilla (*Gorilla*) is associated with a polygamous system. The leader silverback gorilla may be the favored partner for females, but up to four adult males may reside in a gorilla band and adult females can mate with any of them or move on to another band or a lone male—at will. Moreover, the bonds between a silverback male and an adult female are transient and linked to the age of her dependent offspring and her reproductive success. Gorillas then, while technically not promiscuous, have a very loose polygamous arrangement that is very different than a human mating system—even a human polygamous system that is still anchored in a stable arrangement of bonded pairs.
3. The plausibility of the LCA reconstruction was tested with both the relatedness and regularity hypotheses and other strict procedures of this powerful reconstruction procedure that is applicable to any comparative information (see Platnick and Cameron 1977, and Hennig 1966). The control sister group for our cladistic analysis was a sample of well-studied *Cercopithecoidea*, who are, of course, the closest sister taxon to *Hominoidea*.
4. Our findings are in line with other researchers who used different methods to reconstruct the LCA but had similar conclusions. Richard Wrangham

(1987) proposed that ape female dispersal at puberty and a lack of adult female-female bonds was part of an ancestral suite of traits inherited from the LCA population. Foley and Lee (1989) also concur in their reconstruction of early hominin social structure that the lack of adult female-female alliances in extant apes (which, in contrast, is the bedrock for monkey networks) had to rest on male-male bonds and a stabilization of female-male bonds.

5. We should emphasize that a widespread pattern of sexual avoidance is found among virtually all primate species with a variety of strategies to limit close inbreeding between mother and son and between brother and sister.

6. Social species typically build on the social structure they inherit. It is not much of a stretch to assume that savanna-dwelling hominins began with a chimpanzee-like social structure (see Foley and Lee 1989). The alternative model would be a baboon model that is underpinned by a core of kinship-based matrilines. But it would take an act of evolutionary gymnastics for selection forces to undertake such fundamental changes as a shift to a matrilineal kinship system, as it would require a reversal of the female transfer pattern (a rare dispersal pattern but common to all apes) and a weakening of male-male bonds. Selection is conservative and usually takes the easiest pathway to adaptation by working first with what is available. Moreover, radical "macromutations" are very rarely favorable as they disrupt complex genetic associations, and especially so in a mammal as complex as a hominoid. What can be advantageous are small point mutations (see Fisher 1930; Ridley 1996).

7. The female-female ties among *Pan paniscus* are not included here. Bonobos who branched away from the widespread common chimpanzee about 2–3 million years ago comprise a small, isolated population living in the Zaire River basin. While bonobos share female dispersal at puberty and a community organization with common chimpanzees, unrelated females cooperate more than common female chimpanzees. But greater female-female sociality rests on what Kano (1992, 190–92) considers "comparable to copulation between female partners" as they habitually rub their genitals together (i.e., GG rubbing) in what appears to be a stress-releasing mechanism to promote greater tolerance among unrelated females and reduce food competition. This bizarre character is an evolution novelty unique to bonobos and does function to promote greater network density. Our network and cladistic analysis, however, focused on the congruence of deeper-seated affect ties (for discussions on bonobos bonds, see Hohmann et al. 1999, and Hohmann and Fruth 2000).

8. Recently, the Westermarck effect has been observed among chimpanzee brothers and sisters (see Turner and Maryanski 2005, 115ff).

References

Aviezer, Ora, Marinus H. Ijzendoorn, Abraham Sagi, and Carlo Schuengel. 1994. "Children of the Dream Revisited: 70 Years of Collective Early Child Care in Israeli Kibbutzim." *Psychological Bulletin* 116:99–116.

Collins, Randall. 2004. *Interactional Ritual*. Princeton, NJ: Princeton University Press.

Eccles, J. C. 1989. *Evolution of the Brain: Creation of Self*. London: Routledge.

Enhard, W. N. 2002a. "Molecular Evolution of TOXP2, a Gene Involved in Speech and Language." *Nature* 418:869–72.

Enhard, W. N., et al. 2002b. "Intra- and Interspecific Variation in Primate Gene Expression Patterns." *Science* 296:340–42.

Finkelhor, D., G. Hotaling, I. A. Lewis, and C. Smith. 1990. "Sexual Abuse in a National Survey of Adult Men and Women: Prevalence, Characteristics and Risk Factors." *Child Abuse and Neglect* 14:19–28.

Finkelhor, D., and G. T. Hotaling. 1984. "Sexual Abuse in the National Incidence Study of Child Abuse and Neglect: An Appraisal." *Child Abuse and Neglect* 8:23–33.

Fisher, R. A. 1930. *The Genetical Theory of Natural Selection.* Oxford University Press.

Fox, Robin. 1962. "Sibling Incest." *British Journal of Sociology* 13:128–50.

———. 1967. *Kinship and Marriage.* London, Penguin.

———. 1980. *The Red Lamp of Incest.* New York: Dutton.

Foley, R. A., and P. C. Lee. 1989. "Finite Social Space, Evolutionary Pathways and Reconstructing Hominid Behavior." *Science* 243:901–6.

Fromuth, M. E., and B. R. Burkhart. 1989. "Long-Term Psychological Correlates of Childhood Sexual Abuse in Two Samples of College Men." *Child Abuse and Neglect* 13:533–42.

Fritz, G. S., K. Stoll, and N. N. Wagner. 1981. "A Comparison of Males and Females Who Were Sexually Molested as Children." *Journal of Sex and Marital Therapy* 7:54–59.

Geschwind, N. 1965a. "Disconnection Syndromes in Animals and Man, Part I." *Brain* 88:237–94.

———. 1965b. "Disconnection Syndromes in Animals and Man, Part II." *Brain* 88:585–644.

Geschwind, Norman, and Antonio Damasio. 1984: "The Neural Basis of Language." *Annual Review of Neuroscience* 7:127–147.

Goodall, Jane. 1986. *The Chimpanzees of Gombe: Patterns of Behavior.* Cambridge, MA: Belknap Press.

Jennig, W. 1966. *Phylogenetic Systematics.* Urbana: University of Illinois Press.

Hohmann, G., and B. Fruth. 2000. "Use and Function of Genital Contacts among Female Bonobos." *Animal Behaviour* 60:107–20.

Hohmann, G., U. Gerloff, D. Tautz, and B. Fruth. 1999. "Social Bond and Genetic Ties: Kinship, Association and Affiliation in a Community of Bonobos (Pan Paniscus)." *Behaviour* 136:1219–35.

Kano, T. 1992. *The Last Ape: Pygmy Chimpanzee Behavior and Ecology.* Stanford, CA: Stanford University Press.

Lim, M., Z. Wang, D. E. Olazabal, X. Ren, E. F. Terwilliger, and L. J. Young. 2004. "Enhanced Partner Preference in a Promiscuous Species by Manipulating the Expression of a Single Gene." *Nature* 429:754–7.

Lucas, D., V. Reynolds, C. Boesch, and L. Vigilant. 2005. "To What Extent Does Living in a Group Mean Living with Kin?" *Molecular Ecology* 14:2181–96.

Maryanski, Alexandra. 1992. "The Last Ancestor: An Ecological-Network Model on the Origins of Human Sociality." *Advances in Human Ecology* 2:1–32.

———. 1987. "African Ape Social Structure: Is There Strength in Weak Ties?" *Social Networks* 9:191–215.

———. 1995. "African Ape Social Networks: A Blueprint for Reconstructing Early Hominid Social Structure." In *Archaeology of Human Ancestry*, edited by J. Steele and S. Shennan, 67–90. London: Routledge.

Maryanski, Alexandra, and Jonathan Turner. 1992b. *The Social Cage*. Stanford, CA: Stanford University Press.

Maryanski, Alexandra, Stephen Sanderson, and Raymond Russell. Forthcoming. "The Israeli Kibbutzim and the Westermarck Hypothesis." *American Journal of Sociology*.

McLennan, J. F. [1869–1870] 1896. "The Worship of Plants and Animals." In *Studies in Ancient History*;72–108 London: Macmillan.

Miletski, H. 1995. *Mother-Son Incest: The Unthinkable Taboo; An Overview of Findings*. Brandon, VT: Safer Society Press.

Mitani, John, David Watts, and Martin Muller. 2002. "Recent Developments in the Study of Wild Chimpanzee Behavior." *Evolutionary Anthropology* 11:9–25.

Pipping, Knut. 1944. "Who Reads Westermarck Today." *The British Journal Sociology* 35:315–32.

Platnick, N. I., and H. D. Cameron. 1977. "Cladistic Methods in Textual, Linguistic, Phylogenetic Analysis." *Systematic Zoology* 26:380–5.

Pusey, Anne. 2005. "Inbreeding Avoidance in Primates." In *Inbreeding, Incest and the Incest Taboo*, edited by A. P. Wolf and W. H. Durham. Stanford, CA: Stanford University Press.

———. 1980. "Inbreeding Avoidance in Chimpanzees." *Animal Behavior* 28:543–52.

Ridley, Mark. 1996. *Evolution*. Cambridge, MA: Blackwell Science.

Shepher, Joseph. 1971. *Self-Imposed Incest Avoidance and Exogamy in Second Generation Kibbutz Adults*. PhD dissertation. Rutgers University.

Spiro, Melford. 1958. *Children of the Kibbutz*. Cambridge, MA: Harvard University Press.

Stephan, H. 1983. "Evolutionary Trends in Limbic Structures." *Neuroscience and Biobehavioral Review* 7:367–74.

Stephan, H., and O. J. Andy. 1969. "Quantitative Comparative Neuroanatomy of Primates: An Attempt at Phylogenetic Interpretation." *Annals of the New York Academy of Science* 167:370–87.

———. 1977. "Quantitative Comparison of the Amygdala in Insectivores and Primates." *Acta Antomica* 98:130–53.

Talmon, Yonina. 1964. "Mate Selection on Collective Settlements." *American Sociological Review* 29:491–508.

Turner, Jonathan. 2000. *On the Origins of Human Emotions: A Sociological Inquiry into the Evolution of Human Affect*. Stanford, CA: Stanford University Press.

———. 2002. *Face to Face: Toward a Theory of Interpersonal Behavior*. Palo Alto, CA: Stanford University Press.

———. 2010. *Theoretical Principles of Sociology, Volume 2: Microdynamics*. New York: Springer.

Turner, Jonathan, and Alexandra Maryanski. 2005. *Incest: Origins of the Taboo.* Boulder, CO: Paradigm Press.

———. 2008. *On the Origin of Societies by Natural Selection.* Boulder, CO: Paradigm Publishers.

Watts, David, and John Mitani. 2001. "Boundary Patrols and Intergroup Encounters in Wild Chimpanzees." *Behaviour* 138:299–327.

Westermarck, Edward. A. 1891. *The History of Human Marriage.* London: Macmillan.

———. [1891] 1922. *The History of Human Marriage.* 3 vols. New York: Allerton.

Wrangham, R. W. 1987. *The Evolution of Human Behavior: Primate Models.* Edited by W. Kinzey. Albany: State University of New York Press.

9

Darwin and Cousin Marriage in England

Adam Kuper

"Kinship is to anthropology what logic is to philosophy or the nude is to art," Robin Fox famously remarked. "It is the basic discipline of the subject." This aphorism appears in his *Kinship and Marriage*. First published in 1967, and reprinted with astonishing regularity, this audacious combination of textbook and theoretical treatise has triumphantly passed T. S. Eliot's definition of a classic, for it is still widely read after forty years. *Kinship and Marriage* introduced generations of students into the study of this intricate field, to which Robin himself has made a series of major contributions, above all, perhaps, on the questions of incest avoidance and cousin marriage, and always from a Darwinian perspective.

Charles Darwin had been thinking about marriage—although not to anyone in particular—since returning to England after his five-year voyage on the *Beagle*. In July 1838, he took a sheet of paper and wrote, "This is the Question" at the head, and divided it into two columns. "Marry" he wrote at the head of one column, "Not Marry" at the head of the other. He then laid out a balance sheet of arguments for and against.[1]

The arguments in favor were solid, if unromantic:

> Children—(if it Please God)—Constant companion, (& friend in old age) who will feel interested in one,—object to be beloved & played with—better than a dog anyhow.—Home, & someone to take care of house—Charms of music & female chit-chat—These things good for one's health.—but terrible loss of time.—

Yet the bachelor life had its charms:

> Freedom to go where one liked—choice of Society & little of it. Conversation of clever men at clubs—Not forced to visit relatives, & to bend in every trifle.—

And marriage had its drawbacks:

> —to have the expense & anxiety of children—perhaps quarrelling—Loss of time.—cannot read in the Evenings—fatness & idleness—Anxiety & responsibility—less money for books &c—if many children forced to gain one's bread—(But then it is very bad for ones health to work too much)

And where would he make a home?

> Perhaps my wife wont like London; then the sentence is banishment & degradation into indolent, idle fool—

But the alternative was dismal:

> Imagine living all one's day solitarily in smoky dirty London House—Only picture to yourself a nice soft wife on a sofa with good fire, & books & music perhaps—Compare this vision with the dingy reality of Grt. Marlbro' St." At the bottom of the "Marry" column he set down his conclusion: "Marry—Mary—Marry Q. E. D.

Then he moved on to the next question:

> It being proved necessary to Marry
> When? Soon or Late

On this he had consulted his father, Dr. Robert Darwin:

> The Governor says soon for otherwise bad if one has children—one's character is more flexible—one's feelings more lively & if one does not marry soon, one misses so much good pure happiness"—"No putting if off then." "Never mind my boy—Cheer up—One cannot live this solitary life, with groggy old age, friendless & cold, & childless staring one in ones face, already beginning to wrinkle—never mind, trust to chance—keep a sharp look out—There is many a happy slave—".[2]

That settled, another very important question had to be faced. Whom should he marry? Lodging with his bachelor brother, Erasmus, in London, Charles had a few diffident flirtations. His father worried that he showed an interest in the dauntingly intellectual Harriet Martineau. But Charles quickly decided that he wanted to marry a daughter of his favorite uncle, his mother's brother, Jos Wedgwood. Only one of Jos's daughters was unmarried and about the right age. This was the youngest Wedgwood daughter, Emma, who was a year older than Charles.

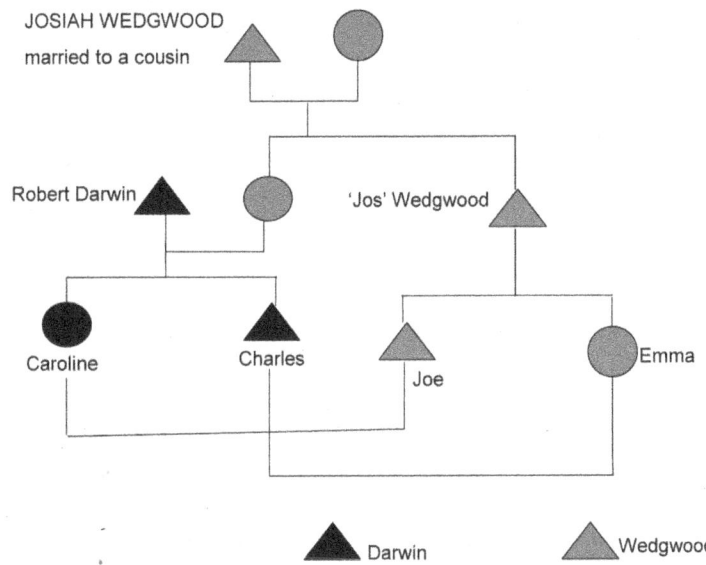

Figure 9.1. Darwin's marriage.

Emma was not only his first cousin, she was also his sister-in-law. Her oldest brother, Joe, had married Charles's sister, Caroline, in 1837.

Other romances had been rumored between the young Wedgwoods and Darwins. According to Charles's sisters—who kept him up-to-date as he voyaged around the world—their elder brother, Erasmus, had shown an interest in Emma as well, and perhaps also in her two older sisters.[3] And three of Emma's brothers had been very attentive to Darwin's sister Susan.

Charles's courtship was awkward. He nerved himself to visit Emma at the Wedgwood home at Maer later that same July. They had a good talk, but he did not commit himself. Then in the first week of November, anxious, headachy, he returned and proposed. Emma was astonished that it all happened so quickly. Rather to Charles's surprise, she accepted at once, but they were both still so overwrought when they confronted the family that one of the Wedgwood aunts was convinced that Emma must have turned him down.[4]

When Darwin wrote to his Cambridge mentor, Charles Lyell, to announce his engagement, he emphasized the family links:

> The lady is my cousin, Miss Emma Wedgwood, the sister of Hensleigh Wedgwood [Darwin's special friend at Cambridge, well-known to

Lyell], and [Emma is also the sister] of the elder brother who married my sister, so we are connected by manifold ties, besides on my part by the most sincere love and hearty gratitude to her for accepting such a one as myself.[5]

The engagement did not come as a surprise to either family. "I knew you would be a Mrs Darwin," one of her psychic Wedgwood aunts wrote to Emma, adding that she was grateful to Charles for saving her from Erasmus.[6] Emma's father—Charles's uncle—wept with joy when Charles asked his permission for the marriage. "I could have parted with Emma to no one for whom I would so soon and so entirely feel as a father," he wrote to Robert Darwin, "and I am happy in believing that Charles entertains the kindest feelings for his uncle-father."[7] It was a match, Emma herself remarked, "that every soul has been making for us, so we could not have helped it if we had not liked it ourselves."[8]

They were married January 29, 1839. John Allen Wedgwood, vicar of Maer, officiated. He was first cousin to both Charles and Emma.

When Emma Wedgwood's friend, Georgina Tollet, heard of the engagement, she remarked, "It is very like a marriage of Miss Austen's."[9] This was not altogether accurate. "The two had no obstacles to overcome," notes Janet Browne, Darwin's biographer, "no delicate flirtations at picnics or dances, no misunderstandings wrenching the heartstrings."[10]

Yet it is true that Jane Austen's novels repeatedly probe and analyze alliances between cousins, most famously in *Mansfield Park* (1814). The principal characters, Fanny and Edmund, are not only children of two sisters. Like another pair of lovers in the novel, Colonel Brandon and his cousin, they have been brought up in the same house, almost as brother and sister. But Fanny and Edmund marry each other in the end. It is hardly surprising that Emma Wedgwood wrote to Darwin, three weeks before their wedding, "I am reading *Mansfield Park* which I find very suitable."[11]

Jane Austen was not unusual in her interest in romances between cousins. Cousin marriage was a recurrent theme in novels published from the late eighteenth century to the end of the nineteenth century. And it reflected the practice of the rising bourgeoisie. Free to mix, unchaperoned, cousins easily fell in love. They often married, usually with the approval, often with the encouragement, of their families. Cousin marriage "was a way of safeguarding the domestic circle against change," Claudia Nelson remarks. "In a society that prized companionate marriage and tended to be suspicious of the outsider, keeping matrimony within the family helped to ensure that partners would understand each other and get along with their in-laws."[12]

For similar reasons, brothers-in-law and sisters-in-law made suitable marriage partners. Emma Wedgwood was not only Charles Darwin's cousin but also his sister-in-law. Two of Jane Austen's brothers married two Lloyd sisters, and her novels feature a number of similar arrangements. In *Emma*, the heroine marries Mr. Knightley, who is the elder brother of her sister's husband. The heroine of *Sense and Sensibility*, Elinor, marries her brother-in-law, Edward Ferrars.

More generally, there was a preference for marriages that sustained an intimate and valued relationship between two families. And marriages bound whole families together. "I protest against the opinions of those sentimental people who think that marriage concerns only the two principals," wrote Charles Darwin's cousin, Francis Galton, "it has in reality the wider effect of an alliance between each of them and a new family."[13] If a marriage between two families paid off, for any reason, yielding financial ties, or simply friendship and intimacy, there was an incentive to reinforce the connection by further marriages. A network of marriages might weave together not two but three, or even more, families, sometimes giving rise to tightly knit clans, such as the Wedgwood-Darwins.

The marriage of first cousins, forbidden by Catholic doctrine, had been legalized in England in 1540. Other Protestant countries also allowed cousins to marry on the grounds that there was nothing against it in the Scriptures. But although royal families had always favored cousin marriages—and the Pope gave dispensations to Catholic monarchs for such marriages—the marriage of cousins was unusual in England until the nineteenth century. In the eighteenth century, only just over 1 percent of aristocratic marriages were between first cousins. In the nineteenth century, however, cousin marriages became much more common, particularly among the upper-middle classes in England. "I have received some statistics from the R[egistrar] G[eneral]," George Darwin noted in 1874 in a letter to his father, Charles Darwin, "& find that cousin marriages are at least 3 times as frequent in our rank as in the lower!"[14] Among people born into the great bourgeois clans of nineteenth-century England, like the Darwin-Wedgwoods, more than one marriage in ten was with a first or second cousin. Marriages between brothers- and sisters-in-law were equally common. Taken together, roughly one marriage in five was within the family circle.

Why did relatives begin to marry with such frequency? Marriages to one another's sisters bound business partners together. Cousins might well be encouraged to marry if they stood to inherit shares in a family concern. But would a bourgeois marry—or be pushed into a marriage—simply to keep the wealth in the family? The cliché was current, and it was sometimes true enough. Yet while the financial side of a marriage was obviously of special importance in business families, even businessmen could seldom dictate the marriage choices of their children. And kinship counted for something in itself. Fathers might emphasize economic considerations, but mothers and sisters were more susceptible to the claims of family. In any case, while material and emotional considerations might pull in different directions, quite often they reinforced each other. As David Sabean remarks, "The flows of sentiment and money operated in much the same channels."[15] Nor was a family business necessarily involved. Marriages between cousins or brothers- and sisters-in-law were just as common in families of doctors, lawyers, and clergymen, or in the Anglo-Indian dynasties of high civil servants, judges, and engineers.

This pattern of marriage came to an end, with the long nineteenth century itself, in the catastrophe of the First World War. But it had lasted for some hundred and fifty years and shaped the new bourgeoisie.

Josiah Wedgwood, the patriarch of the Wedgwood clan, started work at the age of fourteen as an apprentice to his brother Thomas. He wanted to marry a cousin, but his wife's father, a particularly successful potter, thought that his daughter could do better for herself. Josiah was made to wait for years until he could match "guinea for guinea" the £4,000 that his uncle planned to settle on his daughter.[16]

Josiah eventually accumulated this steep bride-price and married his cousin in 1764. He went on to become the most successful of all the potters in Staffordshire. Beginning his career with a legacy of £10, he was worth half a million pounds at the end of his life.[17] It was well-earned. He innovated, experimented with new processes and materials, organized his production along modern lines, and introduced fresh designs. His factory at Etruria made Wedgwood pottery world-famous.

And it was very much a family business. Josiah's brother John became his London representative. The son of a widowed sister was taken on as bookkeeper and was made a partner alongside Josiah's three sons. As supervisor of the works, he hired a cousin. When the business began to stretch his resources, Josiah leased one of his works to another cousin, young Joseph Wedgwood, who married the daughter of another sister of Josiah's.

Yet Josiah's children did not marry cousins. The youngest, Tom, a bohemian, a dabbler in drugs, and an associate of the Lake Poets, died young and unmarried. Josiah's older sons, John and "Jos," married two sisters. Their father-in-law was a wealthy and tyrannical country gentleman, John Bartlett Allen, "domineering and possessed of a vile disposition, quarrelling with his neighbors and making life practically intolerable for his two sons and nine daughters."[18] The Allen sisters, however, were spirited and charming, and very fond of one another.

An alliance with a county family such as the Allens was a step up socially for the Wedgwoods, but Josiah Wedgwood was happier when his favorite daughter, Susannah, married Robert Darwin, the son of his close friend, Erasmus Darwin. Erasmus Darwin was a doctor, a natural philosopher, and a poet. An expansive and unconventional eighteenth-century figure, he was suspected of atheism, and after the death of his wife, he lived openly with a mistress who was also his servant.

Erasmus Darwin's son Robert became a particular friend of his brother-in-law, Jos Wedgwood, the eldest son of Josiah. The two men had an understanding that Jos's eldest son, yet another Josiah Wedgwood, known as "Joe," would marry Robert Darwin's daughter, Caroline, who was, of course, his cousin. Joe was in no hurry to get married, but he went along with his father's wishes, eventually. His marriage to Caroline Darwin was celebrated in 1837. He was forty-two years old, and Caroline was thirty-seven. Obviously they were not slaves to passion, nor were they simply being pushed around by their fathers. But their marriage did make excellent financial sense. Dr. Robert Darwin was not only a prosperous physician: he also operated as a private banker, and he had lent a lot of money to Jos. The two men were involved in joint speculations in canals and later in railways. And Robert Darwin advised Jos on most of his financial arrangements, including those within the family. Because Joe was in line to take over the Etruria pottery works, his marriage to Caroline Darwin would ensure that important debts and obligations were kept within the family. This may have been a consideration for their fathers.

Jos was also perfectly happy when, two years later, his daughter Emma reinforced the alliance with the Robert Darwins by marrying Charles Darwin. Charles had always been a favorite with his uncle, with whom he used to go shooting at Maer, where he was particularly welcome because his Wedgwood cousins were rather sedentary. (Charles called Maer "Bliss Castle.")[19] And it was Jos who had persuaded a reluctant Robert Darwin to allow Charles to sail on the *Beagle*.[20] Like their fathers they were friends, united by exchanges. When the engagement was announced, Jos told Robert Darwin, "You lately gave up a daughter—it is my turn now."[21]

The two fathers made a settlement that allowed the young couple to live independently. "I propose to do for Emma what I did for Charlotte and for three of my sons," Jos Wedgwood wrote to Robert Darwin. He planned to "give a bond for £5,000, and to allow her £400 a year, as long as my income will supply it, which I have no reason for thinking will not be as long as I live."[22] Robert Darwin contributed shares worth £10,000 that provided an income of some £600 a year. (The young couple therefore began life with an annual unearned income of around $100,000 a year in today's terms.)[23] Charles's brother Erasmus and Emma's brother Joe were appointed executors of the trust set up for the couple.[24] The fact that Emma was marrying her cousin made no difference to the marriage settlement. Jos made similar provision for all his married children, some of whom married cousins, while others did not.

Six of Jos's nine children married, four of them to first cousins. At least two of these cousin marriages were poor financial risks, and they were resisted by prudent fathers. John Wedgwood had been Jos's partner in the pottery. But he was a hopeless businessman, so Jos eased him out. John then went into banking, failed, and had to be bailed out by Jos. Jos was not best pleased when Henry, the least promising of his own sons, married John's daughter, Jessie Wedgwood, the beauty of her generation, although Jessie was his niece twice over. She was his brother's daughter. Moreover, his wife and Jessie's mother were sisters. Jessie herself had her doubts about the match. But her mother and her Allen aunts were in favor, and she eventually capitulated.[25]

Hensleigh, another of Jos's sons, fell in love with his mother's sister's daughter, Fanny Mackintosh. Fanny's mother, a third Allen sister, and yet another of Jos's sisters-in-law, had married the rising statesman James Mackintosh. Mackintosh opposed the marriage. He was reluctant to see his daughter leave home, and he thought—as it turned out, rightly—that Hensleigh's worldly prospects were poor. Once again the Allen sisters caballed, and Mackintosh eventually gave

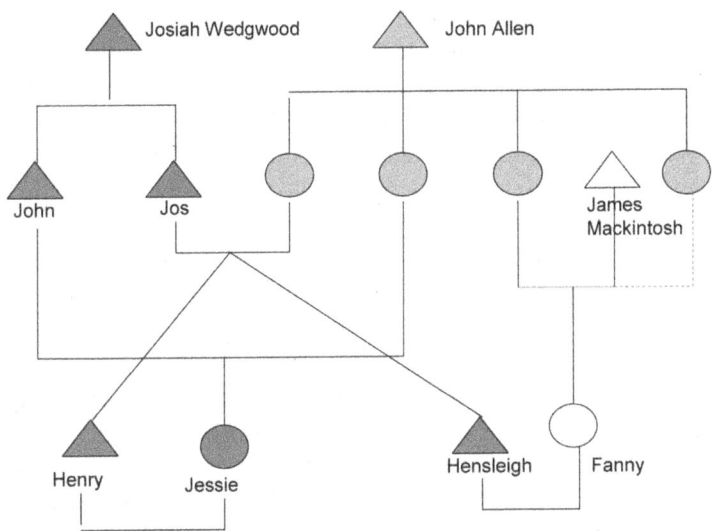

Figure 9.2. The Wedgwoods and the Allens: The Third Generation.

in. (A generation later, Hensleigh's daughter's stepdaughter married Charles Darwin's unpromising son, Horace, again despite the objections of her father.)

So fathers generally paid close attention to financial considerations when their children married, but this was not a necessary reason for cousin marriage, certainly not in the Darwin-Wedgwood clan. Nor was it a sufficient reason, even within the Wedgwood family concern. When Josiah grew old, his cousin Thomas Byerley effectively became the manager of the Etruria works. On Thomas's death, the Wedgwoods took on his son Josiah Byerley as manager. This was at least partly because the young Byerley was the executor of his father's will. They would have to deal with him over Byerley's share in the firm and his debts to it. Yet no marriage was mooted between the Byerleys and their (much grander) Wedgwood cousins.

Finally, in families like the Wedgwoods, fathers might not have the last word on the marriages of their daughters, let alone their sons. A determined pair like the Allen sisters often carried the day.

Families that intermarried over the generations virtually fused together. "You've none of you ever seen a Darwin who wasn't mostly Wedgwood," one of Charles Darwin's sons told his daughter. "Rather sadly," she thought, "as of a dying strain."[26] Outsiders who married into these close-knit clans were immediately enveloped in a web of emotional relationships. When his wife died, James Mackintosh very nearly married yet a fourth Allen sister, Francis, although she was, of course, his deceased wife's sister. She was very much in love with him and acted as his hostess for the rest of his life.[27]

Jos Wedgwood's daughter Charlotte married a clergyman, Charles Langton. After her death, he remarried—to one of Charles Darwin's sisters. To put it another way, his two wives were sisters-in-law to each other: indeed, doubly so, as two of the Wedgwood siblings had married two of the Darwin siblings. They were also, of course, first cousins.[28]

In the inner circles of the clan, relationships could become extremely complicated. Charles Darwin's older brother, Erasmus, never married. His closest friend was his cousin Hensleigh Wedgwood, who had finally overcome James Mackintosh's resistance and married Fanny. Erasmus took to seeing Fanny and her children several times a week. They sometimes went on holidays or trips alone together. Fanny came to stay at his house to nurse him when he fell ill. He took to referring to her as "Missis" and "the wife" and spoke of "our daughters." Fanny's marriage nevertheless survived, and Hensleigh and Erasmus remained friends.[29]

In the next generation, Godfrey Wedgwood, son of Hensleigh's brother Francis, fell in love with Hensleigh's daughter Effie. She rejected him, and Godfrey married someone else. But he pined for Effie, and even confided to his pregnant wife that he remained in love with his cousin. When his wife died in childbirth, he proposed to Effie again. Now a spinster in her midforties, she turned him down once more and almost immediately married Lord Farrer of Abington. But she urged Godfrey to marry her younger sister, Hope, who was in her midthirties. Despite family worries that the relationship between the sisters would be ruined, they remained very close to one another. Hope had a child whom she insisted on sharing with Effie, who was childless, saying she would have two mothers. Effie spoke always of "our child."[30]

Yet although cousin marriage was so common, by the 1860s, medical men were beginning to worry about the possible malign consequences of inbreeding. "I'm not quite sure that it's a good thing for cousins to marry," remarks Dr. Crofts in Trollope's *The Small House of Allington*, published in 1863. "They do, you know, very often," he is reminded, "and it suits some family arrangements."[31] To be sure, the doctor had a personal interest in the matter. A young woman he

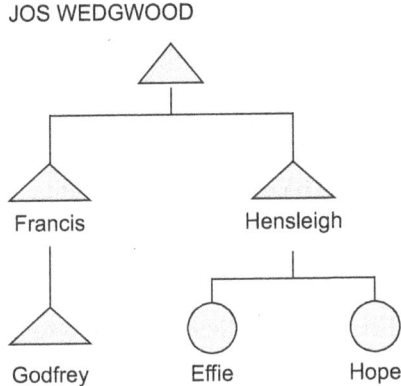

Figure 9.3. Godfrey Wedgwood Effie and Hope.

hoped to marry had just become engaged to her cousin. The British medical press was raising questions about the risks to offspring.[32] A bright young doctor would have been familiar with the professional debates. Dr. Crofts was talking as a responsible medical man. (And in the end he gets his girl.)

But Darwin would have felt that Dr. Croft was on to something. Indeed, that was his private nightmare. His mother, unwell throughout his childhood, had died from an agonizing stomach ailment, probably peritonitis, at the age of fifty-two. Charles was eight years old when she died, and as an adult he was obsessively concerned with his own ill health, particularly the recurrent stomach complaints that recalled his mother's fatal illness. Both his mother and Emma were Wedgwoods, and the Wedgwoods were notorious for their ill health.[33] Whenever one of his children fell ill, Charles was inclined to see the same symptoms in himself and to worry that it exposed a family propensity.

Or were the frequent illnesses of his children and the health problems of the Wedgwoods perhaps the consequence of cousin marriages?[34] This was a growing concern, and not only in scientific circles. "In many families, marriages between cousins are discouraged and checked," Francis Galton noted in 1865.[35] Charles Darwin's son George actually published a note recommending that cousin marriage be avoided.[36]

Worrying reports had appeared in the United States and in France, but the first thorough study of the subject in the United Kingdom was published in 1865 by Arthur Mitchell, deputy commissioner in *Lunacy for Scotland*. Scotland was an obvious choice. It was widely believed that marriage between close relatives was rampant in remote

Scottish regions, particularly the Highlands and islands. Mitchell noted that popular opinion in Scotland condemned "blood-alliances" as "productive of evil."[37] And indeed national statistics showed that nearly 14 percent of "idiots" in Scotland were children of kin. In 44 percent of families with more than one mentally handicapped child, the parents were blood relatives. And 6 percent of the parents of deaf-mutes were close relatives.

Nonetheless, Mitchell was not convinced that this was the whole story. Fewer than 2 percent of marriages in Scotland were between first or second cousins. The rate was indeed higher in some isolated regions, but the evidence for bad effects was uncertain. In one small town on the northeast coast of Scotland, 9 percent of marriages were with first cousins and 13 percent with second cousins. Mitchell acknowledged that the children of these cousin marriages were often unprepossessing, but then many fishing families in the region were "below par in intellect."[38] A more telling case was Berneray-Lewis (now Great Bernera, off the Isle of Lewis). Here 11 percent of marriages were with first and second cousins, yet Mitchell remarked that "instead of finding the island [Berneray-Lewis] peopled with idiots, madmen, cripples, and mutes, not one such person is said to exist in it."[39]

Perhaps environmental factors—"occupation, social habits, etc."—influenced the outcome. One "shrewd old woman" remarked to him, "But I'll tell ye what, Doctor, bairns that's hungert i' their youth aye gang wrang. That's far waur nor sib marriages."[40] Mitchell concluded that close-kin marriage tended to reinforce "evil influences."

Darwin was fascinated. Between 1868 and 1877, he published three monographs on cross-fertilization in animals and plants.[41] In the first of these books, *The Variation of Animals and Plants under Domestication*, he proposed that

> the existence of a great law of nature is almost proved; namely, that the crossing of animals and plants which are not closely related to each other is highly beneficial or even necessary, and that interbreeding [i.e., inbreeding] prolonged during many generations is highly injurious.[42]

Darwin thought this was probably true of human beings, although he was reluctant at first to press the issue. ("Before turning on to Birds, I ought to refer to man, though I am unwilling to enter on this subject, as it is surrounded by natural prejudices.")[43] However, he was bound to consider the implications for his own family. His scientific project and his personal concerns could hardly be separated. "The philosophical difficulties and practical consequences of cousin marriages troubled him for years afterwards," Janet Browne observes. "There was no other theme in Darwin's science that more clearly reflected the personal origins of his intellectual achievement. He could scarcely have arrived at pangenesis without this attention to his marriage, his children's ill health, and his own sickness."[44]

He began to canvass his correspondents. William Farr—the senior statistician in the registrar-general's office—suggested to him that the 1871 census should include a question on cousin marriage.[45] Darwin began to lobby for it. His neighbor and ally John Lubbock had just been elected to Parliament. In the summer of 1870, Darwin asked him to put Farr's proposal to the House. He even drafted arguments for Lubbock to use:

> In England and many parts of Europe the marriages of cousins are objected to from their supposed injurious consequences; but this belief rests on no direct evidence. It is therefore manifestly desirable that the belief should either be proved false, or should be confirmed, so that in this latter case the marriages of cousins might be discouraged. If the census recorded cousin marriages it could be established whether they were less fertile than the average. Later it might also be possible to find out whether or not consanguineous marriages lead to deafness, and dumbness, blindness, &c.[46]

Lubbock put it to the House that "consanguineous marriages were injurious throughout the whole vegetable and animal kingdoms." It was obviously "desirable to ascertain whether that was . . . the case with the whole human race."[47]

The response was unenthusiastic. One member remarked that Parliament was already busy every year debating marriage with the deceased wife's sister: "If there were to be legislation about the marriage of first cousins also, the whole time of the House would be taken up in deciding who was to be allowed to marry anybody else."[48] According to George Darwin, the proposition was rejected, "amidst the scornful laughter of the House, on the ground that the idle curiosity of philosophers was not to be satisfied."[49] Yet forty-five members voted for Lubbock's motion in committee. Ninety-two voted against, but Lubbock remarked in his summing up that virtually everyone who spoke shared his concern.[50]

Farr now proposed to Darwin that an "inquiry might be undertaken through private channels."[51] Darwin agreed. He entrusted the study to his eldest son, George, who was an accomplished mathematician. George was also fascinated by genealogy—he commissioned a genealogy of the Darwins—and he was influenced by the eugenic theories of his cousin Francis Galton. Indeed, he had published a paper that suggested there might be good scientific reasons to prevent the marriage of first cousins and argued that the mentally ill should be kept from marrying.[52] Clearly George was primed for his father's commission.

Darwin laid out the research design. George was to compare the incidence of close-kin marriage in the general population with that among the parents of patients in asylums. If it turned out that marriages between close relatives produced a disproportionate number of "diseased" children, this would "settle the question as to the injuriousness of such marriages."[53]

The first step was to find out how common it was in England for first cousins to marry. Apparently no one knew the answer. George Darwin was given estimates that ranged from 10 percent to one in a thousand. "Every observer," he concluded, "is biased by the frequency or rarity of such marriages amongst his immediate surroundings."[54] He would have to discover the facts for himself. Expert in the new statistical techniques that were being developed by Farr and by Francis Galton, George decided to attempt a scientific survey. It was to be one of the very first statistical studies of a social problem.

Marriage announcements in the *Pall Mall Gazette* seemed a good starting point. Riffling through them, George noticed one marriage between a man and a woman with the same surname. This led him to consult the registrar-general's annual reports. (As the office was created by the Marriage Act of 1836, Darwin's friend Farr had organized the registrar-general's statistics on family and marriage.) These reports were full of valuable and often surprising information. One table gave the proportions of persons who had various surnames. Smith was the most common: one in seventy-three of the population was a Smith. Most surnames, of course, were much rarer. Of a total number of 275,405 people whose names were registered, there was an average of 8.4 per surname. The chance that two unrelated people with the same surname would marry was slight, one in a thousand George Darwin calculated.[55] Returning to the *Pall Mall Gazette*, he and an assistant checked through 18,528 marriage announcements published between 1869 and 1873 and found that 1.25 percent of the couples had the same surname. Very nearly all of these marriages must have been between close relatives on the father's side of the family.

George Darwin now sent out a barrage of questionnaires "to members of the upper middle and upper classes."[56] He also studied the genealogies in Burke's volumes on the peerage and the landed gentry. In this upper-class sample, 4.2 percent of marriages were with first cousins. Marriages between first cousins with the same surname accounted for about a quarter of all first cousin marriages. There appeared to be no preference for one form of cousin marriage over another. Referring back to his data from the *Pall Mall Gazette*, he concluded that 3.5 percent of marriages in "the middle classes" were between first cousins.[57] He then collected a large sample of marriages from the General Registry of Marriages at Somerset House. About 4.5 percent of marriages in the aristocracy were with first cousins; 3.5 percent in the landed gentry and the upper-middle classes; about 2.25 percent in the rural population; and among all classes in London, about 1.15 percent.

The level of cousin marriage in country districts seemed surprisingly low. George Darwin's cousin, Clement Wedgwood, made an inquiry on his behalf among skilled artisans in the potteries. He did not find a single case of first cousin marriage in a sample of 149. "He was further assured that such marriages never take place amongst them," George Darwin noted.[58] Both men must have been familiar with the cousin marriages in the earlier, humbler generations of Wedgwood potters, but they were evidently unusual. (And perhaps their cousin marriages helped to make them so successful.) Except in very isolated districts, such as those investigated by Arthur Mitchell, rural people were not inclined to marry cousins. This conclusion is supported by Alan Macfarlane's study of the marriage records of eight hundred people in East Colne in Essex for the sixteenth to the eighteenth century. He found only one first cousin marriage and two marriages with more distant cousins.[59]

The next step was to gather statistics from mental asylums. Charles Darwin wrote on George's behalf to the heads of the leading institutions. Several provided detailed responses. These indicated that only 3 to 4 percent of patients were the offspring of marriages between first cousins. "For Heavens sake," Charles urged his son, "put a sentence in some conspicuous place that your results seem to indicate that consanguineous marriage, as far as insanity is concerned, cannot be injurious in any very high degree."[60] George complied. "It will be seen [he concluded] that the percentage of offspring of first-cousin marriages [in mental asylums] is so nearly that of such marriages in the general population, that one can only draw the negative conclusion that, as far as insanity and idiocy go, no evil has been shown to accrue from consanguineous marriages."[61]

Other studies suggested that the offspring of cousin marriages were more likely to suffer from blindness, deafness, or infertility. George accepted that these conditions were highly hereditary, but saw no convincing evidence that they were caused by cousin marriage. In fact, first cousin marriages were, if anything, more fertile than others. Presumably a man was more likely to marry a cousin if he had many to choose from. First cousin marriage would therefore be more common among people who came from large—and so presumably fertile—families.[62] Only one small piece of evidence gave George pause. Among men who had rowed for Oxford or Cambridge, men who were obviously the fittest of the fit, sons of first cousin parents appeared slightly less frequently than might have been expected (2.4 percent as opposed to 3–3.5 percent among their peers).[63]

George Darwin was well aware that his conclusions flew in the face of a common and ancient prejudice. He conceded that marriages between cousins might be quite all right for the rich but bad for the poor:

> I may mention that Dr Arthur Mitchell, of Edinburgh, conducted an extensive inquiry, and came to the conclusion that, under favorable conditions of life, the apparent ill-effects were frequently almost nil, whilst if the children were ill fed, badly housed and clothed, the evil might become very marked. This is in striking accordance with some unpublished experiments of my father, Mr. Charles Darwin, on the inbreeding of plants; for he has found that in-bred plants, when allowed enough space and good soil, frequently show little or no deterioration, whilst when placed in competition with another plant, they frequently perish or are much stunted.[64]

In short, cousin marriage caused no harm in the best families. Charles Darwin endorsed these conclusions.[65] In later editions of *Variation* he modified his original rule, weakening the claim: "It is a great law of nature, that all organic beings profit from an *occasional* cross with individuals not closely related to them in blood" (emphasis added). On the other hand, the experience of animal breeders indicated that "the advantage of close interbreeding [i.e., inbreeding], as far as the retention of character is concerned, is indisputable, and often outweighs the evil of a slight loss of constitutional vigor."[66]

The densely intermarried Wedgwoods joked that any hint of laziness or illness was an infallible signs of familial degeneracy.[67] However, the

Darwinian establishment was now convinced that the risks of cousin marriage were slight, at least within prosperous families. Francis Galton wrote enthusiastically to George Darwin that he had "exploded most effectually a popular scare."[68] He added that his cousin could make a fortune from his discovery:

> Thus: there are, say, 200,000 annual marriages in the kingdom, of which 2,000 and more are between first cousins. You have only to print in proportion, and in various appropriate scales of cheapness or luxury: WORDS of Scientific COMFORT and ENCOURAGEMENT To COUSINS who are LOVERS then each lover and each of the two sets of parents would be sure to buy a copy; i.e. an annual sale of 8,000 copies!! (Cousins who fall in love and don't marry would also buy copies, as well as those who think that they might fall in love.)[69]

Galton's protégé, Karl Pearson, made a follow-up study in 1908. He was less systematic than George Darwin, relying on correspondence from readers of the *British Medical Journal*. These select respondents reported a very high incidence of first cousin marriages in their families. A smaller proportion of marriages were with more distant cousins, but Pearson remarked that second and third cousins in these families were also often related in more than one line. He lumped them all together and concluded that "consanguineous marriages in the professional classes probably occur in less than 8 per cent. and more than 5 per cent. of cases." Yet only 1.3 percent of patients in the Great Ormond Street Hospital for Children were the children of cousins. Pearson concluded that "the diseases of children are not largely due to any consanguinity between their parents."[70]

Endorsed by the Darwinian establishment, George Darwin's conclusions reassured many people whose family trees featured marriages between cousins. Englishmen could also rest more easily when they considered that Queen Victoria was married to a first cousin and that several of her descendants had also married cousins. And Darwin's conclusions seemed only common sense to landowners in the House of Lords, who knew that the inbreeding of good stock was sound policy.

Whatever the causes of this pattern on endogamy, the consequences were profound. The political networks of the eighteenth-century aristocracy, like the Whig Cousinhood, were succeeded in the nineteenth century by hundreds of bourgeois dynasties—in business and finance, in the new professions, in the church, in local and national politics, and in intellectual life. Marriages between relatives sustained networks of kin.

Veritable clans emerged and might persist for several generations—in the case of the Darwin-Wedgwoods for over a century, and they were not exceptional, in this respect at least. These webs of relationships delivered enormous collateral benefits, shaping vocations, generating patronage, yielding information, and giving access to capital. A young man with such family connections began his career with a decisive advantage. In short, the prevalence of marriages within the family—between cousins or between in-laws—had much to do with the success of some of the most important Victorian clans.

As these clans were growing in wealth, influence, and prestige, so was their country. In the course of the long nineteenth century, Britain became an increasingly prosperous, secular and democratic land. After the defeat of Napoleon, it was the greatest power in the world. The leading bourgeois clans played a great role in the history of this industrial and imperial Britain. Their preference for marriages within the family circle was a crucial factor in their success. The marriage pattern of the English bourgeoisie therefore played a significant part in making the nineteenth-century world.

Notes

1. Frederick Burkhardt and Sydney Smith, eds., *Correspondence of Charles Darwin*, vol. 2 (Cambridge 1986), 444.
2. Op. ct., 445.
3. Janet Browne, *Charles Darwin: Voyaging* (London, 1996), 392.
4. Op. ct., 391.
5. *Emma Darwin: A Century of Family Letters*, vol. 2, edited by Henrietta Litchfield (London 1915), 1.
6. Barbara Wedgwood and Hensleigh Wedgwood, *The Wedgwood Circle 1730–1897: Four Generations of a Family and Their Friends* (London 1980), 233.
7. *Emma Darwin: A Century of Family Letters*, vol. 2, 2–3.
8. Janet Browne, *Charles Darwin: Voyaging*, 392.
9. Ibid.
10. Ibid.
11. Letter 482—Wedgwood, Emma (Darwin, Emma) to Darwin, C. R., January 3, 1839, *Darwin Correspondence Project*, Cambridge University Library.
12. Claudia Nelson, *Family Ties in Victorian England* (New York 2007), 137.
13. Francis Galton, *Memories of My Life* (London 1908), 158.
14. George Darwin to Charles Darwin, February 5, 1874. *The Darwin Correspondence*, University of Cambridge Library.
15. David Sabean, Simon Teuscher, and Jon Mathieu, eds., *Kinship in Europe* (Oxford 2007), 188.
16. Using the retail price index, this would be about £446,000 in 2007 ($666,000 at the end of 2008). Lawrence H. Officer, "Purchasing Power of British

Pounds from 1264 to 2007," *Measurng Worth*, 2008, www.measurngworth.com/ppoweruk.
17. Barbara and Hensleigh Wedgwood, *The Wedgwood Circle, 1730–1897* (London 1980), 11.
18. Op. ct., 101.
19. Janet Browne, *Charles Darwin: Voyaging* (London 1995), 111.
20. Op. cit.
21. *Emma Darwin: A Century of Family Letters*, vol. 2, 2.
22. Op. ct., vol. 2, 3.
23. Calculating current sterling equivalent (at the end of 2007, with reference to the cost of living index), £5,000 in 1839 would be worth about £339,000 (or $492,000 at the end of 2008); £400 would be worth £27,000 (or $39,000); £10,000 pounds would be worth £678,000 (or $985,000); and £600 would be worth £41,000 (or $60,000). Lawrence H. Officer, "Purchasing Power of British Pounds from 1264 to 2007," *Measuring Worth*, 2008. www.measuringworth.com/ppoweruk.
24. Frank Burkhardt, ed., *The Correspondence of Charles Darwin, Volume 2, 1837–1843* (Cambridge 1986), 119, note.
25. Barbara and Hensleigh Wedgwood, *The Wedgwood Circle*, 209–10.
26. Gwen Raverat. *Period Piece: A Cambridge Childhood* (London 1960), 154.
27. Barbara and Hensleigh Wedgwood, *The Wedgwood Circle*, 211ff.
28. Op. ct., 261–2.
29. Op. ct., 269–70.
30. Op. ct., 310–6.
31. Anthony Trollope, *The Small House of Allington* (London 1863), chapter 20.
32. E.g., James Gardner, "On the Intermarriage of Relations as the Cause of Degeneracy of Offspring," *British Medical Journal* (1861):290; Gilbert Child, "On Marriages of Consanguinity, *British and Foreign Medco-Chirurgical Renew* 29 (1862):461–71.
33. Janet Browne, *Charles Darwin: Voyaging*, (London 1995), 18.
34. Janet Browne, *Charles Darwin: The Power of Place*, 277, 279.
35. Francis Galton, "Hereditary Talent and Character," *Macmillan's Magazine* 12 (1865):319.
36. George H. Darwin, "On the Beneficial Restrictions to Liberty of Marriage," *Contemporary Review* (1873):412–26.
37. Arthur Mitchell, "On the Influence Which Consanguinity in the Parentage Exercises upon the Offspring," 3 parts, *Edinburgh Medical Journal* 1 (Mar./Apr./June 1865):781.
38. Op. ct., 3:1075.
39. Op. ct., 2:907.
40. Op. ct., 2:913.
41. Charles Darwin, *The Variation of Animals and Plants under Domestication*, 2 vols. (London 1868); Charles Darwin, *The Effects of Cross and Self-Fertilization in the Vegetable Kingdom* (London 1876); Charles Darwin, *The Various Contrivances by Which British and Foreign Orchids Are Fertilised by Insects* (London 1877).
42. Darwin, *Animals and Plants*, 144. In the next edition, he dropped the qualification "highly" before "injurious": Charles Darwin, *Animals and Plants under Domestication*, 2nd edition (London 1875), 126.

43. Op. ct., 122.
44. Janet Browne, *Charles Darwin: The Power of Place*, 282.
45. William Farr to Darwin, May 21, 1868, *The Darwin Correspondence*, Cambridge University Library.
46. Darwin to Lubbock, July 17, 1870, Darwin Correspondence, Cambridge. Reproduced in *The Life and Letters of Charles Darwin*, Francis Darwin, ed., 3 vols. (London 1887), 129.
47. Hansard, 3rd ser., cc, col. 817 (July 25, 1870).
48. Op. ct., col. 1009 (July 26, 1870).
49. George H. Darwin, "Marriages between First Cousins in England and Their Effects." *Jl Statistical Soc.* (1875):153.
50. Hansard, 3rd ser., cc, cols. 1006–10 (July 26, 1870).
51. Farr to Darwin, August 6, 1870, *Darwin Correspondence*, Cambridge.
52. George H. Darwin, "On the Beneficial Restrictions to Liberty of Marriage," 424.
53. George Darwin, "Marriages between First Cousins," 153.
54. Op. ct., 178.
55. Op. ct., 155.
56. Op. ct., 156.
57. Op. ct., 162.
58. Op. ct., 164.
59. Alan Macfarlane, *Marriage and Love in England: Modes of Reproduction 1300–1840* (Oxford 1986), 250.
60. Darwin to G. H. Darwin, December 6, 1874, Darwin Correspondence, Cambridge.
61. George Darwin, "Marriages between First Cousins," 168.
62. Ibid., 178.
63. George H. Darwin, "Note on the Marriages of First Cousins." *Jl Statistical Soc.* (1875), 344–8.
64. George Darwin, "Marriages between First Cousins."
65. Darwin, *Effects of Cross and Self Fertilisaton*, second edition, 460–1. Cf. *The Variation of Animals and Plants under Domestication*, 2 vols. (New York 1896), 104.
66. Darwin, *The Variation of Animals and Plants under Domestication*, 1, 94.
67. Barbara and Hensleigh Wedgwood, *The Wedgwood Circle*, 269.
68. Karl Pearson, *The Life, Letters and Labours of Francis Galton*, 3 vols. (Cambridge 1914–30), 188.
69. Karl Pearson, "Cousin Marriages," *The British Medical Jl* (June 6, 1908), 1395.
70. Ibid.

V

Self and Epic

Apes with Existential Questions

And did some sly malicious god,
When an ape first stood and faced the sky,
Prepare a two-edged gift, a rod
It sought to cure this hubris by?
It did, and so the creature choked,
Then straining through its tears it croaked
The first, pathetic, "Why?"

10

The Image of the Good Imperial Education

Alan Macfarlane

I owe Robin Fox a great deal, so it is both a pleasure and an honor to be able to contribute to a volume dedicated to him. The only problem is choosing which of his many interests to focus on. "Kinship and marriage" would be an obvious one, for I attended his brilliant lectures on these topics at the London School of Economics in 1966–1967 and still have my notes on them. I used these and his book *Kinship and Marriage* as the basis for my own lectures for eight years when in 1975 I took over the introductory course on "Kinship and Marriage" previously delivered by Meyer Fortes and Esther Goody.[1] His work on Tory Island, his *Red Lamp of Incest*, *Encounter with Anthropology*, and other books and articles have deeply influenced my thought in anthropology and history.

Let me choose to follow up, however, on some of his more recent work of a more autobiographical kind, in particular his deeply moving and amazingly remembered *Participant Observer*. Here he shows among other things some of the familial and educational pressures that shaped him. It is a riveting account and takes us deep into the culture and ideology of the three decades after the 1950s. This work has more recently led him to an interest in the history of English education, and it is to this that I would like to address myself albeit briefly.[2]

I have long realized that the sending of little boys (and some girls) away to boarding schools is a peculiar and very British institution. Yet I had never really thought of the difference between preparatory schools, dealing with children from eight to thirteen, and public (i.e., private) schools from thirteen to eighteen. Now that I have started to work on my own experience, I have come to suspect that the preparatory schools are in many ways more peculiar and perhaps influential, at least on those who went to them.

The Character of Human Institutions

Many societies have dealt with the problems of changing from child to adult, puberty and its consequences, by the seclusion of children. There are boys' and girls' dormitories or training camps outside the village in many parts of the world. The public school, which traditionally dealt with the period around puberty and the emergence of the adult, can be seen as a form of this institution. Yet I know of very few parallels to the taking of children away from their homes of children from the age of eight to thirteen. Throughout these five years, certainly until the recent dramatic drop in the age of puberty, it was dealing with small children who remained children throughout the period of seclusion.

It is not just comparatively rarer, and more difficult to understand in terms of its function, but its effects on those who go through it are likely to be stronger. We may not completely agree with the view that "A child's character," as a headmaster of Eton emphasized recently, "changes little in essentials after the age of twelve or thirteen." Sir James Barrie went even further: "Nothing," he said, "that happens after we are twelve matters very much."[3] Yet there is some truth in it.

By the age of nearly fourteen, which is when I went on to my public school, much of my basic personality was formed, and many of my attitudes and skills were roughly in place. The period between eight and thirteen was a period of basic learning, turning late infancy into real childhood. Using the metaphor of horticulture, the young tree can still be bent and shaped a good deal in these five years in a way that becomes much less the case in the subsequent five years of boarding. In terms of setting the direction for a life, molding the mind and character, I suspect that more is done in these five years than in the subsequent years.

Both the extreme rareness of such an institutional seclusion, combined with its importance, makes it particularly fascinating to try to understand why this peculiar institution emerged and its function, and how in detail it worked to mold the child and what effects this had.

It is all the more fascinating because it seems such an old pattern in English society. I first encountered it when analyzing the diary of the seventeenth-century *Diary of Ralph Josselin*. All his children left home between the ages of ten and fifteen, some to be educated away from home, others to be servants and apprentices. This led me to investigate this problem more widely, and I found that this was a very widespread phenomenon, as shown in other diaries, listings of inhabitants, and other sources. Many people were sent off to other people's houses as apprentices or to schools from the age of six to ten onward.

The Image of the Good Imperial Education

For example, Elias Pledger went to school in London at the age of six or seven and sent his son off to school at the age of eight; the future Sir John Bramston went away to school at the age of eight; Simon Forman was the same age when he was boarded out at school; as was the son of Mrs Elizabeth Freke. The girls seem to have been a year or two older when they left home. Others were even earlier. The Earl of Cork sent his son away from Ireland to England "to be bred there" when the child was only six and three quarters.[4]

Such a pattern, which we can trace back into the Middle Ages and perhaps back to Anglo-Saxon England, shocked foreigners. An Italian visitor to England in about 1500, who would later become pope, wrote about the custom and gave evidence of its widespread nature and some hints as to its functions, which still seem to apply:

> The want of affection in the English is strongly manifested towards their children; for after having kept them at home till they arrive at the age of seven to nine years at the utmost, they put them out, both males and females, to hard service in the houses of other people, binding them generally for another seven or nine years. And these are called apprentices, and during that time they perform all the most menial offices; and few are born who are exempted from this fate, for every one, however rich he may be, sends away his children into the houses of others, whilst he, in return, receives those of strangers into his own. And on inquiring their reason for this severity, they answered that they did it in order that their children might learn better manners. But I, for my part, believe that they do it because they like to enjoy all their comforts themselves, and that they are better served by strangers than they would be by their own children. . . . That if the English sent away from home to learn virtue and good manners, and took their children away from home to learn virtue and good manners, and took them back again when theyr apprenticeship was over, they might, perhaps, be excused; but they never return, for the girls are settled by their patrons, and the boys make the best marriages they can.[5]

So the phenomenon of sending children away from home from about the age of eight is one of the deepest and most important in English upper-middle-class social structure, unknown anywhere else in the world but with immense consequences on family life, individual psychology, economic and political patterns, the nature of the British Empire, and much else in British history.

My own "participant fieldwork" on this tradition was done in two total institutions in 1950–1960 when I was sent away to boarding school at the age of eight and emerged at eighteen. The first was the famous north Oxford preparatory school, the Dragon School, where I stayed until 1955. The second was the northern boarding school of Sedbergh in Yorkshire, long a grammar school, set in its beautiful but rugged fells of the kind that Robin had been familiar with as a boy. I had been sent home at the age of five from India and for much of this time had been left by my tea-planter parents (who were away in Assam) in the care of my grandparents. It was a Kiplingesque kind of experience, and one I am trying to make sense of now. It affected me deeply, as it did many of the English ruling class for three or four hundred years who went through something similar. But how do we understand it from an anthropological and historical point of view?

At first it is tempting to slot my account into the framework provided by Kathryn Tidrick in her *Empire and the English Character: The Illusion of Authority* (1990). She asks how such a small number of people from a small country could rule the largest empire the world has ever known. Her answer is that it did so by devolving authority, by the "responsibility system" of indirect rule.

She studies examples of the leaders of the British Empire, such as Frederick Courtenay Selous, about whom one obituarist wrote that he was

> of the type of Christian English gentleman who knew how to make friends with backward and coloured peoples, and who consequently were able to gain their respect and obedience. This was the spirit that created the pax Britannica and gave that order, safety and happiness to millions of helpless people in the British Empire, which modern education and so-called democracy strains every nerve to destroy.[6]

The question was, as one administrator wondered aloud, why the British needed only 500 men to rule India, with its population of 300 million, while the French were unable to get by with less than 200 *fonctionnaires* for one and a half million Cambodians.[7]

As E. D. Morel wrote after a visit to Nigeria in 1910,

> When one sees this man managing, almost single-handed, a country as large as Scotland; when one sees that man, living in a leaky mud hut, holding, by the sway of his personality, the balance even between fiercely antagonistic races, in a land which would cover half a dozen of the large English counties; when one sees the marvels accomplished by tact, passionate interest and self-control, with utterly inadequate

means, in continuous personal discomfort, short-handed, on poor pay, out here in Northern Nigeria—then one feels that permanent evil cannot ultimately evolve from so much admirable work accomplished and that the end must be good.[8]

The trick was to accomplish the "difficult task of ruling without actually appearing to rule at all." The essence, wrote a lieutenant-governor of Southern Nigeria, was "authority combined with self-effacement."[9] The archetype of this was the famous imperial hero, T. E. Lawrence, who "was entranced by the conviction that he was controlling the Arabs without their ever realizing it."[10]

The philosophy was put into words by Lugard in *The Dual Mandate*,

> When a few score are responsible for the control and guidance of millions. His courage must be undoubted, his word and pledge absolutely inviolate, his sincerity transparent. There is no room for "mean whites" in tropical Africa.... They lower the prestige by which alone the white races can hope to govern and to guide.

Thus, as Tidrick comments, "By requiring its practitioners to possess the moral prestige necessary to guide, Indirect Rule seemed to ensure that they also possessed the means whereby, in the absence of any overwhelming display of physical superiority, they could govern."[11] This would produce, for example, the ideal district officer—"permanently on tour, manfully resistant to bureaucratic interference from headquarters," and "winning the trust and loyalty of [his] charges by [his] integrity, fairness, firmness, and likeableness."[12]

The characteristics of a person who could combine the integrity, authority, moral conviction, and toughness to become a ruler of the empire are very close to those that I shall shortly outline. And the public school system was clearly effective in producing the type. How was this done?

Tidrick suggests that the mechanism was a powerful mix of a Darwinian struggle for survival in an almost Hobbesian world of "a war of all against all," a tribal gerontocratic system whereby the beaten would finally become the beater, and a toughening and cauterization caused by the deprivation of love.

Tidrick's is an intelligent and intriguing suggestion, and it is worth considering how far the school and my experience within it as described in the previous chapters supports her hypotheses.

Tidrick's first point is that the public schools were based on Arnold of Rugby's philosophy, a mixture of a "politically vital sense of sin" induced by Christianity, with manliness through sport. From my own experience, this is precisely what the Dragon tried to mute. Remembering the lectures, sermons, and exhortations, and particularly the revealing poems read at Remembrance Day as well as the eschewing of a chapel, a cadet force, and the scouts, the Dragon message was subtler. We were not imbued with sin, but much more with a sense of obligation, of returning the kindness and sacrifice of others, especially those who had died for us, or were paying for our education. It is much more like the samurai spirit of Japan with its powerful sense of "on" or obligation to our fathers and forefathers. We were not being inculcated with guilt, but with gratitude and a desire to repay.

Tidrick then writes about the anarchy and survival of the fittest. "Virtually all the accounts we have suggest that the public schools, in spite of Arnold's efforts, continued to exist in something not far removed from a Hobbesian state of nature—or rather, just far enough removed to allow for the development of tribal ritual."[13] Her qualification at the end is sensible, for it was not a Hobbesian world without rules. It was, as anthropologists have described certain kinds of tribes without rulers, what they call "ordered anarchy." It was full of rules, hierarchies, obligations, and reciprocities. So though it may have appeared chaotic from the outside, very soon we realized as pupils that it followed predictable patterns.

Indeed, Tidrick notes this in her next sentence, when she states that "The number of taboos which might unknowingly be broken was terrifying. Some children spent their entire schooldays in unrelieved misery." As Erving Goffman has pointed out for other asylums, the system was filled with regulations and rules. We learned in the preparatory school, as I would have to learn again in my public school and then in universities, that a host of customary and unwritten yet powerful rules surrounded me, rules that I must internalize and then follow. The staff devised some, but the students invented many, as they do in Oxbridge colleges.[14]

Tidrick then makes the valuable point that there was a compensating feature of the system, which is that most people would move from being at the bottom of the pile to becoming rulers. She writes that

> matters were so arranged that for most the outlook was not completely bleak; almost everyone could arrive eventually at a state of

> relative freedom from intimidation and enjoy a measure of authority over others. And when this happy moment arrived, it was crowned with legitimacy, because like many tribal societies the public school was a gerontocracy... the critical fact was that, in the fullness of time, little boys who were beaten by big ones might reasonably expect to do the beating themselves.[15]

Again this is oversimplified, or perhaps just not appropriate for the Dragon. The school did not give prefects the power to beat, or even to have much formal power at all. What one discovered, and this also happened at Sedbergh and at Oxford and Cambridge, is that while one had little formal power, if one lived up to expectations in terms of leadership—integrity, fairness, encouragement of others, generally being "a good chap," and preferably a good game player or singer or good in class—then one had invisible prestige. This was exactly what was needed in the remote reaches of empire. One might only have a few "plucky Gurkhas" to enforce control over a large and warlike edge of empire. One ruled through being "a good chap," fair and decent in the famous mold.

Tidrick then makes another valuable point, which is that what was particularly unusual about the system, a point also noted by George Orwell, was the sharp contrast between the home life of at least the elite and what happened at school. The schools managed

> to keep alive, in boys whose privileged background might have encouraged complacent acceptance rather than active pursuit of power, a keen appreciation of what it was like to have it, and what it was like to be without it. The schools claimed to toughen boys, and they did. By making it possible for a vivid and urgent desire for power to exist alongside a consciousness of being the legitimate and predestined possessor of it, they kept the edge on the governing classes.[16]

Most ruling classes in history tend to lose that edge—the children are loved too much, or at least take their future power for granted in luxurious surroundings. Both the Dragon school, with its motto of *Arduus ad solem* ("Striving for the sun"), and later Sedbergh, *Dura Virum Nutrix* ("A hard nurse of men"), emphasized the struggle, the effort, the overcoming of obstacles. Life was extremely difficult materially, psychologically, and in every way for a little boy of eight going to one of these schools. But through effort and self-control, we could survive and perhaps one day achieve something.

Tidrick suggests that the desire to pursue power was paralleled by an equally powerful psychological pressure caused by the loss of parental love. She points out

> that boys in public schools were chronically deprived of the normal sources of affection. Expelled from the comfort of home usually at the tender age of eight, they were compelled until they left school (or, in some cases, university) to associate almost exclusively with other boys, whose behavior towards them was unpredictable.... To what extent boys were conscious of the loss of love—in its practical and immediate manifestation—is impossible to say: mechanisms of denial come quickly into operation to deal with such enormities.[17]

My own experience suggests that this is again too simple. It is true that many accounts quoted by Brendon and others do suggest the dreadful effects when little children thought they had been abandoned. The classic account by Kipling in "Baa Baa Black Sheep" is well-known.[18] I don't think that my own confidence that I was still loved by my parents is the result of "mechanisms of denial." If I had relied just on memory, as almost all do, then it might appear like that. But the contemporary letters show that children can perfectly well understand that love and separation can be combined. I knew my mother loved me, whatever had happened. So while I did not smile much for two or three years during term time, and put on little weight, and showed other signs of psychological distress, this was not in the end because I felt I was no longer loved.

Tidrick's next comment about how such deprivation of home love led to intense relationships at school does seem to be as I remember it. She writes that

> what is evident is that they often sought affection from the only source which under the circumstances was available—other boys. Friendships developed of a very intense type, sometimes, inevitably, with an explicitly sexual aspect which seems, in spite of the awful fulminations of headmasters, to have produced remarkably little in the way of enduring guilt or sexual abnormality in adult life: it was the emotional intensity of the experience which was remembered, suggesting how deep a displaced need it in fact fulfilled.[19]

This is something which many accounts, including my mother's of her schooling, show. And Brendon and others have also suggested the absence of a necessary link between these same-sex "crushes" and later tendencies toward homosexuality.

We have an interesting dialectic in Tidrick's account. The little child is pushed toward a desire for power over others. This is countered by a desire to be loved by those same others:

> It thus came about that, during the process of a boy's adjustment to public school, two very powerful and not very compatible needs—the need for power and the need for love—were grossly stimulated, in an environment where their satisfaction could not easily be assigned to the usual separate compartments of life.

One outcome, she suggests, was that people give up the struggle and opt for one or the other. She chooses as her example two members of my own college at Cambridge, King's, namely, E. M. Forster and Goldsworthy Lowes Dickinson, who opted for friendship as the supreme value. This example, unfortunately, tends to add to the stereotype of the link with homosexuality, for the Bloomsbury group was famously associated with this activity.

There was, however, one way to resolve the conflict between the desire to pursue power and the need for, and this was put before the child by the school. This resolution would also provide the key answer to the psychological underpinning of the British Empire and how so few people held the largest empire in history together.

Tidrick writes that "there was one orthodox route, supplied by the school itself. This was to learn to exercise power 'responsibly.' In this way power and love might both be enjoyed, as we see them being enjoyed by the heroes of a thousand school stories." One could be both powerful and loved, or at least admired and followed, by other little boys or, later, by vast swathes of the globe. So, Tidrick concedes that given that "the avowed purpose of the public schools was to produce leaders," then "if we are to understand by leaders rulers capable of extracting the voluntary compliance of the ruled, we must concede that they produced them."[20]

This boarding school experience and its link to empire is well described by Edward Thring, a celebrated headmaster of Uppingham, in about 1874, when he wrote to a friend,

> The learning to be responsible, and independent, to bear pain, to play games, to drop wealth and rank and home luxury, is a priceless boon. I think myself that it is this which has made the English such an adventurous race.[21]

Another way to start to understand what happened to me, looking back from sixty years later, is to return to the question of what the school, and others like it, was aiming at. It now seems to me that the purpose of the Dragon was to shape me into a model British gentleman who would be capable of doing well in many spheres. What then was the "Good Dragon" into which they were trying to turn me?[22]

I was to have a *good mind*. This consists of both content and form. The content are the things such as language ability (and language learning), particularly important in foreign lands, writing and expressing oneself clearly, arithmetic, and so on—the three Rs. I was also to have a sense of history, geography, the classics of literature, and a dash of science. This was to give us the tools of thought and expression, to be able to argue, persuade, solve problems, and generally lead confidently. The training was rather general, for it was to train doctors, administrators, lawyers, managers, academics, and anyone whose job it is to take a tough knot of complex issues, unravel them, and then put forward a viable solution—usually choosing the lesser of two evils. Yet while we should work hard and be keen on the development of the intellect, we should not be arrogant if we are successful, and we should not be overly brainy, too obsessive. It should all be achieved as effortlessly (apparently) as possible.

I was to have a *good body*. Given the huge emphasis on the physical disciplining of children, the games, sports, toughening up and beating, it is clear that much of school life was to do with toughening the body. This made sense in a world of premodern medicine, inadequate heating or cooling, and limited food in many remote parts of the globe. This meant that the body had to be really tough and inured to pain to survive. It should be trained to enjoy the physical excitements of sports and games if one was going to overcome the stultifying boredom and loneliness. We should strive hard to be good at games, and respect those who were. But again we should keep this in moderation. Modesty in our achievements, putting more emphasis on commitment and effort rather than attainment, was encouraged. Sport and games were a necessary part of growth, but they could be over emphasized.

I was to learn to lead *a good moral life*. Here the school was setting up goals of virtue, sacrifice, purity of thought and action, avoidance of lying and deceit, of honesty, kindness, and decency. Much of this, of course, was to be taught to us at home, but it was also to be inculcated, mainly indirectly, through our education at school. Much of school life, in its informal aspects as I have discovered, is about ethics, not telling tales, not lying, appropriate sexual misbehavior, but doing the honorable thing, even when no one was watching.

Complementing this, though different, was *the good spiritual life.* This was wider than formal Christianity, though that was a part of it. We were to learn to believe in the value of the human spirit, wherever it was manifested, and to ponder on the meaning of life. We should try to spread good Christian values through practice rather than precept, or as Gandhi would say, a rose does not need to advertise itself, it just smells sweet.

We were to be filled with *good emotions.* This was especially important. Good emotions included things like self-confidence, cheerfulness, overcoming of loneliness, the art of attracting people to one's personality, and of being attracted by them, the arts of love, hate, detachment, and attachment. This is a complex web and particularly difficult because the natural place to develop these emotions, the family, was largely replaced for boarders in an artificially generated setting, the new "quasi-family" of the school. Something that was constructed and nonfamily had to take on some of the warmth and intensity of the blood family.

In these and other areas, the child was being shaped into a sort of model of the English gentleman. He (and sometimes she) was to be tough, trustworthy, humorous, self-deprecating, clever, a leader of men, individualistic yet a team player, able to overcome obstacles in the most difficult situations, a survivor, and a true Christian knight. Bits of these models are in Chaucer and in Shakespeare, and through our teaching in literature we were given instruction. But much of it was to be instilled into us more indirectly. And against all of these models we could set the model of the bad life—the bad sport, the liar, the fanatic, the bully, the libertine, the toady, the swot, the cheat.

Two portraits of the ideal type illustrate this picture. The first is part of some notes written for his daughter by the Old Dragon (former Dragon School pupil) Pat Cotter in 1939. Cotter describes the ideal set before him by one of the teachers, Gilbert Vassal ("Cheese"):

> Cheese's standard of conduct was a simple one; his Good Man was one who was generally believed to be faithful to his wife and reasonably sober, who looked you in the eye and told the truth at awkward times, who was either good at work or games or had enough sense of humour to make you forgive him his incompetence in either (preferably not both) of these respects. This Good Man could be modest about all these accomplishments, and Cheese in his turn was modest about his athletic distinction, his looks, and his prestige both in the school and in the University. My description of his standards may be

cynical, my feelings about Cheese are not. He was and is a gentleman ... and boys from the school do not commonly lose their respect for him as they grow older and discern his failings.[23]

The other is John Betjeman's "Percivall Mandeville," whom he encountered at the Dragon School as described in "Summoned by Bells":

> Percival Mandeville, the perfect boy,
> Was all a schoolmaster could wish to see—
> Upright and honourable, good at games,
> Well-built, blue-eyed; a sense of leadership
> Lifted him head and shoulders from the crowd.
> His work was good. His written answers, made
> In a round, tidy and decided hand,
> Pleased the examiners. His open smile
> Enchanted others. He could also frown
> On anything unsporting, mean or base,
> Unworthy of the spirit of the school
> And what it stood for.[24]

In many ways, I was to become the hero of Kipling's "If," based on his own experience of being abandoned at home by his parents and living through a nightmare of "toughening up" education. The whole poem is a superb outline of the public-school philosophy, but I shall just quote the last verse:

> If you can talk with crowds and keep your virtue,
> Or walk with Kings—nor lose the common touch,
> If neither foes nor loving friends can hurt you,
> If all men count with you, but none too much;
> If you can fill the unforgiving minute
> With sixty seconds' worth of distance run,
> Yours is the Earth and everything that's in it,
> And—which is more—you'll be a Man, my son!

The enormous conditioning, the creation of a certain ruling habitus, through English boarding education is a serious subject—and still having large effects around the world as the new rulers—now from China and India—come to be educated in British boarding schools or in replicas of such schools set up in their own countries. Yet despite the seriousness, it is good to end on a more cheerful and humorous note—for Robin Fox writes with wit and considerable humour about many serious topics.

One way to understand the education I went through is to see the parallels between what we were being made into and several famous depictions of children in English fiction. C. H. Jacques in his *Centenary History of the Dragon* writes,

> One is tempted to wonder whether the young Lionel Charles Liddell was ever visited at the School by an elder sister, some of whose recent adventures in Wonderland and elsewhere might have rubbed off on the embryo Dragon to account for some at least of the odder quirks in its future development.

Peter Snow is surely right that

> Lewis Carroll can hardly be cited as a commentator as the suburb was still being built when he was writing but his work nevertheless provides a superb handbook to the area. It is all still there; the sharp little Alices, the Tweedledum and Tweedledee arguments, the dominating Duchesses and Queens, and the hapless terrified males—the White Rabbits, gardeners and Knaves.

Snow notes that

> Another writer of fantasy, and one interested in dragons, lived for a time at 20 and 22 Northmoor Road (neighboring the Dragon School): J. R .R. Tolkien. There have been various interpretations of Lord of the Rings ... but its rootedness in Oxford and specifically in North Oxford seems to have been overlooked. The hobbit heroes are clearly North Oxford children; they have the bodies of children but the minds of adults; they speak with all the distinctive spry confidence of Dragon School pupils; they are good marksmen (Ouch!); they become extremely distinguished in the outside world: Frodo (Old Dragon, 1929) has done outstandingly well in Mordor. ... There is also a range of other peculiar races and creatures in the novel, odd little particularizations of the British/class system: the orcs are miniaturized Cowley yobs and the wizards are of course superdons, with magical powers.

In the light of all this, it is interesting to note that in 1970 a film unit came down to make a film about Professor Tolkien

> who would naturally be perfectly at ease with any sort of Dragon. So fifty of them, including the Professor's grandson, all Hobbits for the evening, milled around a bonfire on the river bank by the Barge, armed with torches. (233)

Others who were either at school nearby or who lived in neighboring areas and went through similar educations could be cited. One was Kenneth Graham, whose *Wind in the Willows* was supposedly dreamed up just to the north of the Dragon at St. Edwards public school. A later representation in fiction is the world of Narnia imaginedby C. S. Lewis, typical British schoolchildren being the heroes and heroines.

Let me give the last word to another Old Dragon, the novelist Pico Iyer. In an article on "The Playing Fields of Hogwarts," he suggests that the model for J. K. Rowling's Hogwarts is somewhere like the Dragon:

> "What J. K. Rowling has done, with considerable charm and inventive brio, is to take the traditional rituals of English public schools and show them in a light in which they seem as curious to outsiders as the rites of passage of tribal Africa."

Moving on to Eton, Iyer remembers: "the special school train that would be waiting in a London station to transport us to our cells. Once the doors clanged shut behind us, we knew we were inside an alternative reality where none of the usual rules applied—and where there was only one sex, everyone wore tails every day and it was assumed that every boy would partake of Anglican worship twice a day."

Behind all this, of course, there is a somewhat sinister clannishness that makes all these private academies seem like secret societies—the English version of Skull and Bones—designed to train the elite in a system that other mortals cannot follow. When I was at school, it was always assumed that all the years of quasi-military training ("Hard work and pain are the best teachers if you ask me," the Hogwarts caretaker says) were meant to teach us how to rule the Empire and subdue the natives around the world. When we graduated, however, we found that the Empire was gone, and the only natives visible were ourselves.[25]

So it was with me. As I joke to my pupils, I was trained to rule an empire. Yet by the time I came to run it, the empire was gone. So what should I do? Become an anthropologist, of course, and dissect the desiccated bones of that empire in the remote corners of Nepal or Assam. And I could not have a more stimulating start to this further adventure than an encounter with Robin Fox in his early years.

Notes

1. These lectures can be seen in abridged form on www.alanmacfarlane.com or on the Ayabaya channel on *Youtube*.
2. This sketch is taken from a larger project to reconstruct in detail my education (and that of my ancestors), based on personal archives covering the period 1650–2000 and in particular Jamaica, India, and Burma. I threw little paper away from the age of fourteen and before that kept letters from my parents, as they did mine. So there is a large set of primary contemporary materials for this task. The first two volumes of the account, *Dragon Days* and *Dorset Days*, were published in March 2012.
3. Meston Batchelor, *The Cradle of Empire* (1981), xiv.
4. Alan Macfarlane, *The Family Life of Ralph Josselin* (1970), 207–8.
5. Quoted in Macfarlane, "Family Life," 206, from C. A. Sneyd (trans), *A Relation or Rather a True Account of the Island of England. . . . About the Year 1500*, by an Italian, Cam. Soc. Vol. xxxvii (1847), 24–5.
6. Kathryn Tidrick, *Empire and the English Character* (1990), 59.
7. Ibid., 110.
8. Ibid., 204.
9. Ibid., 208.
10. Ibid., 210.
11. Ibid., 213.
12. Ibid., 216.
13. Ibid., 217.
14. Alan Macfarlane, *Reflections on Cambridge* (2009).
15. Tidrick, *Empire*, 217.
16. Ibid., 218.
17. Ibid., 218–9.
18. Vyvyen Brendon, *Prep School Children* (2009); "Baa Baa Black Sheep," in Rudyard Kipling's *Collected Works*.
19. Tidrick, *Empire*, 219.
20. Ibid., 220.
21. Quoted in Batchelor, *Cradle of Empire*, 15.
22. This approach was partly inspired by George M. Foster, "Peasant Society and the Image of Limited Good," *American Anthropologist*, 68, no. 2 (April 1965):293–315.
23. From *Our Father: Pat Cotter*, compiled for the Dragon School Archive by Helen Stell, younger daughter of Patrick Cotter, 2005.
24. John Betjeman, *Summoned by Bells: A Verse Autobiography* (1960), 43.
25. Peter Snow, *Oxford Observed* (1991).
26. Pico Iyer, "The Playing Fields of Hogwarts," *New York Times*, October 10, 1999.

11

The Ethnography of the Self: Anthropologists' Autobiographies

David Jenkins

> *"As I understand it, you have asked me for an honest, introspective—personal—account of how I think about anthropological material, and if I am to be honest and personal about my thinking, then I must be impersonal about the results of that thinking. Even if I can banish both pride and shame for half an hour, honesty will still be difficult."*
> —Gregory Bateson, "Experiments in Thinking about Observed Ethnological Material"

Gregory Bateson's comments must have raised a laugh when he delivered his paper at the Seventh Conference on Methods in Philosophy and Science in 1940. But his point was a serious one. It is as difficult to be an outside observer of one's thoughts as it is to step outside of culture to find solid ground for analysis. Willard Van Orman Quine noted an analogous problem for the study of language. How except through language do we study language? His metaphor for this task, borrowed from Otto Neurath, was that of taking apart a boat at sea while simultaneously staying afloat. At some point in the disassembly and analysis, a last plank of language on which one stands must remain in place.

Anthropologists who write about themselves are faced with a predicament. What plank of self remains after the disassembly? How does that self coincide with the anthropological project?

Bateson illustrated the development of his own thought and its relationship to anthropological analyses across different domains of inquiry, ranging from ethnography to psychiatry to cybernetics. Along the way, he suggested that scientific investigation has two starting points: one based on scientists' observations, the other on relevant scientific fundamentals. As Bateson and others have lamented, in the human sciences, there remain more observations than fundamentals. This situation has led some to believe there are in fact no fundamentals; indeed, any reference to them results in a vaguely wicked or, at least, morally suspicious cultural "essentialism," which along with other "-isms" should be castigated and summarily rejected. One point of rejection is a presumed failure to allow for cultural variation (Fuchs), a failure that cannot be attributed to anthropology. Yet anti-essentialists, seeking to promote a historical vision of unbounded cultural contingency, fail to see the incoherence of their own position, confusing midlevel analytical abstractions with which anthropologists develop comparative work—culture, structure, social organization, symbolic form, kinship ritual, ceremony, and the like, in other words where the essentials reside—with the historically situated ethnographic descriptions of this or that group of people, where cultural essentials may be absent.

In anthropology, cultural diversity is commonly manifested, but human commonality is manifested as well. One way to make sense of human commonalities, against which cultural diversity can be understood, is by recourse to scientific fundamentals, for example, those derived from evolutionary theory (Allen et al.; Chapais). Another way is to refer to culturally specific modes of historical change (White). Yet another is to recognize the role of individual agency in the context of symbolic structures, which are both historically contingent and culturally ordered (Sahlins). None of these approaches are particularly mysterious, let alone wicked, even as they require detailed description and analysis and proceed to accumulate analytical statements about cultural commonalities or—dare one say—essential human qualities.

Bateson provided glimpses of his mode of thought and his style of anthropological theorizing. Other anthropologists, especially those who advance a particular reflexive mood, have written about their own lives in a more sustained fashion. At one extreme, these moody anthropologists insist on inserting themselves into their accounts of complex social worlds. Their work often gives us more information about the anthropologist than we could ever want, while insufficiently describing another culture. The result has provided fodder for endless discussion about the impossibility of finding any outside perspective from which to observe consciousness, language, or culture, leading many anthropologists down the rabbit hole of reflexivity and extreme versions of cultural relativism, from which, unlike Alice, some have not returned (the literature is large; see e.g., Aunger; Behar; Behar and Gordon; Clifford and Marcus; Davies; Myerhoff and Ruby; Rabinow; Rosaldo; cf. Salzman). An obvious and unfortunate side effect of this approach is that comparative analyses are rendered problematic, if not impossible.

The valorization of the individual in contemporary Western thought (Lukes) may account for the reflexive mood as anthropologists elevate their own idiosyncrasies to the level of great theoretical moment. The result is often an ethnographic bonfire of the vanities, emphasis on "vanities," omitting the self-parodic stance that made Tom Wolfe's fictional rendering of American culture so funny. Grumpy reflexivity leads to grumpy anthropology. As Pierre Bourdieu comments, such reflexivity often does not go far enough, leaving us with an "explosion of narcissism sometimes verging on exhibitionism," rather than scientific ethnography (282). Wendy Kaminer may have contemporary anthropology in mind when she states that "Academic fashions locate truth in individual narratives, and falsehood in the quest for objectivity" (5).

But I am not interested here in the genre of reflexive anthropology, scientific or otherwise. My topic is anthropologists' autobiographies, which in their very form require a self-contemplation quite different from reflexive anthropology, but which nonetheless contain their own irrepressible vanities.

A handful of anthropologists have written autobiographies. These include Claude Lévi-Strauss (*Tristes Tropiques*, 1955); Margaret Mead (*Blackberry Winter*, 1972); Loren Eiseley (*All the Strange Hours: The Excavation of a Life*, 1975); Richard MacNeish (*The Science of Archaeology?*, 1978); Christoph von Furer-Haimendorf (*Life among Indian Tribes: The Autobiography of an Anthropologist*, 1990); Edward T. Hall (*An Anthropology of Everyday Life: An Autobiography*, 1992); and Robin Fox (*Participant Observer: Memoir of a Transatlantic Life*, 2004), among others.

I focus on Lévi-Strauss, Eiseley, Mead, and Fox, whose work extends beyond the margins of anthropology and has proven influential in other realms. I wish to examine the boat of self as it is disassembled and laid out on the ocean of contingency, especially that last essential plank upon which the autobiographer stands. As a comparative exercise, I am particularly interested in the floating plank or cluster of planks from which the disassembled life can be viewed, recognizing all the while that it is the relationships between planks that make a boat a boat.

Claude Lévi-Strauss

Claude Lévi-Strauss's autobiographical *Tristes Tropiques* (1955) is less a summing up than a midway marker of his long, productive, and influential intellectual life (Wilcken). It has been reviewed and analyzed so much that there is little I can add. Lévi-Strauss (1908–2009) famously noted that he despised traveling and travel narratives because he found them trivial; he then proceeded to write about his travels. Over a five-year period in the late 1930s, Lévi-Strauss sporadically conducted research in Brazil, later producing what Clifford Geertz called "one of the finest books ever written by an anthropologist" (347). Susan Sontag thought *Tristes Tropiques* "a masterpiece" and "one of the great books of our century" (71). Lévi-Strauss himself was ambivalent about his effort.

Tristes Tropiques of course is not simply a travel narrative. It contains detailed ethnographic descriptions of the Bororo, Nambikwara, and Caduveo, as well as an account of the development of Lévi-Strauss's own thinking about humanity. At the beginning, Lévi-Strauss describes his intellectual restlessness and his inability to retain any interest in topics he had worked on, let alone recall them to mind. Philosophy, to which he was initially drawn, proved impoverishing. Phenomenology and existentialism merely provided alibis for metaphysics, not routes to a rigorous accumulation of knowledge. Existentialism in particular promoted "personal preoccupations to the dignity of philosophical problems." The point, Lévi-Strauss insists, was "to understand being in relation to itself and not in relation to myself" (58). Anthropology opened up the possibilities for such understanding, even as the hegemony of modern anthropology closed out such possibilities with a return to "myself" as the object of anthropological interest.[1] For Lévi-Strauss, Robert Lowie's *Primitive Society* (1920) provided new vistas unhampered by philosophy. "Like a city-dweller transported to the mountains, I became drunk with space, while my dazzled eyes measured the wealth and variety of the objects surrounding me." Thus began his lifelong interest in the cultures of the Americas.

The bulk of *Tristes Tropiques* is devoted to descriptions of local peoples and environments interspersed with details of travel. I am more interested in Lévi-Strauss's remarks on how the ethnographer's experience has consequences for his understanding of the anthropological project. He notes in the conclusion to his book that some of the problems he addressed—for example, how to conceptualize cultural difference and similarity—found their solutions not in Brazil but in the

Chittagong hill tracks of Bangladesh years later where he watched a religious ritual in a Mogh village and reflected on the nature of Buddhism:

> You need not do what I am doing," my companion said to me as he prostrated himself on the ground four times before the altar, and I followed his advice. However, I did so less from self-consciousness than discretion: he knew that I did not share his beliefs, and I would have been afraid of debasing the ritual gestures by letting him think I considered them as mere conventions: but for once, I would have felt no embarrassment in performing them. Between this form of religion and myself, there was no likelihood of misunderstanding. It was not a question of bowing down in front of idols or of adoring a supposed supernatural order, but only of paying homage to the decisive wisdom that a thinker, or the society which created his legend, had evolved twenty-five centuries before and to which my civilization could contribute only by confirming it. (411)

Such confirmation, for Lévi-Strauss, takes a particular form. "Every effort to understand," he explains, "destroys the object studied in favor of another object of a different nature" (411). Confirmation thus requires revising the experientially distant into the conceptually familiar. The process is continual, as the new understanding is itself subject to further reconceptualization, which similarly destroys the prior object, "and so on and so forth until we reach the one lasting presence, the point at which the distinction between meaning and the absence of meaning disappears: the same point from which we began" (411).

Repudiating Western philosophy at the beginning of *Tristes Tropiques*, Lévi-Strauss embraces Eastern philosophy at the end. This transformation may seem mysterious enough, but his general point is that the anthropologist makes sense of distant beliefs, such as an empirically unbelievable supernatural order of things, by making them intelligible and subjectively familiar. Such intelligibility is not precisely that of the native, but results from a shared symbolic capacity with the native. Marshall Sahlins makes the point thus: "By virtue of the shared humanity of anthropologists and their interlocutors, which is also to say their common symbolic capacity, the former replicate in mind, as the meaningful significance of custom, what the latter express in practice" (*Comments*, 275).

In a frequently quoted passage from *The Raw and the Cooked*, Lévi-Strauss provides an early expression of this point of view:

> For if the final aim of anthropology is to contribute to a better knowledge of objectified thought and its mechanisms, it is in the last

resort immaterial whether in this book the thought processes of the South American Indians take shape through the medium of my own thought, or whether mine take place through the medium of theirs. What matters is that the human mind, regardless of the identity of those who happen to be giving it expression, should display an increasingly intelligible structure. (13)

If anthropology is constituted in this way, then all the recent reflexive hand-wringing is quite unnecessary. Moreover, the reflexive self-focus of the anthropologist—analyzing her own complex position in her own social world—is also quite beside the point, for two reasons. First, an individual's self-awareness is inherently limited and inevitably incomplete, as Bateson insisted, Freud demonstrated, and, it hardly needs saying, anthropology has shown to be the case, with its record of cross-cultural comparisons. Where, additionally, would an anthropologist stop his or her self-analysis? Must anthropologists cover all essentials, in kin relations, social organization, class position, educational cohort, birth order, gender, marital status, religious affiliation, medical history, and psychological profile? The reflexive impulse seems to share characteristics with an earlier era, when psychoanalysts themselves had to undergo psychoanalysis. Now it is the anthropologist who has to undergo an analogous analytical procedure to productively engage another culture. "The problem here is," as Sahlins notes in a different context, "that as an intersubjective field of which the people concerned have different social experiences and local perceptions, a cultural life in its complexity, let alone its totality, involves reasons and relationships that no one who lives it can be expected to express" (*Comments*, 273). This observation applies equally well to the self-centered anthropologist—including those of us who write autobiographies.

The second reason to question the reflexive impulse, as Lévi-Strauss playfully says, is that "The self is not only hateful: there is no place for it between *us* and *nothing*" (414). He means that anthropological understanding is inevitably about shared experience, just as all human existence is essentially shared, and that the individual *qua* individual has no secure place outside of human sociability. There is only *us*. Even Lévi-Strauss's own identity is questioned. "Yet," he remarks, "I exist," hastening to add, "not, of course, as an individual." Lévi-Strauss's "*les mythes se pensent en moi*," thus makes sense insofar as an anthropologist provides a locus for the articulation of mythic structure, with his or her construction of meaning, much the same way as he or she provides the locus for symbolic structures of all sorts across all cultures and through all historical periods. Thus the anthropologist analytically replicates the meaningful significance of lived custom, however not without inevitable loss. Adopting, ironically, the voice of the travel narrative, Lévi-Strauss observes, "[O]nce they were in my power, the men and the landscapes I had set out to conquer lost the significance I had hoped they would have for me" (376). Despite the irony, this is for Lévi-Strauss the central paradox of anthropology, which can be overcome in thought but only temporarily. And this paradox is, I imagine, the reason that he ended *Tristes Tropiques* contemplating not humanity but a shared glance with a cat.

Loren Eiseley

Loren Eiseley (1907–1977), widely read in the 1960s and 1970s, is remembered less as an anthropologist than as an essayist with a fine literary gift. He taught at a number of universities, received over three dozen honorary degrees, and was the Benjamin Franklin Professor of Anthropology and History of Science at the University of Pennsylvania. His books include *The Immense Journey* (1957), *Darwin's Century* (1958), *The Firmament of Time* (1960), *The Unexpected Universe* (1969), and *The Night Country* (1971), among ten others. With a few exceptions, Eiseley used the personal essay as a means to write about larger topics, with time and nature forming prominent themes (Wisner). His work influenced natural history writers but had little impact on anthropology, which is why I recite his honors and list a few of his publications. He was, to borrow the title of Harold Orlans's memoir, an anthropologist without a tribe.

In *All the Strange Hours*, Eiseley disassembles his life and leaves the reader with a deeply pessimistic view of humans and their relations to each other. As a young man during the Great Depression—a few years before Lévi-Strauss was in Brazil—he rode freight cars across North America, along with thousands of other out-of-work men looking to alight in more hospitable climes. In one instance, he describes being beaten by a brakeman on a train traveling sixty miles per hour. The brakeman battered his face and tried to push him off the train and under the wheels. A day or two later, his face still showing signs of the beating, Eiseley briefly traveled with another man who advised him about the inevitability of human aggression:

> "Remember this," he said suddenly, dispassionately, as though the voice originated over this shoulder. "Just get this straight. It's all there

is and after a while you'll see it for yourself." He studied me again without expression. "The capitalists beat men into line. Okay? The communists beat men into line. Right again?"

"I reckon," I ventured, more to fill in the silence growing around us than because I had understood.

He pointed gently at my swollen face. "Men beat men, that's all. That's all there is. Remember it, kid. Take care of yourself." He walked away up the dark diverging track. (10)

Eiseley's later graduate training in anthropology at the University of Pennsylvania, where he studied under Frank Speck in the 1930s, did little to dispel his pessimistic view of humans. Speck and Eiseley once spent a day in the nearby Pine Barrens, rather than attend the Anthropological Association meetings in Philadelphia, which Speck thought oppressive. As they walked, Speck related a story about his grandfather, a sea captain:

"These Pineys," Frank swept a hand over the woods through which we tramped, and I knew he was referring to the illiterate inbred woodsmen who inhabited the place, "were wreckers two generations ago. My grandfather's ship was lured onto the shoals by false lights during a storm. Grandfather's body was cast up along with the cargo and some of the crew. In those days, that was the Atlantic, with its false lights, and the piratical people of the shore."

He paused and took a quick breath and went on. "My father had to drive down in a wagon and take the body home. It's odd, you know. I've sat around fires with Pineys whose grandfathers did the job. They would half admit it." (88)

Eiseley wondered whether his mentor held murderous thoughts toward his grandfather's killers, akin to his own murderous thoughts toward the brakeman. Oddly, Eiseley proceeds to use this vignette as a backdrop for a brief observation about the unexpected rise in interest in anthropology in the 1950s and 1960s in the United States, as opposed to the turn of the century, when only a handful of scholars counted themselves as anthropologists. He was unable to explain the interest beyond noting that anthropology may have helped to soften old taboos, offering rationalizations for countercultural behavior. He also provided an incongruous warning about anthropology: "As in the case of any science, not all of its practitioners need be regarded as reasonable or without self-interest" (88). One wonders about to whom this warning was given.

Other stories are similarly pessimistic. As a graduate student, Eiseley took a trip to Washington DC. His international companions included a

Filipino, a Chinese, "an Indian or two," and a Japanese-born American, all good friends. They were unable to find a hotel that would take them, attitudes toward race being what they were. Even the Young Men's Christian Association (YMCA) turned them away. They drove back to Pennsylvania, hoping to find a place for the night en route. They came across a large house with a sign, "Tourists Welcome Overnight." Eiseley and Tachi, a Japanese American friend who was nicknamed "Duke," approached the door and knocked.

> A pinched-faced women with the relentless eyes of a turkey vulture came to the door. I explained our need for rooms. Her eye traveled behind me, focused upon Duke.
> "Is this your man?" she asked.
> Never in America had I previously heard that expression. I thought it was something only to be read in English novels. I was indeed still very naïve.
> "Ma'am," I said, "he is not my man. He is my friend." The door smashed shut as though glass would be spewed over us. (112–3)

This event serves as historical context for a lunch Eiseley shared with Tachi many years later, long after World War II, when a new world order was uneasily in place, new wars were looming, and both men were well into their last years. They talked about their friends from the old days, only one of whom Eiseley had heard from, a Chinese man who was later killed and eaten by a tiger in Tibet. Eiseley wondered about Tachi's demeanor and its relation to his experiences in the war. Tachi, an American citizen, had returned to Japan in 1936 and was lost for a time in the chaos of war. Eventually an American intelligence unit found him. As a biologist he was recruited to help American medical teams in the horrors of the aftermath of the atomic bombing of Hiroshima.

"He had once been different, laughing, eager," Eiseley notes. "Perhaps he now lived with the dead of Hiroshima. I had no right to ask; his calm was beyond my probing" (113).

They parted. Eiseley reflects on their lives with a simple, summary sentence: "Our world was gone."

The theme of loss pervades Eiseley's autobiography and colors his own understanding of humanity. He conceived his life as a life of ruins, from which he selected shards to examine and write about. Despite his central position as longtime chair of the Department of Anthropology and, later, as provost of the University of Pennsylvania, and despite the success of his books, which included translations into a variety of languages, he saw himself as an outsider, a loner, perpetually marginal to the contemporary world. "You are a freak," a colleague once told him, "a God-damned freak, and life is never going to be easy for you" (201). This was said half in warning, half in admiration, and one senses Eiseley concurred.

Lévi-Strauss described himself not as an individual but as a site where events happen, a site where through thought the diversity of distant cultural experiences are rearticulated into new intelligible configurations. Myths thus think themselves through the minds that consider them and thereby demonstrate how the mind works unfettered by empirical concerns. Eiseley, by contrast, described himself as a troubled individual, a monad of sorts, to which things happened. He responded by retreating into himself and writing. In the process, he elevated his personal preoccupations to the status of larger philosophical problems, reasoning thus: "That the self and its minute adventures may be interesting every essayist from Montaigne to Emerson has intimated, but only if one is utterly, nakedly honest and does not pontificate" (178). A focus on the naked self, however, comes with a warning. "One had to stand aloof. Otherwise one was easily destroyed." Eiseley passed his life standing aloof and left a substantial account of what he saw along the way. He lamented life's inevitable destruction with only one resonant exception recorded in autobiography.

Walking home on the evening of a holiday party, "tired of my own skin, of sterilized apartment living," Eiseley happened upon a cat in distress just outside his building, hiding beneath a bush. The vocal cat "was not merely saying he was lost and complaining about it."

> With a perfectly amazing eloquence he was going up and down the scale of animal grievance. If I could not completely make out the words, I could comprehend their gist. This invisible cat was informing me of the nature of the world, of his deliberate abandonment, of his innocence of wrong, and of my duties as a human being. (229)

Eiseley ignored the covenants of his apartment building, took the cat in, and eventually found him a home. With an odd sentimentality verging on the maudlin, he became attached to the cat in ways he never expressed in writing toward humans. The cat provided a brief occasion for Eiseley to become comfortable in his own skin and represented the possibility of a certain egotistical transcendence. "He is still living, may outlive me," Eiseley allows, "but with him I finally outfaced the universe" (235).

Margaret Mead

Eiseley, whose father died from the Spanish flu in 1919, grew up impoverished with a deaf, possibly schizophrenic, mother. By contrast, Margaret Mead (1901–1978) had a relatively comfortable upbringing. Her father was a college professor and her mother was pursuing a PhD at the time of Mead's birth. She grew up in a multigenerational household, rarely attended school, and received much of her formal instruction from her father's mother. One gathers from her autobiography, *Blackberry Winter*, that her comparatively mild traumas were social, the result of being different and not fitting in. These traumas came during her college years and were tempered by her strong sense of self-worth, developed in a household that valued intellect and promoted an egalitarian ethos.

Engaged at seventeen and married at twenty-three, Mead, who kept her own last name, went to Samoa at twenty-four, while her husband, Luther Cressman, traveled to Europe to pursue his own graduate education. In 1925, a decade before Lévi-Strauss ventured to Brazil, and five years before Eiseley rode the rails across the American southwest, Mead made her first field trip. She wanted to go to Tuamotu and study culture change, but Franz Boas thought that too dangerous and insisted she travel to an island that had regular steamer service. He also provided her with a topic: adolescent girls.

"Chance favors none but the prepared mind," Louis Pasteur notes. Chance also favors the well-situated. Mead was a student of Boas, friend of Ruth Benedict, and uniquely positioned to pursue her ethnographic interests. On her way to Samoa she stopped in Hawaii, where a family friend eased her transition.

> When I arrived in Honolulu I was met by May Dillingham Freer, a Wellesley friend of my mother's. She and her husband and daughter were living in their house up in the mountains where it was cooler, but she said I could live in Arcadia, their beautiful big house in the town. The fact that my mother had known May Dillingham and her sister-in-law Constance Freer at Wellesley made all the difference in my comings and goings in Honolulu for many years. May Dillingham was the daughter of one of the original missionary families, and her husband Walter Freer had been governor of the Hawaiian Islands.... [S]he was able to command any resources she needed and her influence, which extended even to Samoa, smoothed my path in a hundred ways. (145–6)

Mead took advantage of the colonial social organization that predated her arrival, but she scarcely referred to it in her own analyses. Instead, her brief comments acknowledged the random elements in any fieldwork. "The factor of accident is great," Mead says about the help of her mother's friend. "Mrs. Freer might have been away from Honolulu when I arrived. Just that" (146). But rather than take the opportunity to reflect on the social relations that provided her entrance into Samoan life, Mead passed over that entrance as if the historical moment did not matter.

But it did matter. Mead had with her "a letter of introduction from the Surgeon General of the Navy." As it happened, the surgeon general had attended the same medical school as Mead's father-in-law; her own affinal relations thus played an unexpected role in her Samoan work. "Without the letter," Mead writes, "I do not know whether I would have been able to work as I wished." The letter of introduction "opened the doors of the Medical Department," which assigned Mead a "young Samoan nurse, G. F. Pete, who had been to the United States and spoke excellent English" (147). Her work facilitated, Mead found it much easier to travel to local villages and set up ethnographic shop. In the back of a medical dispensary on the island of Tau, for example, she interviewed young girls without the complications of Samoan rank relations that would have made such interviews difficult had she lived with a Samoan family. "People knew that when the fleet came in to Pago Pago I had dined on the admiral's flagship," Mead explains. "[T]hat had established my rank" (150–1). Her rank was publicly understood, but she preferred to keep some personal details private, unsure of the ethnographic costs. "[I]n Vaitogi I did not tell them that I was married; I knew too little about what the consequences might be in the roles that would be assigned to me" (148).

Far from standing aloof or conceiving herself as an element in a collectivity, Mead thought it possible to conduct ethnographic research as a *tabula rasa*. "To do it well," she writes, "one has to sweep one's mind clear of every presupposition, even those about other cultures in the same part of the world in which one is working." The technique probably requires practice, but Mead does not describe how she managed it. Once clear of presuppositions, she argues, good ethnography is possible. "Later, when one has come to know the new culture, everything has to be reassimilated into what is already known about other peoples living in that area, into our knowledge about primitive peoples, and into our knowledge about all human beings, *so far*" (143).

Mead's solution to the problem of ethnographic description and analysis is the opposite of Lévi-Strauss's. Mead saw herself as an individual capable of limiting her assumptions about the world and, thus cleansed, to experience others without bias. She had the skill to approach each ethnographic encounter *de novo*. For Lévi-Strauss, by contrast, it was precisely the structure of the mind that was the object of inquiry. Anthropologists, with a shared symbolic capacity of those they study, were in a position to render intelligible the experientially distant and to find common form in the worldwide ethnographic clutter.

On her way to meet her husband after her fieldwork was completed, chance again intervened. Mead sailed from Samoa to Sidney, Australia, and then to England. In Sidney she boarded the SS *Chitral*, whose schedule included a stop in Tasmania to pick up a load of apples. A dock strike in England, however, made it unwise to take on a load of fruit that might spoil if left unloaded. Most passengers disembarked, while Mead, low on funds, stayed onboard waiting for the ship to eventually sail. "Of course," she writes, "I can never know how differently that whole trip—and so my own life—might have turned out had the *Chitral* sailed to Tasmania, as planned, to pick up a cargo of apples" (157).

But change her life did. During the multiweek voyage to England she met Reo Fortune, who was to become Mead's second husband. Fortune engaged in enthusiastic conversation and both created a "state of profound excitement," according to Mead. "He was going to England to meet people who could understand what he was talking about, and I, just emerging from the field, was hungering and thirsting for communication" (158). Those on board thought they were having an affair and shunned them. "We were not, but we were falling in love, with all the possibility of a relationship I found profoundly unsuitable" (161).

Mead eventually returned home, took a job as assistant curator of ethnology at the American Museum of Natural History, wrote *Coming of Age in Samoa*, divorced, and married Fortune. Mead had always intended to have a large family but was told that she had a tipped uterus and would not be able to have children. She rethought her marriage plans. "One of my principal reasons for not wanting to marry Reo was my feeling that he would not make the kind of father I wanted for my children." But without children, Fortune would make an ideal intellectual companion and field colleague (164).

They decided to work in the Admiralty Islands among the Manus, about whom little research had been conducted. At this point in her autobiography, Mead seems to have abandoned the *tabula rasa* ideal of ethnographic fieldwork and articulated her own feelings about the people she studied. Her personal reactions may have affected her ethnographic assessment.

> I was as surprised at the ways in which the Manus were less pleasant than the Samoans as Reo was surprised at the ways in which they were so much more pleasant than the Dobuans. And neither of us identified with them. They were a puritanical, materialistic, driving people and they were driven relentlessly by their ghostly mentors, who punished them for the slightest sexual misdemeanor, like accidentally brushing against a member of the opposite sex when a house floor collapsed, or for gossiping, as when two women were heard talking about their husbands. The ghosts punished people for not meeting their innumerable economic obligations, and if they had met them, for not contracting new ones. Life for the Manus was very much like continually walking up a down escalator. The men died early; they did not live to see their son's children born. . . . The children were delightful, but I always had before my eyes the kind of adults they would soon become. (171–2)

At the end of their New Guinea fieldwork, Mead and Fortune returned to New York City in September of 1929, just before the October market crash signaling the onset of the Great Depression. Mead resumed her position at the American Museum of Natural History, although her salary had been reduced. They were fortunate to have $5,000 in earnings from *Coming of Age in Samoa*, an unexpected best seller. Unlike Eiseley, for whom the Great Depression was a personal trauma, for Mead, "the Depression at first meant very little to me."

Over the next two years, Mead wrote *Growing up in New Guinea* while Fortune completed revisions to *Sorcerers of Dobu* and wrote *Manus Religion* as a doctoral dissertation. They also received two small grants for an ethnographic study of the Omaha Indians. They both found the experience depressing, in large measure because they believed reservation Indians too acculturated. Fortune, however, wrote *Omaha Secret Societies* based on his research.

Mead describes American Indians as less congenial for study than the peoples of Oceania. "The stance of American Indians," she writes, "was very alien to us, accustomed as we were to Oceanic peoples who, however dour and glum they might be, were dour and glum in ways that were more intelligible" (191). Despite their reservations, they later approached Boas with a proposal to study the Navajo. Boas dissuaded them, arguing that Gladys Reichard was already engaged in such study. Chance once more intervened in Mead's plans. Because the various American Indian cultures had been assigned to other anthropologists, she was left with the option of returning to a part of the world she knew well.

In the spring of 1931, Mead and Fortune decided to return to New Guinea, but a critical review of Mead's work on Manus kinship prompted a three-month delay. Angered by the review, Mead responded by writing *Kinship in the Admiralty Islands*, later published in the *Anthropological Papers of the American Museum of Natural History* (1934). With this bit of scholarly competition out of the way, she and Fortune made their way to New Guinea by December 1931. They traveled into the interior with six months of supplies, but their porters abandoned them in a mountaintop village, "So we had no means of reaching the people we had intended to study and no choice but to settle down, build a house, and work with the simple, impoverished Mountain Arapesh, who had little ritual and less art, among whom we now found ourselves" (194).

Among the Arapesh, Mead appears to have forgotten her earlier ideal of approaching new cultures without presupposition.

> As in Manus, our personal responses to this new culture were heavily conditioned by our past experiences—by the Samoans, whom I had enjoyed, by the Dobuans, whose culture Reo had passionately disliked, and by the Manus, to whom neither of us had had any strong responses and among whom we had been able to do good work without any serious clash of temperament or personality.

Yet in 1931–1932, Mead admits that "It had not yet occurred to us that the differences in our experiences—Reo's with Dobu and mine with Samoa—had nearly as much to do with us as individuals, as it had to do with the nature of the cultures we studied" (195). The implications of this revelation would appear later in lengthy discussions of fieldwork with Gregory Bateson, who would become her third husband.

Mead thought Arapesh culture "very thin," and she "loathed" Mundugumor culture "with its endless aggressive rivalries, exploitation, and rejection of children" (205). At the completion of their work among these two groups, Mead and Fortune decided to travel to the Sepik River where they would conduct research on the Tchambuli. At the time Bateson was working among the nearby Iatmul, and all three of them engaged in lively debates about the cultures they had been studying. They began to develop "a new formulation of the relationship between sex and temperament," working out as well the temperamental differences between the anthropologists, an American, an Englishman, and a New Zealander.

> As we discussed the problem, cooped up together in the tiny eight-foot-by-eight-foot mosquito room, we moved back and forth between analyzing ourselves and each other, as individuals, and the cultures that we knew and were studying, as anthropologists must. Working on the assumption that there were different clusters of inborn traits, each characteristic of a particular temperamental type, it became clear that Gregory and I were close together in temperament—represented, in fact, a male and a female version of a temperamental type that was in strong contrast with the one represented by Reo. (216)

All of these mosquito-room discussions of temperament, "heightened by the triangular situation," illuminated the characteristics of each. Likely unaware at the time of each other's inclinations, both Mead and Bateson were bisexual (Mary Catherine Bateson; Dobrin and Bashkow; see also Howard; Caffrey). "Both Gregory and I felt that we were, to some extent, deviants, each within our own culture.... However, Reo did not have as great a sense of revelation about himself" (219). As Mead describes the increasingly awkward circumstances, she and Bateson discovered they shared a kind of temperamental camaraderie, while Fortune now became the odd man out.

Mead had earlier commented about her effect on Fortune and his work. Radcliffe-Brown thought that Fortune's *Sorcerers of Dobu* benefited from Mead's influence and was not the result of Fortune's own hard work. "This has happened," Mead notes, "a good many times in my life."

> Yet people fail to see what should be attributed to me, that is, my capacity to enjoy and appreciate other people's work in a way that seems to give them something like a transfusion of extra energy to complete a piece of research or finish a book. But the fact is, they are happy to work under what is called my influence only as long as they are working at the top of their own capacity. When their own drive fails, so that they no longer can draw on my energy, they feel it to be a reproach or an unwelcome goad, and so repudiate it. (184)

It is unknown whether Fortune's energy and drive may have eventually failed, but it was Mead who delivered the reproach. "After we separated, he wrote only one more monograph, his Arapesh texts, and the Arapesh grammar—and he left that incomplete" (185; cf. Dobrin and Bashkow).

In the spring of 1933, they all left New Guinea. Mead went to New York, Fortune to New Zealand, and Bateson to England. Mead notes that "Reo had repudiated any psychological formulations," and eventually went to teach in China, rather than continue working as an anthropologist. "[W]e were now divorced. . . . Gregory was awarded a new fellowship at Cambridge, and he and I were at last free to meet in Java and begin field work in Bali" (222). The triangular relationship was resolved, and a new dyadic relationship began between individuals temperamentally well suited to each other.

Robin Fox

Lévi-Strauss thought the self "hateful." Eiseley considered himself a "God-damned freak." Mead, by her own analysis, was "deviant." All three, however, in very different ways and to different degrees, produced work that was influential beyond the confines of the scholarly discourses in which it originated. One consequence of crossing discourses, a self-perceived marginality, applies as well to anthropologist Robin Fox.

In *Participant Observer: Memoir of a Transatlantic Life* (2004), Fox presents a history of anthropology as an illuminating cultural production through which the scholar weaves his own life story. As Fox shows, life is never one damn thing after another—at least, not in memory. His vignettes of well-known scholars with whom he interacted over the course of his extraordinarily productive life recasts their work to raise new perspectives about the history of ideas in anthropology. This effort alone makes *Participant Observer* a fine book. What makes it a compelling book is Fox's ability to move from the personal to the social, from details of his own life to theoretical issues germane to the entire field of anthropology, and to do so with verve and humor. If nothing else, anthropology, as the self-awareness of humanity in all of its prehistorical, historical, and contemporary forms, must retain a sense of humor, even as the high seriousness of the discipline remains forefront. Fortunately Fox is funny at the same time that he is serious, simultaneously playful and intellectually rigorous.

Citing Hume, Fox notes that "the very idea of 'self' is a colossal act of faith: an imaginative imposition on the random passing events." His effort, however, is not to write an autobiography, magnifying his persona across passing events in an attempt to solidify historical facts. He is interested in what he remembers, a line of inquiry that follows its own flawed logic. "Memory doesn't respect chronology or topography, but it imposes its own unreliable order; we'll go with that" (47).

What does Fox remember? Perhaps too much. As she reads through the first several hundred pages of *Participant Observer*, written in the third person, the reader realizes that the pronoun case is appropriate because the early self is not the current self and is known only distantly to the one who remembers. The prior self has no real continuity with the present self, the former transformed many times into the latter through erratic metamorphoses as drastic as Kafka's transformation of man into beetle. No continuity obtains, no simple arc from youth to old age, just unexpected jump cuts. As Fox has it, you "dance" and "skate." Fox literally danced as a child for accolades and biscuits from the Woolworth Ladies and also skated as a youth through school in a manner that was both easy, with the exception of mathematics, and pointless in the sense that he apperceived neither direction nor point of rest. Along the way, he experienced unexpected transformations, for example, from believer to unbeliever:

> He still went to church, and in however loose a way, believed. Then it happened. As swift and unexpected as the visitation of the first angel came the second epiphany. He woke up one winter morning with the frost on the windows and the water frozen in the water jug on the dresser of his unheated bedroom (heat in bedrooms was deemed unhealthy). As he stepped out into the cold room watching his breath freeze in the air in front of him, a thought crystallized at the same instant: it's all transparent, blatant nonsense! There was no lead-up of profound thinking and questioning, no agonies of indecision; it was sudden and complete and decisive. It was a complete de-conversion experience. God, if not dead, was at least badly mauled. (82)

For Fox, God and the edifice of religion had evaporated, the self was transformed, and the adults were duped by their own implausible stories. "What was wrong with them?" Fox the younger asked. "They were the adults; they knew everything" (83). Still, Fox the slightly older retained an interest in the big questions. He entered the London School of Economics, discovering anthropology and becoming dissuaded from pursuing difficult inquiry. Apparently as time went by he couldn't help himself. Kinship and incest were possible topics to pursue, with a detour to the United States to study philosophy, which was his stated preference. Chance intervened. Cornell University wrote that funds had dried up for teaching assistants in the philosophy PhD program but that he was still welcome to attend. Instead, Fox altered course to Cambridge, Massachusetts. Fox arrived at Harvard, his second option, "dangerously low on accurate information about what would be required of him" (163).

The transformed student had left LSE and its alpha males—Ernest Gellner, Raymond Firth, Bertrand Russell, Maurice Freedman, and John Barnes—and a passel of Marxist students, and alighted at Harvard among Freudians and new set of alpha males: Evon Vogt, Clyde Kluckhohn, George Homans, Paul Friedrich, and Dell Hymes. He discovered linguistics, had a conversion experience, and shed one carapace to grow another. Although Lévi-Strauss was developing a linguistic model for cultural analysis, Fox could not interest anyone at Harvard in *Anthropologie Structurale* (1958), nor in the "atom of kinship" because the nuclear family and its Freudian implications would be unseated if mother's brother became integral to the oedipal equation (189). Killing off the oedipal dragon would take time.

Another lurching detour—or was it finally a path?—brought Fox to the southwest to work among the Cochiti, a Pueblo society. "Well, he'd survived the Anglicans, the Marxists and the Freudians, he'd even survived Harvard, so far. How hard could the Indians be?" (210). Was he up to the task? There remained a problem to mull over. Fox "hated . . . objectifying [Indians] as things to be studied."

> They were people, not specimens. But this was something he sensed was unresolved by anthropologists generally. You had to be a "participant observer" but how could you participate if you couldn't sleep with the women or take part in the rituals or interfere in any way with the culture? Could you stand by and watch a human sacrifice? Yes, Freedman had said, you watched and took notes. Freedman was a tough character. He remembered Max Gluckman in a lecture saying how he had to watch a man whipped almost to death, as a punishment, in Swaziland. It was a legal punishment said the equally tough Max; one couldn't interfere. (212)

One solution to the problem of objectification was to study Keres, the local language, which Fox set about doing, filling notebooks and tapes and receiving instruction on pronunciation and use. After another year at Harvard, he returned to the Cochiti to continue his linguistic work and generated "a small mountain of notebooks on kinship terms" (249).

Following his increasingly crooked path, Fox left the United States and took a post at the University of Exeter as lecturer in sociology (with special focus on social anthropology). Here he developed lectures on kinship and the incest taboo. He decided to study Gaelic, intending to find a local fieldwork project toward which to direct his restlessness. Tory Island, off the Donegal coast, provided the location. Its three hundred or so Gaelic speakers presented an interesting variation on the human theme. Older men who married late lived with their sisters; their wives lived with their own brothers. Why upset the familiar domestic scene simply to accommodate a late marriage? The practice was once common and included younger couples. Husbands "visited" their wives, who lived with their brothers.

Heeding Firth's advice, Fox did not forget about the Pueblo, or about kinship. He returned to the "atom of kinship" but thought it not to be the basic human unit, as Lévi-Strauss argued. The basic unit, in line with other mammals, was the mother-child bond. This was the primordial relationship. The question was how human males were attached to that unit. The related question was how the mother-child relationship was provisioned and protected.

For the matrilineal Cochiti, the father and mother's brother shared adult male responsibility for a child. On Tory Island, the brother-sister tie was more significant than the husband-wife tie. The patterns were somehow related to the incest taboo, itself related somehow to evolutionary psychology. "Left to their own devices, siblings would not want to mate" (293). Why was this the case? Freud and Lévi-Strauss would have to be addressed eventually (*The Red Lamp of Incest*, 1980). But the path he was on unexpectedly led back to the London School of Economics, which offered him a job.

Primates became an interest, while his interest in kinship persisted. New acquaintances came on the scene and provided new points of intellectual consonance and departure, including David Attenborough, Desmond Morris, and Lionel Tiger, among others. The big questions were still there: the animal origins of human kinship, the transformation of elementary kinship systems into lineage systems, the relationships between language and culture, the nature of human aggression, and the evolutionary significance of male bonding, a topic Tiger fleshed out for Fox.

Chance appeared once more, this time as a job offer from Rutgers University. Fox delivered his Malinowski lecture, packed his bags, gathered up his family (which now included three young daughters), and traveled to America, to New Jersey and a home near the woods.

Again "he had blundered into something with dangerously low information, and too much of a sense that things would somehow work out" (363). Neighborly Princeton asked that he jump ship and join its nascent anthropology department. The resident anthropologists were interested in symbolism and "enamored of Clifford Geertz."

> The whole trend, they told him, was toward a "humanistic" approach rather than a "scientific" one. Then why bother? he asked. You will end up floundering around like the rest of the humanities in a constant state of anxiety over where your authority comes from, why anyone should believe you; constantly looking for saviors to validate your opinions. How, they asked him, would your approach help in the analysis of man's symbolic capacity? Good question. (374)

Fox passed on the Princeton offer and continued wending through the Rutgers thickets. His first books appeared, *The Keresan Bridge* (1967), a study of Cochiti, and *Kinship and Marriage* (1967), an enduring contribution to the field.

What of his sense of self, the colossal act of faith? What is remembered? "This is an accidental life," Fox says of himself. "He pursued his rational path, worked out his ideas, accepted his successes (good reviews and more foreign translations—Hindi, Malay, Japanese) and bemoaned his reversals, but it was out of his hands. Forces set in motion from his cradle . . . were working themselves out" (399). But such forces were not embodied in the relationship of chance and necessity, as Jacques Monod insisted was the biological basis of all life. For an individual human life it is the necessity of chance that reigns. Thus does the later self make sense of the former.

The exception comes when the former Fox is cutting into monkey brains looking for clues. Fox, ever restless, received a National Institute of Mental Health grant to go to Stanford where, with Karl Pribram as guide, he studied neuroanatomy and neurophysiology, which required brain dissection. Memory was one topic of concern, hormonal influence on behavior another. About all of this the later Fox says and apparently remembers little. We will have to go with that.

The big questions continued to tantalize. Evolutionary processes had to be incorporated into any adequate account of human mind and sociability. Lévi-Strauss's work on categories, the pervasiveness of oppositional modes of thought, the human propensity for using natural kinds to stand for social groups, and marriage exchange—all of these needed to be understood against the background of human evolution. How else to make sense of it all?

Tiger's and Fox's *The Imperial Animal* (1971) was published and promoted to general audiences, with talk shows and attendant fanfare. Ashley Montagu, no stranger to the talk-show circuit, advised them that publicity stunts were useless. "You would be better off," said Ashley, "taking a handcart and a bell . . . and hawking copies in the street" (426). The real problem in the 1970s was cultural, not entrepreneurial. The popular and academic response to placing human sociability in an evolutionary framework was one of rejection *tout court*. For the cultural determinists, "any kind of appeal to the innate, whether to innate ideas or innate emotions, or innate social bonding mechanisms, however carefully it avoided the simple-mindedness of the nature/nurture debate, would be vetoed as disreputable and even evil" (430). Vetoed it was, by feminists who disagreed with the evolutionary implications and by academics who disliked seeing culture as anything but *sui generis*, unconfined by biology. But popular and culturally freighted academic responses are not markers of the solidity of ideas. Humans are animals, after all, not rather like animals; we are subject to the constraints of our evolutionary history regardless of how we come to symbolically constitute them. As Bateson foresaw, the problem was how to work out the biological fundamentals while keeping cultural observations intact. This is what Fox and Tiger attempt to do.

Scholarly life, Fox writes, is inevitably "a prolonged peer-review process" in which the culture of contradiction holds court (273). Make a proposition about the human world, no matter how clearly self-evident, and the response will be a foreseeable counterproposition. Promote an argument and someone will promote the opposite argument. Develop a theory and the naysayers will tip it over. Marshal a series of facts and someone will shoot them down one after another. Such is the world of scholarship. The self in this world is a curious artifact, a floating, buffeted plank. "It was too soon for premonitions of death," Fox says of his own buffeted self, "too late to regret being born; it was time to re-group" (461).

Oxford provided the locale to regroup and, with kids in tow, Fox fretted. He "felt less and less any sense of continuity with his old lives or any confidence in those to come." He had a vague sense of direction, but no strong convictions about it. "What was the point of it all . . . the discontinuous self wondered, except perhaps to ask this very question?" (536).

> Perhaps the self has periodically to reconstitute and redefine itself. Mostly this is a case of minor nudges at predictable points in the life cycle, and societies mark these changes with appropriate rituals to help in the redefinition. But sometimes when the points of change are not predictable, the self's equilibrium gets pushed out of whack into a state of near chaos, and the outcome is either self-destruction or a creative reintegration at a different level of selfhood that in turn becomes itself a creative force. That's what he told himself as he tried to come to terms with his sense of loss. But he thought it more likely that the self meandered back and forth between states, never coming to rest, always uncertain where it belonged. (552)

Yet a meandering life still needed tending. Colleagues wanted conversation, students required teaching, children demanded attention, and work, always work, waited to be finished. *Encounter with Anthropology* (1973) appeared, and other books appeared in turn: *The Tory Islanders* (1978), *The Red Lamp of Incest* (1980), *The Search for Society* (1989), *The Violent Imagination* (1989), *The Challenge of Anthropology* (1995), *Reproduction and Succession* (1997), *Conjectures and Confrontations* (1997), *The Passionate Mind* (2000), and *The Tribal Imagination* (2011).

Randomness, a sense of marginality, and the pressure to speak about the world characterize the self-descriptions of Lévi-Strauss, Eiseley, Mead, and Fox. Anthropology tends to promote the marginality of its practitioners. The diverse patterns of human behavior inevitably invite one to ask: Why do I behave thus and not otherwise? Why do I believe this and not that? The self-consciousness of anthropology and the impulse for explanation and interpretation are always incomplete, the more so in social worlds whose trajectories are mutable and unpredictable. Individuals manage to find points of stability—perhaps anthropologists find stability only through their scholarship—but these too are eventually undermined. "Our world was gone," Eiseley says as he reflects on the atomic bombing of Hiroshima. Who cannot make a similar statement about any number of historical junctures?

Lévi-Strauss described and worried over the loss of cultures, his sad tropics, accompanied by the rise of Western civilization. Eiseley lamented humanity's penchant for self-destruction and recognized in himself the impulse to kill another. He ended *All the Strange Hours* with an old man's despair, commenting on his childlessness and apportioning blame to his mother, whose grim mental illness affected his choices. Mead insisted to her American audience that their lives could change for the better if they attended to other places and other cultures and tried to transcend their own limitations, even though she found little to celebrate in some of the "loathsome" cultures she studied. With palpable pessimism, Fox placed human aggression in the context of primate evolution and wondered whether there were ways out.

Yet if one essential statement can be made about humans, it is this: humans persist—abundantly and creatively. From an estimated population of one million to three million hunter-gatherers 20,000 years ago, humans rapidly increased their numbers. By 6,000 years ago there were approximately 86 million humans on the planet. By AD 1750, there were nearly 730 million. In 1950, the figure stood at 2 billion 400 million. Today there are nearly 7 billion, and by the year 2050, estimates put the human population at over 10 billion 200 million (Ausubel; Deevey; Livi-Bacci). One essential quality of an expanding humanity is its resilience, based in large measure on relations of kin. Studies of kinship animated anthropology for a century, and Lévi-Strauss, Mead, and Fox were, in different ways, central to that effort. After an unfortunate decades-long decline in attention to kinship, in which cultural difference was mistaken for an absence of common form, a renewed interest can be found in the work of Nicholas Allen, Bernard Chapais, Maurice Godelier, Per Hage, Doug Jones, and Bojka Milicic, among others. These scholars continue to ask the big questions, increasingly informed by the conjunction of genetics, archaeology, historical linguistics, comparative anthropology, and comparative primatology.[2]

As with much of their professional work, Mead's and Fox's autobiographical accounts also mark the significance of kin. Mead's final chapters in *Blackberry Winter* are about becoming a mother and grandmother, which in her earlier life she had thought impossible. She discovered in herself a way to delight in and commemorate new life. And Fox found his children to be a kind of fulcrum or perhaps a pivot of self, offering new and unexpected ways of being. They provided the occasion to finally end his sustained effort of memory and his search for meaning. Beginning *Participant Observer* with his own unlikely birth, Fox ends with his teenage daughters' mirth:

> As they giggled and laughed, and drank their watered wine, all sense of futility evaporated; the vastations were banished. There was no

longer a mystery. This was the one thing with which he could feel an absolute connection. *This was the point.* (574)

Thus does the boat of self stay afloat.

Acknowledgments

I would like to extend thanks as always to Mona Letourneau who provided fresh insights, critical commentary, and careful editing.

Notes

1. "Hegemony" may be too strong a term—or maybe not. Witness the recent removal of the word "science" from the long-range plan of the American Anthropological Association. The former plan was to "advance anthropology as the science that studies humankind in all its aspects." The new plan is "to advance public understanding of humankind in all its aspects" (Wade).
2. For a review of mathematics as an appropriate language for comparison in anthropology, see Jenkins.

References

Allen, Nicholas J., Hillary Callan Robin Dunbar, and Wendy James, eds. 2008. *Early Human Kinship: From Sex to Social Reproduction.* Oxford: Blackwell.

Aunger, Robert. 2004. *Reflexive Ethnographic Science.* New York: AltaMira Press.

Ausubel, Jesse, and H. Dale Landford, eds. 1997. *Technological Trajectories and the Human Environment.* Washington DC: National Academy Press.

Behar, Ruth. 1997. *The Vulnerable Observer: Anthropology That Breaks Your Heart.* Boston: Beacon Press.

Behar, Ruth, and Deborah Gordon, eds. 1992. *Women Writing Culture.* Berkeley: University of California Press.

Bateson, Mary Catherine. Foreword to *Steps to an Ecology of Mind*, by Gregory Bateson, vii–xv. Chicago: University of Chicago Press, 2003 (1972).

Bateson, Gregory. 2003 (1972). *Steps to an Ecology of Mind.* Chicago: University of Chicago Press.

Caffrey, Margaret M. 1989. *Ruth Benedict: Stranger in this Land.* Austin: University of Texas Press.

Chapais, Bernard. 2008. *Primeval Kinship: How Pair-Bonding Gave Birth to Human Society.* Cambridge, MA: Harvard University Press.

Clifford, James, and George E. Marcus, eds. 1986. *Writing Culture: The Poetics and Politics of Ethnography.* Los Angeles: University of California Press.

Davies, Charlotte Aull. 1999. *Reflexive Anthropology: A Guide to Researching Self and Others.* London: Routledge.

Deevey, Edward S. 1960. "The Human Population." *Scientific American* 203 (197).

Dobrin, Lise M., and Ira Boshkow. 2010. "'Arapash Warfare': Reo Fortune's Veiled Critique of Margaret Mead's 'Sex and Temperament,'" *American Anthropologist* 112:370–83.

Eiseley, Loren. 1975. *All the Strange Hours: The Excavation of a Life.* New York: Charles Scribner's Sons.

Fisher, Michael M. J., and George E. Marcus, eds. 1986. *Anthropology as Cultural Critique: An Experimental Moment in the Human Sciences.* Chicago: University of Chicago Press.

Fox, Robin. 2004. *Participant Observer: Memoir of a Transatlantic Life.* New Brunswick, NJ: Transaction Publishers.

Fuchs, Stephen. 2001. *Against Essentialism: A Theory of Culture and Society.* Cambridge, MA: Harvard University Press.

Geertz, Clifford. 1973. *The Interpretation of Cultures.* New York: Basic Books.

Godelier, Maurice, Thomas R. Trautmann, and Franklin E. Tjon Sie Fat, eds. 1998. *Transformations of Kinship.* Washington DC: Smithsonian Institution Press.

Howard, Jane. 1984. *Margaret Mead: A Life.* London: Simon and Schuster.

Jenkins, David. 2011. "Anthropology, Mathematics, and Per Hage's Contribution to Kinship Theory." In *Kinship, Language and Prehistory: Per Hage and the Renaissance in Kinship Studies*, edited by Doug Jones and Bojka Milicic. Salt Lake City, University of Utah Press. 188–9.

Jones, Doug, and Bojka Milicic, eds. 2011. *Kinship, Language and Pre-History: Per Hage and the Renaissance in Kinship Studies.* Salt Lake City, University of Utah Press.

Kaminer, Wendy. 1999. *Sleeping with Extra-Terrestrials: The Rise of Irrationalism and Perils of Piety.* New York: Pantheon Books.

Lévi-Strauss, Claude. 1969 (1964). *The Raw and the Cooked: Introduction to a Science of Mythology.* Translated by John and Doreen Weightman. New York: Harper and Row.

———. 1973 (1955). *Tristes Tropiques.* Translated by John and Doreen Weightman. New York: Atheneum.

Livi-Bacci, Massimo. 2001. *A Concise History of World Population.* 3rd edition. Malden, MA: Blackwell.

Lukes, Steven. 2006 (1973). *Individualism.* Colchester, UK: ECPR.

Mead, Margaret. 1972. *Blackberry Winter.* New York: William Morrow & Company.

Monod, Jacques. 1972. *Chance and Necessity: An Essay on the Natural Philosophy of Modern Biology.* Translated by Austryn Wainhouse. New York: Vintage Books.

Myerhoff, Barbara, and Jay Ruby, eds. 1982. *The Cracked Mirror: Reflexive Perspectives in Anthropology.* Philadelphia: University of Pennsylvania.

Orlans, Harold. 1981. "An Anthropologist without a Tribe: A Memoir." *The American Scholar* 50:65–78.

Quine, W. V. O. 1960. *Word and Object.* Cambridge, MA: The MIT Press.

Rabinow, Paul. 1977. *Reflections on Fieldwork in Morocco.* Berkeley: University of California Press.

Rosaldo, Renato. 1989. *Culture & Truth: The Remaking of Social Analysis.* Boston: Beacon Press.

Sahlins, Marshall. 1997. "Comments on Robert Borofsky, 'Cook, Lono, Obeyesekere, and Sahlins,'" *Current Anthropology* 38:255–82.

———. 2000. *Culture in Practice: Selected Essays.* New York: Zone Books.
Salzman, Philip Carl. 2002. "On Reflexivity." *American Anthropologist* 104:805–13.
Sontag, Susan. 1966. *Against Interpretation.* New York: Farrar, Straus & Giroux.
Wade, Nicholas. "Anthropology a Science? Statement Deepens Rift." *New York Times.* December 9, 2010.
White, Richard. 1991. *The Middle Ground: Indians, Empires, and Republics in the Great Lakes Region, 1650–1815.* Cambridge: Cambridge University Press.
Wilcken, Patrick. 2010. *Claude Lévi-Strauss: The Poet in the Laboratory.* New York: Penguin Press.
Wisner, William H. 2005. "The Perilous Self: Loren Eiseley and the Reticence of Autobiography." *Sewanee Review* (Spring):84–95.

12

The Universal Epic: A Research Challenge

Frederick Turner

If modernity has ever agreed on any one thing, it is that epic is dead. Historians today like to date modernity all the way back to the Renaissance, a practice that deprives us of some useful if impressionistic language for historical periods. In these terms Giambattista Vico (1688–1744) is already a modern thinker, and he is already, by his famous categorization of history into the age of gods, the age of heroes, and the age of men, implicitly consigning epic to the respected but dismissed childhood of the race. In his footsteps almost every sober, sensible theorist of history has classified epic as the product of a naïve and barbarous era, defining "now" as "not like that."

The tone of that dismissal has changed over the last few centuries. Edward Gibbon and Jean-Jacques Rousseau regret the passing of a nobler and simpler heroic age. Nineteenth- and twentieth-century literary scholars such as W. P. Ker and C. S. Lewis see epic as having decayed into romance or sophisticated itself from the robust old "primary epic" into the self-conscious "secondary epic" and thence into extinction. The novel was to replace the epic; the novel was, in the words of the Marxist scholar John Lukacs, "a typical product of the Bourgeois Age"[1] in our own era—and was in turn slated for revolutionary replacement. "History begins in novel and ends in essay," wrote Macaulay, implying that history had not even begun at all in the prior age of the epic.[2] Lukacs agrees with him, and quotes Ortega y Gasset:

> The novel and the epic are precisely poles apart. The theme of the epic is the past as such: it speaks to us about a world which was and which is no longer, of a mythical age whose antiquity is not a past in the same sense as any remote historical time. . . . [T]he epic past is not our past.[3]

Mikhail Bakhtin was probably the most influential theorist of the novel's triumph over the epic.[4] He argued that while the novel was, like clay, adaptable and suitable to a world of change and evolution, the epic was marble—fixed, hierarchical, sacred, and fit only for a static society, with a hero who is perfect and exists only in his external actions. The novel was "dialogic"—it could contain many different and even conflicting voices; the epic was "monologic." This essay hopes to demonstrate the error of this view, its ignorance of the actual texts and their historical context; but it is to a large extent the contemporary view of the matter.

Some on the left have suggested that the virtues of the novel—its individualism, its power to engage the emotions on behalf of the characters, its acceptance of the social status quo, even while pushing for incremental social reform, its dialogical acceptance of different truths—make it a reactionary bourgeois form, an instrument of sentimental "false consciousness." Perhaps instead epic could be dragged out of the dustbin of history and put to work for the revolution. As Walter Benjamin put it,

> Epic man is only at rest. In the epic, the people rests after the day's labor; it listens, dreams, and collects. Nothing contributes more to the dangerous silencing of the human spirit, nothing stifles the soul of narration more thoroughly than the shameless expansion that the reading of novels has undergone in all of our lives.[5]

Benjamin called for an "epic leftism," using the monologic of epic to weld the people into an instrument of heroic class struggle. After all, he argued, the fascists were already, in Wagnerian Nuremberg style, coopting the old heroic meta-narratives; they were weapons that should rightly belong to the leaders of communist struggle. Berthold Brecht devised an "epic theater" for the same purpose, eschewing the easy identification of audience with bourgeois hero or heroine, reviving the stern clarity of the ancient tribal storyteller. If epic was, as they believed, dead, it might be revived for the sake of the people's revolution. But this view would leave epic in the hands of the perpetrators of the Gulag, the Great Leap Forward, and the Killing Fields.

Postmodern critics, however, their hopes for revolution dashed by the collapse of world socialism, rejected all such "grand narratives." Jean-François Lyotard, the coiner of the phrase, left open the possibility of many little narratives, culture worlds that could not claim a utopian general truth (an idea developed by Michel Foucault in his theory of distinct incommensurable epistemes, local regimes or hegemonies of power and knowledge). Perhaps, though Lyotard and Foucault are not specific, epic could find its place among these local regimes, but only if shorn of its grand pretensions to universality. Epic would be another picturesque tale told around some local campfire. Jean Baudrillard goes further:

> The end of history is, alas, also the end of the dustbins of history. There are no longer any dustbins for disposing of old ideologies, old regimes, old values. Where are we going to throw Marxism, which actually invented the dustbins of history? (Yet there is some justice here since the very people who invented them have fallen in.) Conclusion: if there are no more dustbins of history, this is because History itself has become a dustbin. It has become its own dustbin, just as the planet itself is becoming its own dustbin.[6]

In other words, because the Marxist grand narrative has failed us, all grand narratives must be rejected. All we have left is simulacra. But there is a small ray of hope even here for epic as grand narrative; if the planet is a dustbin of narratives, then maybe we must live in that dustbin and make some kind of home there; and the making of that home might be a fairly grand story in itself. And maybe that was what epic was all along.

One result of these developments in cultural and political theory has been an astonishing and almost total absence of serious literary critical attention to epic for at least the last sixty years. W. P. Ker's *Epic and Romance*[7] was published in 1897; J.R.R Tolkien's lecture "The Monsters and the Critics"[8] was delivered in 1936; C. S. Lewis's *A Preface to Paradise Lost*,[9] the last comprehensive and theoretically serious defense of epic as a serious literary form, came out in 1942. There have since been some good textbook introductions to the subject for students, such as Dennis Tedlock's important preface to his translation of the *Popol Vuh*,[10] and some excellent scholarly articles in the classicist journals dealing with fine points of linguistic and textual detail in Homer and Virgil, but there is nothing to match the enormous output of material in the literary field on other subjects, including really ephemeral texts in the popular media. Here we have a major genre, surely as important as the novel, the lyric poem, or the tragic drama, that has been profoundly neglected.

There are other reasons for this neglect than the consignment of epic to the dustbin of history. One is that classicists and conservative literary scholars have tended, as we have seen in the case of Ker and

Lewis, to set a very high and narrow bar for what constitutes epic at all. Epic, they seem to imply, is a creation of certain high ("Western") civilizations such as Greece, Rome, Italy, France, Germany, and Britain, not naked savages or Oriental despotisms. This territorial tactic (the obverse of that of the Marxist historicists, who regarded epic as admirably barbaric but passé) was bound to misfire when deconstruction, feminism, and postcolonial studies set out to undermine and dismantle the imperialist male Western canon. If epic is the "high" "Western" genre par excellence, the grand narrative of oppression, essentialism, and the marginalization of the subaltern, then it presents a ripe target for dismissal by the aspiring English professor.

Academic specialization largely concealed from such a professor the fact that an enormous variety of nonwestern societies also have works that, if construed without slavish adherence to European classical rubrics, are unmistakably epic. When, as the result of the renewed (and very welcome) interest in "non-Western" cultures that was one good result of the postmodernist movement, literary academics started to pay attention to the larger "non-Western" texts, they had lost the taste and criteria that could have identified some of those texts as epic and placed them in the company of Homer and Virgil.

In my own experience of teaching and writing epic over at least forty years, I have run across an extraordinary variety of reasons why my colleagues reject epic as a proper subject of study and try to put it away in a definitional cage (even if the cage differs radically from one critic to another). They try to cage it to make the world safe—safe for reason, for prose, for the novel, for the lyric poem, for democracy, for the marketplace, for revolution, for non-Western traditional wisdom, for non-narrativity, for nonlinearity, for the hermeneutic incommensurability of local epistemes, for little narratives, for women's stories, for minorities, for unmediated existential experience, for an undamaged natural environment, and for many other endangered causes. Beyond these reasons for the literary dismissal of epic as a legitimate object of critical study is a pervasive sense that epic is for children (or "young adults"), especially boys, and may bring out the worst in them at that, like war toys. Serious poststructuralist professors are embarrassed by the emotions and partisanships and half-remembered nobility and grandeur of the old stories. We are so much more conscious, self-aware, and disillusioned than that now.

Outside literary studies as such there are fields of scholarship that still pay attention to the material of epic. The five most important ones

The Universal Epic

are folklore, oral tradition studies, mythology, religious studies, and anthropology. Here the perverse incentives against the study of epic qua epic work in a different way.

Folklorists are often faithful to the "low" oral culture, defining themselves as champions of the cultural underdog, and are wary of letting literary high-culture types lay claim to their material by means of such markers as epic. The study of oral tradition, a closely related field, has taken a similar position. Felix Oinas's path-breaking collection of scholarly essays on what he calls "folk epic," though valuable, suffers from what I regard as too rigid a distinction between oral epic and literary epic, and an implicit prejudice against the latter as not being truly of the folk.[11] Where this distinction breaks down is in two respects: often written and oral versions of the epic stories have coexisted for decades or centuries, exchanging material and ideas, such as the stories of Rama, the Volsungs, the Nibelungs, Roland, King Arthur, Cuchulainn, the Mayan hero twins, Alexander, Rostam, and Sundiata. Certainly epic cannot be studied adequately without a McLuhanesque attention to its medium. But as in many other ways, epic always, and constitutively, stands at the borders; it does so also between different media and modes of communication and commemoration. Its "always already" implies some kind of fall from an ancient mythic world to a legendary and even historical one, and it generally marks one of the many transitions in media that go along with that fall—from one kind of orality to another (e.g., iconic or ritual to narrative or moralistic), from the oral to the written, from the written to the printed, from the classic language to the vernacular, from verse to prose.

The other consideration that makes the "oral vs. literary," "folk vs. individual," "popular vs. courtly" distinctions, so loved by folklorists, not always useful in understanding the epics themselves, is the matter of the audience. Literary epics can be just as popular, just as much of a folk phenomenon, as oral epics. Scholars and gentlemen are not the only people who read and love literary epic. Consider the popularity of the Mahabharata in India, the Homeric epics in Greece, the Divine Comedy in Italy—the folk culture of those nations is not just shaped by those works, but even constituted by them, so that they would be inconceivable without them. And on the other hand, the implication that the oral poets were not scholars, not conscious of themselves, not individuals, and not conversant with courts and schools, is itself of course an illusion. The folk did not compose epic—particular poets did. The professional modesty of the oral performer—they usually say, "this is how I heard it from the old griots my fathers," or something of the kind—should not deceive us, any more than should similar protestations from the folksingers of our own mountains. Certainly the oral poets were in close touch with their market and possessed a deep intuition into the fundamentals of human nature; if they did not, they would fail. But it is in their individual conscious voice, fully capable of "meta" analysis, that the folk—or rather the human—themes are articulated.

This is not to underestimate the great importance of contemporary scholarship in the oral epic. John Miles Foley, a giant in the field, gives a splendid list of current and recent textualizing projects in his review of Lauri Honko's fine translation of Gopala Naika's *The Siri Epic*:

> the Manas epic and Wilhelm Radloff, the Mohave epic and Alfred Kroeber, the South Slavic epic and Milman Parry and Albert Lord, the Sunjata epic and Gordon Innes, the Anggun Nan Tungga epic and Nigel Phillips, the Annanmaar epic and Brenda Beck, the Palnaadu epic and Gene Roghair, the Son-Jara epic and Charles Bird and John Johnson, the Siirat Banii Hilaal epic and Susan Slyomovics, and the Paabuujii epic and John Smith.[12]

This work is providing a whole new wealth of stories for the enrichment of our perhaps over-refined stock of narrative, and will perhaps be material for epics of the future. The irony is that these very efforts themselves represent the ancient epic event in which the oral and the literate meet, merge, and turn back to examine the transition itself. In these scholarly works, the epic moment of transition from oral to literate continues. And scholarship of this kind, specialized as it must be, except in the work of Foley, cannot yet afford to broaden its purview to include the canonical literary epics and ask itself the meaning of all the remarkable underlying commonalities in epic across the globe.

Similar barriers to a truly comprehensive view of epic also exist in the academic fields of mythology and comparative religion. Mythologists prefer their mythemes and deep structures unmediated and unadulterated by the artistic ambitions, rational reductionism, and ideological biases of courtly epic writers. Religious studies scholars naturally focus their attention on the priestly caste, whether brahminical, scribal, and mandarin or mystical, shamanic and ascetic, and resist the claims of the warrior-ruler caste, the knights, kshatriyas, and samurai, whose exploits are so large in epic. In anthropology there is a traditional split between sociocultural and physical (evolutionary) anthropology that has tended to paralyze epic studies.

I would argue that epic is basically about human evolution—that is, epic is the traditional way we have explained to ourselves as a species our emergence from nature and the stresses within our own nature that result from that emergence and our look back at it. But in the quarrel between sociocultural constructionist anthropologists and naturalist evolutionary anthropologists this fundamental theme of epic is lost. It is lost on one side because cultural and social anthropologists tend to believe that we are more or less a blank slate to be inscribed by social and cultural norms. There is an honorable history to this view, for it is the easiest and most comprehensive rebuff to the scientific racism of much early anthropology. There is also, perhaps, a less admirable subtext, which is that because each society and subculture to be studied is a unique world unto itself, unconstrained by human universals, there will always be significant new material for anthropological fieldwork. So epic, with its powerful myths of the natural underpinnings of our social practices, would seem to imply an essentialist naturalization of unjust status roles and would look much like the enemy of the egalitarian ethic of humanistic anthropology. Epic's cultural universality would both unify a field of study that temperamentally prefers radical diversity and suggest that the "West" (usually the villain of the piece) is not the only "tribe" that has fought, conquered, ordered the world, and subjugated nature. On the other side, the evolutionist anthropologists, who like to look underneath social and cultural conventions and practices to the deep survival drives that have preserved our species, tend to dismiss such cultural genres as religion, art, and epic poetry as "spandrels" in the evolutionary edifice, pretty but insignificant byproducts of the interplay of inherited neural and behavioral traits that confer adaptive advantages. Thus the idea that epic composers may have already second-guessed the evolutionists and conducted their own rather penetrating analysis of how we got to be human would be a little humbling and turn what were the raw materials of scientific study into equal collaborators in it. And if epic composers and their audiences have known about our evolution all along—in traditional symbolic and narrative terms to be sure, but rather useful ones—then who knows how our analysis of underlying evolutionary motives and behavioral drives may have been compromised and nullified by conscious resistance to them or enlistment of them for cultural, strategic, or ideological ends? After all, anthropological evolutionists justify their analysis of human behavioral predispositions on the basis that if we understand them, we can—if they lead to racism or the oppression of women or an unwholesome appetite for sweet things, for instance—control them by social policy. But if the participants in the human drama of evolution were always already canny observers of it, the clarity of the evolutionists' subject and method would suddenly give way to a complex, colorful, and subtle set of puzzles and branching pathways, like the world of epic itself.

Of course, I am here exaggerating the anthropological rift and the extremes to which its participants have gone. Most anthropologists have a more mixed and nuanced view. But the ideological rifting has been enough to leave epic in the resulting limbo between the sides. Two great exceptions to this criticism are Victor W. Turner and Robin Fox. Turner (my father) developed a penetrating analysis of Icelandic saga using his favorite anthropological device of social drama, an analysis with implications for epic tales in general.[13] And Robin Fox, anthropologist and poet, in his *Conjectures and Confrontations* and *The Tribal Imagination*, has brilliantly applied anthropological understandings of sexual competition and male bonding to epic literature.[14] His profound literary knowledge of epic informs much of his other work, and he has implicitly indicated the point of the sense of parallelism increasingly recognized by anthropologists in the great narratives of humankind: they are not many stories, but one.

Beyond the ideological obstacles to the study of epic there are also practical difficulties that stand in the way of a fair, updated, and comprehensive assessment of the value of epic. The problem of academic specialization has already been mentioned; scholars often seem unaware of the rich variety and wide extent of the epic literature, partly because of their confinement within the literary, mythological, folkloristic, comparative religionist, or anthropological worlds, partly because if one is studying a particular culture, one is relatively unaware of others. More immediately to the point, though there are many epics in the world, there are few in any given language; most cultures are blessed with only one or two, if any, that have received the true epic response of a popular audience. Thus a new student of epic must choose to work with translations if any real scope and a good sample of the genre is to be attempted, and even an experienced multilingual scholar will have access to only a small fraction of the literature in the original, often in archaic forms of the language at that. Time and tenure will not wait for the linguist; and the canons of scholarship are contemptuous of work with translations. But rich fields of research lie open if we ignore such cautions and obstacles.

Despite all the discouragements in the secondary academic world of theory, commentary, and criticism, the epic impulse continued unabated for some time in the primary arena of creative art and literature. Wordsworth's *The Prelude* explicitly and implicitly invites the designation "epic," arguing that the history of the individual soul is worthy of epic treatment. Tolstoy's *War and Peace* is plainly epic in conception. Herman Melville's *Moby Dick* adopts the epic rhythms of Christopher Marlowe, William Shakespeare, and John Milton into its prose, and Melville's ambition was arguably more to create the great American epic than the great American novel. Joyce's *Ulysses* reprises Homer. Ezra Pound evoked the great classical epics in his *Cantos*, and in *The Waste Land* Eliot created a marvelously mutilated and condensed mini-epic based on the matter of *Parzifal*. Today the major American poet Julia Budenz is composing an enormous poem in five books, *The Gardens of Flora Baum*, that invokes the ghosts of Virgil and Tasso. The science fiction genre is lavishly epic in scope, inspiration, and action, taking on the ancient themes of world creation, sacrificial heroism, death and immortality, and nature and human nature, without embarrassment. But the avant-garde literary world since the postmodern movement emerged has been largely dismissive of epic.

A new generation has, however, grown up without the prejudices against epic that accompanied the revolt against grand narrative. Even when their elders are content with the elegant little narratives of suburban divorce and private existential struggle, the young are unashamedly epic in their tastes. The very word *epic* is now a live term in their vocabulary for something that is big, exciting, and cutting edge. The cultural genres of Marvel Comics, gothic, anime, multiuser dungeon gaming, summer superhero movies, Civil War reenactments, Renaissance fairs, and the like, reprise all the epic themes and motifs, sometimes consciously, but sometimes as a natural human tropism toward a real human need. Consider *The Wizard of Oz, Star Wars, Star Trek, The Lord of the Rings, Lost, The Matrix, Superman, Harry Potter, Narnia, Batman*; here we find the epic beast-man, the miraculous birth of the hero, the creation myth, the founding of the city, the quest journey, the descent into the land of the dead, the monsters, the trickster, the mystery woman, and all the other epic elements that we shall look at in due course.

A Loose List of Epics

But perhaps at this point the question has been begged: what actual works are we calling epic, and on the basis of what defining characteristics do we so name them? Here the problem for the epic scholar is like that of the biological taxonomist: does one present as confirmation the best specimens of the species one seeks to claim and name—in which case how does one make the choice of specimens? Or does one give one's criteria for describing the species and then pick specimens to fit one's definition?—in which case one stands in danger of imposing an abstract and arbitrary unity and uniqueness on a set of unrelated handpicked individuals. If one claims king penguins as a species on the basis of a collection of specimens, how does one avoid the charge that one just picked, for instance, large long-beaked Adelie penguin individuals? And if one defines the king penguin as being warm-blooded, marine, air-breathing, and predatory, one could end up with penguins, dolphins, whales, walruses, and plesiosaurs as all variants of king penguins. I shall here adopt, as the beginning of a confirmation process, the first strategy, which relies on a strong intuitive sense of family resemblance in choosing a reasonably canonical group of representatives of the genre. Given the fact that I make no appeal to traditional literary authority beyond the use of the term "epic" itself, I beg the reader's provisional assent to the classification, pending later analysis of the features shared by the group, exclusion of nonmembers, and confirmation of the category's organic necessity. This "fresh start" is, I believe, necessary because so many new candidates for the epic canon have emerged through international scholarship that the criteria for admission need to be looked at with an unbiased eye. We may end up with a kind of classicism. But it will not be a European or "Western" one, and it may be very much more exciting and useful than the old one.

To illustrate the cultural universality of epic across multiple remote geographical locations, historical eras, ethnic and linguistic groups, and levels of technological and economic development, I shall classify my proposed list of epics by geographical area, but in no special chronological order.

Africa
Sundiata (Mali)
Mwindo (Congo)
Tambuka (Kenya)

Asia
Gilgamesh (Mesopotamia)
Enuma Elish (Mesopotamia)

Iliad (Asia Minor)
Odyssey (Asia Minor)
Mahabharata (India)
Ramayana (India)

Shahnameh (Persia)
Book of Genesis (Palestine)
Book of Exodus (Palestine)
The Tale of the Heike (Japan)
The Journey to the West, or *Monkey* (China)
King Dongmyeong of Goguryeo (Korea)
King Gesar (Tibet)
Silappathikaram (Tamil India/Sri Lanka)
Manimekalai (Tamil India/Sri Lanka)
David of Sassoun (Armenia)
Manas (Kyrgyz Turkey)
The Secret History of the Mongols (Mongolia)

Europe
Aeneid (Italy)
The Divine Comedy (Italy)
The Liberation of Jerusalem (Italy)
Orlando Furioso (Italy)
The Song of Roland (France)
The Song of the Nibelungs (Burgundy)
The Saga of the Volsungs (Norway)
Njal's Saga (Iceland)
Laxdala Saga (Iceland)
The Peril of Sziget (Hungary)
Kalevala (Finland)
The Poem of My Cid (Spain)
Don Quixote (Spain)
The Cattle Raid of Cooley (Ireland)
Beowulf (England)
The Faerie Queene (England)
The Henriad (Shakespeare's *Richard II; Henry IV,* parts 1 and 2; *Henry V*) (England)
Paradise Lost (England)
The Prelude (England)
The Waste Land (England)

The Kossovo Epic (Kossovo)
The Lusiads (Portugal)
Parzifal (Germany)

Americas
Popol Vuh (Mesoamerica)
The Mohave Heroic Epic of Inyo-kutavêre
Omeros (St. Lucia, West Indies)
The Gaucho Martín Fierro (Argentina)
Hiawatha (USA)
Moby Dick (USA)
The Cantos (USA)
Paterson (USA)
Davenport's Version (USA)
The Gardens of Flora Baum (USA)
The Alamo (USA)
Genesis, an Epic Poem (USA)
The New World (USA)

It would be easy to argue with both the inclusions and the exclusions in this list. Why the *Enuma Elish* but not Hesiod's *Works and Days*? Why leave out Apollonius's *Argonautica*, Lucan's *Pharsalia*, or for that matter Joel Barlow's *Columbiad*? Should recent small-press poems such as John Gery's Davenport's *Version* and Budenz's *The Gardens of Flora Baum* be excluded—or other works with rather small audiences such as Michael Lind's *The Alamo* and my own *The New World* and *Genesis, an Epic Poem*? What about Wordsworth's *Prelude* and Pound's *Cantos*? The former could well be called an extended autobiographical lyric, the latter a collection of cultural reflections without a central narrative. Some of the Asian works may be better classified as king lists or chronicles, especially the *Shahnameh*. Wu Cheng-En's *The Journey to the West*, the Icelandic sagas, and *Moby Dick*, among other works, are in prose. And if we are to include Shakespeare's *Henriad*, why not other extended dramatic works, such as Aeschylus's *Oresteia*? Where would we put the elder *Edda*, the *Morte d'Arthur*, *Sir Gawaine and the Green Knight*, *Orlando Innamorato*, *Ossian*, and the like?

And how do we establish the canonical texts of these works, when so many of them, such as the *Mahabharata*, the Old Testament books, *Gilgamesh*, the *Popol Vuh*, the Tamil version of the *Ramayana*, and the *Kalevala*, are manifestly palimpsested compilations, summaries, abridgements, or translations? My practice in this survey is to treat the more composite texts (as opposed to "signed" final versions such as the *Iliad* or *Paradise Lost*) as musicologists treat folksongs or as Internet users treat corrigible collaborative texts such as *Wikipedia*. The variants, whether as different retellings, such as the various versions of the *Mio Cid* story, or as included in the same text, such as the J, P, and E texts in *Genesis*, or as translations, or as embedded annotations and interpretations such as those of the *Mahabharata*, could perhaps be treated as legitimate elements of the work, contradictions included.

Some traditions, such as those of the classical Greeks, Romans, and Chinese, and those of modern Europe, seem to like to keep the text, once established, as fixed and then generate around it a body of commentary, imitation, and interpretation. Others, such as those of the Hebrews, the Indians, and medieval Europe, prefer to extemporize.

Further objections to my list might legitimately be raised. Where are Oceania and Australasia in this picture? Why are some great civilizations, such as Egypt, absent from the list, and others, such as China and much of Latin America, rather thinly represented while England and Italy are given plenty of candidates? Why did some cycles of story material—the Pele myths of the Hawaiians, the *Chishimukulu* stories I heard as a child growing up among the *Ndembu* people of Zambia, the *Gjeto Bashi Muje* hero legends of Albania and Serbia, or for that matter the Arthurian Round Table—never quite cohere into the definitive epic narrative?

I believe these questions are all relevant and legitimate, but far from being true objections, they are an indication of the richness and value of the epic category itself and an invitation for rewarding readership and scholarly debate. My own ignorance, and that of the literary world in general, is surely to blame for some omissions and the cultural suppression of epic texts and oral traditions—and whole languages—by conquering aliens may have deprived us of many great works. The survival of the *Popol Vuh*, one of the purest and most comprehensive epics in the canon, containing almost all the essential epic elements, was something of a miracle—probably written down in the Mayan hieroglyphics, it was lost (or destroyed by the Spanish with many other Mayan texts) and exists only because a Franciscan friar made a handwritten copy in the 1700s.

But the point is that the very idea that an epic is strangely missing in a great culture—that it might be buried somewhere, or that, on the other hand, it was there all the time but we did not recognize it as such—is a powerful research hypothesis. Further, it may make us think more deeply about epic, in ways that will help us reinterpret the existing canon. Are the Australian songlines actually the Aboriginal version of epic, for instance? Most epics incorporate story explanations of place-names such as Mount Moriah in the Book of Genesis, or Misenum in *The Aeneid*, named after the drowned sailor, or Thorgeir's Ford in *Njal's Saga*, named for Thorgeir Otkelsson, one of Gunnar's unfortunate victims whose floating body ended up at that location. Could it be that instead of epic merely containing place-name stories, it is a place-name story, and the Aborigines have the purest, most fully enacted, and most graphic version of it, its meter here the footsteps of the walkabout? In these terms the Hoares' great garden of Stourhead in Wiltshire, which compels the visitor to symbolically reenact the journey of Aeneas around its exquisite artificial lake, may itself be a walkabout, a sort of epic performative text.

The absence of Egypt from the list perhaps constitutes another critique of our classification. Ancient Egypt surely had the time and stability to produce a poet who could integrate into an epic tale the rich body of myth and story that constitute the soil of any human culture. There are two Egyptian candidates for possible inclusion in our list: the Egyptian creation myth in one of its versions (from Thebes, Heliopolis, Hermopolis, or Memphis) and the Egyptian *Book of the Dead*. Neither incorporates what one might call an epic hero story. The latter is almost a how-to book for negotiating the underworld. But the former bears comparison with the Mesopotamian *Enuma Elish* (on my list) and Hesiod's *Works and Days* (not present on my list), and the latter obviously with Dante's *Divine Comedy* and the underworld journeys in many epics across the world. If the Aborigines' songlines argue that epic is basically place-naming, the Egyptians seem to be arguing that epic is basically a preparation for death, which requires a basic theology of creation if one is to know whom one is meeting in the afterlife. Perhaps the landscape, architecture, history, and funerary ritual of Egyptian civilization were so epic in themselves that no heroic epic was necessary. Again, such issues are more indications of the richness and fertility of the epic category than a refutation of it. If the category provokes questions of great analytical power, then it is worth keeping.

If epic, or at least the epic impulse and a maturing group of epic elements, is so universal, why is it so? What all human cultures have in common is the evolutionary history of our species: perhaps this is the deep subject of all epic, and the reason why all epics converge on certain fundamental themes and forms. The hypothesis, then, is that epic is not beneath serious critical attention, nor even just another legitimate literary form, but the most fundamental and important of all literary forms. It is the *fons et origo* of all the others, the frame within which any literature is possible at all, and a live genre whose reawakening may stimulate a fresh burst of creative literary activity. Epic is the basic story that the human species tells to itself about itself and, using its own narrative and symbolic and folk-science terms, an accurate description of the evolution of the human species seen from the inside and half-remembered in the most graphic and intuitive language. It is a record of the emergence of language and a way to understand the formation of new words and the process of definition and referentiality. This reflection should be a call to begin to repair the great gaps in the literary understanding created by the absence of epic studies—and perhaps offer a permission to future epic writers. Perforce this work must be a close and also wide-ranging analysis of specific passages, themes, plot elements, and symbols in epics from across the globe, which will be the only possible proof of the pudding.

But this is to anticipate. Without a second list, against which we can cross-reference the first—a list of the basic themes, elements, and plot structures of epic, the habits, gifts, and mannerisms, so to speak, by which we recognize the epic family—our list of epic candidates remains only a hypothesis. And to this second list we will now turn.

Elements of Epic: The Super-Attractor

What is needed is an expanded definition of epic, not as focused upon a single attractor, such as W. P. Ker's fine but limited formula, "the defense of a narrow place, against odds," but as tending in its much iteration to fill out the form of a beautiful, shapely, but intricately rich and complex "strange attractor." The proof of the pudding is in the eating, how useful both for anthropological understanding and literary appreciation the "eating," or reading, of the great tales this new definition can be.

The definition is expanded in two senses. One is that it literally takes in works from all over the world, without narrow classicizing boundaries of space or time, as we have seen in our first list The other is that it includes a much larger range of archetypal elements than have been proposed to date. If the choice of examples from so extensive a range would tend to loosen the term *epic*, blur its boundaries, and erode its usefulness, the corresponding expanded specification of epic elements that are demonstrably common and shared will tend to restore the sharpness and value of the word's meaning. Here, then, is the proposed second list, with some important subheadings:

1. *The epic storyteller*
   - The prayer or invocation
   - The appeal to tradition
   - Frame tales
   - Blindness and memory
   - The carrying of the story as itself an epic theme

2. *The Creation Myth*
   - Does it need to be explicit?
   - The dividing of the primal unity
   - Creation by word
   - The rules of recombination
   - False starts
   - The great flood

3. *The Hero*
   - Miraculous birth
   - Obscure origins
   - Blazing the trail: the hero as representing but transcending the cultural norm
   - The heroic code
   - Heroic leadership and its dangers

4. *The Quest*
   - The question
   - The journey
   - Obstacles and enemies
   - Monsters, natural and divine; our own monsterhood
   - Magical helpers, weapons, and talismans
   - Games, rituals, and trials
   - The great battle
   - The noble death or return

5. *Kinship Troubles (includes troubles between in-laws, parents, close kin raised apart, cousins, and half-siblings)*
   - Kinship in human evolution
   - The wrong woman
   - The marriage test
   - Oedipal conflicts
   - Bad gifts and bloody feasts
   - The burning house
   - Tragic kin slaying in ignorance or by intention

6. *Definitions of the Relationship among the Three Worlds*
    - Nature
    - Culture
    - The divine and the covenant
    - Introduction to the divine personalities, their history, relations, and conflicts

7. *Natural Man and the Fall*
    - Knowledge of one's own consciousness
    - Knowledge of one's own death
    - Knowledge of possibility of collective death (a second fall)
    - Sex
    - Drugs
    - Clothes
    - Technology, invention, or shamanic revelation of new technology
    - Mobility, the loss of the home place
    - Loss of one kind of strength, gain of another
    - Domestication of animals
    - Agriculture

8. *The Descent into and Return from the Underworld*
    - The dead companion
    - The need for funeral
    - The hero and the shaman
    - The guardians and the lords of death
    - The use of the talisman
    - The conversation with the dead
    - The prophecy
    - The assignment of the task or duty
    - The return to the land of the living
    - Time anomalies

9. *The Founding of the City*
    - The idea of home
    - The building of the walls and gates
    - Sacrifice and commutation of sacrifice
    - Origin of present rituals, food laws, taboos, mutilations, etc., distinguishing in-group from others
    - Genealogies of gods and humans
    - The establishment of a local language, place names, etc.
    - The creation of a cosmological center
    - The code of laws
    - Boundary markers

10. *The History of the People*
    - Conquests
    - Singled out by the gods

- Faults
- The weak ruler and the superior but faithful follower
- Destiny

11. *Setting an Example—Definitions of Core Values*
    - Good-bad
    - Admirable-despicable
    - Firstness-secondness
    - Primary-meta
    - Wise-foolish
    - Holy-profane
    - Venerable-ridiculous
    - Beautiful-ugly
    - Tragic-comic
    - Honest dealing–trickery
    - Contradictions and choices in the application of these values
    - Building a value language

12. *The New Medium of Communication*
    - From mute to spoken
    - From oral to written
    - From writing to print
    - Record-keeping institutions
    - Unification and fixing of national language
    - Emergence of prose
    - Economic changes in the media of exchange
    - A new religion

13. *Formal Markers*
    - Meter and mnemonics
    - Formulae and mnemonics
    - Story tunes and mnemonics
    - Formalization of meter in written works to preserve the human voice
    - Magnitude
    - Lists and comprehensiveness
    - Boundary conditions

The first objection to this list might be that it has bundled into one category several entirely different kinds of things: creation myths, hero tales, national histories, magical romances, religious scriptures, and the like. Here I shall invoke Wittgenstein's term, *family resemblance*, for the second time. In the family not everyone has Grandfather Edwin's nose, though most do. Young Tom's stammer only seems to occur once or twice in a generation. Great-Aunt Ruby has that odd smile that shows up unmistakably in several cousins, some of whom have

Edwin's nose and some do not. When you know the family well, a newly met member of it is easy to spot. I would argue that the second list is the set of basic epic features, not all of which occur in all epics, but which stamp a work as epic if there is a sufficient critical mass of them—the way to spot whether some work is a member of the epic family. Of special value to the critic and reader is that sometimes one of those family features may be present in a subtle or hidden form, the recognition of which will produce a cascade of insight into a difficult text. Sometimes an epic element is significantly lacking, either because of a special cultural suppression of it or because of the author's intent to make a statement, as when a composer omits an allegro movement or chooses not to make a pause between two movements.

Though the *Mahabharata*, for instance, is not ostensibly a creation myth (such as the Book of Genesis and the *Enuma Elish*), nor does it make a special point of a journey to the land of the dead, nor give prominence to the "beast-man" theme, all three elements are present in relatively brief episodes. The churning sea of milk creation story becomes a microcosm of the creative process of the whole poem. The underworld vision that Yudhishthira experiences in a dream, of Duryodhana enjoying the afterlife while the *Pandavas* languish in darkness, is a significant critique of easy moralistic interpretations of Karma and an important complement to the paradoxes of the *Bhagavadgita* episode.

The story of the horned forest child Rishyasringa, who is so natural, ignorant, and holy that he does not recognize as female the girl who is sent to lure him from the wild, is just a tale told by Yudhishthira to entertain his brothers. But in that it is the wild man whose capture restores the rain to a drought-ridden civilization, it is an important commentary on the healing and fertility that the Pandava brothers bring back from their own sojourn in the forest—a theme that now casts light on the forest exile of Rama in the *Ramayana* and exactly parallels the great myth of the fall of Enkidu from natural innocence in *Gilgamesh*; it illuminates the meaning of the shaggy nakedness of Odysseus when he emerges from his bed of leaves on the shore of Phaiakia (he resembles a "mountain lion") and the transformation of the half-brothers of Hunahpu and Ixbalanque into monkeys exiled to the forest. Meanwhile, the omission of the "wild man" theme in the *Aeneid* (explicitly signaled by Aeneas's prudent decision to leave Polyphemus and the Cyclopes alone) is plainly meant by Virgil—who knows what the theme means—to indicate that his poem is not about the transition from wild nature to human nature but the transition from human nature to lawful civilization. But natural man in the brief Cyclopes episode is still present, *"sous rature,"* as Derrida would say.

Some cultural traditions suppress certain epic themes. Creation myths are scarce, except by remote inference, in the great Christian hero epics of Roland, Parzifal, the Nibelungs, the Arthurian world, and the Crusaders, but that is because the Christian creation story was the canonical and unchallenged possession of the church. The proto-Christian epic of *Beowulf* gives Grendel a provenance not, as we might expect, among the frost giants, but in the Genesis account as a descendant of Cain. The pagan saga of the Volsungs, which preceded the later northern works and supplied them with story material and heroes, begins explicitly right in the midst of the old Nordic creation myth, but that part is omitted from the Christian sagas (though traces of the old creation myths remain in the Icelandic prose sagas, whose subtext is the transition from pagan polytheism to Christianity). The creation theme returns in full theological garb in *Paradise Lost*, Milton having found a way to accommodate the rich material of pagan creation myths as tropes and imagery, carefully criticized for their relative correspondence with Christian truth.

Some cultures, perhaps, have been so disturbed and divided by economic, political, or ecological change that there simply has not been time enough for their proto-epic ingredients—creation myths, trickster tales, funeral rites, heroic tales, animal spirit lore, and so on—to cohere into a single large story. Had the unification of the Hawaiian island chain by King Kamehameha been followed by a couple of hundred years of consolidation and the emergence of a bureaucratic script for recordkeeping, no doubt some courtly maker would have told the great story in fitting language, incorporating ancient legends of the arrival at the islands and the myth cycle of Pelé.

If certain clusters of story elements were unique to specific cultures, another argument might be made against the validity of the expanded epic category as suggested here. That is, if hero tales only occurred in one culture, creation myths in another, and so on—if quests, tricksters, underworld journeys, wild men, and the like were exclusive inventions of particular nations—then the coherence of the epic classification would be in doubt. But though many epics lack significant elements, there are enough epics in widely different locations and times that contain almost all of them for us to be sure that the differences among such works are not differences of kind but choices within a single menu. For instance, as I have already pointed out, the *Popol Vuh* contains almost all of the major elements: the creation, the hero tale, the founding, the quest, the journey to the land of the dead, the wild man or beast-man, the trickster, the wrong woman (Egret Woman), the national history, the gods, the genealogy, the place-names, and so on. Other epics with a full complement include the *Sundiata* of Mali, the *Odyssey*, the *Mahabharata*, the *Tibetan Epic of King Gesar* (at one million lines, the longest epic in the world), and *Paradise Lost*.

In so characterizing these works—as if they were retellings of a story mysteriously known to the poets already, retellings modified by local concerns—I am introducing a method whose validity will need to be proved. I would add, however, an unverifiable but to me compelling observation drawn from my own experience of having composed two narrative poems of epic length and several more of lesser magnitude, and thus having been compelled to invent plot details and symbolic and thematic material to flesh out the story. When my intent was to tell a grand narrative, it was as if episodes, plot points, bones of contention, and situations sprang in full detail to my mind as I proceeded, linking up with each other in a fashion like the architect Christopher Alexander's "pattern language" and guided by an organic sense of rightness. In chaos theory parlance, I was being drawn into certain preexistent basins of attraction.

When this happened I often found later, upon reading an epic from the canon for the first time, that I had reproduced exactly an episode that had been composed hundreds or thousands of years before and in two or three different and, in their time, unconnected parts of the world. Perhaps I was composing clichés; but these were very peculiar clichés if so, as I had not heard them before. Indeed one could argue, as would proponents of the social construction of the self, that I had picked them up as part of my local episteme from forgotten conversations or reading, or on the other hand agree with the evolutionary psychologists that I was simply reporting my innate psychological hardwiring. But if those memes are so pervasive or the genes so persuasive that poets will naturally seek such basins of attraction, then epic is indeed a real category, a super-attractor composed of many such preferred spots in the topology of the human phase space.

Notes

1. John Lukacs, *Historical Consciousness: The Remembered Past* (Piscataway, NJ: Transaction Publishers, 2004), 118.
2. Thomas Babington Macaulay, review of Henry Neele's *The Romance of History: England*, in *The Miscellaneous Writings and Speeches of Lord Macaulay* (Longmans, Green & Co., 1889), 133.

3. John Lukacs, *Historical Consciousness* (Piscataway, NJ Transaction Publishers, 1994), 118.
4. M. M. Bakhtin. 1982. *The Dialogic Imagination* (Austin: University of Texas Press).
5. Walter Benjamin, "The Crisis of the Novel," review of Alfred Döblin's *Berlin Alexanderplatz*, 1930, in *Selected Writings*, vol. 2, edited by Michael Jennings (Cambridge: Belknap Press, 2003), 301.
6. Jean Baudrillard, 1994. *The Illusion of the End* (Stanford University Press), 263.
7. W. P. Ker, *Epic and Romance* (Wilmington: CreateSpace, 2009).
8. J. R. R. Tolkien, *The Monsters and the Critics* (New York: HarperCollins, 1997).
9. C. S. Lewis, *A Preface to* Paradise Lost (Oxford University Press, 1961).
10. Dennis Tedlock, trans., *Popol Vuh: The Definitive Edition of the Mayan Book of the Dawn of Life and the Glories of Gods and Kings* (London: Touchstone, 1996).
11. Felix Oinas, *Heroic Epic and Saga: An Introduction and Handbook to the World's Great Folk Epics* (Indianapolis: Indiana University Press, 1979).
12. John Miles Foley, "Experiencing the Siri Epic," 1985, *Folklore Fellows Communications*, www.folklorefellows.fi/comm/rev/reviewffc264-266.html, 1999.
13. "An Anthropological Approach to the Icelandic Saga," in *On the Edge of the Bush*, edited by Edith Turner (Tucson: University of Arizona Press, 1985), 71–93.
14. Robin Fox, *Conjectures and Confrontations: Science, Evolution, Social Concern* (Transaction, 1997); *The Tribal Imagination: Civilization and the Savage Mind.* (Harvard University Press, 2011).

VI

Nature and Society

Love at First Sight

Although I never saw your face before,
Your image was prefigured in my mind,
Assuring me that one day I could draw
Upon this template, knowing I would find
With instant recognition what I sought.
So when you blazed into my consciousness
The golden message in my brain was caught,
Examined, and in milliseconds "yes"
Came back the answer "this is she who was
And is and always will be coded there."
I did not need to verify because
The answer was confirmed by your brief stare,
And for one terrifying moment we
Were locked in perfect mental symmetry.

13

From Human Nature to Human Society: Why Anthropology Cannot Ignore Biological Constants

Bernard Chapais

> *"As a student I had the litany chanted at me: 'Biological universals cannot explain cultural differentials.'... Even in those days I was plaguing my teachers with the question: If we do not really know what biological universals there are, how can we study the cultural differentials? How can we study the variables without the constants?"*
> —Robin Fox, ([1970] 1989a, 15–16)

The question Fox was plaguing his teachers with is possibly that which best embodies cultural anthropology's most fundamental *raison d'être* as a discipline. Anthropology is indeed uniquely positioned among the social sciences to integrate biological constants (human nature) and cultural variables and propound on this basis unified theories of human behavior. Cultural anthropology is the sole academic specialty that has the required data on "cultural differentials" to do so. From that perspective it may appear a priori paradoxical that this endeavor should have been neglected, if not discarded, by the discipline. Of all time a majority of cultural anthropologists have considered human nature—the universal set of biological predispositions, mental and physical, affecting human behavior—as a marginal entity. Significantly, the idea that human nature could be practically ignored was far from being limited to the cultural relativistic persuasion and its numerous schools of thought. Staunch protagonists of systematic cross-cultural comparatism—people who believed in the existence of general laws governing the cultural realm and hence in humankind's unity—nonetheless minimized human nature. For example, no less a positivist than Marvin Harris proposed a list of "pan-specific bio-psychological principles" that included only four items: the need to eat (high-calorie diets), the sex drive, a preference for energetically less-demanding ways of carrying out physical activities, and the need for love and affection. His main argument for such a succinct list was that "the more parsimonious we are about granting the existence of bio-psychological constants, the more powerful and elegant will be the network of theories emanating from sociocultural strategies" (1979, 63).

To Harris and a host of other comparatists, the laws governing the sociocultural realm stemmed from, and were intrinsic to the sociocultural realm itself; they had little to do with human nature. The work of Claude Lévi-Strauss, possibly the most influential anthropologist of the twentieth century, provides another, particularly significant, example. In stark contrast with the majority of his fellow comparatists, the father of structuralist anthropology was a strong advocate of the idea that cultural diversity reflects universal constraints set by the human mind—by human nature. For all that, Lévi-Strauss consistently limited the content of human nature to a tiny set of "mental structures," such as reciprocity and binary oppositions, and was extremely reluctant to phrase the corresponding processes in terms of biological processes. He also discarded any significant biological influence on social behavior. Thus, although structural anthropology departed drastically from the powerful relativistic school in its appraisal of humankind's psychic unity, both perspectives conceived of human nature as an extremely indeterminate source of influence on behavior.

The reasons underlying that foundational postulate of sociocultural anthropology form an extraordinarily intricate web of ontological, epistemological, philosophical, theoretical, political, and moral factors that have been amply discussed by many, notably by Fox (see in particular, Fox (1989b), a collection of essays, the first of which was written in 1970). Notwithstanding that complex history, the most basic reason may well reflect the conjunction of two factors: an erroneous theoretical conception, combined with a solid empirical finding, the former factor compounding the latter. The theoretical factor was the widespread postulate that biology has deterministic effect on behavior and therefore that a significant human nature must be manifest in the existence of "behavioral universals"—behaviors that are both omnipresent and uniform cross-culturally. The empirical factor was the exact opposite finding, and ethnographic fact, that there are no behavioral universals, that extensive variation is the rule wherever one looks. The contradiction between theory and fact was thus blatant. Moreover, what turned out to be universal were categories that appeared hardly meaningful by virtue of their generality. As remarked by Lévi-Strauss,

> Ethnologists, mostly Americans, have greatly enriched our inventory and proposed a list of universal traits: age gradings, sports, bodily adornment, calendar, toilet-cleanliness, community organization, cooking, cooperative labor, cosmology, courtship, dance, decorative art, and so on. In addition to the bizarre character of an alphabetical repertoire, those common denominators are only vague and meaningless categories. (1983, 61, my translation)

The categories were indeed highly heterogeneous, readily mixing cognitive abilities, social activities, social patterns, social concepts, semantic categories, technological categories, and so on. If such repertoires had the unquestionable merit of imposing a reflexion on the very origin of so many universal phenomena, they said very little about the content of human nature, and almost nothing about the causal relations between human nature and the sociocultural realm. In short, they were not operational. The upshot was that the quest for universals based on the fallacious uniformity premise provided cultural anthropology with what was apparently a solid case for dismissing human nature as an indeterminate entity.

The investigation of human universals had concentrated on universals of substance—or content—and to many anthropologists they had to be defined that way. In the words of Geertz, "to say that 'religion,' 'marriage,' or 'property' are empirical universals is to say that they have the same content, and to say that they have the same content is to fly in the face of the undeniable fact that they do not" (1973a, 39–40). But, as emphasized by Fox more than forty years ago (1989a), if there are universals they are at the level of *process*, not at the level of substance. Borrowing from Wittgenstein, Fox argued that a given process could generate a universal pattern that would take on different forms in different cultures, with some forms lacking certain features present in other forms. To illustrate the principle, Fox considered "the elusiveness of the nuclear family as a universal" and reasoned that "if one takes the component bonds and a theory of the bonding process, then one can see how the process generates the patterns and this would include a theory to explain why in particular instances certain bonds were *not* activated for certain purposes, hence the gaps" (1989c, 117). The universal processes Fox alluded to were some sort of deep structural principles underlying a variety of social forms, for example, principles common to all human kinship and marriage arrangements. Although those principles were not biological or psychological by nature, they were, presumably, the expression of biopsychologial processes.

Mainstream cultural anthropology has since persisted in ignoring human nature. The problem with that position is that from the perspective of theory building it may be the most counterproductive stance ever in the whole history of the discipline. Human nature indeed appears of cardinal importance (1) to characterize humankind's cross-cultural unity, including the deep structuring principles that run through all human societies; (2) to understand the intimate connections between biological constants and the realm of culture, hence the world of symbolic representations and meaning; and (3) to build large-scale—panhuman—theories about human behavior, theories that make sense of cultural *diversity*. In sum, anthropological theory can hardly do without human nature, and this, in combination with the tremendous complexity of sociocultural phenomena, might well explain why the history of anthropological theory over the last century has tended to be mainly substitutive, with competing schools of thought replacing one another, rather than cumulative as in many other sciences. What is needed at this point is a demonstration of the *connections* between biological constants, social organization, and cultural variation. The word *connection* is central. In view of the theoretical and epistemological arguments that have been leveled against biological interpretations of human society, a key issue is the nature of the causal sequence going from biological constants and individual actions to social organization, and from there to cultural variation in social systems.

In this essay I present a preliminary version of a theoretical framework integrating biology, society, and culture. The whole argument holds in four propositions. First, all human societies would share a common denominator, a set of structural and organizational features defining the cross-cultural unity of human society and its uniqueness compared to other animal societies. I refer to that composite denominator as *human society's deep configuration* (or the deep social configuration of humankind). The second proposition is a model of human nature's makeup as far as its impact on social life is concerned. The model states that the biological constants underlying human social behavior and bridging the gap between individual minds and sociological phenomena are mental units made up of a motivational component sustaining a cognitively defined behavioral category, with every such mental unit constituting a *universal psychosocial proclivity*. The third proposition links the previous two. It states that human society's deep configuration is a correlate of human nature, the emergent manifestation of all psychosocial proclivities operating in social settings. The fourth proposition integrates culture with the model. Culture would be the capacity to express psychosocial proclivities in constantly renewed forms and meaning; in other words, culture would provide human nature with a variable content, the implication being that human nature is central for understanding the symbolic realm.

Human Society's Deep Configuration

Human society's deep configuration is not to be confused with any specific human society; it is an abstract entity. But although it is represented by no extant society, it pervades all of them. It is also more than a set of descriptive features; it is a social system—a set of elements forming a coherent whole—and a unique social system in the animal world. Human society's deep configuration is presumably the stem social system from which culture built all past and present human societies. In prior work (Chapais 2008, 2010, 2011a) I described an important aspect of that configuration, the set of principles that, taken together, define the overall structure of human society compared to other primate societies. I was then specifically concerned with social structure. But human society's deep configuration includes much more than that.

Every social species may be described in terms of a number of classes of social components: *behaviors* (e.g., grooming); *social activities* (e.g., courtship, coalition formation); *social relationships*, defined in relation to the age, sex, kinship, and social status of individuals (e.g., mother-offspring bonds, sibling bonds, pair-bonds); *social patterns* (e.g., dominance or kinship structures); and a *social structure* defined in terms of group composition, mating system, residence pattern, and genealogical structure. Moreover, every social species exhibits a relatively specific set of all such components, present in all groups of the same species. In short, every species has a universal and unique social configuration. The human species is no exception to that rule, except that all components—behaviors, activities, relationships, patterns, and structure—now have a highly variable cultural content. Other primates have some cultural traditions, mostly technological ones (McGrew 2004), but social traditions are relatively few: nonhuman primates rarely invent new ways of fighting, courting, playing, or making alliances. The repertoire of courtship acts, for instance, is limited and almost finite in any species. As a result, there is relatively little cultural variation in behavioral forms across groups of the same species (even though there is a good deal of variation in the frequency and intensity of social interactions). Another way of saying this is that social components in other species are mostly monomorphic, culturally speaking, or slightly polymorphic. In humans, by contrast, all components are highly polymorphic. They are open categories constantly filled with new cultural forms. This explains why the search for human universals has proven so frustrating. Human universals are categorical (or classificational); there are no universals of substance. Perceiving universal categories amid their extremely diverse cultural expressions has proven exceptionally difficult.

The most comprehensive repertoire of human universals was compiled by Brown (1991) based on a review of anthropological studies. Brown provided an enumerative description of "the traits that all people, all societies, all cultures have in common," or what he called the *Universal People* (Brown 1991, 130)—a concept reminiscent of Fox's description of a hypothetical primeval group issued from Adam and Eve (Fox 1989a). Brown's description was later published as an alphabetical list by Pinker (2002, 435). The list contained more than four hundred elements. But even that list still lacked several diagnostic features of human society's deep organization. It appears that sociocultural anthropology in its quest for universals was hampered by a number of serious problems that can only be attenuated or resolved by comparing human societies to *nonhuman* societies. One problem is that the cultural expressions of a universal category may be so variable as to conceal its very existence or to lead researchers to question its universal character. The universality of pair-bonding (and of its cultural correlate, marriage) is a case in point. From a primatological perspective, however, enduring breeding bonds between particular males and females are a diagnostic feature of human society. The community of mostly monogamous unions is uniquely human in the primate order, and pair-bonding is the central feature of the human mating system despite the fact that sexual promiscuity (premarital or postmarital) is practiced in all human societies (Chapais 2011b). Another problem is that some universal categories are so evident that they can easily be taken for granted by cultural anthropologists, and their significance missed or underestimated. Such is the case, for example, with the bilateral recognition of kin (Chapais 2008) and the bilateral recognition of affines (Fox 1980; Rodseth et al. 1991), traits that stand out as uniquely human in a comparative perspective. A third difficulty is that some universals can hardly be recognized as features of their own and evolutionarily meaningful phenomena in the absence of information on whether the trait is present or absent in other species. The existence of lifetime bonds between cross-sex kin and the complex suite of traits associated with the brother-sister bond in particular (cross-cousin marriage, sister exchange, levirate, sororate, avuncular relationships) provides a particularly significant example (Chapais 2008, 2010).

Using primate categories to define human society's deep configuration may appear somewhat restrictive in view of the complexity of human society, but a comparative analysis reveals that a large number of uniquely human social features emerged from ancient primate categories either merging together and producing original traits in the process (several examples are discussed in Chapais 2008, 2010) or from primate categories combining with novel biological traits. Among the latter are several cognitive abilities (e.g., the symbolic capacity, theory-of-mind, deductive reasoning), physical abilities (e.g., bipedalism), and life-history parameters (e.g., slower maturation), all of which endowed old primate traits with a new life of their own. For example, the capacity to transport objects—a correlate of bipedalism—set the stage for the evolution of a wide array of cooperative activities involving the capacity to provision others. From that perspective, human society appears as an extremely elaborate outgrowth of primate social categories.

Table 13.1 presents a list of universal social patterns characterizing human society. Because of obvious space constraints, it is not possible to present other aspects of human society's deep configuration such as the equally significant list of panhuman social activities (Chapais n.d.).

Table 13.1. *Universal social patterns—culturally polymorphic categories—characterizing human society's deep configuration. All patterns reflect human nature. Asterisks indicate patterns also present in other primates.*

Stable breeding bonds (pair-bonding)*
Multifamily groups
Monogamy/polygyny mix as modal configuration of marital unions
Extramarital (extra bond) sexual activity*
Male competition over mate retention*
Female competition over mate retention
Exogamy and dual-phase residence (premarital/postmarital)*
Flexible residence/dispersal patterns (one sex or two sexes stay or move)
Extensive bilateral kin recognition
Recognition of mutigenerational kinship links (lineage recognition)
Kin favoritism*
Incest avoidance*
Provisioning of offspring (extending over adolescence)
Biparental care of offspring*
Sexual division of labor between spouses
Parental transmission of
- wealth (inheritance)
- information (teaching)
- beliefs (including moral education)
- status (hereditary succession)*

Grandparenting (bilateral)
Cooperative labor among
- close female kin
- close male kin
- distantly related/unrelated males

Pattern of reciprocal resource sharing between families
Co-occurrence of several social orders with status differentials based on
- wealth (socioeconomic stratifications)
- physical skills
- mental skills
- knowledge

Status-based structures of influence or authority (domain specific)
Competition for status within social orders*
Alliance formation based on
• relative status (revolutionary, co-optive, conservative)*
• age and sex similarity (play groups, fraternities)
• shared ideas (ideational alliances)
Continuous segmentation of ideational alliances
Staged competitive games (physical or mental) between males
Group membership–limited access to resources*
Lifetime bonds between kin living in distinct groups (multigroup kinship networks)
Recognition of affines on both the husband's and the wife's sides
Cooperative mate selection (marital arrangements)
Matrimonial exchange
Brother-sister kinship structure
• Lifetime bonds between brothers and sisters
• Mate selection biases (cross-cousin marriage, sister exchange, levirate, sororate)
• Special relationships between uncles and nephews
Federated organization (between-group alliances)
Nested organization of social groups
Nested structure of solidarity at all levels of organization
Between-group exchange (trade)
Between-group coordination in relation to other groups
Between-group military alliances
Ingroup/outgroup distinction (intragroup solidarity)*
• Parochialism, ethnocentrism, nationalism

The most distinctive feature of human societies compared to other primate societies is perhaps that they are multilevel organizations. From a primatological viewpoint, human societies may be defined as *nested communities of multifamily groups*. The basic (modal) social unit is the multifamily group, or community of conjugal families. Multifamily groups always combine to form more inclusive social entities (e.g., villages belonging to the same band), which in turn combine to form still more inclusive entities (e.g., bands belonging to the same tribe) and so on. At each level of organization, groups act in a coordinated manner in relation to others. Thus human societies are both federated and nested entities. In our closest relatives (chimpanzees and gorillas), the local group is the largest existing social entity; there are no supragroup social structures. A small number of primate species do have a multilevel structure, with a number of polygynous units forming a cohesive group (called a band) and such groups combining to form larger aggregations (Stammbach 1987; Swedell 2011). However social bonds between individuals living in distinct groups are weak, if existent, and levels of coordination between groups are loose.

Human social organization may thus be described at various levels of network and multigroup social entities. Table 13.1 includes social patterns pertaining to all levels or organization. The list is not exhaustive but is nonetheless sufficient to pursue the general argument that, however complex it is, human society's deep organization is a product and correlate of human nature.

A Model of Human Nature

What follows is an attempt to describe the universal biological predispositions generating human society's deep organization. My objective, in a nutshell, is to show that a small number of biologically hardwired socioemotional systems, in interaction with a wide array of cognitive processes, produce a large number of universal mental units (called universal psychosocial proclivities) that, taken together, bridge the gap between human biology and human society—between individual-level factors and the sociological realm.

Evolutionary psychology conceives of the human mind as comprising a large number of specialized mechanisms that evolved to solve specific problems that early humans faced on a recurrent basis—acquiring mates, retaining them against competitors, rearing offspring, forming alliances, trading resources and services, and so on. Each of these problems in turn includes many sub-problems. For example, mate selection involves discriminating between potential partners according to their fertility, parental potential, genetic quality, and degree of kinship (Neuberg et al. 2010). The corresponding psychological mechanisms would include processes for perceiving particular cues that reveal significant categories such as kinship, fertility, disease, or inequity, and for activating particular emotional and cognitive processes, thereby inclining individuals toward particular behaviors (Neuberg et al. 2010). Many evolutionary psychologists further put forth a domain-specific, or modular, conception of the brain, according to which the mind is "made up of functionally distinct (albeit linked) cognitive, emotional and behavioral mechanisms—each adapted to a set of specific fitness relevant challenges" (Neuberg et al. 2010, 764; see also Boyer and Barrett 2005, Hagen 2005).

The present model accords with the view that there exist evolved psychological mechanisms dealing with particular problems. But it places the emphasis on how motivational systems translate into behavioral responses through the mediation of cognitive processes, regardless of the extent to which cognition is domain-specific (modular) or domain-general. The model posits the existence of a finite set of hardwired *prime social movers*. A social prime mover is a biologically hardwired link between an emotion, or a motivation, and a particular category of social contexts. Examples include *dispossession-induced anger* (experienced when one's possession is taken away against one's will through theft, extortion, or deprivation); *resenting disloyalty* (a mixture of pain, anger, and other emotions felt when one's actual social partner shows a preference for a third party, at a cost to ego); *sexual jealousy* (a particular form of the previous category, discussed below); *ostracism-induced distress* (pain associated with being excluded from an alliance by common consent, whatever the nature of the alliance); *the enjoyment of social superiority (winning)* (discussed below); *sexual attraction*; *romantic love*; the *Westermarck effect* (an expression coined by Fox, 1962—the ontogenetic process through which persons raised in close intimacy from childhood lack a sexual attraction for each other); *the enjoyment of generosity* (discussed below); *resenting nonreciprocation* (discussed below); *attraction to high-status individuals* (discussed below); *outgroup hostility* (a variable mixture of a priori mistrust, fear, and aggressiveness felt toward outgroup and unfamiliar individuals); and *parental attachment/love* (discussed below). It should be noted that all social prime movers pertain to and regulate a small number of basic social processes (competition and cooperation) and fundamental behavioral categories (reproduction and parenting).

Various lines of evidence support the existence of social prime movers: functional, phylogenetic, ontogenetic, ethnographical, and neurobiological. Functional evidence involves testing hypotheses on the adaptive design of social prime movers such as resenting cheating and inequity in social exchange (Cosmides and Tooby 2005). Phylogenetic evidence is based on a social prime mover being present in other species (e.g., sexual jealousy, the Westermarck effect, parental attachment) and the similarities reflecting homologies, homoplasies, or both.

Ontogenetic evidence refers to the prime mover being manifest at a very early age in ontogeny. For example, the motivation to cooperate (to help and share emotions and information with others) is already present in eighteen-month-old children and manifest in the spontaneous pointing of objects and events to particular individuals (Warneken and Tomasello 2006; Warneken et al. 2006; Tomasello 2008). Ethnographical evidence rests on the cross-cultural distribution of a social prime movers's behavioral manifestation. For example, ethnographic data and economic games indicate that reciprocity is valued cross-culturally (Gurven 2004; Heinrich et al. 2004; Heinrich et al. 2006). Finally, neurobiological evidence for the existence of social prime movers lies in the possibility of testing specific hypotheses about social motives. For example, individuals witnessing others' failures may ostensibly show empathy for them, but neuroimaging studies revealed that witnessing others' failures actually stimulate reward neural systems (Dvash et al. 2010). As another example, it was found that donations stimulate the neural circuitry of reward systems in the same manner that receiving donations does (Moll et al. 2006; Harbaugh et al. 2007; Fehr and Camerer 2007). This supports the view that generosity is adaptive as a means to initiate cooperative partnerships. A third example is the finding that inequity is punished by observers, even at a cost to those inflicting punishments (Gardner and West 2004; Fehr and Fischbacher 2004), but that such altruistic punishment stimulates the neural circuity of reward systems (de Quervain et al. 2004; Buckholtz et al. 2008).

Social prime movers are construed as evolved psychological mechanisms and hence as Darwinian adaptations. For example, sexual jealousy is an emotional response to the possibility (real or imaginary) that one's partner is unfaithful. Sexual jealousy thus involves a cognitive component enabling ego to assess the relevant characteristics of the social context and an emotional component motivating ego's behavioral responses. I am not so much concerned here with the cognitive processes involved in assessing social contexts, as with those regulating ego's behavioral responses. A basic assumption of the present model is that in the human cognitive environment every social prime mover has access to the whole set of cognitive potentialities of the human brain, even if the brain is modular. It is thus assumed that modules have access to information from other modules (see Hagen 2005). From this it follows that any social prime mover may translate into several cognitively differentiated behavioral responses, which I refer to as *universal psychosocial proclivities*. For example, sexual jealousy would sustain the following proclivities: acting to stop unfaithful interactions by one's partner when they are taking place; acting to prevent the reoccurrence of infidelity after it has taken place, that is, punishing infidelity; preventing unfaithful behavior by monitoring one's partner; preventing partner's infidelity through verbal prescriptions and proscriptions (about attitudes, behaviors, appearance); displaying or advertising one's sexual partnership; engaging in negative gossiping about unfaithful individuals in general; and so on. All psychosocial proclivities stem from the same emotional system but recruit distinct sets of cognitive abilities. Thus, regardless of the issue of modularity, human cognition is seen as providing a large number of cognitive means for the actualization of every social prime mover.

Psychosocial proclivities are universal because their building blocks—the underlying motivational system, the various cognitive processes involved, and the corresponding social contexts eliciting sexual jealousy—are themselves universal. Thus although psychosocial universals are biologically grounded, they are not necessarily evolved psychological mechanisms and Darwinian adaptations—contrary to social prime movers. Many of them, if not a majority, might be the emergent manifestations of interactions between specific emotions and cognitions. This evolutionarily parsimonious view remains to be empirically validated. Another important point is that every psychosocial proclivity is an open behavioral category; it is not a specific behavioral response. As will be discussed later, the exact form taken by the behavioral response, for example, punishing infidelity, is a matter of cultural context and historical background.

Parental love provides another example. In the human cognitive environment, parental love is manifest under an unprecedentedly wide array of cognitively differentiated behavioral categories: protecting children against social aggressors and physical threats; provisioning children; transmitting information to children about both the physical and social environments (teaching); imparting children with one's beliefs; providing children with behavioral directives (e.g., in relation to the value of prospective mates); planning the posthumous transfer of one's possessions to one's children (inheritance); and so on. As in the previous example, a unique motivational system recruits several distinct sets of cognitive abilities to generate a number of universal psychosocial proclivities. This example will serve to illustrate a further principle: any psychosocial proclivity may affect several distinct social domains concurrently. Imparting one's beliefs to children universally involves the transmission of beliefs about supernatural entities and about what is morally acceptable or unacceptable in various contexts, whatever the exact cultural content of those beliefs. Likewise, providing behavioral directives to children universally involves prescriptions and proscriptions relating to contributions to domestic work, sibling interactions, the suitability of potential mates, and so on. The existence of several universal domains of application for each psychosocial proclivity considerably increases the number of biologically grounded mental units regulating social behavior. On this view, biological predispositions for social life are hierarchically organized, with each social prime mover generating several cognitively differentiated psychosocial proclivities, and each psychosocial proclivity affecting several domains simultaneously. One is far from Harris's four "pan-specific bio-psychological principles."

A third example relates to competition. In humans, status competition has multiple bases besides sheer physical power, as in other primates. Those bases include athletic skills, technological abilities, accumulated wealth, verbal skills, and knowledge, among many others. Any individual may thus compete for status in a number of different arenas, simultaneously or sequentially. Status competition appears to stem from a general motivation that I refer to as the *enjoyment of social superiority* (or enjoyment of winning). It is the pleasure of winning a contest, or gaining more than others; it is also the pain of losing contests and having less. The enjoyment of winning thus involves cognitive abilities enabling a comparison of one's performance with those of others. But as in the previous examples, I am specifically concerned here with how the enjoyment of winning generates various behavioral responses through the mediation of cognitive processes. The corresponding psychosocial proclivities include the following: seeking to win contests or gain more than others; monitoring others' performances; displaying or advertising one's own level of performance; devaluing the performances of competitors, or engaging in negative gossiping about them; and exhibiting a tendency to overevaluate one's performance when telling about it.

The enjoyment of social superiority also appears to generate secondary social emotions that sustain other behavioral responses. Among those emotions are *envying* more successful individuals, experiencing *pride* when being praised by third parties, experiencing *shame* when receiving negative critiques by third parties, and *gloating* (enjoying a competitor's failures). All such secondary emotions apparently stem from the same social prime mover. Basically it is because social superiority is experienced as pleasurable that individuals find it enjoyable to be praised about their performance (pride), or to learn about a competitor's failures (gloating), and it is because losing is painful that individuals find it painful to recognize that others have more than they have (envy), or to be told by others that they are less competent (shame). Secondary social emotions are uniquely human because they involve uniquely human cognitive abilities such as the capacity to know that other individuals have knowledge, opinions, and beliefs about oneself (theory-of-mind, discussed below). (For information on social contexts eliciting secondary emotions and their neural correlates, see, for example, Izuma et al. 2008; Shamay-Tsoory et al. 2009; Takahashi et al. 2009; Tracy et al. 2010.)

Attraction to high-status individuals provides a final example. Like the three social prime movers just discussed, attraction to high-status individuals is present in other primates but in simpler forms; in primates, it translates essentially into attraction to top-ranking individuals in the dominance hierarchy. In the human cognitive environment, by contrast, attraction to high-status individuals operates in multiple social arenas, including physical power, physical dexterity, athletic performance, resource control, expertise, artistic skills, intellectual skills, and so on. Whatever the exact competitive arena considered, attraction to high status generates the following universal psychosocial proclivities: monitoring the activities of high-status individuals; imitating them (i.e., adopting their physical appearance, behavior, and beliefs); attempting to ally with them (through various means including instrumental help and information sharing); displaying such alliances; and exhibiting a tendency to obey or follow the advice of high-status individuals.

According to the present model of human (social) nature, the total number of universal psychosocial proclivities characterizing human beings would be equivalent, roughly speaking, to the number of distinct cognitive means available to express every social prime mover, summed over all social prime movers. Put very simply, it would be the summation of the mathematical "products" of emotions and cognitions. Compared to other species, human cognition greatly enriched the realm of psychosocial proclivities by providing a particularly rich array of cognitive tools for the expression of prime movers. In other species, social acts aim to affect what others will *do*: playing, helping, having sex, and so on. In humans, social acts aim, in addition, to affect what others *know* (by informing, narrating, teaching, censuring, gossiping, bragging, denouncing, etc.), what they *believe* (by persuading, proselitizing, deceiving, etc.), and what they *feel* (by praising, commending, blaming, accusing, etc.). In short, human sociality encompasses *ideational objectives*, in addition to emotional and behavioral ones.

Basically, ideational objectives reflect the operation of two major sets of cognitive abilities: symbolic communication and mental state attribution—or theory-of-mind (Premack and Woodruff 1978). Mental state attribution is the capacity to attribute intentions, knowledge, and beliefs to other individuals, and hence to act upon those mental states. It is the capacity of ego to know that others know something, that others know that ego knows something, and so on. Although other species exhibit some building blocks of mental state attribution and symbolic communication, both capacities are uniquely human (Cheney and Seyfarth 2007; Penn and Povinelli 2007; Call and Tomasello 2008).

From Human Nature to Human Society

The complex route going from biopsychological proclivities to complex social phenomena involves the creation of collective entities with properties of their own, distinct from the properties of the mental entities themselves. It is the conversion of multiple individual actions into social patterns and sociological properties. In anthropology, that topic has been neglected because the discipline's main interest has consistently been the reverse causality: the molding effect of supra-individual factors (cultural institutions) on inter-individual actions and individual psychology. Accordingly, the bulk of social analyses has concentrated on relationships between institutions, not on relationships between individuals. A sociology concentrating on relations between institutions is perfectly legitimate, and in fact unavoidable, in a species in which individuals are able to recognize and conceptualize social patterns (e.g., social stratifications), modify them, and even create new ones through normative decisions. But complex social patterns are also common in other species, in which they are *not* recognized as entities of their own, or incompletely so. This strongly suggests that social regularities predated and provided the blueprint of social institutions, hence the importance of understanding how social regularities originate from individual actions. Owing to our present state of knowledge and to space constraints, it is not possible to present a complete picture of how human society's deep organization unfolds from universal psychosocial proclivities. It is nonetheless possible to lay down a number of propositions about the processes involved.

From Human Nature to Social Bonds

One such proposition is that many universal social patterns (table 13.1) are emergent phenomena stemming from regularities in the content of dyadic social bonds. This implies that human nature generates a universal and uniquely human set of dyad types defined in relation to the intrinsic characteristics of individuals (age, sex, and kinship). That set of dyad types includes, for example, spouses, same-sex siblings, cross-sex siblings, same-sex cousins, cross-sex cousins, brothers-in-law, sisters-in-law, cross-sex siblings-in-law, adult male friends, adult female friends, and so forth. The proposition also implies that each dyad type has its own specific behavioral profile. This is obviously not to say that all pair-bonds, or all sibling bonds, are the same cross-culturally, but that all pair-bonds share a common set of features which, taken together, differ from the set of features characterizing bonds between brothers, between sisters-in-law, or between unrelated adult male friends. Human nature would produce a specific set of social bonds for the same reason that "chimpanzee nature" generates a chimpanzee-specific set of social bonds.

The reasoning starts with the idea that human life-history traits (in particular, longevity, generation length, and mean birth interval), in combination with the main feature of the human mating system (stable breeding bonds), generate a uniquely human *genealogical environment*. The defining characteristic of that environment is the conjunction of bilineal kinship recognition and bilateral recognition of affines among three to four generations of co-residing kin. Two types of bonds, the pair-bond and the mother-child bond, engender all other kin types through developmental associative processes (discussion in Chapais 2008). Briefly, the conjunction of these two types of bonds brings about father-child recognition. Mother-child and father-child bonds in turn generate sibling bonds and bilateral grandparental bonds. Sibling bonds generate bonds between aunts and uncles, nieces and nephews, cousins, and so on with more remote kin types. Kinship bonds and pair-bonds jointly give rise to affinal kinship. Brothers-in law, for instance, are connected to each other through the same female who is a sister to one and a wife to the other. In small-scale societies, most group members are kin or affines (Hill et al. 2011). The human-specific set of dyad types reflects the specificity of human life-history traits, group composition, and residence patterns.

The next step in the reasoning is that age, sex, and kinship markedly affect the likelihood of competition, cooperation, reproduction, and parenting between any two individuals. Although the three factors always act in conjunction in any dyad, I consider their effect separately for the sake of clarity. Other things being equal, *closeness in age* between two individuals is expected to promote cooperation between them because similarly aged partners share similar characteristics, similar levels of competence, and similar goals. At the same time and for the same reason, closeness in age is expected to favor competition between individuals who value and seek the same categories of resources. Thus, age similarity would create biases for the formation of cooperative bonds exhibiting a significant competitive dimension. On the contrary, *age discrepancy* would decrease opportunities for both cooperation and competition, while constituting a source of power asymmetry, hence control, between partners.

Like partners close in age, *same-sex* partners, share similar characteristics, competence levels, and goals and are therefore biased for cooperating with each other. But because males and females differ in their characteristics and goals, they are expected to focus on somewhat different cooperative activities. Considering age and sex simultaneously, same-sex partners close in age would thus be disproportionately biased for cooperating with each other. They would also be biased for competing over the same resources, for example, sexual partners. Correlatively, *cross-sex dyads* are not expected to foster high levels of cooperation, except in the case of breeding alliances (pair-bonds), in which case partners share important (reproductive) goals precisely because they are not of the same sex. In contrast with same-sex status, cross-sex status would promote differences in the contribution of each partner—some level of sexual specialization—because males and females differ in their characteristics and goals more than same-sex individuals do. Cross-sex status would also constitute a significant source of power asymmetry based on physical dimorphism and aggressiveness, but not necessarily on other factors.

Turning to the kinship factor, a correlate of many kinship bonds is *developmental familiarity*, as between parents and children, siblings, grandparents and grandchildren, or cousins. Developmental familiarity *per se* markedly promotes cooperation between partners, if only because it creates regular and predictable opportunities for mutual help, in a wide array of contexts, and over extensive periods of time. Because developmental familiarity is a usual correlate of biological kinship, it is also likely that it favors cooperation and *unilateral altruism* based on processes that evolved through kin selection. High levels of developmental familiarity also foster the Westermarck effect, preventing breeding alliances between partners. Developmental familiarity may also characterize relationships between unrelated (or distantly related) partners, as in the case of friendships between young same-age peers.

Given, then, (1) that there exists a human-specific set of dyad types; (2) that age, sex, and kinship determine the likelihood of competition, cooperation, reproduction, and parenting for any dyad type; and (3) that universal psychosocial proclivities regulate the forms taken by competition, cooperation, reproduction, and parenting in humans (cf. previous section), every dyad type would have its own specific behavioral profile. To illustrate the principle, I briefly describe the behavioral profile of three types of bonds: spouses, same-sex siblings, and same-sex friends. Human nature alone generates pair-bonds that have the following traits: sexual attraction; attachment potentially based on romantic love; high levels of cooperation resulting both from common reproductive goals and habitual coresidence, and hence high levels of mutual sharing of services, resources, and information; some level of sexual specialization in cooperation; high levels of reciprocity expectations owing to the spouses' high degree of interdependence, and hence conflicts over reciprocity issues; high levels of jealousy owing to the important costs of infidelity in terms of paternity confidence and economic dependence; and relatively low levels of competition between partners. This specific behavioral profile arises solely from interactions between human psychosocial proclivities and the effect of age and sex on cooperation and competition in the context of human life-history traits. It is not a cultural construct, even though it is culturally modifiable.

A markedly distinct behavioral profile is that of same-sex siblings bonds, which includes the following traits: a high propensity for cooperation resulting from extensive developmental familiarity, especially among siblings close in age; similar types of contributions due to same-sex status; significant levels of unilateral altruism (e.g., protection) owing to kin selection, and hence higher levels of tolerance to unbalanced reciprocity; relatively high levels of competition and conflicts resulting from same-sex status, but also from a history of shared dependence in relation to common caregivers; and marked power differentials between immature siblings owing to age difference. Thus, considering only the effect of kinship, age, and sex, bonds between same-sex siblings offer a unique mixture of cooperation, altruism, competition, and control. No less distinct is the behavioral profile of bonds between unrelated, adult, same-sex friends, defined by a high propensity for cooperation in association with substantial levels of competition because of age similarity and same-sex status; similar contributions to cooperative activities; low levels of unilateral altruism and, concomitantly, high expectations with regard to reciprocity and equity; and low levels of age-related power asymmetry. Arguably the same type of analysis applies to all other dyad types, with the whole set of behavioral profiles amounting to "humankind's unitary configuration of social bonds."

From Human Nature to Complex Social Patterns

In the present model, dyadic social bonds are the single most important intermediary step in the causal chain linking psychosocial proclivities to complex social patterns. Regularities in social bonds are expected to give rise to collective social patterns that are more than the sum of their constituent bonds. A simple example is the cooperation bias stemming from closeness in age, a bias expected to give rise to cooperative networks connecting similarly aged individuals, that is, age groups and corresponding conceptual categories such as *age grades*. A more specific example is the bias for cooperating with same-sex individuals, for example, among females. In association with other aspects of human nature—notably, nepotism, the bipedality-based capacity to provision others, and the high costs of maternity because of the protracted dependency of human children—the female cooperation bias is expected to translate into kin-biased, cooperative breeding networks among females. More generally, in the human cognitive environment, female cooperative bonds are expected to give rise to various forms of *sororities* (in the generic sense of the word)—as many different ones as there are distinct underlying activities and goals. The same reasoning applies to male cooperative bonds, which should translate into various forms of cooperative labor, alliances, and *fraternities*. Sororities and fraternities are complex social patterns with properties of their own. Nonetheless they are all governed by rules, implicit or explicit, expressing psychosocial proclivities relating to sharing, reciprocating, equity, loyalty, and comformity to the group's distinctive attributes, such as physical identity symbols, beliefs, and rituals. These universal attributes of sororities and fraternities are products of human nature; they are not cultural constructs.

A further example concerns the origin of group-wide kinship structures from regularities in social bonds. As pointed out earlier, the pair-bond and the mother-offspring bond alone produce humankind's specific genealogical environment in the context of human life-history traits. But a genealogical structure is not a social structure. How, then, do socially differentiated kinship structures arise from mere genealogical structures? As argued elsewhere (Chapais 2008), all that is needed is the existence of enduring (e.g., lifetime) parental favoritism. In the human genealogical environment, all individuals recognize their mothers and fathers. Let us consider a small-scale society in which all individuals are related to each other either through their mother, their father, or both. In such a context, parental favoritism alone, whatever the form it takes, generates a conspicuous pattern of dyadic (parent-offspring) bonds that connects all individuals and maps upon the group-wide genealogical structure—parental favoritism reveals the whole genealogical structure. Moreover, if parental favoritism includes the transmission of any entity—objects, information, status— from parents to offspring, this translates into multigenerational links between lineal relatives, a de facto *pattern of descent*. In theory, descent may be either unilineal (through the male line only or the female line only) or bilineal. Unilineal and bilineal descent patterns reveal *lineage structures*. They make it possible for two individuals, two cousins for instance, to trace their ancestry back to a common ancestor. In all probability, many complex social patterns, such as lineages and descent groups, were born as de facto entities well before they were recognized as such, institutionalized, and acted upon (Chapais 2008). The important point here is that matrifiliation and patrifiliation, the core of descent structures, appear to have originated from a limited number of psychosocial proclivities and to have created initial biases for cooperation among lineage members.

Another example concerns the development of complex social orders (hierarchies) based on the psychosocial proclivities regulating competition, notably the enjoyment of social superiority. Because all individuals enjoy social success, because they all do so by comparing themselves to others (and by being compared to others by third parties), and because they all differ in their personal competence levels in any particular domain, they end up being ranked in relation to each other, whether from their own perspective or from that of observers (audiences). Multiple social comparisons in any particular domain aggregate and translate into several de facto, domain-specific social orderings. Social orders in turn have properties of their own, the most important of which is the existence of enduring status inequalities that have a profound impact on an individual's life. Status variance is a property of social orders; it is not a property of psychosocial proclivities and individual minds. For all that, the formation of social orders and the origins of social inequalities are unintelligible in the absence of information on human nature.

When the enjoyment of social superiority is considered in conjunction with another social prime mover, parental attachment and its correlate, parental favoritism, one obtains a new phenomenon: heredity-based social orders, or hereditary succession. For example, in a society where individuals differ in wealth, the preferential transmission of property from parents to offspring is expected to bring about the inheritance of economic status, and hence some level of socioeconomic stratification based on heredity (birth status). Heredity-based socioeconomic stratification is a group-wide phenomenon with major properties of its own. It is nonetheless the outcome of the concurrent operation of two psychosocial proclivities. This brings up an important issue. If heredity-based socioeconomic stratifications are the expression of universal psychosocial proclivities, they are not universal for all that; economic stratifications are absent or incipient in foraging societies. But the contradiction is only apparent. Parental favoritism and the enjoyment of social success are consistently at work in all human societies wherein they produce different types of hereditary social orders, depending on the particular measure of social success. In societies with minimal wealth differentials, there can be no significant socioeconomic stratification. Nonetheless, heredity-based social orders are manifest in the inheritance of other transferrable currencies, for example, knowledge, physical skills, psychological abilities, prestige, and so forth. Thus, psychosocial proclivities produce group-level organizational processes, and the particular form taken by the latter is a matter of cultural content (discussion below).

I end this discussion of the emergent character of human society's deep organization with one last example, the existence of structures of authority or influence. In human societies, high-status individuals have more influence or more power compared to lower-status individuals. This property of social orders is not self-evident. Social orders impose status differentials among individuals in multiple domains, but they do not necessarily impose influence or authority differentials. According to the present view, structures of influence or authority are a further dimension of social orders brought about by the joint operation of a specific social prime mover, attraction to high-status individuals, which sustains a number of proclivities for monitoring, believing, obeying, imitating, and allying with high-status individuals. Through such behavioral processes, low-status individuals are actually investing high-status individuals—athletic champions, top hunters, rock stars, wealthy people, army chiefs, religious leaders, and so forth—with influence or authority. In other primates, top-ranking males and females are highly attractive but do not exercise authority on others because individuals lack the cognitive abilities for recognizing other individuals' thoughts and beliefs, hence for adopting their views (theory-of-mind), and for commanding others explicitly (symbolic communication). Human cognition created conditions in which simple social hierarchies, in whatever domain, acquired further properties, including a dimension of differential authority or influence. As in the previous examples, the particular form taken by authority structures, from lax forms of leadership to despotic forms, is a matter of cultural content.

Culture as Multiform Expression of Psychosocial Proclivities

I have postponed discussing culture until now in order to establish that individual actions regulated by a number of universal psychosocial proclivities may generate complex social patterns in the absence of cultural prescriptions, norms, and institutions. The articulation of culture in the present framework hinges on the idea that cultural diversity is essentially the expression of psychosocial proclivities in continually renewed forms and meanings. Culture would be the imparting of *content* to psychosocial constants. Two types of content are differentiated because they have distinct, though related, evolutionary histories. The *formal* content of culture (hereafter *formal culture*) refers to variation in behavioral form and includes both behavior patterns and technology; the *semantic* content of culture (hereafter *semantic culture*) relates to variation in meaning and is uniquely human. Primate studies indicate that formal culture predated semantic culture and paved the way for it.

Formal Culture and Psychosocial Proclivities

From the perspective of human evolution, formal culture is a primitive phenomenon; many other animal species, notably the great apes, exhibit it. Formal culture reflects the operation of two sets of cognitive abilities supporting, respectively, the capacity to innovate (creativity) and the capacity to learn by observing others (social learning). Empirical studies indicate that creativity in animals is inventing novel behavioral ways and technical means to satisfy individual needs, drives, and goals. For example, chimpanzees have invented tools and techniques to collect termites, crack hard nuts, and hunt mammals (McGrew 2004). Creativity here appears to work through simple associative processes—for example, the fortuitous insertion of a twig inside a termite, leading the performer to recognize the association between the behavior and its consequences. Whatever its cognitive basis, creativity is innovation and behavioral flexibility at the service of an individual's needs and drives. As to social learning, it encompasses a wide array of cognitive processes, including social facilitation, observational conditioning, goal emulation, true imitation, and many others (1998). Social learning allows animals to bypass individual trial-and-error learning and benefit from the inventive capacity, or chance discoveries, of others. Basically, then, behavioral culture results from individual innovations being adopted by others and spreading to the whole group.

The observation that culture in other animals is the adoption of novel behavioral patterns to satisfy individual needs and drives strongly suggests that humanlike culture also originated in that function and was, at least initially, the multiform expression of human biological constants, including psychosocial proclivities. The ethnographical and historical repertoire of the behavioral manifestations of a single prime mover, sexual jealousy, will serve to illustrate the reasoning. Sexual jealousy is felt by both sexes in humans, but for the sake of simplicity, I focus here on male jealousy.

Male competition for females is generalized in animals and manifest in the formation of short-term bonds (consortships) or long-term ones (monogamous or polygynous). In all situations, males closely monitor their females and seek to prevent them from interacting with other males. In any particular species, male sexual control is manifest under a limited number of behavioral forms across groups of the same species. By contrast, in the human cognitive environment, male sexual jealousy sustains several cognitively differentiated psychosocial proclivities, each of which is manifest in a great variety of cultural forms (a sample of which is given in parentheses in the following list): (1) praising and prescribing fidelity (on sentimental, aggressive, moral, legal, religious, or hygienic grounds); (2) monitoring a wife's fidelity in absentia through technological means (wife confinement, chastity belts, physical devices hindering a wife's mobility, infibulation, clitoridectomy); (3) monitoring and ensuring fidelity through third parties (chaperones, gossiping, private investigators, DNA-based paternity tests); (4) controlling the attractiveness of one's wife (prescriptions and proscriptions about wife's physical appearance, use of garments to conceal wife's physical attributes); (5) dyadic punishments of infidelity (extremely variable degrees of physical and psychological violence); and (6) punishment of infidelity through third parties and public audience (attacks on wife's reputation, public sanctions).

All cultural forms of sexual control spring from the same social prime mover interacting with universal cognitive abilities, and the specific forms observed at any time in any group result from a particular history. The multifarious and heterogeneous character of the list is a direct reflection of human cognitive potentialities. Among other things, symbolic communication makes it possible to direct the behavior of others (wives and third parties) at a distance thanks to verbal statements, while mental state attribution (theory-of-mind) enables one to reason about others' desires, intentions, and beliefs and take precautionary measures on the basis of that knowledge. The list of means at one's disposal is in principle infinite, its boundaries set by the limits of imagination and cultural innovation.

The same reasoning applies to the whole set of human psychosocial proclivities: multiformity across cultures is the rule. Equally significant, and by way of consequence, multiformity also characterizes human society's deep structural principles (table 13.1). Humans have invented innumerable ways to form enduring breeding bonds, carry out the sexual division of labor, express status differentials, and so forth. They have produced myriad versions of human society's deep organization. The observed variation is limitless, it grows cumulatively and ceaselessly, but it is nonetheless highly constrained in that it consistently revolves around the same set of psychosocial constants.

Semantic Culture and Psychosocial Proclivities

Variation in the behavioral dimension of culture is only the minor reason why the search for human universals has proven so frustrating. A more important reason stems from the phylogenetically more recent aspect of culture: meaning. As a property of the human mind, meaning is inescapable. Every human action is an integral part of a particular system of beliefs shared by a group and recognized by them as shared (collective) knowledge. Beliefs are interpretations about the nature of relations between objects, individuals, and events; they are rationalizations about reality, including causality. The world of meaning thus truly embodies the symbolic realm; it is a correlate of the symbolic capacity. To interpretive anthropologists such as Clifford Geertz this entailed that meaning must have little, if anything, to do with human nature. Geertz reasoned that if human nature were to impinge on the realm of meaning, this must translate into cross-culturally unitary meanings—for example, about motherhood, kinship, or marriage. But given that meanings are extremely variable across groups, that every human action has a stratified—or "thick"—structure of meanings, and that every culture has its own system of beliefs, human nature must be irrelevant for understanding meaning (Geertz 1973a). This entailed that the realm of meaning has its own causality, unrelated to biological constants, and that it is the symbolic world itself that determines human action. Variants of this reasoning characterize other theoretical perspectives, notably postmodern anthropology.

A diametrically opposed view was that of Fox for whom "anthropologists, time after time in society after society, come up against the same processes carried out under a variety of symbolic disguises" so that "once one gets behind the surface manifestations, the uniformity of human behavior and of human social arrangements is remarkable." (1989a, 18–19). In that vein, the view espoused here is that the realm of meaning does determine human action to a large extent but that it is largely determined by human nature. To conceive of the symbolic realm as an entity largely freed from human nature makes no biological sense. If formal culture is the capacity to devise an infinite number of behavioral ways to express psychosocial proclivities, it is likely that a similar principle applies to semantic culture. A mind capable of generating symbolic rationalizations about the world may be expected to be strongly biased for generating ideas, beliefs, and rationalizations that are congruent with, support, and satisfy human psychosocial proclivities. According to this principle, psychosocial constants would constitute the primary, if not paramount, source of meanings; the symbolic realm would predominantly tap and diffuse human nature. Sperber (1996) propounded a similar principle but in relation specifically to the cognitive components of human nature. Sperber argued that to explain culture is to explain why some symbolic representations are more easily adopted than others and more likely to stabilize as cultural traits—why some ideas are more "contagious" than others. Sperber's general answer was that "contagious" ideas are those that are compatible with human cognitive constraints. According to the present view, contagious ideas are congruent with psychosocial proclivities, each of which has both an emotional and a cognitive basis.

The incest avoidance prime mover provides an illustration of the congruence principle. One expects symbolic representations about incest to be congruent both with the observance of the incest taboo ("it is normal, good, or moral not to commit incest") and with its transgression (it is bad, dangerous, or bizarre to commit incest). A recent analysis by Fox (2011) exemplifies how meanings about incest accord with human nature. Assuming that incest avoidance has deep biological roots, Fox reasoned that "we can expect the tensions in it, and our fascination with it, to resonate in our imaginations and to be reflected in our stories and dramas," and he provided a comprehensive inventory of "literary imaginings on incest" from the Old Testament and Sophocles, to Emily Brontë and Vladimir Nabokov. The classic literature, in effect, proves to be filled with incestuous characters: sisters feeling a sexual passion for their brothers, brothers raping their sisters, sons enamored with their mothers, daughters falling in love with their fathers and tricking him into sleeping with them, fathers raping their daughters, and so on. But it is also filled with the psychological sufferings and terrible consequences befalling those experiencing incestuous fantasies, or acted out relationships: frustration, guilt, suicide, murder, divine punishment, and catastrophes.

Perhaps the most important point here is that the specific *content* of symbolic representations has no bearing on the congruence principle. Any symbolic rationale condemning incest, whether it invokes spiritual, religious, moral, mythological, political, economic, or medical reasons, will do, provided (1) it adheres to the underlying psychosocial constant by inducing one to avoid incest or to condemn it, and (2) it is in harmony with other aspects, for instance, mythological, of the conceptual framework from which it is issued. The exact content of the corresponding symbolic elaborations is irrelevant. That content is somewhat like the copious decorative illuminating of alphabet letters. Such embellishments may effectively blur or even conceal the significance of the underlying letter, but they do not erase it. On theoretical grounds, therefore, one expects variation in meaning to be limitless, yet highly constrained by the congruence principle. Because the realm of symbolic representations lends itself wide open to innovation and social learning, one also expects systems of beliefs to evolve cumulatively and differ extensively across cultures, with any human action exhibiting a highly stratified (deep) structure of meanings. Thus, Geertz's argument that meanings are incommensurate across cultures is untenable. Highly variable meanings go hand in hand with a unitary human nature. (Nowhere is this more evident than in Geertz's (1973b) own analysis of Balinese cockfighting, which is taken to exemplify the incommensurability of meaning but which radiates human nature from everywhere.)

The Costs of Ignoring Biolog3ical Constants

Let us come back to Fox's complaint (chapter epigraph) that anthropology can hardly study cultural differentials without knowing about biological universals, that it is handicapped in its analysis of variables if it ignores constants. This essay was an attempt to pinpoint the problem raised by Fox. The reduction of human nature to a few biological drives and cognitive processes opened the way to two distinct types of errors: the misinterpretation of humankind's unity and the misinterpretation of cultural diversity. To illustrate the reasoning, I consider a classic among classics, the incest taboo as it applies to siblings. For the sake of the argument, I assume that the taboo is the cultural expression of an underlying biological constant, the Westermarck effect (low sexual attraction because of high levels of developmental intimacy). Any model integrating that constant would posit that it accounts for the universality of sibling incest avoidance. Accordingly, the model would treat actual occurrences of sibling incest as exceptions to the rule, exceptions that require their own explanations in terms of various factors interacting with the Westermarck effect. Among such factors are the special status of certain categories of siblings (as in the case of sibling marriage in royal families) or low levels of developmental intimacy between siblings in certain contexts (Fox 1980; general discussion in Chapais 2008).

Misinterpreting Humankind's Unity

Dismissing the role of the Westermarck effect in the existence of a universal rule of sibling incest avoidance entails invoking a *cultural constant* to account for the effect of the ignored biological constant. For example, Lévi-Strauss (1969) recognized the incest taboo as a universal phenomenon, but having rejected all biological explanations, he interpreted the taboo as a cultural invention, the purpose of which was to ensure that individuals marry out of their family and establish beneficial alliances with other families. Although the alliance dimension of marriage is real, it hardly explains the very origin and existence of the incest taboo. Ethological and primatological studies indicate that incest avoidance predated marriage, exogamy, and marital exchange (Fox 1967, 1980; Chapais 2008). Thus, ignoring biological constants does more than produce incomplete explanations: it automatically introduces major errors in the corresponding theories through the introduction of erroneous cultural constants.

Misinterpreting Humankind's Diversity

That biological constants might account for humankind's unity makes sense intuitively, but that the same constants might be relevant for understanding cultural *differences* is much less evident. As Kroeber remarked, "granted that we knew the full biochemistry of the sex drive, we would still know nothing of why a thousand human populations are likely to practice five hundred distinguishable kinds of marriage besides innumerable varieties of extramarital sex behavior" (1952, 111). Leslie White stated the same argument more formally, exemplifying his reasoning with variation in musical behavior (M) across cultures (C): M_1 in C_1, M_2 in C_2, and so on. Referring to the organism (O) as a constant, he gave the following type of formulas: $O \times C_1 \rightarrow M_1$; $O \times C_2 \rightarrow M_2$; and so on, before concluding that "since ... the organism is a constant factor in all of our equations we may eliminate it entirely from a consideration of variations of behavior. Thus we strike out the O and rewrite our equation thus: $C_1 \rightarrow M_1$; $C_2 \rightarrow M_2$; etc." (White 1949, 138–9). In other words, behavioral differences are determined by cultural differences, and human nature may be totally ignored.

White's mathematical analogy is logical but incomplete. His reasoning applies exclusively to variation in *content* (form or meaning). As argued previously, any psychosocial proclivity may be expressed under a wide array of forms and meanings, in which case biological constants are irrelevant for explaining the observed variation. Answers to such questions belong to history, among other domains. As Fox put it, "if all you want to explain is why in America girls wear their dates' fraternity pins while in Fiji they put hibiscus flowers behind their ears, that is fine ... but these are simply ways of getting the same courtship job done" ([1970] 1989a, 16). Biology here is irrelevant. That said, cultural diversity involves sources of variation other than differences of content. The absence of sibling incest in some cultural contexts, and its presence in others, may result from *interactions* between the Westermarck effect and other factors, including the social status of siblings and their degree of intimacy, those factors *modulating* the effect of the biological constant and generating the observed variation. Specifically, according to the present view, in the majority of cultural contexts, the Westermarck effect is not opposed by other factors and hence prevails (no sibling incest), whereas in other cultural contexts (e.g., sibling incest in royal families) the Westermarck effect is effectively opposed by other factors and its effect diluted, although not eliminated—it appears to decrease sexual attractiveness between spouses and cause various problems as a result. Because the observed variation reflects interactions between the Westermarck effect and other variables, explanations must necessarily integrate the biological constant. The constant cannot be "stricken out of the equation," as in the case of differences of content—for example, differences in beliefs about the consequences of incestuous relationships. White's reasoning implicitly assimilated the entirety of cultural variation to differences of content, neglecting the effect of interactions between biological constants and other factors.

Every psychosocial proclivity is subject to modulation by factors conflicting with its expression. Cultural practices might conflict with, and more or less hinder, the control of children by their parents in some contexts, the role of romantic love in the formation of pair-bonds, the exercise of sexual control by husbands, or the feasability of status competition in some contexts. In all situations the outcome will be a good deal of cultural variation, but models concerned with that variation must integrate the underlying psychosocial constants because they are always at work, even when their effect is modulated.

The impact of the marginalization of human nature on anthropological theory remains to be fully assessed, but the corresponding costs—theoretical, ontological, and epistemological—are certainly substantial, and the integration of human nature to social theory is all the more urgent. Twenty years ago Fox wrote that he had "no idea where all this will end, except perhaps in the development of a natural science of society that simply bypasses the social sciences as we know them" (1989c, 4). Such a science appears, in effect, to be emerging in bits and pieces in various disciplines, subdisciplines, and research areas, and is growing at a rapid pace. It remains to be seen how it will impact cultural anthropology in the long run.

Acknowledgments

I thank Bernard Bernier, Robert Crépeau, and Shona Teijeiro for helpful comments on the manuscript. This essay owes much to Robin Fox, whose pioneering work on the significance of primate studies for sociocultural anthropology in the 1970s was deeply inspirational to me. That so many of Robin's ideas were to be vindicated by subsequent research testifies to the visionary character of his thinking at a time when the primate data base was rather scanty, and attempts to bridge the biological and sociocultural realms were generally met with skepticism or indifference, at best.

References

Boyer, P., and H.C. Barrett. "Domain Specificity and Intuitive Ontology." In *The Handbook of Evolutionary Psychology*, edited by D. M. Buss, 96–118. Hoboken, NJ: Wiley.

Brown, D. S. 1991. *Human Universals*. Boston: McGraw Hill.

Buckholtz, J. W., C. L. Asplund, P. E. Dux, D. H. Zald, J. C. Gore, O. D. Jones, and R. Marois. 2008. "The Neural Correlates of Third-Party Punishment." *Neuron* 60:930–40.

Call, J., and M. Tomasello. 2008. "Does the Chimpanzee Have a Theory of Mind? 30 Years Later." *Trends in Cognitive Sciences* 12:187–92.

Chapais, B. 2008. *Primeval Kinship: How Pair-Bonding Gave Birth to Human Society*. Harvard University Press.

———. 2010. "The Deep Structure of Human Society: Primate Origins and Evolution." In *Mind the Gap: Tracing the Origins of Human Universals*, edited by P. M. Kappeler and J. B. Silk, 19–51, Springer.

———. 2011a. "The Deep Social Structure of Humankind." *Science* 331:1276–7.

———. 2011b. "The Evolutionary History of Pair-Bonding and Parental Collaboration." In *The Oxford Handbook of Evolutionary Family Psychology*, edited by C. A. Salmon and T. K. Shackelford, 30–50. New York: Oxford University Press.

Cheney, D. L., and R. M. Seyfarth. 2007. *Baboon Metaphysics: The Evolution of a Social Mind*. Chicago: The University of Chicago Press.

Cosmides, L., and J. Tooby. 2005. "Neurocognitive Adaptations Designed for Social Exchange." In *The Handbook of Evolutionary Psychology*, edited by D. M. Buss, 584–627. Hoboken, NJ: Wiley.

de Quervain, D., U. Fischbacher, V. Treyer, M. Schellhammer, U. Schnyder, A. Buck, and E. Fehr. 2004. "The Neural Basis of Altruistic Punishment." *Science* 305:1254–8. J. Dvash, G. Gilam, A. Ben-Ze'ev, T. Hendler, and S. G. Shamay-Tsoory. 2010. "The Envious Brain: The Neural Basis of Social Comparison." *Human Brain Mapping* 31:1741–50.

Fehr, E., and C. Camerer. 2007. "Social Neuroeconomics: The Neural Circuitry of Social Preferences." *Cognitive Sciences* 11:419–27.

Fehr, E., and U. Fischbacher. 2004. "Third Party Punishment and Social Norms." *Evolution and Human Behavior* 25:63–87.

Fox, R. 1962. "Sibling Incest." *British Jl of Sociology* 13:128–50.

———. 1967. *Kinship and Marriage: An Anthropological Perspective*. Harmondsworth: Penguin Books.

———. 1989a. "The Cultural Animal" (1970). In *The Search for Society: Quest for a Biosocial Science and Morality*, 11–34. New Brunswick, NJ: Rutgers University Press.

———. 1989b. *The Search for Society: Quest for a Biosocial Science and Morality*. New Brunswick, NJ: Rutgers University Press.

———. 1989c. "The Disunity of Anthropology and the Unity of Mankind: Introducing the Concept of the Ethosystem." In *The Search for Society: Quest for a Biosocial Science and Morality*, 106–25. New Brunswick, NJ: Rutgers University Press.

———. 1989d. "Introduction: Bearing the Bad News." In *The Search for Society: Quest for a Biosocial Science and Morality*, 1–10. New Brunswick, NJ: Rutgers University Press.

———. 2011. *The Tribal Imagination*. Harvard University Press.

Gardner, A., and S. A. West. 2004. "Cooperation and Punishment, Especially in Humans." *American Naturalist* 164:753–64.

Geertz, C. 1973a. "The Impact of the Concept of Culture on the Concept of Man." In *The Interpretation of Cultures*, edited by C. Geertz, 33–54. New York: Basic Books.

Gurven, M. 2004. "To Give and to Give Not: The Behavioral Ecology of Human Transfers." *Behavioral and Brain Sciences* 27:543–83.

Hagen, E. H. 2005. "Controversial Issues in Evolutionary Psychology." In *The Handbook of Evolutionary Psychology*, edited by D. M. Buss, 145–73. Hoboken, NJ: Wiley.

Harbaugh, W. T. 2007. "Neural Responses to Taxation and Voluntary Giving Reveal Motives for Charitable Donations." *Science* 316:1622–5.

Harris, M. 1979. *Cultural Materialism: The Struggle for a Science of Culture*. New York: Random House.

Heinrich, J., R. Boyd, S. Bowles, C. Camerer, E. Fehr, and H. Gintis. 2004. *Foundations of Human Sociality: Economic Experiments and Ethnographic Evidence from Fifteen Small-Scale Societies*. London: Oxford University Press.

Heinrich, J., R. McElreath, A. Barr, J. Ensminger, C. Barrett, A. Bolyanatz, J. C. Camilo, M. Gurven, E. Gwako, N. Heinrich, C. Leserogol, F. Marlowe, D. Tracer, and J. Ziker. 2006. "Costly Punishment across Human Societies." *Science* 312:1767–70.

Hill, K. R., R. S. Walker, M. Božičević, J., Eder, T. Headland, B. Hewlett, M. A. Hurtado, F. Marlowe, P. Wiessner, and B. Wood. 2011. "Co-residence Patterns in Hunter-Gatherer Societies Show Unique Human Social Structure." *Science* 331:1286–9.

Izuma, K., D. N. Saito, and N. Sadato. 2008. "Processing of Social and Monetary Rewards in the Human Striatum." *Neuron* 58(2):284–94.

Kroeber, A. L. 1952. "White's View of Culture." In *The Nature of Culture*, 110–7. Chicago: University of Chicago Press.

Lévi-Strauss, C. 1969. *The Elementary Structures of Kinship*. Beacon Press. Translation of *Les structures élémentaires de la parenté*, 1967, 2nd edition. Paris: Mouton.

———. 1983. *Le regard éloigné*. Paris: Plon.

McGrew, W. C. 1998. "Culture in Nonhuman Primates." *Annual Review of Anthropology* 27:301–28.

———. 2004. *The Cultured Chimpanzee: Reflections on Cultural Primatology*. Cambridge: Cambridge University Press.

Moll, J., F. Krueger, R. Zahn, M. Pardini, R. de Oliveira-Souza, and J. Grafman. 2006. "Human Fronto-Mesolimbic Networks Guide Decisions about

Charitable Donation." *Proceedings of the National Academy of Sciences* 103:15,623–8.

Neuberg, S. L., D. T. Kenrick, and M. Schaller. 2010. "Evolutionary Social Psychology." In *The Oxford Handbook of Evolutionary Psychology*, edited by R. I. M. Dunbar and L. Barrett, 761–96. Oxford University Press.

Penn, D. C., and D. J. Povinelli. 2007. "On the Lack of Evidence That Nonhuman Animals Possess Anything Remotely Resembling a 'Theory Of Mind.'" *Philosophical Transactions of the Royal Society B* 362:731–44.

Pinker, S. 1997. *The Blank Slate*. New York: Penguin Books.

Premack, D., and G. Woodruff. 1978. "Does the Chimpanzee Have a Theory of Mind?" *Behavioral and Brain Sciences* 1:515–26.

Rodseth, L., R. W. Wrangham, A. M. Harrigan, and B. B. Smuts. 1991. "The Human Community as a Primate Society." *Current Anthropology* 32:221–54.

Shamay-Tsoory, S. G., M. Fischer, J. Dvash, H. Harari, N. Perach-Bloom, and Y. Levkovitz. 2009. "Intranasal Administration of Oxytocin Increases Envy and Schadenfreude (Gloating). *Biological Psychiatry* 66:864–70.

Sperber, D. 1996. *Explaining Culture: A Naturalistic Approach*. Wiley-Blackwell.

Stammbach, E. 1987. "Desert, Forest and Montane Baboons: Multilevel-Societies." In *Primate Societies*, edited by B. B. Smuts, D. L. Cheney, R. M. Seyfarth, R. W. Wrangham, and T. T. Struhsaker, 112–20. Chicago: University of Chicago Press.

Swedel, L. 2011. "African Papionins: Diversity of Social Organization and Ecological Flexibility." In *Primates in Perspectives*, 2nd edition, edited by C. J. Campbell, A. Fuentes, K. C. MacKinnon, S. K. Bearder, and R. M. Stumpf, 241–77. New York: Oxford University Press.

Takahashi, H., M. Kato, M. Matsuura, D. Mobbs, T. Suhara, and Y. Okubo. 2009. "When Your Gain Is My Pain and Your Pain Is My Gain: Correlates of Envy and Schadenfreude." *Science* 323:937–9.

Tomasello, M. 2008. *Origins of Human Communication*. Cambridge, MA: MIT Press.

Tracy, J. L., A. F. Shariff, and J. T. Cheng. 2010. "A Naturalist's View of Pride." *Emotion Review* 2(2):163–77.

Warneken, F., and M. Tomasello. 2006. "Altruistic Helping in Human Infants and Young Chimpanzees." *Science* 31:1301–3.

Warneken, F., F. Chen, and M. Tomasello. 2006. "Cooperative Activities in Young Children and Chimpanzees." *Child Development* 77:640–63.

White, L. 1949. *The Science of Culture: A Study of Man and Civilization*. New York: Grove Press.

14

The Changing Nature of Human Nature

H. Dieter Steklis

Arguably, compared to practitioners in other academic disciplines, anthropologists have always had an overarching interest in understanding human nature—the essence of being human. Not surprisingly, our idea of what constitutes human nature necessarily changes with new scientific discoveries, methods, and theories. My aim here is not to recount this history, but rather to focus on particular recent research and theory integrating the fields of genetics, development, and evolution (popularly referred to as "evo-devo") that I will argue are calling for a radical transformation of our present, widely accepted concept of human nature. This transformation, I will also argue, has profound normative and ethical implications for human society, both local and global.

To properly frame what I suggest is a radically new idea of human nature, I will need to describe some key developments—roughly over the past forty years—particularly within anthropology that bring us to our present idea of human nature. The anthropologist Robin Fox, in my estimation, is a central figure in this recent history of defining human nature. And he perhaps more than others has taken pains to pursue the wider social, legal, and ethical implications of the science of anthropology and the study of human nature in particular, often at a cost to himself. Consequently, I am happy in my present task to stand firmly on his broad intellectual shoulders. I will begin with a brief personal reflection on Fox's work and my association with him, as it conveniently exposes how—primarily from within anthropology—we came to our present idea of human nature. From there, I will proceed to key examples of present research that compel us to rethink human nature and to draw out some ethical implications.

How We Got Here: A Personal Reflection

No one would disagree that the span of Robin Fox's intellectual interests and contributions is vast, ranging far beyond the traditional borders of anthropology (e.g., Fox 1989). This proclivity of his to let his mind travel freely no doubt drew me—as a fellow freethinker—to him and to his program at Rutgers. Early on in graduate school I had been encouraged by my advisor and mentor Sherwood Washburn to fearlessly explore any number of areas or disciplines outside anthropology as part of my training in biological anthropology and primatology. We were encouraged to be "thinkers without borders." Indeed, the promise of unfettered cross-disciplinary study is what attracted me to do graduate work in anthropology and afterward to Rutgers to work with Fox and others (especially his lifelong colleague Lionel Tiger) to help build within anthropology a strong "biosocial" approach to the study of human behavior (Fox 1975). I had trained in primate neurobiology, and there was in the early 1970s great interest within anthropology to incorporate studies on the primate brain into a fuller understanding of human nature (e.g., Laughlin and D'Aquili 1974; Fabrega 1979).

These were heady days as new research on primate brain evolution and the neurobiological and hormonal bases of primate social behavior began to shed light on the biological specializations (or, in ethological terms, "proximate mechanisms") that had evolved in the service of social life. At the same time, there were also important developments in evolutionary theory (or "metatheory") concerning social life, such as kin selection, reciprocal altruism, and parent-offspring conflict, to name a few. These developments in evolutionary theory—the ethologists' "ultimate causes" of behavior—provided and encouraged a new synthesis (i.e., combining proximate and ultimate levels of explanation) in our understanding of the evolutionary origins of human social behavior. Tiger and Fox (1966)—after their providential meeting at the London Zoo—early on and in a prescient way recognized the importance of such developments in the biological and social sciences for stimulating new research agendas and ultimately for our understanding of human nature. What they called "The Zoological Perspective in Social Science" indeed began to transform our ideas about human nature by viewing it in the wider context of primate (especially great ape) behavior and studies of animal socioecology generally. Tiger and Fox rightly pointed out that this perspective is in essence a modern ethological one—that is, the integrated study of proximate and ultimate causes of behavior

(Hinde 1982). We might argue that, as such, "biosocial anthropology" should simply have been called "human ethology." However, at the time "ethology" was generally equated with the study of animal behavior in natural circumstances (i.e., outside the laboratory), perhaps reflecting the historical origins of ethology as a reaction to the dominant "dissecting table" tradition of mid-nineteenth-century natural scientists (Jaynes 1969). Further, the field of "human ethology," also on the rise in the 1970s (Eibl-Eibesfeldt 1989), was largely concerned with the description of "natural" human behavior and its phylogenetic derivation, with little attention devoted to integrating ultimate levels of explanation with proximate ones (e.g., genetics, neurobiology). Fortunately, clans of "neuroethologists" and "cognitive ethologists," who sprang up in the last half of the twentieth century, filled in this gap in our ethological understanding of behavior by showing how proximate mechanisms have been shaped by natural selection to yield behavioral adaptations.

In short, by the mid-1970s, progress in these fields, along with the growing richness of the hominin fossil record, allowed us to articulate a well-rounded, newly informed, if not often well-received, notion of human nature (e.g., Wilson 1978). This encompassed our understanding of what is unique about being human (e.g., language, division of labor) and how these unique features evolved. It is fair to say, certainly within anthropology (though I think his influence went far beyond its borders), that Robin Fox was not only an eminent and prolific spokesperson for a holistic (essentially ethological) approach to human behavior as key to uncovering human nature but was also one of its principal architects. At the risk of some oversimplification, our idea of human nature can be summarized as follows: using the structure of human language as an analogy, human nature generally could be construed as an evolved set of deep-rule structures—a "biogrammar" (Tiger and Fox 1971)—from which the diversity of expressed human behavior was generated. In the same way that the human genome generates species-typical human rather than chimpanzee phenotypes, the idea of a universal biogrammar, reflecting human brain structure and function, seemed to account well for the existence of numerous cross-cultural universals (Brown 1991)—or recurrent themes—alongside of (surface-level) variations in cultural practices or beliefs. In this view, there is one universal human nature—a basic rule structure for behavior—that is variably expressed in response to local environmental conditions. Further, this universal rule structure for behavior, reflecting shared genetic-developmental programs, was designed by natural selection to solve adaptive problems faced by our ancestors long before the invention of agriculture and the complexities of modern life. Human population genetic data—showing overall relatively low amounts of genetic variation and small between-population variation—was seen as consistent with the concept of a universal human nature and lack of significant recent genetic-behavioral adaptation to local conditions.

In my focus on this view of human nature from within anthropology, I don't mean to ignore or underestimate the obvious and considerable contributions to elucidating human nature from other disciplines, such as evolutionary biology (e.g., sociobiology, Wilson 1975; Alexander 1979), many of which were cross-disciplinary thrusts that included anthropologists (e.g., Chagnon and Irons 1979). Perhaps the greatest and sustained influence on our concept of human nature came from psychology. By the mid-1980s, evolutionary psychologists, influenced by developments in cognitive science, had brought considerable specificity to and focus on the nature of human universal mental adaptations (Barkow et al. 1992), which spawned prolific research programs and led to the founding of graduate departments and training programs in evolutionary psychology. Like sociobiology earlier, evolutionary psychology also drew many anthropologists into its fold. This may be because the evolutionary psychological account of human nature did not in its essence deviate from the idea of biogrammar that anthropologists had previously articulated. Thus, much of mainstream evolutionary psychology then and now champions an adapted mind that is universally the same, having been shaped in an ancient ancestral environment, and with local culture "evoking" or calibrating its components in situationally appropriate ways (Tooby and Cosmides 1990a). Influenced by developments in cognitive science, evolutionary psychologists, however, brought precision to the earlier idea of a human biogrammar by postulating that the universal components of the human mind consist of separate information-processing modules that are each specialized to solve particular adaptive problems regularly encountered by our ancestors, such as finding mates or competing for status (Buss 2009). Importantly, this conception of human nature treats individual or between-population level variation in mental adaptations as unimportant or as "noise" (Tooby and Cosmides 1990a). I will now turn to a critique of this notion of human nature in light of recent research.

Where We Are Now

From where we stand today, this concept of human nature no longer seems to fit with the results from several recent research programs on both gene-culture co-evolution (cf. Richerson and Boyd 2005) and the adaptive nature of individual differences in life-history strategies and developmental trajectories. In this section, I will describe key results from these lines of research that I believe place us on the threshold of a radically altered view of human nature from the one I have been describing. As I hope to show, these findings compel us to think anew about what is universal about human nature, what is uniquely human, and about the evolutionary-developmental processes that shape both the consistency and diversity in human psychology and behavior.

I don't claim that there are no human universals (see Brown 1991, for a list of these), especially at the psychological level, but rather that a strict focus on a universally uniform psychology has distracted us from evolutionarily significant adaptive differences within and between human populations. While some features of human psychology have been clearly established as universals—e.g., mate preferences (Buss 1989)—other aspects previously believed to be uniform across cultures are not (e.g., reasoning style, self-concept; see Henrich et al. 2010). Part of the problem of identifying universals is the level of analysis (see Norenzayan and Heine 2005). For example, humans reason everywhere, but the use of or perceived importance of reasoning in behavior, or the style of reasoning (e.g., analytic vs. holistic, etc.) varies across cultures. Similarly, a multifactor personality structure can be identified in a large number of human societies, suggesting that personality structure and personality differences are meaningful constructs and of significance in the lives of people. However, while five factors or dimensions of human personality structure (the "Big 5") can be identified in a large number of human societies, some cultures have fewer or more factors, and cultures vary in mean levels of personality traits and in the level of importance given to individual differences in personality as both explanatory and predictive of behavior (e.g., particularly in collectivist vs. individualist cultures, see below, and Heine and Buchtel 2009, for review). Thus, depending on our level of analysis and what importance we attach to it, we can see human nature as either uniform or variable. Evolutionary psychologists have stressed the uniform components of human nature because they see these as the relevant adaptive features of the human mind. There is good reason, however, to regard individual and population differences in psychology as equally, if not more salient features for adaptation to past and present environmental conditions.

There is growing evidence for significant cultural differences in aspects of cognition, emotion, motivation, and attention, and for a link between variation in these psychological traits and variation in allele frequencies, gene expression, brain function, or neural connectivity, which together provide the basis for culture-environment adaptation (Kitayama and Uskul 2011, for review). Variation in this "psychological genetic-neuro" complex has been systematically linked to cultural differences along the dimension of individualistic versus collectivistic values (or independence vs. interdependence). While this dimension most commonly distinguishes East-West cultures, more fundamentally (as we will see shortly) it differentiates equatorial societies from ones at higher latitudes (see Fincher et al. 2008). In brief, collectivist cultures value beliefs, attitudes, and behaviors that promote social conformity, coordination, and cohesion, while individualist cultures value self-promotion and expression and have a relatively higher tolerance for deviance from cultural norms or traditions. Many of the well-established differences in cognition (e.g., self-construal, mode of reasoning), emotion (e.g., perception and production of facial expressions), or attentional bias (e.g., attention to context) are consistent with the individualist-collectivist dimension (Kitayama and Uskul 2011).

While cultural differences in psychology have long been known to anthropologists and psychologists, only recently has it come to light that such variation in psychological function is "deeper" than anticipated. A burgeoning number of brain-imaging studies have demonstrated that cultural differences in psychology are systematically related to variation in brain function and connectivity, giving rise to a "New model of neuro-cultural interaction where culture modifies brain" (Kitayama and Uskul 2011). In this model, neural connectivity is modified during the course of development through an individual's sustained cultural practices. This does not rule out the contribution of genetics to such culturally induced modifications in neural machinery, and, indeed, population genetic differences have been linked, for example, to cultural variation in neural function and emotionality. The neurotransmitter serotonin regulates emotionality (i.e., negative vs. positive emotional tone or mood) via brain structures such as the amygdala. The amount of serotonergic neurotransmission is determined by two variants of the serotonin transporter gene (the "s" and "l" alleles, named respectively for short and long coding regions) that are found in significantly different frequencies in collectivist and individualist societies: The s-allele is relatively more frequent in collectivist cultures, while the converse is true for the l-allele (Chiao and Blizinsky 2010). Individuals carrying the s-allele show relatively exaggerated amygdala activation (i.e., negative emotional arousal) in response to pictures of angry or fearful faces (Hariri et al. 2002), and are generally prone to negative emotion, depression, and a variety of anxiety-related traits, including a higher attentional bias to negative information (Chiao and Blizinsky 2010; Homberg and Lesch 2011).

This population difference in the s-allele raises the interesting question of how the s-allele's high frequency could be maintained in light of its apparent "negative" effects on emotion and health (Homberg and Lesch 2011). As it turns out, the suite of emotional features, alongside the other psychological characteristics, are adaptive in a collectivist society but are relatively disadvantageous in an individualist society. Thus, in individualist cultures (e.g., North America), the lower frequency s-allele genotype is correlated with anxiety and depression-related clinical disorders, while in collectivist societies (e.g., Japan), the higher frequency of the s-allele is associated with a lower incidence of such disorders, yielding an overall, global negative association between frequency of s-allele carriers and prevalence of anxiety and mood disorders (Chiao and Blizinsky 2010). One way to understand how the s-allele can lead to an advantageous behavioral and psychological phenotype is in viewing the underlying neuro-psychological state as one of "hypervigilance" to both positive and negative stimuli, which, depending on the context or task at hand, can lead to enhanced functioning (Homberg and Lesch 2011). S-allele carriers, for example, outperform l-allele carriers in a variety of social-cognitive tasks (such as decision making, response inhibition, risk aversion, etc.) that promote social conformity (Homberg and Lesch 2011). Their increased emotional reactivity or vigilance enhances both monitoring and responding to subtle signals of social approval and disapproval. As such, s-allele carriers see themselves and are regarded by others as valued members of a collectivist society.

Our discussion so far well illustrates how culture and biology work together (or interact) to promote individual adaptive functioning, but it raises the question of what selection pressures favor collectivist vs. individualist societies, assuming that these represent different population-level adaptive strategies. Here, too, recent theory and analyses nicely close the loop in the culture-gene co-evolution cycle. Pathogen prevalence in the local environment and the associated risks of disease transmission and individual fitness costs account well for cross-cultural variability in the individualism-collectivism dimension (Fincher et al. 2008). The latter authors estimated the prevalence of nine pathogens detrimental to reproductive fitness in ninety-three geopolitical regions (as proxies for "societal cultures") across the globe and found that, as predicted, pathogen prevalence (especially in the past) was negatively correlated with individualism and positively correlated with collectivism. Importantly, the differences between individualist vs. collectivist societies in values, beliefs, and practices—and their grounding in the specific neuropsychological features we have been detailing—are consistent, with antipathogen defense strategies. For example, the tendency for collectivists to be more xenophobic (i.e., a greater in-group vs. out-group distinction) and conformist (e.g., adhering to traditions of food preparation) compared to individualists is consistent with the different ecological pressures posed by pathogen prevalence.

There are two major implications of this work on the adaptive qualities of cultural differences in psychology and behavior. One is that the human mind (or human nature) is not everywhere the same, but rather that its (neural) structure and function vary significantly, having been adaptively shaped in response to different ecological pressures. The second is that human neuro-behavioral adaptive plasticity has been underestimated, in that both gene expression and brain function and connectivity are open to—albeit not open-ended—to environmental regulation. This first implication, of course, flies in the face of mainstream evolutionary psychological thinking, and many perhaps will find it to be politically incorrect because of what it says about recent human evolution and biologically rooted population differences in psychology and behavior. I want to pursue the second implication first because further discussion of examples of adaptive plasticity at the individual level are pertinent to a fuller understanding of the mechanisms of adaptive diversification of the human mind in recent human evolution.

Adaptive phenotypic plasticity in response to specific environmental conditions is a well-studied, well-established phenomenon in a variety of animal species, especially insects (for review, see West-Eberhard 2003). Such plasticity is commonly understood in terms of "developmental switches" that are activated by particular environmental stimuli or cues during an organism's developmental trajectory, such that alternate phenotypes develop as contingent adaptive responses to ecological conditions. The "switching" thus is an epigenetic process, entailing the environmental regulation of gene expression, and thereby affording the organism a degree of adaptive phenotypic plasticity without the necessity of changes in structural DNA. The capacity for and range of phenotypic plasticity are themselves evolved properties that have selective value, therefore, only for some organisms in particular kinds of environments (especially historically variable or unpredictable ones), a point that is often overlooked. We must therefore look at a species' past and present ecologies to understand the evolutionary reasons for adaptive plasticity.

Human adaptive plasticity has been traditionally understood as a process mediated via cultural learning and transmission, that, in retrospect, was too often mistakenly seen as not involving or necessitating biological (i.e., genetic, neurobiological) changes. As I have already shown, this view is flawed in that human adaptive plasticity is the result of an interdependent feedback process between culture and biology. How this works at the level of the individual, demonstrating individual phenotypic plasticity, has been laid bare by several recent multidisciplinary lines of research that illustrate how environmental cues alter children's developmental trajectories. In this work, developmental psychologists have benefitted from incorporating an evolutionary perspective (Moore 2008; Ellis et al. 2011a), which profitably treats developmental trajectories in the context of Life History Theory (LHT). To situate and engage this work properly, we must, therefore, first make a short foray into LHT.

LHT has emerged as a powerful theory in evolutionary biology in that it brings together under one conceptual framework the manifold organismal attributes that contribute to fitness and helps us understand how variation in these attributes reflects differences in the organism's ecological and social environments. Traditionally, LHT has focused on the evolution of species differences in reproductive life-history components (e.g., number and timing of offspring, onset of reproduction) in relation to ecological stability or quality (e.g., stable vs. unstable food supply, high vs. low predator pressure). The power of this theory rests on the simple observation that an organism's limited lifetime energy resources are strategically allocated to investment in its reproduction and survival so as to achieve the greatest possible lifetime fitness. Tradeoffs between energy devoted to reproduction (e.g., reproducing early and often) vs. survival (e.g., investing in somatic growth and delaying reproduction) are well captured, for example, by the classic r vs. K selection model. In simplified form, r and K represent end points of a continuum, respectively, between "fast" and "slow" life-history strategies, with "fast" strategies capturing relatively high investment in reproductive effort (e.g., reproducing early and often at the expense of somatic growth and longevity) and "slow" strategies entailing relatively high investment in somatic growth (e.g., delaying maturation, increasing lifespan) at the expense of reproduction (e.g., reproducing late and producing fewer offspring). In this model, r life history strategies evolve under unstable, harsh, or unexploited ecological conditions, while K strategies are favored in more predictable, resource-stable conditions or ones of high conspecific population density and high competition for resources. Rabbits and elephants, respectively, roughly illustrate the two extremes of the r and K continuum. In comparison to other mammalian orders, primates are relatively K-selected (e.g., small litter size, high parental care, delayed maturation, long-lived).

Traditionally, LHT has been applied toward understanding species differences in life-history component tradeoffs and their connection to variation in ecological and social conditions. Among primates, for example, there is substantial variation among species in K-selected life-history characteristics that reflect predictable differences in socioecological conditions. More recently, however, attention has been productively focused on life-history variation between individuals in human (mostly Western) populations and its relationship to socioenvironmental conditions. In life-history terms, we regard individual-level variation as an evolved capacity to adjust the strategic allocation of lifetime resources to reproduction and survival so as to achieve the best possible fitness outcome. Because humans, like many other primate species, have a delayed maturation schedule, including unusually long periods of juvenility, we should expect that the extensive temporal "sampling" of the social and ecological environment during immaturity allows for calibration or adjustment of life-history strategy (i.e., variation in K-selected life-history components). Much research has therefore been devoted to human life-history adjustment in response to variation in aspects of the developmental environment from infancy through adolescence (e.g., family stability, father absence, parent-child relationships, poverty; see Ellis et al. 2009).

A particularly apt example is the work by Ellis and colleagues (Ellis et al. 2011b) on children's differential susceptibility to variations in rearing environment. From a traditional clinical perspective (i.e., a developmental psychopathology model), children's susceptibility to environmental stress (e.g., parental neglect) is seen as linked to endogenous characteristics (e.g., of genetics, physiology) that mediate vulnerability or resilience to adverse rearing environments. Thus, compared to resilient children, when exposed to adverse rearing environments, "vulnerable" children reach puberty and commence sexual activity earlier, which predicts functional impairments or pathology in later life (e.g., depression, drug abuse, high risk taking). It turns out, however, that "vulnerable" children have a clear advantage over resilient children when reared in supportive environments. In supportive environments, they delay puberty and do not suffer impairments as adults, but instead go on to lead happy and productive lives. Resilient children, by comparison, do not alter their maturation schedule in either adverse or supportive environments, nor do they capitalize on or benefit from a supportive environment in the manner of "vulnerable" children. Ellis and colleagues rightly interpret this differential response to rearing environment not as vulnerability or resilience per se, but rather as environmentally cued distinct adaptive developmental responses ("conditional adaptation"). They showed that compared to resilient children (who they likened to "dandelions"), vulnerable children (likened to "orchids") have an endocrine stress physiology that promotes heightened sensitivity to both adverse and supportive environments. In harsh environments, they make the best of a bad situation, while in supportive environments their heightened sensitivity allows them to excel. As in our earlier example of s- and l-allele carriers, "vulnerability" and pathology are clearly environmentally contingent outcomes, and from an evolutionary perspective are perhaps more meaningfully treated as alternate ("orchid" vs. "dandelion") life-history strategies.

The idea of adaptive individual life-history adjustment has also received strong empirical support in the work of Figueredo and colleagues (see Figueredo et al. 2006, for an overview). As said earlier, humans are a relatively K-selected species; however, there is significant and evolutionarily meaningful individual-level variation in the K dimension (i.e., low to high or slow to fast). Figueredo and colleagues have demonstrated that a single common factor (named "K-Factor" on a fast to slow life history continuum) predicts variation in a cluster of life-history parameters, including sexual, reproductive, and parental behaviors in response to socioecological conditions experienced during development (e.g., parental absence or attachment, divorce, material resources). Significantly, for both sexes and different cultural groups, they also linked the K-Factor to several psychometric and social traits. Although females predictably have higher K-Factor scores, for both sexes low K-Factor scores (i.e., fast LH) are positively associated with high mortality, decreased birth intervals, earlier reproduction and maturation, increased number of offspring, and lower parental effort, as well as with higher impulsivity and risk taking, and other measures indicating lower "executive control" (i.e., frontal lobe functioning). Further, low K-Factor (fast LH) scores are associated with high neuroticism/anxiety and psychoticism, along with poorer physical health and reported lower overall well-being. Here, too, our common inclination and the traditional view of our medical and legal institutions is to disvalue the characteristics of low K individuals and to regard them as dysfunctional phenotypes requiring ameliorative treatment or medical attention, if not incarceration. (I will pursue the ethical implications shortly.) From an evolutionary perspective, however, these may well be equally valid adaptive phenotypic adjustments to different social circumstances (what has been called adaptive social "niche picking"; Figueredo et al. 2011), assuming that each strategy has fitness benefits.

Having further defined the nature and range of human adaptive plasticity, we can now turn to consider when and how this adaptive capacity arose in the course of human evolution. As mentioned earlier, the mainstream evolutionary psychology viewpoint has been that there are no deep mental differences between human populations (Tooby and Cosmides 1990b). This is predicated on the assumption that an essentially uniform human nature—consisting of a universal set of adaptive problem-solving modules—evolved during the Pleistocene when as hunter-gatherers all humans faced similar socioecological challenges. A further assumption is that there has been insufficient time for the evolution of significant genetic and psychological population differences since the wide geographic spread of modern humans. To put it simply, all present-day humans have managed to populate and flourish in all corners of the earth with a Stone Age mind. This conception of human nature is of course politically palatable in that it undermines perpetual arguments about racial differences that have long plagued social and biological scientists.

This concept of human nature, however, is inconsistent with empirical evidence from human psychology and development—as we have already seen—and evolutionary population genetics. Recent comparison of the human and chimpanzee genomes points to significant recent positive selection for adaptive substitutions in the human genome that are linked to rapid cultural evolution within the past 10,000 years (Hawks et al. 2007). The genetic evidence indicates that human evolution proceeded at a relatively slower rate in the distant past, but then accelerated recently with human geographic expansion and cultural diversification and complexity. In particular, the population explosion that accompanied the transition to agriculture likely increased the number of mutations available for selection and thus dramatically accelerated the rate of human adaptive evolution (see Cochran and Harpending 2009). Hence the rate of genetic differentiation among human populations is in large part dependent on the strength of local selection pressures.

The significance of genetic differences among populations has oftentimes been dismissed by pointing to the relatively small amount of genetic variance between populations (about 15 percent) compared to the variance within populations (about 85 percent). However, as we have seen, even minor allelic variants (as in the serotonin transporter gene) can produce relatively large phenotypic effects. The logic is the same for the oft-quoted chimpanzee-human DNA base-pair difference (estimated at around 2 percent), which nevertheless accounts for large phenotypic differences. More importantly, what appears to be ignored in these comparisons is the evolved "epigenome"—the patterned interactions between genes and their environment—that results in differential expression of identical DNA sequences. Study of the epigenome is still in its infancy, particularly where species differences are concerned, but already there are solid demonstrations from several species, including humans, of the sensitivity of genomic expression—especially early in development—to specific social and other environmental stimuli (Champagne and Mashoodh 2009; Cole 2009). For a few species, the pathways from environmentally induced modification of gene expression to alterations in neural function to behavior have been delineated (see Meaney 2010, for review).

All in all, study of the epigenome is revealing a far greater potential for adaptive phenotypic plasticity than we previously imagined from the standpoint of primarily mutation-regulated phenotypic variation. While speculative, it now seems likely that human phenotypic plasticity—in part due to individual and population-level genetic variation—evolved in response to both different ecological pressures (e.g., temperature, food resources, pathogens) and sociocultural pressures (e.g., cultural norms, mating, and resource competition). While technological advances likely buffered human groups from harsh or unpredictable ecological conditions, the growing size and complexity of the human social environment perhaps presented a constant, unpredictable, or uncontrollable mix of both harsh and favorable circumstances that selected for environmentally contingent life-history trajectories and reproductive strategies. In sum, the key to human adaptation on a global scale, we might say, was the evolution of not one universal human nature but rather of diverse human natures. Hagen (2009) has rightly called this an "unsettling specter of distinct African, Asian, and European essences, or natures."

Some Ethical Considerations

In this final section, I wish to pursue certain "unsettling" aspects of the demonstrated variation in human adaptive strategies as evident within and between cultures. Here I am referring to our valuation of and response to the kinds of biologically significant individual and cultural differences I have described. In pursuing the ethical implications of these findings, I stand in the company of other scientists—particularly Chisholm (1999) and Fox (2000/2001)—who have argued, respectively, that fully understanding human nature, has "therapeutic" and "human rights" implications. Of course, as scientists we are enculturated to believe that the ethical implications of scientific findings fall outside the borders of science proper—or that the practice of science is "value-free" because it deals with the discovery of "facts" about the natural world, not the value of these facts. As many philosophers have pointed out, there are no value-free facts, in the same way that there is no thought without emotion, but rather everything we do and think about is "drenched" in values, whether explicit or implicit. And because what we value and our moral dispositions themselves have been shaped by natural selection (Hauser 2006), the ethical implications of scientific facts, I believe, do fall within the domain of science (see also Harris 2010).

A principal difficulty arises in treating what is "natural" as desirable. While the term "natural" has potentially many different, often intangible, meanings (e.g., anything not altered by humans, such as the "wild" parts of the environment, or natural foods), for the present purpose I will restrict it to refer to the adaptive features of the human mind. Some of these are uncontroversial (e.g., the desire to mate) because they are both natural and desirable to (nearly) everyone. Other features, however, are in many cases—at least today—generally undesirable both within and across societies (e.g., rape, slavery), and we regard our individual and collective capacity to suppress and interdict such evolved dispositions as instances of moral progress. For some this kind of "moral victory" over our evolved impulses may be illustrative of our capacity to (consciously) decide what we ought to do in the light of facts about our nature. This was, no doubt, the original intent behind the well-known "naturalistic fallacy"—the injunction against logically deriving (or deducing) an "ought" from an "is." In exposing the naturalistic fallacy as a logical error, neither Moore nor Hume, however, ever intended that humans should not follow their natural inclinations, only that they need not nor should not *slavishly* follow them. Indeed, Hume believed that passion trumped reason in human affairs, which arguably anticipated the central arguments of evolutionary psychologists. What Hume could not anticipate is the modern nondichotomous view of passion and reason, the notion of passion *within* reason. We have evolved to be passionate about reason and to reason passionately. Moreover, our capacity to inhibit, to regulate our desires, to follow an "ought," is also a part of our nature—an evolved psychological capacity. It is a desire to control our desires. Hence, in the modern context of evolutionary biology, the naturalistic fallacy reduces to a mere acknowledgement or reminder of our capacity for self-regulation.

There are many instances where the interests (or rights) of the collective override those of the individual, entailing the subversion of individual (reproductive) interests (e.g., socially imposed monogamy vs. individually favored polygyny; see Fox 2000/2001). This is especially problematic when individual rights are defined in such a way that they reflect the narrow interests of power elites rather than those of the community at large, which, as Fox points out, is often the case in our present nation-state societies. In smaller scale societies, such as foraging bands, the interests of the collective—because it consisted of kin-related individuals—usually overlapped the (reproductive) interests of the individual.

But if individual reproductive interests (or strategies) fundamentally vary within a society, on what basis do we then decide what is acceptable or unacceptable from a societal standpoint? On a global level, the same question arises in taking seriously the deep cultural differences in psychological adaptations and hence cultural practices. How do we avoid a slide into hopeless moral relativism? Don't individuals and cultures have a "natural right" to pursue their respective adaptive behavioral strategies? In the examples provided earlier of variation in individual life-history—essentially reproductive—strategies, our evolutionary viewpoint should move us away from labeling low K strategies (i.e., high risk taking, early reproduction, low parenting) as abnormal or pathological behaviors requiring therapeutic interventions to reverse or "normalize" such behaviors. In other words, our discovery that such strategies represent adaptive responses to localized environmental conditions does seem to be a scientifically valid argument for discarding a "pathology" label. Given the widely distributed, multigenerational social costs of such behaviors, however, a low K strategy still can be rightly viewed as socially undesirable by society as a whole, although legal and therapeutic interventions should then be aimed at altering the environmental conditions known to provide the salient cues for individual life-history adjustment. That's a tall order of course, but it is a more rational and humane intervention than severe punishment or incarceration.

I am suggesting that the ethical standard for adjudicating the socially acceptable from the unacceptable—or the rights of individuals—is the impact (cost vs. benefit) of behavior on society as a whole. In other words, to the extent that specific human cultures have evolved as adaptations to environmental factors (e.g., pathogen prevalence), the individual fitness gains of a few should not reduce the overall fitness of society as a whole if the society (or culture) is the basis for ecological adaptation. Another way to put this is to argue that, regardless of variation in individual life-history strategies, all humans everywhere wish to achieve a basic or minimal level of individual flourishing or avoidance of suffering (see also Chisholm 1999)—reproductive opportunities, health, and nutrition—and that the goals of the collective therefore must be aligned to achieve at least this level of flourishing for all its members. On this view, the collective has the right to define the rights of (or grant rights to) individuals in such a way that the highest overall level of flourishing is attained. Unfortunately, we are still far from achieving even this minimal standard for most human societies.

The same ethical principle, I believe, can be applied to a global human society consisting of diverse sets of psychological and cultural adaptations. Some cultural practices may well morally offend us (e.g., high value placed on nepotism in Arab culture). As well, in the West we have strong ideas about intrinsic human rights based on our idea of human nature, especially the idea of an essentially universal human nature, which may not "export" well to other cultures. Thus, in light of the deep neuro-psychological differences between cultures, our expectations about what is shared in people's values, attitudes, and desires should be questioned, especially if we wish to find common ground. I suggest that there are two sets of shared values that can serve as a means for functioning as a global society and for adjudicating harmful (immoral) cultural practices. One is the previously described universally shared desire for minimal individual flourishing. This means that, as in the case of a particular culture, the "global society" must strive toward the highest overall level of flourishing for all people. And to the extent that the practices of an individual culture (e.g., enslavement, unequal economic and reproductive opportunities, genocide) reduce the flourishing of its own members (and thereby a proportion of the world's community), the global community has a right and responsibility to denounce and ban such practices.

Because of our patent, growing political and ecological global interdependence, the state of flourishing and indeed ultimate survival of any society is more and more linked to that of others. Hence, a second set of shared values emerges, in which societies wish to flourish and survive in a necessarily interdependent global society. This then provides the motivation for societies, like individuals within societies, to adjust or regulate their practices so as to be consistent with the widest global good. And as is the case in individual societies, our designation and granting of some human rights may need to be adjusted, for example, to enable continued global levels of human flourishing in the context of changing natural resources. The hopeful assumption in all this is that the same psychological adaptations that serve us well in promoting within group cooperation and self-regulation will be successfully co-opted for inter-group cooperation and regulation (similar to Singer's idea of "the expanding circle," 1981). This, too, is a tall order, and a social experiment of the future.

Before closing, I want to expand briefly on our evolved capacity for self-awareness, self-monitoring and regulation, empathy, and cooperation because these key components of human nature—though they vary in the extent of their expression among individuals and groups—are necessary for the sort of moral deliberation and progress I have been describing. Evolutionary psychologists not uncommonly are skeptical about the role of self-awareness and the influence of conscious thoughts or "will" on behavior, given that the major part of human cognitive operations lies outside of consciousness. Perhaps, like some "hard-wired" optical illusions, we can get to consciously understand that they are illusions, but consciousness is ineffective in altering the illusion. Similarly, we may discover facts about our evolved behavioral dispositions, but perhaps our conscious awareness of these facts about ourselves is ineffective in altering our dispositions. This assessment may be true in a general way, as witnessed by human history, but it does not discount the evolutionary value of conscious awareness or conscious agency in human decision making. (Here I do not need to enter into the difficult terrain of the meaning and varieties of "free will," but require only that conscious thought is causally related to immediate or short-term behavior, which is well-supported by present evidence.) (Baumeister et al. 2011). Even in the case of "hard-wired" optical illusions, our conscious insight into these allows us to alter or adaptively adjust our behavior. Similarly, insight into our irrational choice behavior can alter our decisions (e.g., Ariely 2009). At the same time, it makes no evolutionary sense to say that we can "override" or contravene what is in our fitness interests (at one or more levels—genes, individual, and group), so consciousness and a sense of agency must themselves have selective value, unless we believe these to be entirely epiphenomenal, or side-products (a "spandrel") of some other adaptive feature.

An epiphenomenalist view is inconsistent with and ignores the evident specialized and complex neuropsychological machinery for conscious "mind reading"—both our own and other minds (i.e., "theory-of-mind")—and for self-awareness and emotional-behavioral regulation (Steklis and Lane, in press, for review). In the absence of a specialized adaptive purpose, there is no a priori necessity for us to be consciously aware of our emotions, motives, behavior, and so on. After all, the vast majority of animal species pursue their reproductive strategies in the absence of any indication that they are consciously aware of what they are doing or of why they are doing it. Indeed, humans may be unique at least in the degree to which we are self-aware of our own mental states, including the construction of a (language-dependent) narrative self, and the capacity for mental "time travel"—that is, retrospection and prospection (Steklis and Lane, in press)—and in our desire to share our mental states with others (Higgins and Pittman 2008).

In light of the specialized neural machinery, primarily in expanded frontal and temporal lobes, responsible for these high-level, conscious representational abilities, adaptationist explanations are warranted. Because awareness of one's own mental content is linked to reading other minds (Frith and Frith 2010), or what is commonly known as constructing a "theory-of-mind," self-awareness may have evolved because of the fitness benefits derived from using such information for Machiavellian purposes (e.g., deception, manipulation; e.g., see Byrne and Whiten 1988; Geary 2005). Another—not mutually exclusive—idea is that this elaborate human "mentalizing" machinery promoted human cooperation, effective information sharing and transmission (i.e., teaching), and hence was responsible for rapid cultural evolution and diversification as a means of ecological adaptation (e.g., Tomasello 2008). Along with language, mentalizing abilities were a crucial component of the human move into a "cognitive niche" (Pinker 2010). Prospection—constructing scenarios of a third-person view of oneself in the future—for example, may be advantageous for assessing environmental risk and uncertainty (Chisholm 1999), despite the evident inaccuracies inherent in predicting future events and one's own adjustment to them (Gilbert and Wilson 2007). Our "executive brain" machinery takes a long time to mature—well into late adolescence (Steinberg 2007)—but it is critical to inhibition of impulses, rule-governed behavior, and observing of social norms, even when these are at an immediate cost to self. Conscious thought and deliberation thus play a vital role in our self-monitoring and adjustment to social norms and what we internalize as desirable behavior for ourselves. These conscious processes thus provide for both self-accountability (e.g., review and construction of an ongoing narrative of our egoic self) and social accountability (e.g., providing reasons for our behavior). Collectively, these evolved capacities are thus the foundation for human cultural adaptive diversification and provide hope for our future as a cooperative, sustainable global society.

Acknowledgments

I am grateful to my wife, Netzin G. Steklis, fellow intellectual traveler and collaborator, for her comments on the manuscript and for her contribution to many of the ethical points expressed herein.

References

Alexander, R. D. 1979. *Darwinism and Human Affairs*. Seattle: University of Washington Press.
Ariely, D. 2008. *Predictably Irrational. The Hidden Forces That Shape Our Decisions*. New York: Harper Collins.
Barkow, J. H., L. Cosmides, and J. Tooby, eds. 1992. *The Adapted Mind*. New York: Oxford University Press.
Baumeister, R. F., E. J. Masicampo, and K. D Vohs. 2011. "Do Conscious Thoughts Cause Behavior?" *Annual Review of Psychology*. 62:331–61.
Brown, D. E. 1991. *Human Universals*. New York: McGraw Hill.
Buss, D. M. 1989. "Sex Differences in Human Mate Preferences: Evolutionary Hypothesis Tested in 37 Cultures." *Behavioral and Brain Sciences* 12:1–49.
———. 2009. "The Great Struggles of Life." *American Psychologist* 64(2):140–8.
Byrne, R. W., and A. Whiten. 1988. *Machiavellian Intelligence: Social Expertise and the Evolution of Intellect in Monkeys, Apes and Humans*. Oxford: Clarendon Press.

Chagnon, N., and W. Irons, eds. 1979. *Evolutionary Biology and Human Social Behavior: An Anthropological Perspective*. North Scituate, MA: Duxbury Press.

Champagne, F. A., and R. Mashoodh. 2009. "Genes in Context: Gene-Environment Interplay and the Origins of Individual Differences in Behavior." *Current Directions in Psychological Science* 18(3):127–31.

Chiao, J. Y., and K. D. Blizinsky. 2010. "Culture-Gene Coevolution of Individualism-Collectivism and the Serotonin Transporter Gene." *Proceedings of the R.oyal Society. B* 277:529–37.

Chisholm, J. S. 1999. *Death, Hope and Sex*. Cambridge: Cambridge University Press.

Cochran, G., and H. Harpending. 2009. *The 10,000 Year Explosion: How Civilization Accelerated Human Evolution*. New York: Basic Books.

Cole, S. W. 2009. "Social Regulation of Human Gene Expression." *Current Directions in Psychological Science* 18(3):132–7.

Eibl-Eibesfeldt, I. 1989. *Human Ethology*. New York: Aldine de Gruyter.

Ellis, B. J., A. J. Figueredo, B. H. Brumbach, and G. L. Schlomer. 2009. "Fundamental Dimensions of Environmental Risk." *Human Nature* 20(2):204–68.

Ellis, B. J., W. T. Boyce, J. Belsky, M. J. Bakermans-Kranenburg, and M. H. van Ijzendoorn. 2011a. "Differential Susceptibility to the Environment: An Evolutionary-Neurodevelopmental Theory." *Development and Psychopathology* 23(1):7–28.

Ellis, B. J., E. A. Shirtcliff, W. T. Boyce, J. Deardorff, and M. J. Essex. 2011b. "Quality of Early Family Relationships and the Timing and Tempo of Puberty: Effects Depend on Biological Sensitivity to Context." *Development and Psychopathology* 23:n85–99.

Fabrega, H. 1979. "Neurobiology, Culture and Behavior Disturbances: An Integrated Review." *Journal of Nervous and Mental Disease* 168:467–74.

Figueredo, A. J., G. Vasquez, B. H. Brumbach, S. M. R. Schneider, J. A. Sefcek, I. R. Tal, D. Hill, C. J. Wenner, and W. J. Jacobs. 2006. "Consilience and Life History Theory: From Genes, to Brain to Reproductive Strategy." *Developmental Review* 26:243–75.

Figueredo, A. J., J. A. Sefcek, C. J. Black, R. A. Garcia, and W. J. Jacobs. 2011. "Evolutionary Personality Psychology." Chapter 390. In V. S. Ramachandran, ed., *Encyclopedia of Human Behavior*, 2nd edition. New York: Academic Press.

Fincher, C. L., R. Thornhill, D. R. Murray, and M. Schaller. 2008. "Pathogen Prevalence Predicts Human Cross-Cultural Variability in Individualism/Collectivism." *Proceedings of the R.oyal Society. B* 275:1279–85.

Fox, R., ed. 1975. *Biosocial Anthropology*. London: Malaby Press.

———. 1989. *The Violent Imagination*. New Brunswick, NJ: Rutgers University Press.

———. 2000/2001. "Human Nature and Human Rights." *The National Interest* 62 (Winter):77–86. Reprinted in *The Tribal Imagination*, Harvard University Press, 2011.

Frith, U., and C. Frith. 2010. "The Social Brain: Allowing Humans to Boldly Go Where No Other Species Has Been." *Philosophical Transactions of the Royal Society B* 365:165–76.

Geary, D. C. 2005. *The Origin of Mind*. Washington DC: American Psychological Association.

Gilbert, D. T., and T. D. Wilson. 2007. "Prospection: Experiencing the Future." *Science* 317(5843):1351–4.

Hagen, E. H. 2009. "Human Natures—A Review of the 10,000 Year Explosion." *Evolution and Human Behavior* 30:453–5.

Hariri, A. R., V. S. Mattay, A. Tessitore, B. Kolachana, F. Fera, and D. Goldman. 2002. "Serotonin Transporter Genetic Variation and the Response of the Human Amygdala." *Science* 297:400–3.

Harris, S. 2010. *The Moral Landscape. How Science Can Determine Human Values.* New York: Free Press, Simon and Schuster, Inc.

Hauser, M. 2006. *Moral Minds: How Nature Designed Our Universal Sense of Right and Wrong.* New York: Ecco.

Hawks, J., E. T. Wang, G. M. Cochran, H. C. Harpending, and R. K. Moyzis. 2007. "Recent Acceleration of Human Adaptive Evolution." *Proceedings of the National Academy of Sciences*, 104(52):20,753–8.

Heine, S. J., and E. E. Buchtel. 2009. "Personality: 'The Universal and the Culturally Specific.'" *Annual Review of. Psychology* 60:369–94.

Henrich, J., S. J. Heine, and A. Norenzayan. 2010. "The Weirdest People in the World?" *Behavioral and Brain Sciences* 33:61–135.

Higgins, E. T., and T. S. Pittman. 2008. "Motives of the Human Animal: Comprehending, Managing, and Sharing Inner States." *Annual Review of Psychology* 59:361–85.

Hinde, R. A. 1982. *Ethology: Its Nature and Relations with Other Sciences.* New York: Oxford University Press.

Homberg, J. R., and K. P. Lesch. 2011. "Looking on the Bright Side of Serotonin Transporter Gene Variation." *Biological Psychiatry* 69:513–9.

Jaynes, J. 1969. "The Historical Origins of 'Ethology' and 'Comparative Psychology.'" *Animal Behaviour* 17(4):601–6.

Kitayama, S., and A. K. Uskul. 2011. "Culture, Mind, and the Brain: Current Evidence and Future Directions." *Annual Review of Psychology* 62:419–49.

Laughlin, C. D., and E. G. D'Aquili. 1974. *Biogenetic Structuralism.* New York: Columbia University Press.

Meaney, M. J. 2010. "Epigenetics and the Biological Definition of Gene X Environment Interactions. *Child Development* 81(1):41–79.

Moore, D. S. 2008. "Integrating Development and Evolution in Psychology: Looking Back, Moving Forward." *New Ideas in Psychology* 26:327–31.

Norenzayan, A., and S. J. Heine. 2005. "Psychological Universals: What Are They and How Can We Know?" *Psychological Bulletin* 131(5):763–84.

Pinker, S. 2010. "The Cognitive Niche: Coevolution of Intelligence, Sociality, and Language." *Proceedings of the National Academy of Sciences*, 107(Suppl. 2):8,993–9.

Richerson, P. J., and R. Boyd. 2005. *Not by Genes Alone.* Chicago: University of Chicago Press.

Steklis, H. D., and R. D. Lane. In press. "The Unique Human Capacity for Emotional Awareness: Psychological, Neuroanatomical, Comparative and Evolutionary Perspectives." In *Comparative Perspectives on Animal and Human Emotions*, edited by S. Watanabe. New York: Springer.

Steinberg, L. 2007. "Risk Taking in Adolescence: New Perspectives from Brain and Behavioral Science." *Current Directions in Psychological Science* 16(2):55–59.

Singer, P. 1981. *The Expanding Circle.* Princeton, NJ: Princeton University Press.

Tiger, L., and R. Fox. 1971. *The Imperial Animal.* New York: Holt, Rinehart and Winston.

Tomasello, M. 2008. *Origins of Human Communication*. Cambridge: MIT Press.
Tooby, J., and L. Cosmides. 1990a. "On the Universality of Human Nature and the Uniqueness of the Individual: The Role of Genetics and Adaptation." *Journal of Personality* 58:17–67.
———. 1990b. "The Past Explains the Present: Emotional Adaptations and the Structure of Ancestral Environments." *Ethology and Sociobiology* 11:375–424.
West-Eberhard, M. J. 2003. *Developmental Plasticity and Evolution*. Oxford: Oxford University Press.
Wilson, E. O. 1975. *Sociobiology*. Cambridge: Harvard University Press.
———. 1978. *On Human Nature*. Cambridge: Harvard University Press.

15

Science and Anti-Science in Anthropology: A Look Back

Melvin J. Konner

I was an intense but wet-behind-the-ears graduate student when Irven DeVore put in front of me an extraordinary paper by two anthropologists. It was called "The Zoological Perspective in Social Science," and its authors' names were part of the shock and part of the fun: *Lionel Tiger* and *Robin Fox*. I mean, *really*. Did they invent these pseudonyms so they could personify not two but four noble nonhuman creatures? Or did their real names somehow urge them inexorably toward their subject, as perhaps happened with the philosopher John Wisdom and the neurologist Lord Brain?

Once you'd read the paper, the question was moot, and it was no joking matter. This was a declaration of war against the conventional social science of the time, and its normative practitioners never knew what hit them. Tiger and Fox were heralds as well as senior officers in the earliest part of the campaign, which was about to change my life and the lives of many others interested in the study of human behavior.

In retrospect, the intellectual program they announced hardly seems stunning. They argued simply that, humans being animals, there was much to be gained by considering them as such. We were clearly not the only animals with social relations, and because many other species had societies as well—in the case of our near relatives, often rather complex ones—why forgo the possibility of developing a more general science that would include their societies and their relationships as well as ours?

Or perhaps they were putting it more strongly: *social scientists, ignore the nonhuman at your intellectual peril.* The previous year, Fox had published the first edition of *Kinship and Marriage*, a major contribution to the most central subject of social anthropology. While it was too soon to position the book on a foundation of kin selection and inclusive fitness theory, by putting the mother-offspring relationship at the heart of all the systems, Fox was able to both unify the alliance and descent perspectives that at the time divided the kinship field and to negate the claim of his colleagues that human kinship had nothing to do with biology. His command of the classic analytical social anthropology of kinship was such that they could say little against his claim.

Meanwhile, Lionel Tiger was working on the soon-to-be-published first edition of *Men in Groups*, which was the first great modern work of comparative sociology. As Fox had shown in the realm of kinship, Tiger would show in that of all-male groups that the laws of human social relations not only extended beyond humans, they derived in the end from much more general laws.

In any case, they went on doing things separately and together that helped to make the scientific case for the program just about airtight. And all along they were inspiring others, me included.

That was certainly the case when they published *The Imperial Animal* in 1971. This was a book-length broadside in favor of understanding humans in Darwinian terms, and it inspired me and many others to try to do similar things. For me it was important that they didn't just look at the human animal from the outside, but also understood that evolutionary logic became relevant to human behavior partly in terms of the biological mechanisms underlying and interacting with our behavior.

Little was known about the specifics back then, but the logic inspired me enough to devote my professional life to helping to figure all this out. And when I came out with my own book about human nature a decade later, I quoted a signal passage from *The Imperial Animal*:

> Many of our intellectuals rush to quell our fears by telling us that theoretically none of this has to happen, that violence is not part of human nature that it occurs only because of evil intentions and circumstances that we can eradicate. They are the Christian Scientists of sociology; and they have not as yet solved the paradox: if we are not by nature violent creatures, why do we seem inevitably to create situations that lead to violence?

I used this as the epigraph for my chapter about human rage and aggression. It was a delicious skewering of all the pretensions of the anti-biology social scientists and scholars. And it named them for what they were: deluded deniers of the biology of the organism that was an increasingly obvious and necessary component of explaining who we are. And their religious allusion served another function: it shined a bright light on the claims of all those in the social "sciences" and humanities to the effect that humans are so unique that no information about other animals is relevant to us.

This was a twentieth-century, allegedly atheistic version of the idea of the finger of God touching this one animal species and making it, well, really, really special. Tiger and Fox laid down not one but two gauntlets before the "Christian Scientists of Sociology," who reacted as fundamentalists generally do: they closed ranks, collectively salved their hurt pride, and waged holy war against the infidels.

But by that time two starkly divergent trends had begun, and they would result in the amassing of two opposing intellectual armies. Both were committed, vigorous, numerous, courageous in their way (let's not confuse this with the courage of real soldiers) and determined. But, alas, this was not to be an equal battle. One side was armed to the teeth with the most modern weapons. The other, by deliberate choice, had gone back to the Stone Age, or at least to the premodern era of intellectual-weapons technology.

These were known by the misnomer of postmodernism, but in reality they were gamely if hopelessly reverting to *pre*-modern methods; their quarrel, ultimately, was not with Charles Darwin or any other leading modern biologist, it was with Francis Bacon, who ushered in the attitudes and stance of modern science almost half a millenium ago. What was this?

It *was* the extraordinary claim that there is something out in the world—something real—to gain knowledge about, and that furthermore there were methods and techniques that could be more or less relied upon to get you closer and closer to a good model of what that real world is. This is the four centuries distant dawn of modern science, and the central fact about it, the one thing you have to know after you have forgotten the names Bacon, Copernicus, Galileo, and Leewenhoek, much less anyone who came after them, is *be skeptical of what you think you know.*

Why is this important in the allegedly postmodern era? Because the postmodernists claimed to have found out that it is necessary to be skeptical of everything that scientists say.

In other words, they decided to teach scientists, especially social and behavioral scientists, that it is necessary for all of us to be skeptical of scientific claims. In other words, they ignored half a millennium of scientific skepticism, ignored the fact that the very essence of scientific method is to question science's claims, made themselves oblivious to the young scientists who in every generation make their reputations by refuting the claims of older ones—because they have a better telescope, a better microscope, a better database, a better computer, a better statistic, a better theory, or, yes, a better mind—and attempted to replace all that with an even broader skeptical claim, an even more trenchant revolution: *there is no knowable reality.*

This of course was for them especially true in the social realm. Human beings were, they said, autonomous agents, not automatons. So as soon as you try to describe or predict their actions, those actions will elude you because you have willfully ignored the actors' autonomy, and—clearly, you're "bad"—even their humanity. Don't describe them; ask them what they think. Don't try to array them and their experience and their actions in some sort of vast and organized system or theory. This effort is futile because it attempts to destroy their humanity. Don't even try to compare sexes or social classes or cultures and come up with generalizations that you laughably but insidiously refer to as "science"; this is inevitably an algorithm for ongoing oppression.

Nowhere in this philosophy was there a place for the idea that human beings might be better off if actual knowledge of them and their social lives were closer to reality, because that very reality was mythological. In fact, a leader of this movement, Richard Schweder, wrote in *The New Times Book Review* that ethnographies are works of fiction that anthropologists write after their year or two of fieldwork.

My reaction? I love fiction, and read a lot of it. But when I choose which fiction to read, my criteria do not lead me to read anthropologists. Their writing is not good enough. Thus, I will only take an interest in reading what might be called (no doubt arrogantly, and I freely admit that I must be an arrogant person) "anthropological nonfiction."

The other of the two trends had begun not only with comparative social anthropologists such as Fox and Tiger—not to mention anthropological primatologists such as DeVore—but also with scientific approaches in ecological, economic, and psychological anthropology. Some of these, especially the last, were to stumble badly on the postmodern bump in the road. However, they were enormously invigorated by the theoretical work of William Hamilton, Robert Trivers, Eric Charnov, and others who were not modeling human behavior at all, but rather that of bees and lizards. Surely no one could be insensitive enough to try to apply such theories to their fellow human beings?

Actually, there were many of us who, in the spirit of "The Zoological Perspective in Social Science," were prepared to do just that, and even—heaven forbid!—to apply the theories first of all to ourselves. In fact, the only way to avoid this eventuality was to posit the most improbable evolutionary discontinuity between our very nearest animal relatives and ourselves, and such a gap was becoming more implausible every day.

Contrary to what the postmodernists and other anti-Darwinians claimed, this *did not* involve (except perhaps in their very idealistic—read not "optimistic" or "generous" but "Platonic"—minds) diminishing human beings in the eyes of (broad sense) philosophy. It involved in the first place elevating animals to the place they deserved to have in behavioral science and, second, looking squarely at ourselves, not with a jaundiced, but with an honest eye. The result? Relentless confirmation of continuity.

Meanwhile, the cherished mechanics of the mills of biology—often, like Michael Faraday in physics, working-class or middle-class kids who liked to tinker but who turned out to have very outsized sorts of tinkering minds—kept on grinding, and in the end they have ground exceedingly small. They have sequenced the genomes not just of humans but of scores of species close to those pivotal in the path of our evolution—among others, amphioxus, which resembles our pre-vertebrate ancestor of 600 million years ago; the platypus, an egg-laying mammal resembling those that began the record of that warm-blooded group of our relatives; and the chimpanzee, our closest relative of all, the molecular genetics of which are vital to understanding our own.

These efforts vindicate the science of evolution. Indeed you might say they continually confirm hypotheses that Darwin would have formed if he could have seen the technologies of the future. But the question of the genes underlying behavior was also being vigorously addressed. It is not a simple one. Opponents of sociobiology used to say that the only known genetic influences on behavior were mutations of single genes that have utterly dire consequences for both brain and mind. Well, it doesn't take a genius to figure out that these tragic anomalies would have to be the simplest to analyze and that in due course behavioral processes within the normal range would come under the steely gaze of molecular genetics.

The complex things, it turns out, whether normal or abnormal, result from the convergent influences of many genes, not one or two. Conversely, genes that matter often do many different things. But that did not and does not make them inaccessible to study.

When I became the first chair of the Department of Anthropology at Emory, I insisted on a commitment from my colleagues and from the college to build the department in equal balance between cultural and biological anthropology. We built state-of-the-art laboratories for the analysis of hormones in human blood and wild primate feces, and we found funding for research on the contribution of sexism to population growth in Nigeria and on the desperation of drug-dependent children in Bolivia. This was not conceived as a simple project, and there was no expectation that it could be addressed by one simple theory.

But what we saw was something like this: Traditional social thought—Marx, Weber, Durkheim, Malinowski, Boas, Lévi-Strauss—had a piece of the truth. But the most scientific approach was to try to reconcile their theories with much larger ones; notably, the one conceived by the young Charles Darwin when Marx was still a schoolboy and the rest of them had not even been born. Why did Marx attempt (unsuccessfully) to get Darwin to allow him to formally dedicate *Das Kapital* to the famous senior biologist? Because he grasped that Darwin's theory, like his own much less rigorous one, was a materialist theory, a way of conceptualizing human life as, like the life of all other animals, a more or less adaptive response to the changing daily compulsions that were dealt to us by our relentless confrontation with our planetary environment.

Darwin's rebuff of Marx was no doubt founded partly on the fact that the elder scientist, a hopelessly bourgeois fellow, could not in good conscience wholly reject bourgeois society—unlike Marx and Engels who, despite enjoying all the then-mod cons of bourgeois life, paradoxically but gamely spilled much ink on behalf of scuttling it. The rebuff was also no doubt founded on Darwin's judgment that Marx was not a scientist.

Why not, despite the fact that generations of Russian and Chinese children would be taught that he was?

Simply because he did not believe in Bacon's method. He did not submit his grand schemes to challenge by potentially frustrating data. He did not in the least way seek the destruction of his own cherished hypotheses to form a more perfect concept of the world. He did not purge himself of ideology to gain understanding—a strategy that in the end would have served suffering humanity much more effectively.

No. What he did was to form an ideology, which drove his theory, which in turn organized his perception of the facts. And the result was, in the end, through much indirection, the deaths of tens of millions and the suffering of much higher, still untold numbers. Yet, amazingly enough, such ideologically driven "science" was at the time standard fare.

Indeed, in retrospect, Tiger and Fox had proposed an unprecedentedly radical program for social science: *get ideology out of the way*. It was unprecedented because almost all prior social science had been motivated by something resembling Karl Marx's dictum, carved into his massive Hyde Park gravestone: *Philosophers have only tried to interpret the world in various ways. The point however is to change it.* Not everyone who has pursued social science in the name of improving the world has had Marx's disastrous impact, and not every dictum carved in stone has ended with its letters dripping blood. Nor, by any means, is every ideologically motivated philosopher left of center. But every one of them has tried very hard to make a real social science impossible.

Of course, as the song goes, we all want to change the world. But if social science is to be science, it must first of all renounce ideology long enough to glean and organize the facts. And that must be done in the context of theories of proven scientific and heuristic value, not in the name of passionately held beliefs about a better world. The point, indeed, *is* ultimately to change the world, just as it is in physics and medical science. But we can only do that if we interpret the world sensibly and accurately first. Even Marx understood that, for social science, this effort must be grounded in Darwin's theory, but he had no real grasp of it.

Now that we do understand it, we can build a real social science in the light of it, and ultimately that will be the key to building a better life for real human beings in a very real and—as Marx and Darwin both understood—very material world.

I have to confess something: the pace of public and culture-wide acceptance of the effects of genes in the past few decades took me by surprise. I should have known better.

The acceptance of genetic explanations of behavior was trivially easy in the last part of the nineteenth and the first half of the twentieth century. Ordinary people, scientists, and governments all seemed to hunger for them. It seemed so simple. Human problems stemmed from weak, criminal, and otherwise defective people, whose behavior depended on genes; eliminate those people or prevent them from reproducing and you improve the species and the world.

That view culminated in one of the largest mass murders in history. But unfortunately for simplicity, a seemingly very different ideology, one based on the denial of genes, also resulted in the murders of millions, both in Stalin's USSR and Mao's China. However, these deaths were by-products and casualties of programs of "education" and "re-education," not eugenics, and "survival of the fittest"—not, incidentally, Darwin's phrase—had nothing at all to do with them.

So in any case I should not have been surprised by the late-twentieth-century success of neo-Darwinism, nor by the greater and greater reliance on genes as explanations—by the general public as well as by scientists—for disease, health, skills, talents, proclivities, personality, and intelligence. This was a continuous process, but a kind of watershed came for me in the form of a special issue of *Newsweek* devoted to child development; splashed across the top of two pages was a prominent banner that read, "Scientists think that no more than fifty percent of personality is determined by the genes."

I was stunned. No more than 50 percent? I remembered when you would be excoriated for suggesting that genes might account for 10 or 20 percent of any aspect of behavior. Now a major magazine was saying defensively, *50 percent at most*. Of course, such estimates are not terribly helpful. Calculations of heritability depend heavily on the relative variation in the genetic and environmental components. Study genetically varied individuals in similar environments and you will seem to increase heritability; study the same trait in genetically similar individuals in varied environments and you will seem to decrease it. Some traits, such as the ability of a young child to learn her first language in a normal expectable environment, are largely genetic despite low variability. Others, such as vocabulary size at age two, have both genetic and environmental influences. Still others, such as which word you use in your corner of the world to mean what English speakers mean when they say, "dog," have genetic components essentially equal to zero.

Nevertheless, it is not a terrible violation of truth or sense to think of 50 percent as the amount of variation accounted for by genes, averaged over many traits and many kinds of studies. The good news is that half the variation is nongenetic, which leaves a large scope for conventional cultural and educational influences. The other good news is that in the not-too-distant future it will be possible to counteract genetic influences (if we want to) with new interventions based on new, often molecular, knowledge.

Let us turn, though, to a different subject: the equally impressive rapid rise of evolutionary anthropology—especially but not exclusively the neo-Darwinian kind—at the same time that postmodernism was exerting its anti-science influence. Cultural and social anthropology, even in the modern era, had matured in opposition to both genetic and evolutionary influences. The whole enterprise of worldwide ethnography had proven that culture, not genes, was what was needed to explain the differences in human behavior observed among different peoples. Many theories arose as to how such differences arose and were maintained, but all of them had to do with traditions, not biology.

In addition, the late-nineteenth-century enthusiasm for arraying the range of human cultures in evolutionary sequences was moribund by the 1920s, as Franz Boas, Bronislaw Malinowski, A. R. Radcliffe-Brown, and their disciples deployed around the globe to document exotic cultures. Their wise and painstaking approach reinforced the conclusion that cultures, however "primitive," must be understood and (if at all) judged according to their own lights and logic. It made no sense to see the Kwakiutl and the Trobriand Islanders as way stations going toward the alleged cultural heights of the United States or England in the late nineteenth century. Such efforts (by Lewis Henry Morgan, Edward Tylor, and others), which often cast themselves as evolutionary, were not really Darwinian, but instead largely products of the Victorian age's understanding of progress, and they helped to create an intellectual climate that justified imperialism.

Twentieth-century anthropology did something like the opposite, despite the unfair attacks it would later receive from postmodern critics. Yet neither the evolutionism nor the materialism of the nineteenth century died out completely. For one thing, there was still such a thing as history, not only in the local sense that made it wrong to reify cultures as static entities existing outside of time, but also in the larger sense of old adaptations being partially superseded by newer ones.

Archeologists, in particular, could not deny this kind of evolutionism; once upon a time all humans were hunter-gatherers, then some became horticulturalists and pastoralists, then some plow-and-irrigation agriculturalists, then industrialists. Historical and archeological evidence showed that these ways of earning a living had consequences for demography, social structure, political forms, and organized violence. It was not an insult to the Samoans or the Nuer to think that, because they represented adaptations in the human past, they might shed some light on some aspects of that past. It also did not mean that they were being reified as throwbacks frozen in time; they had adaptations that worked and were still working. It just meant that we might learn something from them about how we adapted and survived as a species, in addition to what they were teaching us about the marvelous variety of contemporary human cultural forms. This approach would culminate in the work of people such as Allan Johnson and Timothy Earle, building on that of Julian Steward, Elman Service, and others, and of William Durham, whose grand synthesis of cultural and biological evolution seemed in itself to demand a unified anthropology.

There was, necessarily, a materialist implication in this kind of evolutionism. The Marxists were clearly wrong in their lock-step view of history as a series of vast cataclysms due to the successive eventual failure of once-adaptive economic forms. Yet the means of earning a living, and the endless inventiveness of human beings in trying to do that better and, inevitably, differently, had something to say about the shape of society and culture in different times and places. Marvin Harris at times took this notion to extremes, but his contribution in highlighting the influence of demography, ecology, economy, and technology on those forms was valid and important, and this approach too helped to keep the science of society responsive to archeological findings.

Against this methodological and theoretical background, the convening in 1964, by Irven DeVore and Richard Lee, of the "Man the Hunter" conference, resulting four years later in a volume with the same name, was a signal development. It brought together a variety of ethnographers, archeologists, and what were coming to be called human ecologists with an interest in people, recent or distant in time, who gathered plants, hunted, and fished for a living. This was no attempt at simplification; lively debates about proposed generalizations were preserved in the volume, and there were exceptions to every one of them. (One generalization, that in warm climates hunter-gatherer women brought in 70 to 80 percent of the food, appeared to belie the title, and later publications by others went on to explore further and appropriately emphasize the central role of women—although women's and men's contributions to subsistence is now known to be more like half and half.)

Empirical studies of the remaining people hunting and gathering for a living proceeded apace, despite the scoffing of the postmodernists, and those studies got better and better. Some of them, such as those of the !Kung (Jun/twasi), Efe, Baka, and Agta, continued to rest on the quantitative methods of ecology, ethology, and scientific psychology; others, such as those of the Hadza and the Ache, were explicitly framed around neo-Darwinian questions and models in kin selection, sexual selection, and life-history theory.

But hunter-gatherers were only a small part of the story. Human ecologists and true ethnological scientists such as Laura Betzig, Monique Borgerhoff-Mulder, Paul Turke, and others were applying the same body of theory to other kinds of nonindustrial cultures and succeeding beyond most of our wildest dreams. The three coedited an influential volume in 1988 called *Human Reproductive Behavior: A Darwinian Perspective*. In addition to their own contributions on the Kipsigis of Kenya and the Western Pacific island of Ifaluk, the volume represented the contributions of Napoleon Chagnon on the Yanomamo, Mark Flinn on the Caribbean island of Dominica, Barry S. Hewlett on the Aka of the Central African Republic, and Bobbi S. Low on the worldwide distribution of polygyny in relation to pathogen load, among other studies. Overviews by influential elders William Irons and Richard Alexander were also included. By 1997, Betzig was able to publish a collection of "classic" papers in human sociobiology, together with commentaries and updates by the authors of those papers, looking back at them. Clearly the field had matured brilliantly. Among other developments, Donald Symons wrote a foundational book on the evolution of human sexuality, James Chisholm (one of Fox's students) was applying life-history theory to variation in child-rearing methods, suggesting that some of what we think of as deprivation can be seen as a signal for alternate paths of development. Fox's *The Red Lamp of Incest* was an important reformulation of a classic problem in an evolutionary light, and Tiger and Shepher's work on the return of traditional women's roles in Israeli kibbutzim (among other evidence) suggested that radical feminist attempts to erase biological differences, even in theory, were doomed to fail.

Meanwhile, anthropological primatology was also maturing, as perhaps best exemplified by Sarah Blaffer Hrdy's empirical and theoretical work, but also by that of Jeffrey Kurland, Richard Wrangham, John Mitani, Karen Strier, and Barbara Smuts, all of whom were influenced to one degree or another by neo-Darwinian theory. Kurland was perhaps the first to show kin selection operating in a monkey group, Smuts highlighted friendship in baboons as a path to reproductive success, Wrangham and Mitani showed the dark side of chimpanzee male coalitions, and Strier, in addition to her work on muriqui monkeys in Brazil, contributed a foundational textbook,

Primate Behavioral Ecology, which has and will shape the views of subsequent generations.

It is impossible here to give a complete account of how this and other similar work has transformed anthropology. Suffice it to say that it now rests on a base of evolutionary fact and theory and that there is now a successful branch of scientific ethnology that is continuous with biological anthropology. That latter field, for its part, has grown to include human endocrinology, brain imaging, genomics, and other methods that give rich mechanistic reality to the processes that interest evolutionists and provide an ever-wider and more complex interface between biological anthropology and real social science.

So how can it be that, at this writing, the American Anthropological Association voted to strike the word "science" from its statement of purpose?

The answer is that the organization has drastically departed from the goals of its founders and now joins the two postmodern themes of critical ethnography and politicization of all research in an effort to push science aside. This does not just affect evolutionary anthropology, but any quantitative or even systematically empirical approach to human behavior and the variety of human cultures—psychological anthropology, demography, economy, subsistence ecology, medical anthropology, anything that might involve measurement, precise verbal description, hypothesis testing, or other scientific methods. Ironically, there was a time in the early days of cultural anthropology's abandonment of science when ethnographers complained that the National Science Foundation was less and less interested in supporting their work. But with the latest decision to take "science" out of the program, they seem ready at last to own the consequences of their drift.

Roy D'Andrade, a leading psychological anthropologist who, with Naomi Quinn, Susan Seymour, Bradd Shore, and others has maintained scientific approaches to that subfield, said to me in 1987 that postmodernism would last for one generation. They criticize, he reasoned, all that went before them, but they have nothing to teach their graduate students. I wondered whether their graduate students would start criticizing them. Some have, but on the whole they have just got on with other things.

Still, even if D'Andrade's prediction was prescient, much damage has been done to the field as a whole. Departments have split bitterly, precious research opportunities have been lost, and some who in their early careers half a century ago saw an opportunity for a unified science of anthropology have become discouraged about that prospect. But in fact that unified science has been founded, in spite of those who chose to drop out of it. They can continue to "do their thing," which they now freely declare is not science, but they cannot stand in the way of a new generation of anthropologists who have Bacon's method and Darwin's theory guiding their hands and minds.

Reference

Konner, Melvin J. 2010. *The Evolution of Childhood: Relationships, Emotion, Mind.* Cambridge, MA: Harvard University Press.

VII

Finale

Mandelbrot Sonnet

A small initial difference (*a blink
so nondescript it might have passed unseen
had mild intention not produced a wink*)
can have gigantic outcomes that had been
unknown at their inception (*how predict
the mild flirtation pregnant with design
would spawn a dynasty that would inflict
misery on millions*) with no sign
of their impending order (*yet contained
within the gesture consequences down
to final victim*) lawfully constrained
(*imagine if the wink had been a frown*)
both unpredicted yet determinate
exquisite fractal geometry of fate.

16

The Consumerist Cosmos

Howard Bloom

We are told that materialism is our curse. We are told that our greed for material goods has made us plunderers of the planet that gave us birth. But materialism is not our sin; it's our gift. It's our tool for doing nature's work. For 2.5 million years, the human spirit has climbed on stairs of material possession, on the rungs of gadgets, tools, and toys. From stone tools to signet rings, the human spirit has ascended on piles of material things. The spear, the plow, the fireplace, the coat, the boat, the brick, the book, and the laptop helped us create words, concepts, metaphors, religions, creation myths, tales of legendary heroes, sagas of triumphs and defeats, ecstatic contacts with divinity, new aspirations, new worldviews, and new dreams. The domestication of sheep gave us not just the wealth of wool and mutton, but the concept of caring for your flock. The straight walls of Catal Huyuk's brick apartment complexes ten thousand years ago and of the pyramids' blocks of stone five thousand years later gave us geometry, and that geometry gave us the mathematical tools with which 250 generations later we would reach the moon. Innovations of the spirit and the mind grow from jolts of material creativity.

Nature herself is a blatant consumer, an obsessive materialist. We think that we have plundered the pitifully small pool of resources on this earth and that now we must make sacrifices to appease a nature angered by our transgressions. We are wrong. What we call nature is a radical re-inventor, constantly reassembling herself. How does she pull off her acts of creativity? By acts of manic mass production and of appalling mass destruction. By acts of waste and of unacceptable devastation. By acts of rampant materialism, acts of rampant ingenuity. Nature builds stars by the quadrillions, and then murders them off in nova death. She uses their agonies to create and to make new forms of atoms this cosmos has never seen. And she has killed off every living thing she ever produced, then has tossed its body away, turning its corpse into scrap, garbage, and decay.

Nature creates by consuming and reconstructing material things. Then by throwing them away. On this planet, nature creates by what we've mistakenly called rape. Nearly four billion years ago, she violated octillions of virgin atoms of rock and water to make the mud at the bottom of the seas. She used microbes to rape the naked earth beyond the waters, piercing its cloak of stone. She used microbes to produce chemicals that turned this planet's coat of rock into powder. She used microbes to defecate mineral particles from which new rocks would be made. And she used microbes to open cracks in the planet's pristine stone. Then she used plants to dig roots into the microscopic slits and to split the virgin rock. Was this rape? Was this massive pileup of new material goods and of new material litters a sin?

If Charles Darwin is right, every fruitful field now covered with soil was the product of a massive landscaping effort left to us by millions of generations of earthworms who sinned against nature by doing plastic surgery on our untouched planet's face, then by littering it with their droppings. The earthworms turned jagged outcrops and crevasses into gentle hills, slopes, and valleys. They left the trail of their waste, their feces wherever they went. We use the worms' violation of Mother Nature and their sewage to grow our plants. And we worship the worms' legacy rainforests and greenery.

Nature is the mother of all consumption and the mother of all refuse heaps. She is also the mother of all brutality. She has run this planet through over 142 mass extinctions. And her taste for species slaughters hasn't ceased. She puts this orb through wobbles and precessions that blast this earth with massive weather shifts every 22,000, 41,000, and 100,000 years. She whirls our solar system around the core of our galaxy once every 226 million years, sending us on a journey whose dangers make the adventures of Frodo the Hobbit look like a quiet game of Parcheesi. In our galactic circling, we trudge through clouds of space dust and through spiral arms, hazards that stomp our climate, turning plains into swamps and transforming coasts like those on which our cities rest to the beds of seas.

Nature is not testing our ability to respect her. She is testing our ability to outwit her. She is testing our creativity. And she is testing our audacity. So far, we have met that challenge handsomely. There have been sixty glaciations since the days of *Homo erectus* two million years ago. Sixty ice ages. And there have been twenty global warmings in just the last 120,000 years. Massive ones. Warmings in which the temperature has pole vaulted up by as much as eighteen degrees in ten years or less. Even the sun has tossed us challenges, growing 43 percent brighter, 43 percent hotter than it was when the Earth began.

We became human by inventing our way out of these calamities. We were born without the fur and the more regulatory systems that allow wolves and caribou to brave the Arctic cold. And we were born with a hunger for meat. Yet we were not equipped to bring down prey like the beasts with claws and saber teeth. We survived that trial by inventing material goods: stone tools—artificial claws and canine teeth. We met that challenge by hacking the skins off animals and inventing the vain display of cloaks and capes. We met that challenge by marching north from Africa to Europe and Asia, and by taunting nature, living on the edge of her glacial sheets. We met that challenge by building tents with mammoth tusk poles and mammoth rib struts. We covered those tents with mammoth skins. Then we made beads out of mammoth bones, sewed them on our leather vests, and flaunted our material luxuries even in the midst of ice.

Nature rewards those who overcome her. Around 3.85 billion years ago, bacteria colonies invented ways to twist the photons of the sun and the molecules of the sea into cell membranes and energy. But those bacteria had a problem. Toxic waste. They farted what they could not digest into the air and seas. After two billion years of flatulence, the toxic gases poisoned the planet's atmosphere and threatened to exterminate the polluters. What organisms survived the resulting die-off? Those that turned the toxic effluents into food, fuel, and a power base. Those who learned to milk treasure from a murderous cast-off, from gaseous garbage called oxygen.

Today, there are 1.097 trillion cubic meters of rock beneath our feet aching to be recruited into the process of life. For every ounce of biomatter on this planet, there are 200 million ounces of inanimate stuff waiting to be seduced into the grand project of cells and DNA. Then there are the resources we haven't yet touched, the resources hanging above our heads. A single asteroid has a trillion dollars' worth of raw materials, a treasure worth more than the gross domestic product of South Korea. And the solar energy available in orbit around the earth in a year is more than all the energy humanity has tapped in its 2.5 million year history.

Mother Nature's way is instability and catastrophe. She killed off stars, and she has killed off more species than we can count. She is as willing to discard industrialists, environmentalists, socialists, bankers, and you and me as she was to toss away trilobites, Ediacarans, raptors, and tyrannosaurs.

What does nature demand of you and me? Take as many inanimate molecules as you can grab and press-gang them into the family of cells and DNA. Be fruitful and multiply. Turn poisons into delicacies and barren wastes into candy. Turn trash into treasures. Be consumerist as hell. Be materially rapacious. Make as much of this inanimate globe as you can into biomass. Do what quarks, atoms, galaxies, and stars have done. Defy disorder. Shatter the rules of entropy. Make new things. Reinvent reality.

17

Last Word: The Razor's Edge

Robin Fox

In the introduction to *The Tribal Imagination* I told the following story when discussing the various uses and misuses of "civilization":

> My favorite story about Oxford involves an irredeemably judgmental use of the word. The time is World War I and militant ladies are roaming the streets of Oxford giving out white feathers of cowardice to young men of fighting age who are not at the front. (Yes, they did that.) They invade a college quad where a young don in cap and gown is walking across the lawn reading Virgil. Thrusting the white feathers at him one of the ladies demands: "Young man, why are you not out there fighting for civilization?" Without hesitation and with devastatingly correct grammar he replies: "Madam, I *am* the civilization for which they are out there fighting."

I was thinking of this story when I was asked to write something on why we should try to revive the teaching of "Western Civilization" courses in our universities and colleges. Civilization is always a work in progress. Like the process of evolution, like the universe itself in Howard Bloom's description, civilization is a constant defiance of entropy. Every civilization is an experiment in how far we can shift ourselves from the evolutionary norm of the small, kinship-integrated tribal society governed by ritual and custom, to any kind of society either more complex in structure or less tribal in foundation. We assume that given intelligence and foresight there is no limit to where we can move. We can write our own rules, design our own futures. The wise among us have determined that in effect we have reached the perfect resolution of development in Western liberal representative democracy based on

---

This chapter is based on an article that first appeared in *Academic Questions* 25:1, 11–27, 2012, and the material used here is reproduced with the permission of Springer Verlag.

free-market economies, and that the whole world will shift inevitably in this direction. Thinkers from all bands of the spectrum agree that this is inevitable because it is somehow in our natures as human beings to live this way and that only repressive regimes prevent its realization. We invade other nations and at crippling cost try to make them over in our image because we know this is really how they want to be and will be once their bully-boy dictators and enforcers are ousted. Even those of us who are doubtful about the method do not usually question the logic: freedom and free elections are the natural state of man, and all we need to do is liberate these impulses to have free, democratic societies everywhere on earth.

But the liberal democratic societies we regard as the natural outcome of natural human impulses are dangerously late arrivers on the human scene and, to be brutal, they are still fragile experiments whose viability has not been sufficiently tested. Far from being natural outcomes of human nature, they are heroic attempts to defy human nature, and nature itself. They live on a razor's edge, and the state of balance is precarious.

Every civilization in the past has failed. Bits and pieces of them remain and these fragments we shore against our ruin. But as operating entities they are gone. Their song is ended; only the melody lingers on. Some of them lasted a long time and then declined slowly, ossified or imploded, or were overrun by Arnold Toynbee's "external proletariat": the barbarian hordes. Perhaps we think that "Western civilization" is inherently different, that somehow it has solved the problems of the past and can live on without fear of decline? Perhaps we are right. But at the very least it is too early to say. Perhaps a healthy dose of skepticism about our chances is our best bulwark against failure, and our best reason for taking ourselves seriously.

Here we come up against our inability to decide whether we like our own civilization or hate it. Is it worth saving? If it is not worth saving then it is probably not worth studying. This is the easy way out that many among us take, although it ignores the fact that we can only make such a judgment if we have done the necessary study. But our own intellectual tradition (a melody lingering on from the Greeks) militates against this. Some of the people who have studied Western civilization in the most intense way have been its most severe critics. They, like Karl Marx or T.S. Eliot or H.G. Wells, have not liked what they saw, but needed to know what was wrong and why it was wrong. They have needed to understand it so that they could know what to do about it.

For one thing that characterizes us (we members of this civilization) is our need to do something about it. We are not fatalists, despite some of our religious beliefs that would suggest that we might be. Predestination is after all the ultimate in fatalism. The paradox of how religious ideas about ineradicable fate could turn into a driving desire for worldly success (and the reordering of society in the process) was at the heart of Max Weber's analysis of how capitalism and science, secular rationality and progress, became guiding traits of our civilization. The vast majority of us take the result of this process more or less for granted; we can simply enjoy it. The problems it presents for us are practical, not intellectual: how to get the most out of it. Those who refuse to take it for granted and want to do something about it are those most in need of knowledge about its foundations and development—its inner logic. The people who should study it most intently are not those who like it, but those who are most dissatisfied with it. Marx would have agreed.

Marx would also have agreed that they should study it in the context of the other civilizations of the world and even of pre-civilized societies. This would not have been on the grounds of cultural relativism or multiculturalism or any such nonsense, but because he saw these "others" as important clues to the origins and development of our own state of capitalism. It was Marx's attempt to delineate "primitive communism" and the "oriental mode of production" and the transition from mercantile capitalism to free-market capitalism that pushed Weber to reanalyze the same facts. The great basic question of sociology became, "Why did the Oriental societies not make it to the next stage?" Of course, now we are disinclined to see this as a matter of stages. But even if Marx and Weber did not get it all right, their questions remain fundamental. Even if cultural relativists want to regard the Western development not as an advance in civilization but as a giant step sideways, they still have to understand it, not just condemn it, if they want to do something about it.

You will not get much of an argument from the Marxists on this point. They are firmly in the Western-rationalist tradition. They regard their "radical" multicultural brethren as wooly minded, unscientific, *lumpen* socialists. But there are few of the Marxist purists left with whom to have a meaningful debate, while the wooly minds are clogging the arteries of the educational system. Is it worth the trouble of educating our young people in the history and culture of the West? Would we perhaps not be better off making sure that they are computer literate and doing much better in math and science rather than studying art history and classical literature, even in translation?

One immediate answer is that math and science are part of the Western tradition that makes it unique. Even so, the pessimist in me wonders, do they need to know this in any detail or can they not take it for granted and get on with the science and technology that will save us? The quick answer is that they can, but that someone somewhere should be the guardian of the Western secret or we may just lose it, and the science and technology will be for nothing. Does it matter as long as the Guardians have the secret?

I think it does, because if we leave it only to the Guardians—a small, powerful, and fully educated elite—then we are shirking the challenge of democracy: that knowledge and decisions based on it should be open to all, and that all should have the means to assimilate and benefit from them. We would be retreating from our open society into a Platonic closed society with a sharp division between the Guardian elite and the Helots that suited Plato but should not suit a national culture that stems from Jeffersonian rationalism and an ideal of free and universal education. The problem with this is that it all takes time and time is precious.

In the past in Western Europe it has not really been an issue. A system of Guardians was accepted, and they received a pretty intensive education in Western culture—including its classical and modern languages, sciences, and history—through school and university, but mostly the former; not all that many went to university. The rest, those not of the mandarin elite, were given an adequate education and rendered functionally literate and numerate, were given opportunities for upward mobility, and that was enough. With such a system, England ruled a quarter of the globe with a pitifully small cadre of classically educated governors, as Alan Macfarlane has described for us. America, while having a class of similarly educated Guardians, has also undertaken the massive task of trying to bring a reasonable level of education to everyone, including instruction in the foundations of the civilization to which we were thought to be privileged to belong.

But in this we were always coming up from behind. The Guardians of European culture did not so much learn it as live it. The fact that we feel it necessary to give courses in Western Civilization shows up the difficulty we have. European universities, for example, would never have even thought of having a compulsory course on "Western Civilization." It is probably different now, but the students at Heidelberg or Cambridge, Salamanca or the Sorbonne, Bologna or Utrecht *were* Western Civilization: like the young don in the Oxford story.

They would have had to prove in their entrance exams that they were conversant with classical and modern languages, for example, even if they were to concentrate on science once accepted. Their family histories *were* the history of Western art and diplomacy and music and finance and business (like the Macfarlane tea planters.) Even those who rebelled against their own class were pretty well versed in what they were challenging. The Cambridge-educated Soviet spies Burgess, Philby, and Maclean could not have had better Western Civilization qualifications, and their mentor, Sir Anthony Blunt, was curator of the Royal Art Collection.

I think of my own socialization into Western culture in a northern provincial town in the England of the 1930s through the 1950s. Some of this came from formal education, and a very good one, but most of it came by osmosis, by sheer immersion in the flow of the cultural stream—and I was not a child of privilege. One even physically lived in it: from the Iron Age remains on the moorlands, through the Saxon, Norman, and Gothic churches, to the castles, the walled towns, the canals and railways. Its country manors and great houses (open to the public) were living monuments of passing time. Playing in the ruined monasteries and abbeys took one to the heart of the Reformation, as did membership in the Church of England—one wing of the holy trinity of the Bible, Shakespeare, and Milton. There was an immediate connection with the Tudor England of the Book of Common Prayer and the huge feast of music opened up for a chorister. There was an unbelievably rich musical life, with up to forty performances of Handel's *Messiah* alone each Christmas, and everything else in the sacred music repertoire and beyond, including the amazing local brass bands. Traveling operas gave regular performances (all in English, as was the way then) and a bewildering array of local amateur choral, operatic, and dramatic societies put on everything from *Die Fledermaus* to *Naughty Marietta*. Gilbert and Sullivan ran through our bloodstreams.

The town Repertory Theater did a different play each week, from J. B. Priestley to Tennessee Williams (two seats for the price of one on Mondays.) The municipal amateur Civic Theater (featured in the film *Room at the Top*) did Shaw and Ibsen plays and showed Bergman and Nouvelle Vague movies. The municipal Reference Library was well stocked and free, and the Technical College, and the City Museum and Art Gallery had libraries and lectures and exhibitions. The very institutions one lived with unthinkingly—the monarchy, the free press, the local and national elections, the courts of common law, the parish system, the guilds and trade associations (through which most of my friends passed to professional life), the forms of local government (aldermen still sat on the bench)—all had deep roots in the past. The city itself, old in foundation but in effect a product of the Industrial Revolution, was a living history to be experienced.

Even without a formal education, the immersion was massive. Above all there was the BBC, an amazing treasure trove of information, with music, drama, world news, and uplift on all levels. Again, this was open to everyone. The Promenade Concerts were broadcast live and had a huge audience. The local cinema palaces were just as full for Olivier's Shakespeare films as for John Wayne movies.

The town proletariat with its mechanics institutes, technical colleges, trade unions, cooperative societies, clubs, and nonconformist chapels was equally rich in history reaching back beyond the Levelers and Parliamentarians. Despite serious class differences, a kind of homogeneity still existed in English society in those pre-immigration days. Even in insular England, wars had brought us into close contact with continental Europe. My first experience with foreign languages was with German and Italian prisoners of war working as virtually unguarded farm laborers. It was from the prisoners that I learned that all operas were not written in English. The Italians told me they had municipal opera houses with a repertory company doing a different work each week, as cheap as local cinema. To this rich informal mix add the history and languages, science, and literature that were taught in the very good secondary schools (mine being a country grammar school dating from 1673)—the *gymnasia* and *lycées* on the continent—and the cultural immersion is complete.

I apologize for this strongly personal note, but I am trying to emphasize that there is really no substitute for enculturation when it comes to "learning" Western Civ. There is no way that even a yearlong course can compare to being immersed in it. In the United States, much the same held true until the waves of immigration and the great expansion westward of the nineteenth century, when the need to educate a rapidly growing, at best semiliterate and often non-English-speaking community threw the burden of enculturation almost entirely onto the school system. The system responded bravely, but mostly—except of course for the WASP elite, which modeled its education on the European systems—it was trying to socialize and educate at the same time. It was trying to create basic-English speakers out of the fragmented material of European and Asian peasantry and artisans. The immigrant society that America became could not take any kind of "cultural literacy" for granted and go from there. It had to inculcate cultural literacy along with personal hygiene.

It was also a society oriented almost entirely to the future. The old generation of immigrants who never quite developed English fluency and stuck to their old ways, languages, and identities was not regarded by assimilating youngsters with any kind of awe as a repository of civilization. On the contrary, this was something to be thrown off in the effort to become "Americans." These Americans, after all, had thrown off the political yoke of Europe and were being encouraged by the idea makers of the nineteenth century to throw off the cultural yoke also.

Emerson, in 1860, responded testily to a woman teacher's definition of a "suitable education for girls" as "anything that gets them to Europe." Can we not, he asked, "get the tape-worm of Europe out of the minds of our countrymen?" He had already declared America's intellectual independence in his "American Scholar" speech in 1837. But of the three pursuits he demanded of the transcendental scholar, one was to study "the mind of the past"—its literature, art, and institutions. Both Henry James and T. S. Eliot were totally immersed in them to the point of reabsorption. In sum, the attitude of America toward Western civilization was always ambivalent. Americans were conscious of being the heirs to much that was admirable in that tradition, while at the same time were self-consciously trying to distance themselves from it. For the Emersonians, it was a delicate balancing act in which they really saw themselves as part of the tradition but wanting to be an "American voice," both within the tradition and then transcending it—something absolutely distinctive.

The voice was Whitman's democratic voice—the voice that didn't reject the tradition but "said" it in a different way:

> Sail, sail thy best, ship of Democracy,
> Of value is thy freight, 'tis not the Present only,
> The Past is also stored in thee,
> Thou holdest not the venture of thyself alone, not of the
>   Western continent alone,
> Earth's *résumé* entire floats on thy keel O ship, is steadied by thy
>   spars,
> With thee Time voyages in trust, the antecedent nations sink or
>   swim with thee,
> With all their ancient struggles, martyrs, heroes, epics, wars, thou
>   bear'st the other continents . . .

The whole of "Thou Mother with Thy Equal Brood" in *Leaves of Grass* is worth looking at as a statement of the problem, for although "Royal feudal Europe sails with thee," it remains a question whether you still need any of it. Whitman can't make up his mind on this:

> It to eventuate in thee—the essence of the by-gone time
>   contain'd in thee,
> Its poems, churches, arts, unwitting to themselves, destined with
>   reference to thee;

Europe then is simply America *in potentia*:

> Thou but the apples, long, long, long a-growing,
> The fruit of all the Old ripening to-day in thee.

And yet Whitman can't be sure whether what is happening is truly a ripening, or whether the old apples are simply rotten.

> Brain of the New World, what a task is thine,
> To formulate the Modern—out of the peerless grandeur of the modern,
> Out of thyself, comprising science, to recast poems, churches, art,
> (Recast, may-be discard them, end them—may-be their work is
>   done, who knows?)

Who knows indeed? To find a literary "voice" that was not beholden to European—particularly English—literature. Did Whitman do it? Hemingway, Fitzgerald? The jury is still out. Did America ever find a "serious" composer who did not sound like a European knockoff (especially of Dvořák)? When the voice was eventually found in George Gershwin's incomparable *Porgy and Bess*, the critics were uniformly dismissive, and it took decades to become established. The truly original American musical voice, jazz, was not taken seriously except as a source for "themes." Copland and Ives (and others) have been touted as genuine American voices, but they were almost totally derivative of European music despite playing with American themes. I think the great stage musicals, *Porgy and Bess, Showboat, Oklahoma* and *West Side Story* definitively broke the musical voice barrier from the mid-1930s onward; but that is just a personal opinion.

"American cultural anthropology" is really an import from German romantic nationalism and the idea of the unique *Kultur* of the unique *Volk* (and thus the first-cousin of Fascism). American philosophy and literary theory inevitably retreat from their natural pragmatic character to go a-whoring after strange European gods. The only truly American religion, Mormonism, did an about-face from its communalistic-polygamous-utopian roots to morph into a bastion of conservative bourgeois respectability. Americans have problems with their own exceptionalism: they boast of it but seem afraid to pursue it—afraid to cut the cord. Whitman is a secularized Blake still talking the poetical language of the familiar "thee" and "thou" and the vocative "O" and using French as a marker of sophistication.

But old Walt would still have wanted his brothers and sisters of the democracy to know what it was they were recasting and discarding, at least at the stage before a truly unique voice could be found. The ambivalence about Western civilization never led to a complete discarding of it. The critics were all sensible enough to know this was impossible: they were part of it for better or for worse, and they should know it and understand it. For the Guardians, taking their cue from Emerson and inspired by Whitman, it should be known so that it could be improved upon.

But what about the huddled masses: how much of the base culture was needed to put them on the path of that same improvement?

It was in the very process of learning English that the immigrants absorbed at least a version of it. Shakespeare, Gilbert and Sullivan, and Dickens were immensely popular in the American West, and Westerners even liked Oscar Wilde. Anyone having learned English (or starting with dialectical spoken English and learning to read) being then taken by a conscientious schoolteacher through all of McGuffey's excellent *Readers* would pick up a damn good notion of English literature, as Henry Ford understood when he published and distributed them at his own expense, although he was probably equally drawn by their heavy Christian moralizing. There was no idea then of doing this through the learner's indigenous language. Learning English was part of becoming American, and if you were to get out of your ghetto, you had to master it, and in mastering it you—or at least your descendants—picked up a large amount of the heritage by osmosis, too. And it was a heritage if anything enriched by access to at least one other European language besides English.

This learning of culture through language was a model of acculturation: the native heritage (as it were) was still there, but melded with the dominant English heritage being learned. And even if only the Guardians had the fine details of the dominant heritage, the rest got enough to be able to navigate an open democratic society. They had something that welded them together in a common linguistic and, one hoped, nationalistic culture. After the first two generations most of the immigrants were thoroughly "Americanized"—perhaps retaining a deep attachment to their particular heritage, often through religion, but seeing it as a contributor to the American whole.

The annual Polish festival I sometimes attend in Orange County, New York (through my Polish in-laws), is a riot of Polish food, songs, dances, and crafts until the final evening, when it becomes a vigorous and moving chorus of American patriotism, sung in English. The current Hispanic immigrants are resisting this linguistic absorption, and we pander to them partly from left-wing guilt and partly from commercial greed. But this is a mistake, and it may cost us dearly. We can only hope that, as with Asian immigrants, the subsequent generations will more readily integrate (and intermarry) while maintaining their cultural identity.

But this is something they essentially should work out for themselves, as other immigrant groups have done, with our encouragement but without our patronization and pandering. In the process they will become more Americanized, and we shall become a little more Hispanicized, just as we became more Gaelicized, Italianate, Sinocized, and Nordified, and this is how it should be. One of my favorite New Jersey eateries (sadly gone) had this charming legend above its door: "Italian-American-Chinese Restaurant: All Our Wines are Chilled." And no one should miss New York's Chinese-Kosher delicatessens. Not perhaps what Emerson was after entirely, but getting there in its own gustatory way.

This cultural absorption was indeed extended to the Asian immigrants who came without the advantage of any European language and from countries with no traditions whatsoever of democracy (Whitman's "Venerable priestly Asia"). Their strong traditions of deference to age and tradition were something that had kept them from joining the modern world. But they had huge energy and great natural intelligence, and a dedication to worldly success that outshone the Protestant ethic. More recently, the immigrants from India bring something remarkable. Most of them have a sound education in the English manner born of their long association with Great Britain. They mostly speak better English and have a better English education than the rest of us, and they, like us, have a history of shedding the British yoke while retaining the best of British institutions: in particular a respect for the process of common law and the exercise of democracy. They are a gift that we should nurture to their and to our own advantage.

What I am describing is unabashed cultural absorption that blends the various sources into a new whole with a common language and a common set of values and institutions. This new blend, if Whitman and Emerson's hopes are to be realized, will rise to a higher plane of civilization than Europe was able to achieve, even if it is far from that goal at present. The absorption has been a great success, and the public schools and state colleges and universities managed to do the double job of giving a utilitarian education to many people while initiating them into the values of a free society. These were the values of an unabashedly free democratic open society founded on the English model with its tradition of free elections and the rule of law, themselves the result of a long process of social, economic, and political development. To move beyond them we had to know them.

What I am saying used to be commonplace, and a cause for congratulations. It was the American miracle: the melting pot. Those astonishing children of the European Enlightenment, the Founding Fathers, took the English Glorious Revolution of 1688 and brought it to fruition here. It was the actualization of the *potentia* that Emerson and Whitman saw in that model, but that was still imperfect in the home country. It was why Edmund Burke could support the American Revolution for defending the liberties of Englishmen, while condemning the French Revolution for robbing Frenchmen of theirs. It was the city set on the hill. "We Americans," as Herman Melville wrote in *White-Jacket*, "are the peculiar, the chosen people—the Israel of our time; we bear the ark of the liberties of the world."

This is now all called into question, as we know. Most of my academic colleagues (at this point almost always younger) would be of the opinion that I should be embarrassed to write such nonsense. Have I not heard of deconstruction, multiculturalism, colonialism, imperialism, orientalism, globalization, hegemony, neo-liberalism, inequality, sexism and the rest, including my favorite "altericity"? Indeed I have. But I am an immigrant myself, for whom joining this society was a conscious choice; they mostly are not and so can be more free to reject it. I had to weigh these things in the balance and make a decision, and having made it to make sense of it. I was the young don and brought Western Civilization with me to be sure, and on September 11, 2001, I saw it under vicious attack in my own backyard.

I don't have to be told its faults and contradictions. I have lived with many of them, including the aftermath of World War I, the Great Depression, World War II with its consequent austerity and flirtation with state socialism, and the Cold War with its exacerbation of the paranoid streak in our society. My father fought for the colonialist British Raj in imperial India—and against the barbaric Nazis in that Second World War. I know about inequality: I was born on the dole, and my mother grew up in a country where women did not have the vote. I know about slavery, discrimination, and the oppression of native peoples, especially my maternal people the Irish. I was weaned on the Marxist critique of capitalism, and saw up close the fall of the tyranny of Communism. The birth pangs of an open civilized society can be horrendous.

But do we abandon the baby because the birth was painful? With tears and struggle, guilt and sacrifice we have overcome these things, and from Bartolomé de Las Casas through William Wiberforce to Martin Luther King we saw that they were wrong, and—often kicking and screaming—we tried to right them. For Melville we bear the ark of the liberties of the world. This ark was horribly hard to come by. Yet it survived, and we have it.

What is on the tablets in Melville's ark? It is the secret of how our Western civilization achieved, and how we maintain, the democratic open society that we now enjoy, with all its faults and missteps. It is also the secret of its Achilles heel that we need to know in order to preserve it from all too easily slipping off the razor's edge. An open society, like civilization itself, is also a work in progress—a messy, fragmented, difficult, frustrating, often unjust, and sometimes scary work in progress. The very openness that is its virtue lays it open to fatal fragmentation.

Our human psychological and social default system is tribal, and that is where we are most secure. The messier and more frustrating the open system becomes, the more likely that many of its members, including some of our intellectuals, will long for the security of the closed morality and authoritarianism of the tribe: for the simple solution. They embrace the rule of those Guardians (or would-be Guardians), who assure them that all is known and all will be taken care of and that their unbearable individual moral responsibility will be lifted.

Sigmund Freud saw how we needed to be relieved of the burden of the superego with its ever more in-turned aggression: the major discontent of civilization. George Orwell saw us longing for the certainty of Big Brother and could only see our salvation lying with the proles (the working class.) H. G. Wells saw mind as being "at the end of its tether" and seeking the same relief. When looking at the virtues of

American democracy, Alexis de Tocqueville in *Democracy in America* also saw its weakness:

> In democratic times enjoyments are more lively than in times of aristocracy, and immeasurably greater numbers taste them. But, on the other hand, hopes and desires are much more often disappointed, minds are more anxious and on edge, and trouble is felt more keenly.

Tocqueville was anticipating Durkheim on *anomie*, Marx on alienation, Freud on *Angst*, Fromm on the fear of freedom, Eliot on the disassociation of sensibility, and Weber on the fall of the rational before the power of charisma: everything that Popper saw in Freud's inevitable "strain of civilization."

If I had to put only one tablet in the ark it would be my old teacher Karl Popper's *The Open Society and Its Enemies*. Popper's open society was of course Western democratic society, with free elections, a free press, free markets, freedom of speech, universal literacy, freedom of scientific activity, and a rule of law that ensured due process and that enforced contracts. Its enemy was the closed society of tribalism, where taboo and custom governed everything and where the ends of society were fixed. In an ideal open society for Popper, everything should in principle be in doubt, up for grabs, open to question; all hypotheses should be capable of falsification: it was the only way science could occur and knowledge cumulate. You had, in other words, to embrace the idea of being wrong: not something monarchs, prelates and politicians (or current academic humanists) really understand or welcome. But scientists and the scientific method live by it.

This was a startling new way of looking at the world: science was a strict democracy of knowledge and it needed a political democracy in which to thrive. Such a social context was needed for science, and particularly experimental science on which technological advances depend, to flourish. Science *as a form of knowledge*—as opposed to the unchallengeable certainties of religion, magic, and metaphysics—was the product of the "disenchantment" of society consequent on the Renaissance and Reformation. It happened in one place and at one time in the world's history, and what brought us to that point is something we must understand, as well as what fused and transformed itself to make us what we are (or what we can be).

The nearest we have come to a realization of this kind of sociocultural system has been the free democratic societies of northern Europe. But this is an almost impossibly difficult world to live in; it is totally foreign to that tribal default nature at the center of our being. It can be made to work, but it is a constant juggling act along the razor's edge. When it goes right and prosperity follows, it can seem like a formula for paradise on earth. When it fails—as with capitalism in stagflation and depressions and recessions and world wars, or with welfare socialism, when living on the public credit card leads to national bankruptcy—it can scare us to death. Then it can shuffle in the demand for a savior and a doctrine and a retreat to the dumb security of the tribal womb, where everything is settled and the future is known.

As Popper saw to his dismay, from the very beginnings in democratic Athens there have been traitors to the open society: those very intellectuals who were its Guardians. With their unhealthy passion for the various *-isms* that promise absolute knowledge of the future and demand control of the present, they are, like Plato, as much a threat as the barbarians at the gate. And they have often indeed preferred those barbarians to their own messy democracies, from the Athenians who preached the virtues of the Scythians and Spartans to those who today redeem their collective cultural guilt by embracing neo-primitivism and denigrating rational science. This leaves science, the most precious of our civilization's gifts, open to attack from a bizarre coalition of strange bedfellows in the reactionary religious Right and the radical academic Left: they hate each other, but they hate science more.

What "the West" did to the indigenous peoples was not pretty, but what those peoples were doing to each other was not much prettier. There was no Las Casas, no University of Salamanca, among the Aztecs protesting at seventy thousand human sacrifices a year. The expansion and then collapse of the colonial enterprise was a stage in development that had to be gone through. It is something any of the other societies of the world would have done if they had had the chance—and many had already tried it. Colonialism, like slavery, was not invented by the West. It is as old as conquest itself. The very virtues of the West made its effort much more successful than the previous conquerors and plunderers had been, although the Arabs run a close second. But the fact that they stayed in place and tried to bring something of Western political organization to the colonized people meant that in many places they left behind the makings of democratic societies. These now are fighting their own harsh battles with the tribalism from which they are still struggling to emerge.

It is certainly a good thing to teach the music, art, and literature that we think of when we say, "Western civilization." But it is perhaps more important to understand them in the context of the social and political development of which they were and are a part. Music, art, and literature are common to all advanced civilizations, but the scientific method that we depend on and that was a unique aspect of the Western miracle—and the kind of state where it could flourish—were, as we have seen, unique to northern Europe, particularly England.

Francis Fukuyama, in *The Origins of Political Society*, sees three institutions as the cornerstones of the political development of Protestant England as it emerged from Catholic Europe: a strong state, the rule of law, and the accountability of the governors to the governed through that rule of law. The idea of a rule of law to which even the rulers were subjected, Fukuyama rightly notes, was a product of Catholic Christianity. The resulting combination was unique to England, with Holland following closely and the rest gradually catching up. It was exported to North America and became the foundation of the civilization that Whitman and Emerson saw could be the fulfillment of its innate promise.

That was on the political front. On the cultural-economic front we continue to work out the implications of Weber's insight that capitalism and science, and even the rationality that allowed the development of both music and bureaucracy, were products of the Protestant ethic. Other civilizations had some aspects of this magical mix (like the strong state in China, and political assemblies in Hungary), but none put them together to make for the more-than-magical democratic open society that we inherited from northern Europe and especially England. The world would like to embrace its material benefits, but the world lacks the secret of the mix that produced the society that makes these benefits possible. We have the enormous advantage of knowing and living the secret.

If we must teach Western Civilization from the outside—if we no longer can depend on it being absorbed by osmosis through the cultural pores—then we should not teach it simply as an end in itself: get your dose of music, art, and literature, children. When I see a thirteen-year-old immigrant Chinese girl in a flower-print dress playing an impossibly superb version of a Beethoven violin sonata, I know that this bit of Western civilization is safe for a while. We can pass on the content to a generation of talented youngsters. We should certainly be concerned to teach the content; that will get done in bits and pieces as it always has. But we should try also to teach Western civilization as an idea: as the apples of history and culture that ripened into the open society we value, and why we value it, and why it is so difficult to maintain.

We should not confuse the open society with a particular set of democratic political arrangements, although democracy is fundamental to it. It seems to work best, for example, in constitutional monarchies, where the hereditary monarch is a focus for national unity independent of political parties. Openness needs anchors in tradition: not unswerving devotion to form, but recognition that traditional forms have an evolved wisdom to them by their very survival. They should not be discarded lightly, even if they should always be open to question. Such systems (like traditional universities) seem to combine enough of the virtues of the closed society with the aspirations of the open one to maintain a creative balance. The open society is something to be constantly aspired to, and the political arrangements can be tweaked to make it more possible. Nothing should be written in stone: even the revered American Constitution has been amended twenty-seven times.

We must not be ashamed, as Sam Huntington has said, to emphasize that Western civilization is valuable, not because it is universal, but because it is unique. It is what Ernest Gellner called, in *Plough, Sword and Book*, "the miracle": the improbable concatenation of circumstances that produced a brilliant but flawed civilization, difficult to maintain, but because of its very openness remarkably resilient. Every disaster presents a new opportunity that we can grasp because we do not work to a rigid tribal formula (however much some of us would like to), and hence the future is always open and undetermined.

When we do teach Western civilization, then we should certainly teach its many and serious flaws so that we do not repeat them or perpetuate them. We should teach its virtues so that we may defend and preserve them, especially from our own zealots on the left and the right. We should teach it in the context of the other great civilizations (and the pre-literate tribal societies, to be sure—as I do for a living). We must do this both to understand their great intrinsic worth and to understand why, with all their brilliance, they did not make it: why the miracle did not happen there. But why, having learned it from us, they may work their own miracle that might eclipse us if we are not vigilant.

We should teach our civilization not as a settled doctrine but as a risky enterprise that indeed requires eternal vigilance and eternal renewal. We should teach it as a society approaching that rare balancing act on the razor's edge: a society in which everything should be open to question and where no one has the last word. Perhaps this is the truly transcendental society that Whitman and Emerson saw as our potential? We should teach the idea to as many as possible and not just to the Guardians, because they are as susceptible as the masses to the lure of tribal certainty. We must spread the intellectual risk. We are trying not to fall into internal barbarism and to keep the barbarians from the gate at the same time. We are fighting human nature to do this.

Our only hope, as befits our role as a future-oriented society, is in the young. Civilizations that fail, as we know, fail from within. Our education has to be a judicious mix of information and initiation; it has to initiate without indoctrinating. It has to teach us not a fixed set of rules to live by, but how to use our knowledge of ourselves to help us take intellectual chances. We have been very good so far at creating this unique enterprise; let us not hesitate now to preserve it and pass it on, when we most need to get it right.

Contributors

Howard Bloom is the author of *The Lucifer Principle: A Scientific Expedition into the Forces of History, Global Brain: The Evolution of Mass Mind from the Big Bang to the 21st Century*, and *The Genius of the Beast: A Radical Re-Vision of Capitalism*. He is a former Core Faculty Member, The Graduate Institute, Recent Visiting Scholar—Graduate Psychology Department, New York University; founder of the International Paleopsychology Project; founder of the Space Development Steering Committee; Member of the Board of Governors, National Space Society; founding board member of the Epic of Evolution Society and the Darwin Project; founder of The Big Bang Tango Media Lab; and member of many learned societies.

Bernard Chapais is a biological anthropologist and primatologist who received his PhD from Cambridge University in 1982. He has since then been a professor of anthropology at the University of Montreal. After conducting experimental research on primate social behavior—on kinship and dominance in particular—for over twenty years, he turned his attention to the evolution of human social organization by carrying out a detailed comparative analysis of primate societies and human societies. This resulted in the book *Primeval Kinship: How Pair-bonding Gave Birth to Human Society* (HUP, 2008), which presents the first description of human society's deep structure and a comprehensive account of its evolutionary history. He is now working on a new book that pursues further the bridging of biological and sociocultural anthropology.

Michael Egan is a former English professor and Scholar in Residence at Brigham Young University, Hawaii. He is the author/editor of eleven books, including *The Tragedy of Richard II, Part One, a Newly Authenticated Play by William Shakespeare, Edited, Introduced and with Variorum Notes* (2006), which won the 2006 Adele Mellen Prize for Distinguished Contribution to Scholarship. He is the editor of *The Oxfordian*.

Anne Fox was educated in the United Kingdom, France, and the United States, did a degree in Russian at George Washington and Leningrad universities, and a PhD in anthropology at Imperial College London. After a brief career in journalism and bookselling in the United States, she founded Galahad SMS Ltd., a UK firm specializing in research and education on substance abuse. She does educational work for the Ministry of Defense, the Home Office, and the Youth Justice Board, and is currently developing a curriculum in anthropology for primary and secondary schools. She is the editor, with Mike MacAvoy, of *Expressions of Drunkenness: Four Hundred Rabbits* (2009).

Kate Fox was educated in the United Kingdom, United States, France, and Ireland and read anthropology and philosophy at Cambridge. She is a Director of the Social Issues Research Centre in Oxford, United Kingdom, and a Fellow of the Institute for Cultural Research. Her work has involved research on subjects as varied as drinking, flirting, body image, gossip, violence, and mobile phones. She has lectured at many universities in the United Kingdom, United States, and elsewhere, most recently at Brown University and the University of Pisa, Italy. She published *Drinking and Public Disorder* with Dr Peter Marsh (1990) and *The Racing Tribe: Watching the Horsewatchers* (1999). Her *Watching the English: The Hidden Rules of English Behaviour* (2004) became an international bestseller.

Sir Antony Jay CVO was educated at St. Paul's school and Magdalene College, Cambridge. He is famous as the coauthor with Jonathan Lynn of the TV satirical comedies *Yes, Minister* and *Yes, Prime Minister*. He has had a distinguished career in broadcasting and public service, for which he was knighted in 1988, and which included writing two documentaries on the royal family. He was made a CVO—awarded for personal services to the monarch. He is the author of several books, including *Management and Machiavelli* (1967), *Corporation Man* (1973), and most recently, *The New Great Reform Act* (2009).

David Jenkins has a variety of publications that span a range of topics, including myth, social organization, kinship, exchange networks, museums, ethnographic photography, environmental values, endangered species, resource exploitation, and the use of mathematical models in anthropology. He has conducted anthropological research in the highlands of Peru and coastal British Columbia, and over the last decade has conducted research on coupled human and natural systems in various sites in North America. He has taught at the Massachusetts Institute of Technology and Bates College, among other institutions. He currently resides in Anchorage, Alaska, where he researches environmental policy and traditional subsistence cultures.

Melvin J. Konner is Samuel Candler Dobbs Professor in the Department of Anthropology and the Program in Neuroscience and Behavioral Biology at Emory University. He studied at Brooklyn College, CUNY, and Harvard where he earned his PhD in biological anthropology in 1973. He did two years fieldwork among the Kalahari San Bushmen, studying infant development, hormones, lactation, and fertility, then after six years on the Harvard faculty, he went to Harvard Medical School and received his MD in 1985, a story told in his autobiographical *Becoming a Doctor* (1987). After medical school he became chair of the Anthropology Department at Emory. In 1982 he published *The Tangled Wing: Biological Constraints on the Human Spirit* (revised 2002), and in 1988, with his wife, Marjorie Shostak, and S. Boyd Eaton, he published *The Paleolithic Prescription*. His other books include *Medicine at the Crossroads*, *Why the Reckless Survive*, *Unsettled: An Anthropology of the Jews*, *The Jewish Body*, and most recently *The Evolution of Childhood* (2010).

Adam Kuper is an anthropologist, and author of a number of books, most recently *The Chosen Primate, Culture: The Anthropologists' Account*, and *Incest and Influence: The Private Life of Bourgeois Britain*, all published by Harvard University Press. He is a Fellow of the British Academy and was formerly professor of anthropology at Brunel University.

Charles J-H. Macdonald obtained his PhD at the Sorbonne in 1974 and his "Thèse d'Etat" in 1984. He has been with the Center for Scientific Research (CNRS)–France since 1974 and is now Senior Fellow Emeritus. He was a founder and director of the Institute for Southeast Asian Studies in Aix-en-Provence (CNRS–Université de Provence), the founding director of the Maison Asie-Pacifique in Marseilles, and a fellow of the Institute for Advanced Study, Princeton. He has done fieldwork with the Palawan of the southern Philippines as well as with the Raglai of Southern Vietnam and has published on Palawan ethnography and on kinship, social structure, mythology, rituals, religion, shamanism, and material culture. His interests include mythology, phenomenological psychology, linguistic anthropology, religion, general comparative theory, suicide and anarchic, egalitarian, and peaceful societies. Recent publications include: *Uncultural Behavior: An Anthropological Investigation of Suicide in the Southern Philipines* (2007), *Asian Names: History, Culture and Identity* with Zheng Yangwen (2009), and *Anarchic Solidarity: Autonomy, Equality and Fellowship in Southeast Asia* (2011.)

Alan Macfarlane was born in India in 1941. He has an MA and D.Phil. in history at Oxford, an M.Phil. from the London School of Economics (where he attended lectures by Robin Fox), and a PhD from the School of Oriental and African Studies. He is currently Emeritus Professor of Anthropological Science at the University of Cambridge and a Life Fellow of King's College. He was elected a Fellow of the British Academy in 1986. He has done work in English history and as an anthropologist in Nepal, India, China, and Japan. He has published more than twenty books, including *The Origins of English Individualism* (1978), *Letters to Lily: On How the World Works* (2005), *Japan through the Looking Glass* (2007), and *The Riddle of the Modern World* (2000). His most recent work, with a friend, is a trilogy of books about his early life and schooling titled *A Dragon Triptych* (2012). His website is www.alanmacfarlane.com.

Michael T. McGuire MD is married and has five children. He is Professor Emeritus in Psychiatry and Biobehavioral Science, University of California at Los Angeles. His education took place at the Universities of Rochester, California, Harvard, and the Massachusetts Institute of Technology. The majority of his professional work focused on the behavior and physiology of nonhuman primates, particularly the effect of external information on the brain's neurotransmitter and the body's hormone systems. He has authored numerous book and scientific articles and was the founding editor of *Ethology & Sociobiology*. Currently he is president of the Biomedical Research Foundation, a director of the Bradshaw Foundation and the Gruter Institute for Law and Behavior, and manages his cattle and grape ranch in Northern California.

H. Dieter Steklis PhD is co-Division Chair at the University of Arizona South and Professor of Psychology and Adjunct Professor of Family Studies and Human Development at the University of Arizona. His present research includes the comparative study of primate family systems, with a particular focus on paternal behavior, life history, and personality in mountain gorillas. His research also includes the study of human-animal relationships, and the evolution of cognitive and emotional differences between apes and humans. Steklis earned his PhD in Anthropology from the University of California, Berkeley. He joined Rutgers University in 1974, retiring in 2004 as Professor Emeritus of Primatology. His research, scholarship, and publications span several disciplines, including comparative primate neurobiology, primate behavior and conservation, and the evolution of human behavior. Steklis held several science and conservation leadership positions with the Dian Fossey Gorilla Fund International. He began his long-term research with mountain gorillas while serving as director of the Karisoke Research Center in Rwanda (1991–1993). He collaborates with his wife, Netzin G. Steklis, on many projects, and their joint work has been featured in scholarly journals and books, national and international magazines, radio programs, and numerous television broadcasts (including *National Geographic*).

Linda Stone is Professor of Anthropology Emerita at Washington State University in the United States. She received her PhD in anthropology from Brown University in 1977. Along with kinship, her research has focused on South Asian cultures, gender, and medical anthropology. She is author of *Kinship and Gender: An Introduction* (2009), coauthor (with Paul F. Lurquin and L.L. Cavalli-Sforza) of *Genes, Culture and Human Evolution* (2007), editor of *New Directions in Anthropological Kinship* (2001), and coeditor (with Robert Parkin) of *Family and Kinship: An Anthropological Reader* (2004).

Lionel Tiger is Charles Darwin Professor of Anthropology Emeritus at Rutgers University. He has taught at the Universities of Ghana and of British Columbia. He was co-Research Director of the Harry Frank Guggenheim Foundation with Robin Fox. Among his books are *Men in Groups: The Imperial Animal* (with Robin Fox); *Women in the Kibbutz* (with Joseph Shepher); *Female Hierarchies* (ed.); *Optimism: The Biology of Hope*; *The Manufacture of Evil: Ethics, Evolution and the Industrial System*; *The Decline of Males*; and *God's Brain* (with Michael T. McGuire MD).

Robert Trivers has a BA in history and a PhD in biology from Harvard (1972). He has been an evolutionary biologist since 1965 when he first learned that natural selection is the key to understanding life and that it favors traits that give individuals an advantage (in producing surviving offspring). In 1996 he learned of Hamilton's kinship theory, which extended one's self-interest to include not only one's own offspring but also those of relatives, each devalued by the appropriate degree of relatedness. He has contributed to building social theory based on natural selection: a general system of logic that applies to all creatures and vastly extends the range of relevant evidence. He published a series of papers on social topics, reciprocal altruism (1971), parental investment and sexual selection (1972), the sex ratio (1973), parent-offspring conflict (1974), kinship and sex ratio in the social life of insects (1976), summarized in his book *Social Evolution* (1985). His latest book is *The Folly of Fools: Deceit and Self Deception in Human Life* (2011). In 2006 he wrote *Genes in Conflict: The Biology of Selfish Genetic Elements* with Austin Burt, and in 2007 was awarded the Crafoord Prize in Biological Sciences of the Royal Swedish Academy of Sciences.

Frederick Turner, Founders Professor of Arts and Humanities at the University of Texas at Dallas, is a poet, cultural critic, literary scholar, playwright, and philosopher of science, aesthetician, essayist, and translator. Born in England in 1943 to the anthropologists Victor W. and Edith L. B. Turner, he grew up in Central Africa and was educated at Oxford University. A former editor of *The Kenyon Review*, he has authored thirty-one books, including *The Culture of Hope, Genesis, Hadean Eclogues, Shakespeare's Twenty-First Century Economics, Paradise*, and *Natural Religion*. He is a winner of many poetry and literary prizes and has been nominated internationally over forty times for the Nobel Prize in Literature. He is or has been a member of several research groups, on subjects including the biological foundations of esthetics, artificial intelligence, ecological restoration, time, interdisciplinarity, the sociological study of emotion, chaos theory, game theory, philanthropy, and ecopoetics. His essay (with Ernst Poppel) on the neurobiology and cultural universality of poetic meter has been widely cited and reprinted, as have his essays for *Harper's* on modernism, education, and environmentalism.

Index

A

Academic anthropologists, 54
Academic hierarchies, 48–49
Adaptive phenotypic plasticity. *See* Phenotypic plasticity
The Aeneid, 262
African Genesis (Ardrey), 89, 95
Age, closeness in, 290
Age discrepancy, 290
Alcohol. *See also* Drinking rituals in British Army
 in African cultures, 80
 ancestor worship and, 80
 in British Army. *See* Drinking rituals in British Army
 consumption, 62
 in Mexico, 80
 as transformative substance, 79
 in warrior-hunter male process of bonding, 83
Alcoholics Anonymous (AA), 114–116. *See also* Felicity in human organizations
Alexander, Christopher, 269
al-kol or *al-ghol* (alcohol), 79
Allen, John Bartlett, 189
Allen, Nicholas, 153–154
All the Strange Hours (Eiseley), 227
American Anthropological Association, 31
American Indians, 234–235
American Museum of Natural History, 233
Amphioxus, 333
Amygdala activation, s-allele in, 313
Ancestors, 176
Ancestor worship, 80
Angela's Ashes (McCourt), 10
Anonymity in Alcoholics Anonymous (AA), 114–116. *See also* Felicity in human organizations

Anthropologie Structurale (Lévi-Strauss), 239
Anthropologists, on humor, 118
Anthropology. *See also specific entries*
 psychological, 113
Anthropology Today, 54, 61
Antigone, 136
Antistructure, 118
Arapesh culture, 235
Archeologists, 337
Ardrey, Robert, 89–90, 95
Arnold of Rugby, 209
Ashcroft, Peggy, 91
A Study of History (Toynbee), 12
Attenborough, David (*Life on Air: Memoir of a Broadcaster*), 10–11
Audience, 93–95, 98
 absolute numbers, 93
 concentration and dispersal, 93
 darkness for mood setting, 94
 primitive tribal gathering, 106, 108
 principal performer, 94
 for television, 95
Austen, Jane, 186
Autobiographies, 221–245
 Eiseley, Loren, 227–230
 Fox, Robin, 237–245
 Lévi-Strauss, Claude, 10, 224–227
 Mead, Margaret, 231–237
Automatism, 106
Aztec goddess Tlazolteotl, 78

B

Baboons, 136, 142, 179, 339
Bacon, Francis, 331
Bakhtin, Mikhail, 124, 250
Barrie, James, 206
Bateson, Gregory, 221–222, 235

Battle, emotion of, 82
Beer. *See also* Drinking rituals in British Army
  importance for British soldiers, 69–70
  survey, 70
  views by infantry sergeant, 70
Beer tokens, 69
Behavior, genetic influences on, 333
Behavioral Biogrammar, 29
Behavioral universals, 274–275
Benjamin, Walter, 250
Bergson, Henry, 94
Betjeman, John, 216
Beyond Freedom and Dignity (Skinner), 31
Bhagavadgita, 267
Bianquis-Gasser, Isabelle, 81
Binomial naming system, 115
Biogrammar, 309
Biological constants, 276–277
  cost of ignoring, 300–302
  cultural diversity and, 301–302
Biosocial Anthropology (Fox), 14
Biosocial approach
  to human behavior, 308
  to kinship, 136–139
Blackberry Winter (Mead), 231
Bloch, Maurice, 152
Boarding schools. *See* English boarding education
"Boat race" drinking game, 75
Bond. *See* Social bonds
Book of Genesis, 262
Book of the Dead, 262
Bourdieu, Pierre, 223
Bramston, John, 207
Brecht, Berthold, 250
British Army, drinking habits of. *See* Drinking rituals in British Army
British Electrical Equipment Federation Chairman, 92
British Medical Journal, 199
Brothers-in-law, 187
Browne, Janet, 186, 195
Browning, Robert (*Sordello*), 9–10
Budenz, Julia, 257

C

Calamities, 346–347
Calming functions of nervous system, 76
Cantos (Pound), 257
Carnivals, 125
Cartesian Meditations (Husserl), 46

Cavalli-Sforza. L. L., 145
Cenobites, 113–114
Centenary History of the Dragon (Jacques), 217
The Challenge of Anthropology (Fox), 15, 20, 48
Chance, Michael, 234–235
Chance and Necessity (Monod), 16
Chanoyuists, 117
Chapais, Bernard, 142–144, 146–147, 149
Chemical spillover, 76
Children
  incest and, 164–165, 174
  marriage choice and childhood, 186–199
  seclusion of, 206
  social relations of, 47
Chimpanzees
  primal horde, 169–171
  stronger ties in, 169
Christianity, 215
  and laughter/merriment, 126
"Christian Scientists of Sociology," 331
Civil religion, 81
Closeness in age, 290
Code of Conduct in the Armed Forces, 71
Cognitive environment, 284–288
Cohesion, 71–72
Collectivist cultures, 312
  antipathogen defense strategies in, 314
  s-allele in, 313
Collier, Jane, 139
Combat readiness, 71
Comedy, 108
  beneficial biochemical change in patients, 91
  and laughter, 91
  strength of, 97
  styles of Peter Ustinov/Frankie Howerd, 96
Comic character, 106
Coming of Age in Samoa (Mead), 233–234
Communal drinking by young soldiers, 81
Communitas, 77
Complex social patterns, 292–295. *See also* Social prime mover; Society
  descent patterns, 293
  fraternities, 292
  kinship structures, 292–293
  social orders, 293–294
  sororities, 292

Index

Conceptual Processes, 47–48
Conjecture, 103
Conjectures and Confrontations (Fox), 15, 256
Consumerism. See Nature
Content, 214
Conviviality, 113–114. See also Felicity in human organizations
Cooperation bias, 292
Corporate anthropologists, 56
Cotter, Pat, 215–216
Courtesy, 124
Cousin marriage, 183–200. See also Marriage, of Darwin
  business partnership and, 188
  Catholic doctrine and, 187
  childhood and, 186–199
  consequences of, 193–194
  financial considerations in, 188–191
  royal families and, 187
Cross-sex dyads, 290
Crow-Omaha systems, 153–154
Cultural anthropology, 67, 273–274
  kinship, 147–150
Cultural diversity, 222
  biological constants and, 301–302
Cultural evolution, 108
Cultural remission, 71
Culture, and psychosocial proclivities, 295–300
  formal content, 295–297
  multiform expression, 295
  semantic culture, 297–300

D

Dancing for the Woolworth Ladies, 9–10
D'Andrade, Roy, 340–341
D'Aquili, Eugene, 75–76
Darwin, Caroline, 189
Darwin, Charles, 183–200, 346
Darwin, Erasmus, 189
Darwin, George, 187, 195–199
Darwin, Robert, 184, 189–190
Das Kapital (Marx), 334
Decline and Fall of the Roman Empire (Gibbon), 12
de Garine, Igor, 80
Detribalization, 105
de Unamuno, Miguel *(Tragic Sense of Life)*, 46
Developmental familiarity, 290–291
DeVore, Irven, 338

Diary of Ralph Josselin, 206
Dickinson, Goldsworthy Lowes, 213
Dispossession-induced anger, 283
Divine Comedy (Dante), 262
Douglas, Mary, 62, 77
Dragon School, 208
Drama, 108
Drinking, 62
Drinking rituals in British Army. See also Alcohol, Beer
  alcohol defining status/identity, 71
  battle and hunt, 82–84
  "boat race" drinking game, 75
  cohesiveness, developing, 71
  cultural remission, 71
  "digestive biscuit" game, 75
  elite regiments, 74–75
  ergotrophic functions, 76
  group drinking of soldiers, 70
  hemispheres function, 76
  male bonding, 74–75
  modern warfare, 82–83
  negative features, 74–75
  new member in group, 74
  official ban, 74
  organizational influence on, 71
  ritualization, 73–81
  "soggy biscuit," 75
  training purposes, 78
  trophotrophic function, 76
Drug-taking sessions, 81
Drunkenness, 72
  extreme, feminine aspects, 72
The Dual Mandate (Lugard), 209
Dupa religion (Northern Cameroon), 80

E

Earl of Cork, 207
Ecstasy, Ritual and Alternate Reality (Goodman), 79
Egyptian epic, 262
Eiseley, Loren, 227–230
Elite regiments in British Army, 74–75
Emetics, 80
Emma, 187
Emotion of battle, 82
Emotions, 215
  bonds and, 171–173
  inbreeding and, 175–176
Empire and the English Character: The Illusion of Authority (Tidrick), 208
Enclaved aggregates, 113–114

Encounter with Anthropology, 14, 20
Energy-expanding functions of nervous system, 76
Energy reducing functions of nervous system, 76
English boarding education, 214–218
   in fiction, 217–218
   life in, 211
   morality and, 214
   objective of, 213–215
   physical discipline and, 214
   portraits of, 215–216
   preparatory schools *vs*., 205
   shaping children as models, 215
   spirituality and, 215
English upper-middle-class social structure, 207
Enuma Elish, 262
Epic, 249–269
   criticism, 250–252
   cultural universality of, 255
   elements of, 263–269
   folk, 253–254
   human evolution and, 255–256
   ideological rifting, 256
   list of, 258–263
   mythological *vs*. religious, 254
   new generation, 257
   novel *vs*., 250
   oral *vs*. literary, 253–254
   teaching and writing, 252
Epic and Romance (Ker), 251
Ergotrophic function of nervous system, 76
Eskimo society, 121
Essentialism, 222
Ethics of community, 113
Ethnic groups, 113
Ethnographers, 67
Ethnographical evidence, of social prime mover existence, 284
Ethnology, 111
Ethology. *See* Human ethology
Ethosystem, 144
Etiquette in tea ceremony, 117
European Commission, 59
Evolutionary anthropology, 336–337
Evolutionary biology, 310
Evolutionary theory, 308
"The Evolution of Kinship Systems and the Crow-Omaha Question," 153

Exogamy, 178
Exogamy complex, 143
Exotic cultures, 337

F
Family bonding, and marriage, 187
Faraday, Michael, 333
Farr, William, 195
Father abuse of sons, 174
Felicity in human organizations, 111–128
   anonymity in Alcoholics Anonymous (AA), 114–116
   conviviality, 113–114
   human social organization, Charles Macdonald on, 111–112
   humor, 118–120
   inuit humor, 120–122
   Japanese tea ceremony, 116–118
   laughter and grotesque, 124–127
   Palawan humor, 122–124
Fellowship of Alcoholics Anonymous (AA), 114
Feminism and kinship, 139–142
Figueredo, A. J., 317
Financial considerations, in cousin marriage, 188–191
First-name basis, 115
Foley, John Miles, 254
Folklore, 95, 116, 118
Forced social relationship, 78
Forman, Simon, 207
Forster, E. M., 213
Fortes, Meyer, 205
Fortune, Reo, 233–237
Foucault, Michel, 250–251
Fox, Robin, 135–136, 183, 205, 329–330
   academic hierarchies, 48–49
   Antony Jay on, 90
   autobiography, 7–8, 237–245
   biography, 6–8
   biosocial science, 17–20
   career as anthropologist, 4–5
   Charles Macdonald on, 111–112
   colleagues and students, 16–17
   comedy writer, 90
   education, 4
   on emotional male bonding in Western epics, 72–73
   ethosystem, 144
   final grades, 35–36
   friends, 5–6

on incest taboo, 150–151, 163–164
innate conservatism, 33–35
interests, 11–13
later years, 32–33
management writer, 90
on natolocality, 152
as private intellectual, 36–38
The Tribal Imagination, 112
work, 5–6
writing on human condition, 42
Freke, Elizabeth, 207
Freud, Sigmund, 13, 150
Frost, David, 93
The Frost Report, 93
Functional evidence, of social prime mover existence, 283

G
Galton, Francis, 187, 193, 196
Games. *See* Sports
The Gardens of Flora Baum (Budenz), 257
Gasset, Ortega y, 249
Geertz, Clifford, 81, 297–298
Genome, 309
Gibbon, Edward *(Decline and Fall of the Roman Empire)*, 12, 249
Global warmings, 346–347
Godelier, Maurice, 154
Goffman, Erving, 77–78, 210
Goodall, Jane, 170
Goodman, Felicitas, 79
Goody, Esther, 205
Graham, Kenneth, 218
Grandmother hypothesis, 149. *See also* Matrilocality
Great Depression, 234
Greco, Juliette, 94
Grooming, 77
Grotesque, laughter and, 124–127
Grotesque body, defined, 125
Group drinking of soldiers, 70
Group synchronicity, 77
Growing up in New Guinea (Mead), 234

H
Halloween, 125
Hamadryas baboons, 136, 142
Harris, Marvin, 274
Hart, Keith, 61
Heath, Dwight, 62
The HFG Foundation, 31–32

The History of Human Marriage (Westermarck), 161–162
The Hollow Crown, 91
Home audience, 95
Hominin fossil record, 309
Homosexuality, 212–213
Honko, Lauri, 254
Horticulture, as metaphor, 206
Howerd, Frankie, 96
Hrdy, Sarah Blaffer, 339
Human community, 105
Human ecologists, 338
Human ethology, 309
Human exogamy, 18
Human nature/behavior, 307–325
  adaptive phenotypic plasticity, 314–315, 319–320
  animal socioecology and, 308–309
  biogrammar, 309–310
  cultural differences and, 312
  ethical considerations, 320–325
  ethology and, 309
  evolutionary biology and, 310
  evolutionary origins of, 308
  evolutionary psychology and, 310
  genetics and, 318–319
  holistic approach to, 309
  hominin fossil record, 309
  life-history and, 316–318
  model of, 282–288
  personality structure and differences, 311
Human social organization, Charles Macdonald on, 111–112
Humility, 115–116
Humor, 118–120. *See also* Felicity in human organizations
  Inuit, 120–122
  Palawan, 122–124
Hunter-gatherers, 338–339
Husserl, Edmund (*Cartesian Meditations*), 46
Hypothesis, 103

I
Ideology, 334–335
The Imperial Animal (Tiger and Fox), 16, 29–31, 90, 330
Imperial education. *See* English boarding education
Inbreeding, and incest taboo, 175–178

Incest avoidance, 298–300
Incest: Origin of the Taboo (Maryanski and Turner), 161, 165, 178
Incest taboo, 5, 7, 18–19, 33, 150–151, 299–300
  data on, 173–175
  Fox on, 163–169
  inbreeding and, 175–178
  Westermarck's thesis on, 162–163
Indirect Rule, 209
Individualist cultures, 312
  antipathogen defense strategies in, 314
  s-allele in, 313
Innate conservatism, 33–35
Institutional seclusion, 206
Intentional communities, 114
Inuit humor, 120–122. See also Felicity in human organizations
Iyer, Pico, 218

J
Jacques, C. H., 217
Japanese tea ceremony, 116–118. See also Felicity in human organizations
Jay, Antony (on laughter). See Laughter, Antony Jay's article on
The Jesus Tapes: We Are Not Alone (Fox), 16
Joking, 119

K
Kamehameha, King, 268
Kaminer, Wendy, 223
Kate Fox on anthropology. See Popular anthropology
Ker, W. P., 249
The Keresan Bridge (Fox), 14
Kinship, 135–136
  biosocial approach to, 136–139
  cultural anthropology, 147–150
  feminism and, 139–142
  hominid, 146
  incest taboo, 149–150
  large-game hunting, 146–147
  matrilineal societies, 151–152
  matrilocality, 148–150
  pair-bonding and, 146
  patrilineal societies, 152–153
  primate, 136–139, 142–146
  psychological disposition, 152
  terminology systems, 141
  tetradic theory, 153–154

Kinship and Marriage (Fox), 13, 23–25, 135–136, 183, 205, 329–330
Kinship bonds, 289
  developmental familiarity, 290–291
Knight, Chris, 148
Kuper, Adam, 138–139
Kurland, Jeffrey, 339

L
L-allele carriers, 313
Langton, Charles, 192
Language ability, 214
Large-game hunting, 146–147
La Rire (Bergson), 107
Laughter
  against anger and violence, 121
  and grotesque, 124–127. See also Felicity in human organizations
Laughter, Antony Jay's article on, 89–108
  absence of laughter, 98
  behavioral evolution, theory of, 90
  drama and comedy, 108
  efforts of writers, 98–99
  emotional state, 100
  government meeting, funnier side of, 100
  influence of Robin Fox, 90–91
  National Film Theatre, 92
  population, 104
  summary of plays, 102
  in television, 93
  tribal phenomenon, 105
L'Avare (Molière), 98
Lawrence, T. E., 209
Lee, Richard, 338
Lévi-Strauss, Claude, 224–227, 274
  contention, 111
  death, 19, 83
  dedication to, 38
  and kinship analysis, 24
  and Robin Fox, 19
  Tristes Tropiques, 10
Lewis, C. S., 218, 249, 251
LHT. See Life History Theory
Life History Theory (LHT), 315–316
  fast and slow life strategies, 316
Life on Air: Memoir of a Broadcaster (Attenborough), 10–11
Light, 6
Light Entertainment Department, 93
Lineal masculinity, 148

Index

Littlewood, Roland, 17
Live shows, 98
Lord Farrer of Abington, 192
Lorenz's contention, 82
Lubbock, John, 195
Lukacs, John, 249
Lyell, Charles, 185
Lyotard, Jean-François, 250–251

M

Macdonald, Charles, 111–128. *See also* Felicity in human organizations
Mackintosh, Fanny, 190–191
Mahabharata, 267
Male-male bond, 73–75
Malinowski, Bronislaw, 19
Man: The Journal of the Royal Anthropological Institute, 26
Management and Machiavelli (Jay), 89
Mansfield Park (Austen), 186
"Man the Hunter" conference, 338
Manus Religion (Fortune), 234
Margaret Mead Award, 67
Marlowe, Christopher, 257
Marriage, 119. *See also* Cousin marriage
  of Darwin, Charles, 183–200
  family bonding and, 187
  financial side of, 188–191
Marriage Act of 1836, 196
Marsh, Peter, 58
Martineau, Harriet, 184
Marx, Karl, 335
Marxists, 90
Mass drinking sessions, 72
Materialism, 345. *See also* Nature
Matrilateral cross-cousins, 119
Matrilocality, 148–150
McLennan, John, 178
Mead, Margaret, 231–235
Mella, John, 6
Melville, Herman, 257
Men in Groups (Tiger), 30, 330
Mental state attribution, 288
Merriment, 118, 120
Military strategy, 71
Mills, David, 54, 61
Milton, John, 257
Mitani, John, 339
Mitchell, Arthur, 193–194
Moby Dick (Melville), 257
Modern warfare, frustration of, 83

Modesty, 214
Monod, Jacques *(Chance and Necessity)*, 16
Monogamous unions, 279
"The Monsters and the Critics," 251
Moral life, 214
Morel, E. D., 208–209
Morgan, Lewis, 148
Mother-son incest, 174. *See also* Incest taboo
Much Ado about Nothing, 101
Mundugumor culture, 235
The Myth-Ritual Complex by Eugene d'Aquili (1993), 75–76

N

Naika, Gopala, 254
Naming systems, 115
National Film Theatre, 92
National Science Foundation, 340
Natolocality, 152
Natural History, 30
Naturalistic fallacy, 321
Natural resources, 347
Natural selection, 162
Nature, 345–348
  demand, 348
  as materialist, 345–346
  rewards, 347
Nayar of southwest India, 151
Needham, Rodney, 138
Nelson, Claudia, 186
Neo-Darwinian theory, 339
Neonate Cognition (Mehler and Fox), 14
Nested communities of multifamily groups, 281
Neurath, Otto, 221
Neurobiological evidence, of social prime mover existence, 284
Neurological processes, 76
New York Review of Books, 31
Niche construction framework, 144–145
Nonenclaved aggregates, 113
North Alaska Eskimos, 121
Nuclear families, 176

O

Obligation, sense of, 209
Ockham's Razor, 27
Oedipus Rex, 106
Oinas, Felix, 253

Ontogenetic evidence, of social prime mover existence, 284
Opie, Kit, 149
Opposite-sex siblings, and incest, 164
Ordered anarchy, 209
Orgiastic group-drinking behavior, 70
Orwell, George, 211
Ostracism-induced distress, 283
Othello, 106
The Outline of History (Wells), 12

P

Palawan humor, 122–124. *See also* Felicity in human organizations
Pall Mall Gazette, 196–197
Parental love, 285–286
Participant Observer: Memoir of a Transatlantic Life (Fox), 9–11, 35, 205, 237, 238
The Passionate Mind (Fox), 15–16, 35
Pasteur, Louis, 231
Pathogens, 313–314
Patrogenesis, 148
Pedagogy, 54
Peer group, sexual attraction, 174–175
Performers, 94
Peribasa (courtesy), 124
Personality traits, 311
  individual differences, 311
Pete, G. F., 232
PhD fieldwork, use of, 60–61
Phenotypic plasticity, 314–315
Phylogenetic evidence, of social prime mover existence, 283
Physical fitness, 214
Piaora humor, 120
Pipper, Knut, 163
"The Playing Fields of Hogwarts," 218
Plays, 92–98
Pledger, Elias, 207
Pleistocene, 318
Pop anthropology. *See* Popular anthropology
Popol Vuh, 251, 261, 268–269
Popular anthropology
  about author's work, 53
  blurbs for catalogs and leaflets, writing, 58–59
  conflicts in, 64
  ethnography, 60
  image problem, 66–67
  methods, role of, 64

nonacademic readers, 63
PhD fieldwork, use of, 60–61
preservation of anthropology, 55–56
reviews, 54
Social Issues Research Centre (SIRC), 59–60
training by Robin Fox, 56–58
Populations, 104
Power, Camilla, 149
A Preface to Paradise Lost (Lewis), 251
The Prelude (Wordsworth), 257
Preparatory schools, 205
Primate Behavioral Ecology (Strier), 340
Primate kinship, 136–139, 142–146
Primatology, 339–340
Primeval Kinship (Chapais), 19, 142–143
Primitive tribal gathering, 106, 108
The Prince (Machiavelli), 103
Prudishness, 118, 120
Psychoactive substances, 76
Psychological anthropology, 113
Psychology
  cultural differences, 312–313
  evolutionary, 310
  universally uniform, 311
Psychosocial proclivities, 284–288
  culture and, 295–300
  formal culture and, 295–297
  semantic culture and, 297–300
Puberty, 206
Public school, 206
Purists, 56

Q

Queen's Regulations, 74
Quine, Willard Van Orman, 221
Quinn, Naomi, 340

R

Racial differences, 318
The Racing Tribe, 60, 63
Ranked society, 115
The Raw and the Cooked (Lévi-Strauss), 225–226
Reasoning, 311
Rebellion, form of, 72
Red Lamp of Incest, Encounter with Anthropology (Fox), 14, 46, 161, 205
Reproduction and Succession (Fox), 14
Reproduction *vs.* survival, 315–316. *See also* Life History Theory

Index

Research on drinking habits by Anne Fox, 69
Resenting disloyalty, 283
Resources, natural, 347
Reward systems, 284
Rituals, drinking, 73–81
Rodesth, Lars, 140–141
Rousseau, Jean-Jacques, 249

S

Sabean, David, 188
Sacred principle, 115
Sahlins, Marshall, 225–226
S-allele
  carriers, 313
  collectivist and individualist cultures, 313
  higher frequency of, 313
  population difference in, 313
Same-sex partners, 290
Same-sex siblings bonds, behavioral profile of, 290–291
Schneider, David, 138–139
School for Scandal (Sheridan), 98
Schweder, Richard, 332
Scientific skepticism, 332
The Search for Society (Fox), 14, 20
Selection pressures, 176
Self-less(ness), in AA, 115
Selous, Frederick Courtenay, 208
Sense and Sensibility (Austen), 187
Sense of obligation, 209
Sexuality and aggression, 82
Sexual jealousy, 283
Seymour, Susan, 340
Shakespeare, William, 257
Shapiro, Judith, 30
Shoguns, 118
Shore, Bradd, 340
Sibling bonds, 289
Sibling Incest (Fox), 13, 163
Siblings
  incest, 174
  sexual love, 162
The Siri Epic (Naika), 254
Sisters-in-law, 187
Skinner, B. F. (*Beyond Freedom and Dignity*), 31
The Small House of Allington (Trollope), 192–193
Smuts, Barbara, 339
Snow, Peter, 217

Social anthropologist, 66
Social bonds, 289–292
  alcohol and, 71
  behavioral profile of, 291–292
  developmental familiarity, 290–291
  emotions and, 171–173
  kinship, 289–291
  sibling, 289
Social conformity, 313
Social Issues Research Centre (SIRC), 59
Social life, comic dimension of, 120
Social patterns, complex, 292–295
Social prime mover, 283. *See also* Society
  cognitive environment and, 284–288
  ethnographical evidence, 284
  existence of, 283–284
  functional evidence, 283
  neurobiological evidence, 284
  ontogenetic evidence, 284
  parental love, 285–286
  phylogenetic evidence, 283
  psychosocial proclivities, 284–288
  social superiority, 286–287
  status competition, 286
Social psychology, 60
Social rituals, 62
Social science, 68, 335
Social species, 277–278
Social superiority, 286–287
Society. *See also* Social prime mover
  complex social patterns, 292–295
  deep configuration, 277–282
  multifamily groups, 281–282
  overview, 276–277
  primate categories and, 279
  sexual promiscuity in, 279
  as social system, 277
  universal patterns, 278–281
Society (journal), 4, 19
Sociocultural anthropology, 274
Solar energy, 347
Sorcerers of Dobu (Fortune), 234, 236
Sordello (Browning), 9–10
Souza, Paulo, 138
Sperber, Dan, 152
Spiritual life, 215
Sports, 214
Status competition, 286
Stepdaughter-stepfather incest, 174
Step-siblings incest, 174
Strier, Karen, 339–340

381

Symbolic communication, 288
Syntagm, binomial or trinomial, 115

T
"Taming the Savage Mind," 4
Tea ceremony, Japanese, 116–118. *See also* Felicity in human organizations
Tedlock, Dennis, 251
Television, 93, 98
  audience, 95
The Territorial Imperative (Ardrey), 89, 95, 104
Tetradic theory, 153–154. *See also* Kinship
Theatre, 92–95
  comic character, 106
  design by Rumford, 105
Thring, Edward, 213
Tidrick, Kathryn, 208–210
Tiger, Lionel, 3–4, 16, 329–330
Tlazolteotl, Aztec goddess, 78
Tolkien, J. R. R, 251
Tollet, Georgina, 186
Tory culture, 151–152
The Tory Islanders (Fox), 15
Tragic Sense of Life (de Unamuno), 46
Training, 57
Tribal gathering, primitive, 106, 108
The Tribal Imagination: Civilization and the Savage Mind (Fox), 11, 16–17, 112, 256
Tribal societies, 113
Tribes, 105, 116
Trinomial naming system, 115
Tristes Tropiques (Lévi-Strauss), 10, 224–225, 227
Trivers, Robert, 17
Trophotrophic function of nervous system, 76
Turner, Victor W., 77–78, 256
Twelfth Night, 101
Tylor, Edward, 145

U
Ulysses (Joyce), 257
Unilateral altruism, 290
Unit cohesion, 72

Universal psychosocial proclivities. *See* Psychosocial proclivities
Ustinov, Peter, 96

V
Van Gennep, Arnold, 80
The Variation of Animals and Plants under Domestication, 194
Vico, Giambattista, 249
The Violent Imagination (Fox), 5, 15–16, 19, 44–47

W
War and Peace (Tolstoy), 257
The Waste Land (Eliot), 257
Watching the English: The Hidden Rules of English Behaviour, 53–54
Wedgwoods and Darwins, 184–192
Wells, H. G. (*The Outline of History*), 12
Westermarck, Edward, 7, 13, 150, 161–163
Westermarck effect, 164, 283, 302
Whiting, John, 163
Wilson, David Sloan, 18
Wilson, E. O., 9–10, 17–19
Wind in the Willows (Graham), 218
"Wine and Men in Alsace, France" (Bianquis-Gasser), 81
Wood, Peter, 19
Works and Days (Hesiod), 262
Wrangham, Richard, 140–141, 339

Y
Yanagisako, Sylvia, 139
Yes, Minister, 98
YMCA (Young Men's Christian Association), 229

Z
Za arts, 117
Zen temples, 117
"The Zoological Perspective in Social Science," 329, 333
Zoon Politikon, 28–29